Concurrency

ACM Books

Editor in Chief

M. Tamer Özsu, *University of Waterloo*

ACM Books is a series of high-quality books for the computer science community, published by ACM and many in collaboration with Morgan & Claypool Publishers. ACM Books publications are widely distributed in both print and digital formats through booksellers and to libraries (and library consortia) and individual ACM members via the ACM Digital Library platform.

Concurrency: The Works of Leslie Lamport

Dahlia Malkhi, *VMware Research* and *Calibra*
2019

Providing Sound Foundations for Cryptography: On the work of Shafi Goldwasser and Silvio Micali

Oded Goldreich, *Weizmann Institute of Science*
2019

The Essentials of Modern Software Engineering: Free the Practices from the Method Prisons!

Ivar Jacobson, *Ivar Jacobson International*
Harold "Bud" Lawson, *Lawson Konsult AB (deceased)*
Pan-Wei Ng, *DBS Singapore*
Paul E. McMahon, *PEM Systems*
Michael Goedicke, *Universität Duisburg–Essen*
2019

Data Cleaning

Ihab F. Ilyas, *University of Waterloo*
Xu Chu, *Georgia Institute of Technology*
2019

Conversational UX Design: A Practitioner's Guide to the Natural Conversation Framework

Robert J. Moore, *IBM Research–Almaden*
Raphael Arar, *IBM Research–Almaden*
2019

Heterogeneous Computing: Hardware and Software Perspectives

Mohamed Zahran, *New York University*
2019

Concurrency

The Works of Leslie Lamport

Dahlia Malkhi, editor

VMware Research and *Calibra*

ACM Books #29

Concurrency: The Works of Leslie Lamport

Dahlia Malkhi, editor

books.acm.org

http://books.acm.org

ISBN: 978-1-4503-7270-1   hardcover
ISBN: 978-1-4503-7271-8   paperback
ISBN: 978-1-4503-7273-2   eBook
ISBN: 978-1-4503-7272-5   EPUB

Series ISSN: 2374-6769 print   2374-6777 electronic

DOIs:

10.1145/3335772 Book
10.1145/3335772.3335773 Preface
10.1145/3335772.3335774 Introduction
10.1145/3335772.3335775 Paper 0
10.1145/3335772.3335776 Chapter 1
10.1145/3335772.3335777 Chapter 2
10.1145/3335772.3335778 Chapter 3
10.1145/3335772.3335779 Chapter 4
10.1145/3335772.3335780 Chapter 5

10.1145/3335772.3335781 Chapter 6
10.1145/3335772.3335782 Paper 1
10.1145/3335772.3335934 Paper 2
10.1145/3335772.3335935 Paper 3
10.1145/3335772.3335936 Paper 4
10.1145/3335772.3335937 Paper 5
10.1145/3335772.3335938 Paper 6
10.1145/3335772.3335939 Paper 7
10.1145/3335772.3335940 References/Index/Bios

A publication in the ACM Books series, #29
Editor in Chief: M. Tamer Özsu, *University of Waterloo*

This book was typeset in Arnhem Pro 10/14 and Flama using ZzTEX.

First Edition

10 9 8 7 6 5 4 3 2 1

Contents

Preface

This book is a collective work of many contributors. Leslie Lamport gave the world his work. Chapter authors, listed at the beginning of each chapter, volunteered their time and expert knowledge. Additional people contributed comments or portions of chapters, including: Mani Chandy, Vassos Hadzilacos, Jon Howell, Igor Konnov, Daphna Keidar, Butler Lampson, Kartik Nayak, Tom Rodeheffer, Fred Schneider, Yuan Yu, Lidong Zhou. Ted Yin edited the bibliography and helped typeset the biography chapter. Ruth E. Thaler-Carter provided preliminary biographical notes. Mimi Bussam and Fred Schneider provided several photos of Lamport for this book. The ACM and Turing series editor Tamer Özsu initiated this work and provided support and resources for it. Leslie Lamport developed LaTeX, the typesetting macro environment used for writing this book.

Leslie Lamport at his uncle's wedding, seated in front.
He is about six years old in this photo.

Leslie Lamport at the National Academy of Sciences
induction, Washington, April 28, 2011.

Photo and Text Credits

Photos

Page viii   Richard Morgenstein Photography, © Association for Computing Machinery, Inc. 2014

Page xviii   Photo courtesy of Leslie Lamport

Page xviii   Photo courtesy of Leslie Lamport

Page 27   © Dag Johansen, Photo courtesy of Leslie Lamport

Page 28   Photo courtesy of Leslie Lamport

Page 170   Photo courtesy of Leslie Lamport

Page 170   © Keith Marzullo 2001

Page 171   Photo courtesy of Leslie Lamport

Page 172   Photo courtesy of Leslie Lamport

Page 172   Photo courtesy of Leslie Lamport

Page 343   Photo courtesy of Dahlia Malkhi

Text

Page 1   "Introduction" by Dahlia Malkhi and Idit Keider. Copyright © Dahlia Malkhi and Idit Keider. Reprinted by permission of Dahlia Malkhi and Idit Keider.

Page 13   Leslie Lamport. 2015. Turing lecture: The computer science of concurrency: the early years. Commun. ACM 58, 6 (May 2015), 71–76. DOI: https://doi.org/10.1145/2771951

Page 29   "Shared Memory and the Bakery Algorithm," Hagit Attiya and Jennifer L. Welch, Copyright © Hagit Attiya and Jennifer L. Welch. Reprinted by permission of Hagit Attiya and Jennifer L. Welch.

Page 47   "The Notions of Time and Global Sstate in a Distributed System" by Karoloa Antoniadis and Rachid Guerraoui. Copyright © Karoloa Antoniadis and Rachid Geurraoiu. Reprinted by permission of Karoloa Antoniadis and Rachid Guerraoui.

Page 67   "Byzantine Faults" by Christian Cachin. Copyright © Christian Cachin. Reprinted by permission of Christian Cachin.

Introduction

Dahlia Malkhi, Idit Keidar

Back in the days when the world's first multiprocessor computers were being built and clouds existed only in the sky, Leslie Lamport ruminated about a bakery. He observed that in order to be served one at a time, customers had to solve a mutual exclusion problem, and discovered a way for them to do so without the baker's help. The resulting Bakery algorithm foreshadowed some of the most important developments in multiprocessor programming for years to come. Lamport's works have since been interwoven with four and a half decades of evolution of digital computing technology, while multiprocessing and distributed computing have become increasingly commonplace.

The body of Lamport's works lays formal foundations for concurrent computations executed by multiple processes—be they threads running on a shared memory multicore platform or autonomous agents communicating via message passing. He put forward fundamental concepts, such as causality and logical time, atomic shared registers, sequential consistency, state machine replication, Byzantine agreement, and wait-freedom. Some of his algorithms have become standard engineering practice for fault-tolerant distributed computing—distributed systems that continue to function correctly despite failures of individual components. He developed a substantial body of work on the formal specification and verification of concurrent systems, and has contributed to the development of automated tools applying these methods.

This book begins with an article covering Lamport's A.M. Turing Award lecture, which he gave at the PODC Conference in 2014. The article was published in the *Communications of the ACM* in 2015. It recalls the cradle of concurrency from 1965 to 1977, with forty years of hindsight. The first concurrent computing problem formulated was mutual exclusion. Next came producer-consumer algorithms and their extensions, and then distributed algorithms. With these problems as examples, the article illustrates different approaches to describing concurrent algorithms and to reasoning about them. Lamport dedicated this historical review to Edsger Dijkstra, who played a fundamental role in the study of concurrency.

This introduction is followed by two parts. Part 1 includes technical chapters centered around five key topics addressed in Lamport's works: Chapter 1, shared memory and the Bakery algorithm for mutual exclusion; Chapter 2, state machines and event ordering; Chapter 3, Byzantine protocols; Chapter 4, fault-tolerant replication; and Chapter 5, formal methods. Each of the chapters presents an expert's retrospective on Lamport's original ideas. They explain how Lamport tackled certain problems and also underscore a number of common themes that recurred throughout his career.

One prominent characteristic of Lamport's work is that to approach specific problems, he develops novel and more general foundations. Time and time again, the experience of devising concurrent algorithms and the challenge of verifying their correctness led him to focus on the basic premises that would enable a mathematical study of multiprocessor behavior. For example, working on the Bakery algorithm (Chapter 1) led Lamport to define the semantics of memory "store" and "load" operations in multiprocessors. Lamport later said, "For a couple of years after my discovery of the Bakery algorithm, everything I learned about concurrency came from studying it" [Lamport and Levin 2016a]. Another example is the Byzantine generals problem, an agreement problem in a model that characterizes faulty (or "buggy") processor behavior. This concept emerged while working on a fault-tolerant multicomputer system for executing avionics software. All in all, many of the abstractions and principles that Lamport invented in order to tackle specific problems ended up becoming theoretical pillars of concurrent programming.

A second theme in Lamport's work is addressing practical problems. Indeed, spending his research career in industrial research environments was not an accident. "I like working in an industrial research lab, because of the input," Lamport said. "If I just work by myself and come up with problems, I'd come up with some small number of things, but if I go out into the world, where people are working on real computer systems, there are a million problems out there. When I look back on most of the things I worked on—Byzantine generals, Paxos—they came from real-world problems" [American Mathematical Society 2019a].

Lamport's works are also characterized by the use of amusing metaphors and associated parables to explain new solutions to problems. Lamport adopted this approach from another prominent computer scientist of that era, Edsger Dijkstra, who popularized a multiprocess synchronization problem by casting it in terms of philosophers competing for dining utensils. On his "My Writings" page [Lamport 2019], Lamport writes, "The popularity of the dining philosophers problem taught me that the best way to attract attention to a problem is to present it in terms of a story." As noted above, Lamport used a bakery metaphor for his solution of Dijkstra's mutual exclusion problem. To explain the challenge of coordinating multiple bug-prone computers, he used the metaphor of an attack by Byzantine generals. And his solution for fault-tolerant state replication was explained using the story of the island of Paxos and its imaginary part-time parliament.

The chapters of Part I are described below. They are organized roughly in chronological order of the literature they cover. The last chapter in Part I describes Lamport's professional biography. It provides the context in which his pioneering work arose and sheds light on the people involved with breaking the new ground.

This book would not be complete without a glimpse onto the works themselves. A small selection of the original papers introducing the key notions discussed in the contributed chapters is given in Part II. Yet within the scope of a single book we cannot hope to cover all of Lamport's important contributions. We therefore encourage readers to visit Lamport's "My Writings" page [Lamport 2019], where he gives a complete list of his papers accompanied by historical notes that describe the motivation and context of each result.

Chapter 1: Shared Memory and the Bakery Algorithm

Lamport's influential works from the 1970s and 1980s came at a time when the fundamental issues of concurrent programming were not well understood. Chapter 1, by Hagit Attiya and Jennifer L. Welch, starts with the seminal Bakery algorithm [Lamport 1974a] for solving "mutual exclusion," a fundamental requirement in multiprocessor programming. After developing the Bakery algorithm, Lamport used it as a vehicle for formalizing a number of concepts that facilitate reasoning about concurrent programs. The chapter further covers related concepts that Lamport developed while studying the Bakery algorithm.

At the time, it was known that correct execution may require parallel activities to exclude one another during "critical sections" when they manipulate the same data, in order to prevent undesired interleaving of operations. The mutual exclusion problem originated from Edsger Dijkstra's pioneering work, which includes his solution [Dijkstra 1965]. Dijkstra's algorithm, while correct, depends on shared memory accesses being atomic—that one processor reading when another is writing will be made to wait, rather than returning a possibly garbled value. In a sense, it constructs a high-level solution out of the low-level mutual exclusion already implemented by the hardware.

Lamport's Bakery algorithm does not depend on low-level mutual exclusion. In particular, when one processor reads data from a shared variable while the same variable is being updated by another processor, it is acceptable for the former to read garbage, and the algorithm still works! The Bakery algorithm has become textbook material, and most undergraduates in computer science encounter it in the course of their studies.

Among the conceptual contributions emanating from the study of the Bakery algorithm is the notion that processes can make progress independently of the speed of other processes. Rather than preassign turns to processes in a rotation, the Bakery algorithm assigns turns to processes in the order of their arrival. Using the bakery analogy, preassigning turns would be akin to arriving to an empty bakery and being asked to wait for a customer who hasn't even arrived at the bakery yet. Independent progress is a crucial concept that has been used in the design of many subsequent algorithms and in memory architectures. *Wait-freedom*, a condition requiring independent progress despite failures, has its clear roots in this notion and the Bakery doorway concept. It was later extensively explored by Herlihy [1991] and others.

The Bakery algorithm also led Lamport to wonder about the precise semantics of memory when multiple processes interact with shared data. The result is the abstractions of atomic, regular, and safe registers [Lamport 1986c, 1986d].

A register is basically a shared memory location that can be read (loaded) and written (stored) by multiple processes concurrently. Lamport's theory gives each operation on a shared register an explicit duration, starting with an invocation and ending with a result. The registers can be implemented by a variety of techniques, such as replication of the register's data to tolerate faults. Nevertheless, the interactions of processes with an atomic register are supposed to "look like" serial accesses to actual shared memory. The theory also includes semantics of interaction weaker than atomicity, namely, those of regular and safe registers. A regular register captures situations in which processes read different replicas of the register while it is being updated. At any moment in time, some replicas may be updated while others are not, and eventually, all replicas will hold the updated value. The even weaker notion of safe registers allows reads that overlap a write to obtain an arbitrary value. Importantly, these weak semantics suffice for achieving mutual exclusion: the Bakery algorithm works correctly with safe registers.

It is worth noting that Lamport's study of atomic objects covered in Chapter 1 was restricted to registers, which support only read and write operations. The notion of atomicity was generalized to other data types by Herlihy and Wing [1990], and their term *linearizability* became synonymous with it.

Before the theory of shared registers was completed, Lamport worked on a condition for coherent cache behavior in multiprocessors. That work brought some order to the chaos in this field by introducing sequential consistency [Lamport 1979b], the last concept covered in the chapter. This simple and intuitive notion provides just the right level of "atomicity" to allow software to work and has become the gold standard for memory consistency models. Today, we design hardware systems with timestamp ordering or partial-store ordering, with added memory fence instructions that allow programmers to make the hardware appear sequentially consistent. Sequential consistency underlies the memory consistency models defined for programming languages like Java and C++. Thus our multicore software runs based on principles described by Leslie Lamport in 1979.

In addition, essentially all nonrelational storage systems developed by companies like Amazon, Google, and Facebook adopt linearizability and sequential consistency as their data coherence guarantees.

Chapter 2: The Notions of Time and Global State in a Distributed System

A prominent type of concurrent system is a distributed one, where processes use messages to interact with each other. Chapter 2, by Karolos Antoniadis and Rachid Guerraoui, covers powerful notions introduced by Lamport that have shaped the way we think about distributed systems as well as the engineering practices of the field.

The first of these is "logical clocks" and the corresponding "logical timestamps," which, in fact, are often referred to as "Lamport timestamps." Many people realized that a global notion of time is not natural for a distributed system, but Lamport was the first to formalize a precise alternative. He defined the "happened before" relation on events—a partial order capturing the causality induced by message exchange. Consider, for example, a process in San Francisco that reads the temperature from a sensor, and a process in London that prints the temperature in San Francisco on a screen. If the Californian process sends a message after reading the sensor and this message is received in London before the temperature is presented on the screen, then it is possible that the sensor read in San Francisco has "caused" a specific temperature to be printed out in London. Lamport's logical clocks capture this potential causality, stipulating that the sensor read happened before the temperature was printed.

Logical clocks are defined in the paper "Time, Clocks, and the Ordering of Events in a Distributed System" [Lamport 1978b] ("Time/Clocks"), which has become the most cited of Lamport's works. The paper won the very first Principles of Distributed Computing Influential Paper Award (later renamed the Edsger W. Dijkstra Prize in Distributed Computing) in 2000 and an ACM SIGOPS Hall of Fame Award in 2007.

At the time of the invention, there was no good way to capture the communication delay in distributed systems except by using real time, and hence the work has become so influential. Lamport realized that the communication delay made those systems very different from shared-memory multiprocessors. The insight came when reading a paper on replicated databases [Johnson and Thomas 1975] and realizing that its logical ordering of commands might violate causality.

Originally, Lamport introduced logical time as a tool to synchronize the copies of replicated service, though it became a powerful notion by itself. Today, this ordering of events is widely used for intuitive proofs of concurrent synchronization algorithms.

In order to correctly replicate a service, Lamport introduced in the same "Time/ Clocks" paper one of his most significant contributions, the state machine replication (SMR) paradigm. This paradigm abstracts any service as a centralized state machine—a kind of universal computing engine similar to a Turing machine. A state machine has an internal state, and it processes commands in sequence, each resulting in a new internal state and producing a response. Lamport realized that the daunting task of replicating a service over multiple computers can be made remarkably simple if you present the same sequence of input commands to all replicas and they proceed through an identical succession of states. Chapter 2 describes an SMR solution introduced in Lamport [1978b], which uses logical timestamps to replicate an arbitrary state machine in a distributed system that does not suffer from failures. Fault-tolerant solutions came later, and are the focus of Chapter 4.

A related problem is that of consistently reading the state (taking a "snapshot") of an arbitrary distributed system. If the global system state is constructed by probing all system components, but due to communication delays they are physically probed at different times, how do we know if that picture is consistent? In a joint work with Mani Chandy, Lamport observed that once you define causal order, the notion of a "consistent global state" naturally follows [Chandy and Lamport 1985]. In a nutshell, if one event happens before (i.e., causally precedes) another, then the global state should not reflect the latter without the former. This notion is also covered in Chapter 2 along with the Chandy and Lamport [1985] algorithm for obtaining such a consistent snapshot. This is such a powerful notion that others later used it in different domains, like networking, self-stabilization, debugging, and distributed systems. The paper received the 2013 ACM SIGOPS Hall of Fame Award and the 2014 Edsger W. Dijkstra Prize in Distributed Computing.

Chapter 3: Byzantine Faults

Before Lamport developed a full solution for fault-tolerant SMR, he addressed a core ingredient, namely, distributed agreement. Chapter 3, by Christian Cachin, describes the work formulating the agreement problem.

The work arose at SRI International, which had previously been called Stanford Research Institute, in the 1970s. Lamport was part of a team that helped NASA design a robust avionics control system. Formal guarantees were an absolute necessity because of the mission-critical nature of the task. Safety had to be assured against the most extreme system malfunction one could imagine. One of the first challenges the team at SRI was asked to undertake was proving the correctness of a cockpit control scheme that NASA had designed. The scheme relied on three computers replicating the computation and using majority voting to mask any single faulty component.

The team's work resulted in several foundational concepts and insights regarding these stringent types of robust systems. It included a fundamental definition of robustness in this setting, an abstraction of the coordination problem that underlies any replicated system to date, and a surprising revelation on the prerequisites for three computers to safely run a mission-critical cockpit.

In two seminal works published by Lamport, Marshall Pease, and Robert Shostak [Pease et al. 1980, Lamport et al. 1982], the team first identified a somewhat peculiar vulnerability. They posited that "a failed component may exhibit a type of behavior that is often overlooked—namely, sending conflicting information to different parts of the system." More generally, a malfunctioning component could function in a manner completely inconsistent with its prescribed behavior, and might appear almost malicious.

The new fault model needed a name; thus the Byzantine generals tale was born, and the name *Byzantine failure* was introduced to capture an arbitrary computer malfunction. Reaching far beyond the mission-critical avionics system for which it was conceived, the Byzantine fault model is still in use for capturing the worst mishaps and security flaws in systems.

In 1980, Pease, Shostak, and Lamport formulated the problem of reaching coordination despite Byzantine failures [Pease et al. 1980], and in 1982 named it *Byzantine agreement* [Lamport et al. 1982]. Their succinct formulation expresses the control coordination task as the problem of agreeing upon an individual bit, starting with potentially different bits input to each component. One can use it repeatedly in order to keep the system coordinated. In the papers, they show that in the system settings for which NASA designed, four computers are needed for a single bit in the face of a single malfunction. Three are not enough, because then a faulty unit may send conflicting values to the other two units and form a different majority with each one. More generally, they showed that $3t + 1$ units are needed in order to overcome t simultaneously faulty components. To prove this, they used a beautiful symmetry argument now known as the *hexagon argument*. This archetypal argument has been subsequently used in additional settings where a malfunctioning unit that sends conflicting information to different parts of the system looks indistinguishable from a symmetrical situation in which the correct and faulty roles are reversed.

The papers additionally demonstrated that $3t + 1$ units are enough, presenting an algorithm that reaches Byzantine agreement among $3t + 1$ units in $t + 1$ synchronous communication rounds. They further showed that if you use digital signatures, $2t + 1$ units are sufficient and necessary.

The Byzantine agreement problem and its solutions have become pinnacles of fault-tolerant systems. Most systems constructed with redundancy use agreement internally for replication and coordination. Lamport himself later used it to develop fault-tolerant SMR, which is the topic of Chapter 4.

The 1980 paper [Pease et al. 1980] was awarded the 2005 Edsger W. Dijkstra Prize in Distributed Computing, and the 1982 paper [Lamport et al. 1982] received the Jean-Claude Laprie Award in Dependable Computing.

Working on synchronous algorithms for Byzantine agreement made Lamport realize that it is necessary to synchronize clocks among the processes. The chapter also includes a brief recollection of another seminal work [Lamport and Melliar-Smith 1985] in which Lamport, together with Michael Melliar-Smith, formalized the Byzantine clock synchronization problem and gave its first solutions.

The last topic covered in the chapter is a "one off" work Lamport did in cryptography, one-time signatures based on one-way functions.

Chapter 4: State Machine Replication with Benign Failures

The first SMR solution Lamport presented in his 1978 "Time/Clocks" paper assumed there are no failures, and it made use of logical time to step replicas through the same command sequence. With the growing understanding of reaching agreement in distributed systems, it was time for Lamport to go back to state machine replication and address failures and lack of synchrony. This is the topic of Chapter 4, by Robbert van Renesse.

In 1989, Lamport designed a fault-tolerant algorithm called Paxos [Lamport 1998a]. Continuing his trend of humorous parable-telling, the paper presents the imaginary story of an ancient parliament on the Greek island of Paxos, where the absence of any number of its members, or possibly all of them, can be tolerated without losing consistency.

Unfortunately, the setting as a Greek parable made the paper difficult for most readers to comprehend, and it took nine years from submission to publication in 1998. But the 1989 DEC technical report did get noticed. Lamport's colleague Butler Lampson evangelized the idea to the distributed computing community [Lampson 1996].

Paxos stitches together a succession of agreement decisions into a sequence of state machine commands in an optimized manner. Importantly, the first phase of the agreement component given in the Paxos paper (called Synod) can be avoided when the same leader presides over multiple decisions; this first phase needs to be performed only when a leader needs to be replaced. This insightful breakthrough accounts for much of the popularity of Paxos, and was later called Multi-Paxos by a Google team that implemented the algorithm [Chandra et al. 2007]. Lamport's Paxos paper won the ACM SIGOPS Hall of Fame Award in 2012.

SMR and Paxos have become the de facto standard framework for designing and reasoning about replication methods. State machine replication à la Paxos is now widely offered and deployed as an external service via libraries and toolkits such as Google's Chubbie [Burrows 2006], Apache's open-source ZooKeeper [Hunt et al. 2010], the popular open-source etcd/raft library, and more. Virtually all companies building critical information systems, including Google, Yahoo, Microsoft, and Amazon, have adopted the Paxos foundations. The engineering of reliable systems led to several important variants and modifications of Paxos. The chapter briefly describes Disk Paxos [Gafni and Lamport 2003], Cheap Paxos [Lamport and Massa 2004], Vertical Paxos [Lamport et al. 2009a], and Stoppable Paxos [Lamport et al. 2010].

Chapter 5: Formal Specification and Verification

Even before he worked on the Bakery algorithm, Lamport learned, through an erroneous manuscript he submitted for publication, the importance of rigorously specifying and proving algorithms correct. Chapter 5, by Stephan Merz, describes his quest for good foundations and tools to describe solutions and prove their correctness.

Lamport has made central contributions to the theory of specification and verification of concurrent programs. He was the first to articulate the notions of safety properties and liveness properties for asynchronous distributed algorithms. These were the generalization of "partial correctness" and "total correctness" properties previously defined for sequential programs. Today, safety and liveness form the standard classification for correctness properties of asynchronous distributed algorithms.

Another work, with Martin Abadi, introduced *prophecy variables*: an abstraction that can be added to an algorithm model in order to handle a situation where an algorithm resolves a nondeterministic choice before its specification does. These complement the previously suggested notion of *history variables*, auxiliary variables that record past actions of the algorithm. Abadi and Lamport [1991] pointed out situations where such problems arise and developed the foundations needed to support this extension to the theory. Moreover, they proved that whenever an algorithm meets a specification, where both are expressed as state machines, the correspondence between them can be proved using a combination of prophecy and history variables. This work won the 2008 LICS Test-of-Time Award.

Lamport realized that computer scientists need more than foundational notions for reasoning about concurrency. They need languages to formally express solutions and tools for verifying their correctness. Chapter 5 gives an overview of the TLA (temporal logic of actions) logic and the specification language TLA$^+$ Lamport developed for modeling and verifying distributed algorithms and systems. TLA and TLA$^+$support specification and proof of both safety and liveness properties using notation based on temporal logic.

Lamport has supervised the development of verification tools based on TLA$^+$, notably the TLC model checker built by Yuan Yu. TLA$^+$ and TLC have been used to describe and analyze real systems. For example, TLA$^+$ was used to find a major error in the coherence protocol used in the hardware for Microsoft's Xbox 360 prior to its release in 2005. They were also used for the analysis of cache coherence protocols at DEC and Intel. To teach engineers how to use his formal specification tools, Lamport wrote a book [2002] and also developed the PlusCAL [2009] formal language and tools for use in verifying distributed algorithms. At the time of this writing, Leslie Lamport continues to work actively on enhancing and evangelizing the TLA$^+$ toolset.

Chapter 6: Biography

Chapter 6, by Roy Levin, tells of Lamport's career. It views his works in historical perspective, providing the context in which they arose during four decades of an evolving industry: from the introduction of the first personal computer to an era when parallel and distributed multiprocessors are abundant. Through this lens, it portrays their long-lasting impact.

The biography also tells of LaTeX, perhaps Lamport's most influential contribution outside the field of concurrency. As a prolific author, Lamport would naturally wish for a convenient typesetting tool. He did not just wish for one, he created one for the entire community. Lamport's LaTeX system [Lamport 1994b] is a set of macros for use with Donald Knuth's TeX typesetting system. In creating LaTeX, Lamport brought to TeX three concepts that he borrowed from Brian Reid's Scribe system and comprehensively elaborated:

- The concept of "typesetting environment"
- A strong emphasis on structural rather than typographic markup
- A generic document design, flexible enough to be adequate for a wide variety of documents

LaTeX is a system that provides the quality of TeX and a lot of its flexibility, but is much easier to use. It has became the de facto standard for technical publishing in computer science and many other fields.

Several other works of Lamport's that are omitted from the technical chapters of this book surface in the biography chapter. The chapter underscores a lifetime achievement and the long-lasting impact Lamport has had on the computer science field. It paints a picture of how his timeless impact on the foundations of concurrency formed. It threads Lamport's thought process as he developed solutions for the challenges he tackled.

The biography chapter gives a glimpse into the professional interactions, and even some conflicts, that the pioneers of the concurrency arena had as they broke new grounds. The chapter concludes by giving a voice to the people behind the achievements, notably Lamport himself and additionally the colleagues around him, who have inspired, collaborated, and helped him drive worldwide impact.

Closing Remarks

If one could travel back in time to 1974, perhaps one would find Leslie Lamport arranging a queue for customers at his busy local neighborhood bakery to be served one at a time via the Bakery algorithm. This and Lamport's other pioneering works—many with amusing names and associated parables—have become pillars of computer science. His collection forms the foundation of broad areas in concurrency and has influenced the specification, development, and verification of concurrent systems. Any time you access a modern computer, you are likely to be impacted by Leslie Lamport's algorithms.

This book touches on a lifetime of contributions by Leslie Lamport to the field of concurrency and on the extensive influence has he had on people working in the field. Those who have collaborated with him have often found the experience remarkable and sometimes even career-altering.

And all of this work started with the quest to understand how to organize a queue at the local bakery.

The Computer Science of Concurrency: The Early Years

Leslie Lamport (Microsoft Research)

28 February 2015

To Edsger Dijkstra

It is insufficiently considered that men more often require to be reminded than informed.

—Samuel Johnson

1 Foreword

I don't know if concurrency is a science, but it is a field of computer science. What I call *concurrency* has gone by many names, including parallel computing, concurrent programming, and multiprogramming. I regard distributed computing to be part of the more general topic of concurrency. I also use the name *algorithm* for what were once usually called programs and were generally written in pseudo-code.

This is a personal view of the first dozen years of the history of the field of concurrency—a view from today, based on 40 years of hindsight. It reflects my biased perspective, so despite covering only the very beginning of what was then an esoteric field, it is far from complete. The geneses of my own contributions are described in comments in my publications web page.

The omission that would have seemed most striking to someone reading this history in 1977 is the absence of any discussion of programming languages. In the late 1960s and early 1970s, most papers considered to be about concurrency were about language constructs for concurrent programs. A problem such as mutual exclusion was considered to be solved by introducing a language construct that made its solution trivial. This article is not about concurrent programming; it is about concurrent algorithms and their underlying principles.

2 The Beginning: Mutual Exclusion

2.1 The Problem

While concurrent program execution had been considered for years, the computer science of concurrency began with Edsger Dijkstra's seminal 1965 paper that introduced the mutual exclusion problem [5]. He posed the problem of synchronizing N processes, each with a section of code called its *critical section*, so that the following properties are satisfied:

> **Mutual Exclusion** No two critical sections are executed concurrently. (Like many problems in concurrency, the goal of mutual exclusion is to eliminate concurrency, allowing us to at least pretend that everything happens sequentially.)

> **Livelock Freedom** If some process is waiting to execute its critical section, then some process will eventually execute its critical section.

Mutual exclusion is an example of what is now called a *safety* property, and livelock freedom is called a *liveness* property. Intuitively, a safety property asserts that something bad never happens; a liveness property asserts that something good must eventually happen. Safety and liveness were defined formally in 1985 [1].

Dijkstra required a solution to allow any computer to halt outside its critical section and associated synchronizing code. This is a crucial requirement that rules out simple, uninteresting solutions—for example, ones in which processes take turns entering their critical sections. The 1-buffer case of the producer-consumer synchronization algorithm given below essentially is such a solution for $N = 2$.

Dijkstra also permitted no real-time assumption. The only progress property that could be assumed was *process fairness*, which requires every process that hasn't halted to eventually take a step. In those days, concurrency was obtained by having multiple processes share a single processor. One process could execute thousands of steps while all other processes did nothing. Process fairness was all one could reasonably assume.

Dijkstra was aware from the beginning of how subtle concurrent algorithms are and how easy it is to get them wrong. He wrote a careful proof of his algorithm. The computational model implicit in his reasoning is that an execution is represented as a sequence of states, where a state consists of an assignment of values to the algorithm's variables plus other necessary information such as the control state of each process (what code it will execute next). I have found this to be the most generally useful model of computation—for example, it underlies a Turing machine. I like to call it the *standard model*.

The need for careful proofs should have become evident a few months later, when the second published mutual exclusion algorithm [9] was shown to be incorrect [10]. However, incorrect concurrent algorithms are still being published and will no doubt continue to be for a long time, despite modern tools for catching errors that require little effort—in particular, model checkers.

2.2 The First "Real" Solution

Although of little if any practical use, the bakery algorithm [11] has become a popular example of a mutual exclusion algorithm. It is based on a protocol sometimes used in retail shops: customers take successively numbered tickets from a machine, and the lowest-numbered waiting customer is served next. A literal implementation of this approach would require a ticket-machine process that never halts, violating Dijkstra's requirements. Instead, an entering process computes its own ticket number by reading the numbers of all other synchronizing processes and choosing a number greater than any that it sees.

A problem with this algorithm is that ticket numbers can grow without bound. This shouldn't be a practical problem. If each process chooses a number at most one greater than one that was previously chosen, then numbers should remain well below 2^{128}. However, a ticket number might have to occupy more than one memory word, and it was generally assumed that a process could atomically read or write at most one word.

The proof of correctness of the algorithm revealed that the read or write of an entire number need not be atomic. The bakery algorithm is correct as long as reading a number returns the correct value if the number is not concurrently being written. It doesn't matter what value is returned by a read that overlaps a write. The algorithm is correct even if reading a number while it is changing from 9 to 10 obtains the value 2496.

This amazing property of the bakery algorithm means that it implements mutual exclusion without assuming that processes have mutually exclusive access to their ticket numbers. It was the first algorithm to implement mutual exclusion without assuming any lower-level mutual exclusion. In 1973, this was considered impossible [1, page 88]. Even in 1990, experts still thought it was impossible [21, question 28].

One problem remained: How can we maintain a reasonable bound on the values of ticket numbers if a read concurrent with a write could obtain any value? For example, what if reading a number while it changes from 9 to 10 can obtain the value 2^{2496}? A closely related problem is to implement a system clock that provides the current time in nanoseconds if reads and writes of only a single byte are atomic, where a read must return a time that was correct sometime during the read operation. Even trickier is to implement a cyclic clock. I recommend these problems as challenging exercises. Solutions have been published [12].

2.3   A Rigorous Proof of Mutual Exclusion

Previous correctness proofs were based on the standard model, in which an execution is represented as a sequence of states. This model assumes atomic transitions between states, so it doesn't provide a natural model of the bakery algorithm with its non-atomic reads and writes of numbers.

Before I discuss a more suitable model, consider the following conundrum. A fundamental problem of interprocess synchronization is to ensure that an operation executed by one process precedes an operation executed by another process. For example, mutual exclusion requires that if two processes both execute their critical sections, then one of those operation executions precedes the other. Many modern multiprocessor computers provide a Memory Barrier (MB) instruction for implementing interprocess synchronization. Executing an instruction A then an MB then instruction B in a single process ensures that the execution of A precedes that of B. Here is the puzzle: An MB instruction enforces an ordering of two operations performed by the same process. Why is that useful for implementing interprocess synchronization, which requires ordering operations performed by different processes? The reader should contemplate this puzzle before reading the following description of the *two-arrow* model.

In the two-arrow model, an execution of the algorithm is represented by a set of *operation executions* that are considered to have a finite duration with starting and stopping times. The relations $\longrightarrow$ and $\dashrightarrow$ on this set are defined as follows, for arbitrary operation executions A and B:

$A \longrightarrow B$ is true iff (if and only if) A ends before B begins.

$A \dashrightarrow B$ is true iff A begins before B ends.

It is easy to check that these relations satisfy the following properties, for any operation executions A, B, C, and D:

1. (a) $A \longrightarrow B \longrightarrow C$ implies $A \longrightarrow C$ ($\longrightarrow$ transitively closed)
   (b) $A \nrightarrow A$. ($\longrightarrow$ irreflexive)

2. $A \longrightarrow B$ implies $A \dashrightarrow B$ and $B \not\dashrightarrow A$.

3. $A \longrightarrow B \dashrightarrow C$ or $A \dashrightarrow B \longrightarrow C$ implies $A \dashrightarrow C$.

4. $A \longrightarrow B \dashrightarrow C \longrightarrow D$ implies $A \longrightarrow D$.

The model abstracts away the explicit concept of time and assumes only a set of operation executions and relations $\longrightarrow$ and $\dashrightarrow$ on it satisfying A1–A4. (An additional property is needed to reason about liveness, which I ignore here.)

Proving correctness of the bakery algorithm requires some additional assumptions:

- All the operation executions within a single process are totally ordered by $\longrightarrow$.

- For any read R and write W of the same variable, either $R \dashrightarrow W$ or $W \longrightarrow R$ holds.

Each variable in the algorithm is written by only a single process, so all writes to that variable are ordered by $\longrightarrow$. We assume that a read that doesn't overlap a write obtains the correct value. More precisely, if a read R of a variable satisfies $R \longrightarrow W$ or $W \longrightarrow R$ for every write W of the variable, then R obtains the value written by the latest write W with $W \longrightarrow R$.

With these assumptions, the two-arrow formalism provides the most elegant proof of the bakery algorithm that I know of. Such a proof of a variant of the algorithm appears in [14].

The conundrum of the MB command described at the beginning of this section is easily explained in terms of the two-arrow formalism. Suppose we want to ensure that an operation execution A in process p precedes an operation execution D in a different process q—that is, to ensure $A \longrightarrow D$. Interprocess communication by accessing shared registers can reveal only that an operation execution C in q sees the effect of an operation execution B in p, which implies $B \dashrightarrow C$. The only way to deduce a $\longrightarrow$ relation from a $\dashrightarrow$ relation is with A4. It allows us to deduce $A \longrightarrow D$ from $B \dashrightarrow C$ if $A \longrightarrow B$ and $C \longrightarrow D$. The latter two $\longrightarrow$ relations can be ensured by using MB instructions, which enforces $\longrightarrow$ relations between operation executions by the same process.

3 Producer-Consumer Synchronization

3.1 The FIFO Queue

The second fundamental concurrent programming problem to be studied was producer-consumer synchronization. This form of synchronization was used at the

```
--algorithm PC {
    variables in = Input, out = ⟨ ⟩, buf = ⟨ ⟩;
    fair process (Producer = 0) {
        P: while (TRUE) {
            await Len(buf) < N ;
            buf := Append(buf, Head(in)) ;
            in := Tail(in) }}

    fair process (Consumer = 1) {
        C: while (TRUE) {
            await Len(buf) > 0 ;
            out := Append(out, Head(buf)) ;
            buf := Tail(buf) }} }
```

Figure 1   Producer-consumer synchronization.

hardware level in the earliest computers, but it was first identified as a concurrency problem by Dijkstra in 1965, though not published in this formulation until 1968 [6]. Here, I consider an equivalent form of the problem: a bounded FIFO (first-in-first-out) queue. It can be described as an algorithm that reads inputs into an N-element buffer and then outputs them. The algorithm uses three variables:

in   The infinite sequence of unread input values.

buf   A buffer that can hold up to N values.

out   The sequence of values output so far.

A *Producer* process moves values from *in* to *buf,* and a *Consumer* process moves them from *buf* to *out*. In 1965 the algorithm would have been written in pseudo-code. Today, we can write it in the PlusCal algorithm language [15] as algorithm *PC* of Figure 1. The initial value of the variable *in* is the constant *Input*, which is assumed to be an infinite sequence of values; variables *buf* and *out* initially equal the empty sequence. The processes *Producer* and *Consumer* are given the identifiers 0 and 1. In PlusCal, an operation execution consists of execution of the code from one label to the next. Hence, the entire body of each process's **while** loop is executed atomically. The **await** statements assert enabling conditions of the actions. The keywords **fair** specify process fairness.

Figure 2 shows the first four states of an execution of the algorithm represented in the standard model. The letter *P* or *C* atop an arrow indicates which process's atomic step is executed to reach the next state.

$$\begin{bmatrix} in & = \langle v_1, v_2, \ldots \rangle \\ out & = \langle \, \rangle \\ buf & = \langle \, \rangle \end{bmatrix} \xrightarrow{P} \begin{bmatrix} in & = \langle v_2, v_3, \ldots \rangle \\ out & = \langle \, \rangle \\ buf & = \langle v_1 \rangle \end{bmatrix} \xrightarrow{C}$$

$$\begin{bmatrix} in & = \langle v_2, v_3, \ldots \rangle \\ out & = \langle v_1 \rangle \\ buf & = \langle \, \rangle \end{bmatrix} \xrightarrow{P} \begin{bmatrix} in & = \langle v_3, v_4, \ldots \rangle \\ out & = \langle v_1 \rangle \\ buf & = \langle v_2 \rangle \end{bmatrix} \xrightarrow{P} \cdots$$

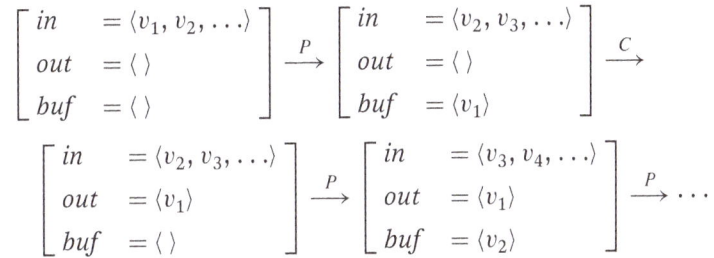

Figure 2   An execution of the FIFO queue.

Algorithm PC is a specification; a bounded FIFO queue must implement that specification. A specification is a definition, and it makes no formal sense to ask if a definition is correct. However, we can gain confidence that this algorithm does specify a bounded FIFO queue by proving properties of it. The most important class of properties one proves about an algorithm are invariance properties. A state predicate is an *invariant* iff it is true in every state of every execution. The following invariant of algorithm PC suggests that it is a correct specification of an N-element bounded queue:

$$(Len(buf) \leq N) \wedge (Input = out \circ buf \circ in)$$

where $Len(buf)$ is the length of the sequence buf and $\circ$ is sequence concatenation.

The basic method for proving that a predicate *Inv* is an invariant of a concurrent algorithm was introduced by Edward Ashcroft in 1975 [2]. We find a suitable predicate I (the inductive invariant) and prove that (i) I is true in every initial state, (ii) I is left true by every step of the algorithm, and (iii) I implies *Inv*. It is easy to prove that the state predicate above is an invariant of algorithm PC. The appropriate inductive invariant I is the conjunction of this invariant with a predicate asserting that each variable has a "type-correct" value. (PlusCal is an untyped language.)

3.2   Another Way of Looking at a FIFO Queue

The FIFO queue specification allows only a single initial state, and executing either process's action can produce only a single next state. Hence the execution of Figure 2 is completely determined by the sequence $P \to C \to P \to P \to \cdots$ of atomic-action executions. For $N = 3$, all such sequences are described by the graph in Figure 3. The nodes of the graph are called *events*, each event representing an

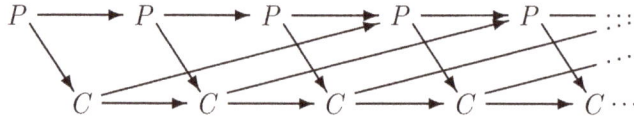

Figure 3   An event history for the FIFO queue with $N = 3$.

atomic execution of the algorithm step with which the event is labeled. The graph defines an irreflexive partial order $\prec$ on the events, where $e \prec f$ iff $e \neq f$ and there is a path through the graph from event e to event f. For want of a standard term for it, I will call such a partially ordered set of events, in which events are labeled with atomic steps, an *event history*.

This event history describes all sequences of states that represent executions of algorithm PC in the standard model. Such a sequence of states is described by a sequence of infinitely many P and C events—that is, by a total ordering of the events in the event history. A total ordering of these events describes a possible execution of algorithm PC iff it is consistent with the partial order $\prec$. To see this, observe that the downward pointing diagonal arrows imply that the ith P event (which moves the ith input to the buffer) must precede the ith C event (which moves that input from the buffer to the output). The upward pointing diagonal arrows indicate that the ith C event must precede the $(i + 3)^{\text{rd}}$ P event, which is necessary to ensure that there is room for the $(i + 3)^{\text{rd}}$ input value in the buffer, which can hold at most 3 elements.

We can view the event history of the figure to be the single "real" execution of algorithm PC. The infinitely many different executions in the standard model are artifacts of the model; they are not inherently different. Two events not ordered by the $\prec$ relation—for example, the second C event and the fourth P event—represent operations that can be executed concurrently. However, the standard model requires concurrent executions of the two operations to be modeled as occurring in some order.

3.3   Mutual Exclusion versus Producer-Consumer Synchronization

Producer-consumer synchronization is inherently deterministic. On the other hand, mutual exclusion synchronization is inherently nondeterministic. It has an inherent race condition: two processes can compete to enter the critical section, and either might win.

Resolving a race requires an *arbiter*, a device that decides which of two events happens first [3]. An arbiter can take arbitrarily long to make its decision. (A well-

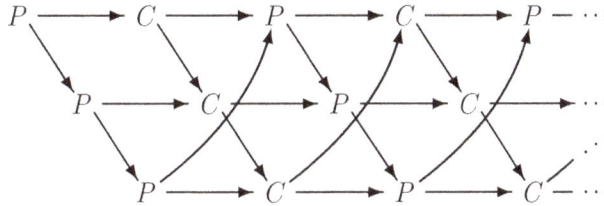

Figure 4   Another view of the FIFO queue for $N = 3$.

designed arbiter has an infinitesimal probability of taking very long.) Any mutual exclusion algorithm can therefore, in principle, take arbitrarily long to allow some waiting process to enter its critical section. This is not an artifact of any model. It appears to be a law of nature.

Producer-consumer synchronization has no inherent nondeterminism, hence no race condition. It can be implemented without an arbiter, so each operation can be executed in bounded time. It is a fundamentally different class of problem than mutual exclusion.

3.4   The FIFO Queue as an *N*-Process System

The graph in Figure 3 is drawn with two rows, each containing the events corresponding to actions of one of the two processes. Figure 4 is the same graph drawn with three rows. We can consider the three rows to be three separate processes. If we number these rows 0, 1, and 2 and we number the elements in the *Input* sequence starting from 0, then the events corresponding to the reading and outputting of element i of *Input* are in row i mod 3. We can consider each of those rows to be a process, making the FIFO queue a 3-process system for $N = 3$, and an N-process system in general. If we were to implement the variable *buf* with an N-element cyclic buffer, each of these processes would correspond to a separate buffer element.

In the event history model, any totally ordered subset of events can be considered a process. The standard model has no inherent notion of processes. In that model, an execution is just a sequence of states. Processes are an artifact of the way the sequence of states is represented. The set of executions of algorithm PC can also be described by an N-process PlusCal algorithm.

3.5   Generalized Producer-Consumer Synchronization

The generalization of producer-consumer synchronization is marked-graph synchronization. Marked graphs were introduced by Holt and Commoner in 1970 [8].

A marked graph is a directed graph together with a *marking* that assigns a finite set of indistinguishable tokens to each arc. A node is *fired* in a marking by removing one token from each of its input arcs and adding one token to each of its output arcs (producing a new marking). A *firing sequence* of a marked graph is a sequence of firings that can end only with a marking in which no node may be fired. (By definition of firing, a node can be fired iff it has at least one token on each input arc.)

A marked graph synchronization problem is described by labeling the nodes of a marked graph with the names of atomic operations. This specifies that a sequence of atomic operation executions is permitted iff it is the sequence of labels of the nodes in a possible firing sequence of the marked graph. For example, the following marked graph describes the FIFO queue for $N = 3$.

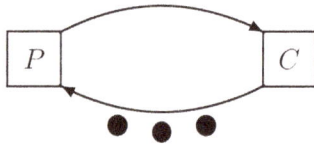

A token on the top arc represents a value in the buffer, and a token on the bottom arc represents space for one value in the buffer. Observe that the number of tokens on this marked graph remains constant throughout a firing sequence. The generalization of this observation to arbitrary marked graphs is that the number of tokens on any cycle remains constant.

All executions of a marked graph synchronization algorithm are described by a single event history. Marked graph synchronization can be implemented without an arbiter, so each operation can be executed in a bounded length of time.

Marked graphs can be viewed as a special class of Petri nets [18]. Petri nets are a model of concurrent computation especially well-suited for expressing the need for arbitration. Although simple and elegant, Petri nets are not expressive enough to formally describe most interesting concurrent algorithms. Petri nets have been used successfully to model some aspects of real systems, and they have been generalized to more expressive languages. But to my knowledge, neither Petri nets nor their generalizations have significantly influenced the field of concurrent algorithms.

3.6 The Two-Arrow Formalism Revisited

Let $\mathcal{E}$ be an event history with partial order $\prec$. Suppose we partition $\mathcal{E}$ into nonempty disjoint subsets called *operation executions*. We can define two relations $\longrightarrow$ and $\dashrightarrow$ on the set of operation executions as follows, for any operation executions A

and B:

$$A \longrightarrow B \text{ iff } \forall\, e \in A, \ f \in B : e \prec f.$$
$$A \dashrightarrow B \text{ iff } \exists\, e \in A, \ f \in B : e \prec f.$$

It is straightforward to see that these definitions (and the assumption that $\prec$ is an irreflexive partial order) imply properties $A1$–$A4$ of Section 2.3. Thus, we can obtain a two-arrow representation of the execution of an algorithm with non-atomic operations from an event history whose events are the atomic events that make up the operation executions. The event history does not have to be discrete. Its events could be points in a space-time continuum, where $\prec$ is the causality relation introduced by Minkowski [17].

4 Distributed Algorithms

Pictures of event histories were first used to describe distributed systems. Figure 5 is an event history that appeared as an illustration in [13]. The events come from three processes, with time moving upwards. A diagonal arc joining events from two different processes represents the causality relation requiring that a message must be sent before it is received. For example, the arc from q_4 to r_3 indicates that event q_4 of the second process sent a message that was received by event r_3 of the third process.

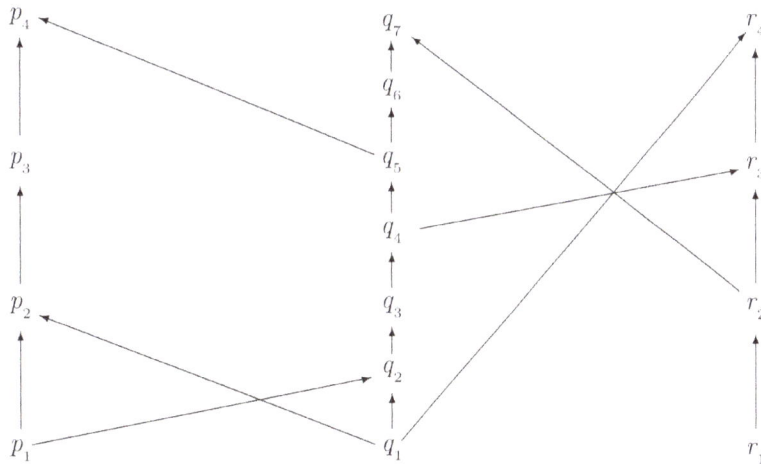

Figure 5   An event history for a distributed system.

In general, executions of such a distributed system can produce different event histories. For example, in addition to the history of Figure 5, there might be an event history in which the message sent by event q_1 is received before the message sent by event q_4. In such a case, there is true nondeterminism and the system requires arbitration.

Let a *consistent* cut of an event history consist of a set C of events such that for every two events c and d, if event c is in C and $d \prec c$, then d is in C. For example, $\{p_1, q_1, q_2, r_1, r_2\}$ is a consistent cut of the event history of Figure 5. Every consistent cut defines a global state of the system during some execution in the standard model—the state after executing the steps associated with the events in the consistent cut.

An event history like that of Figure 5 allows incompatible consistent cuts—that is two consistent cuts, neither of which is a subset of the other. They describe possible global states that, in the standard model, may not occur in the same execution. This shows that there is no meaningful concept of a unique global state at an instant. For example, there are different consistent cuts containing only events q_1 and q_2 of the second process. They represent different possible global states immediately after the process has executed event q_2. There is no reason to distinguish any of those global states as *the* global state at that instant.

Because the standard model refers to global states, it has been argued that the model should not be used for reasoning about distributed algorithms and systems. While this argument sounds plausible, it is wrong. An invariant of a global system is a meaningful concept because it is a state predicate that is true for all possible global states, and so does not depend on any preferred global states. The problem of implementing a distributed system can often be viewed as that of maintaining a global invariant even though different processes may have incompatible views of what the current state is at any instant.

Thinking is useful, and multiple ways of thinking can be even more useful. However, while event histories may be especially useful for helping us understand distributed systems, the best way to reason about these systems is usually in terms of global invariants. The standard model provides the most practical way to reason about invariance.

5 Afterwards

After distributed systems, the next major step in concurrent algorithms was the study of fault tolerance. The first scientific examination of fault tolerance was Dijkstra's seminal 1974 paper on self-stabilization [7]. However, as sometimes happens with work that is ahead of its time, that paper received little attention and was essentially forgotten for a decade. A survey of fault tolerance published in 1978 [20] does not mention a single algorithm, showing that fault tolerance was still the province of computer engineering, not of computer science.

At about the same time that the study of fault-tolerant algorithms began in earnest, the study of models of concurrency blossomed. Arguably, the most influential of this work was Milner's CCS [16]. These models were generally event-based, and avoided the use of state. They did not easily describe algorithms or the usual way of thinking about them based on the standard model. As a result, the study of concurrent algorithms and the study of formal models of concurrency split into two fields. A number of formalisms based on the standard model were introduced for describing and reasoning about concurrent algorithms. Notable among them is temporal logic, introduced by Amir Pnueli in 1977 [19].

The ensuing decades have seen a huge growth of interest in concurrency—particularly in distributed systems. Looking back at the origins of the field, what stands out is the fundamental role played by Edsger Dijkstra, to whom this history is dedicated.

References

[1] Bowen Alpern and Fred B. Schneider. Defining liveness. *Information Processing Letters*, 21(4):181–185, October 1985.

[2] E. A. Ashcroft. Proving assertions about parallel programs. *Journal of Computer and System Sciences*, 10:110–135, February 1975.

[3] J. C. Barros and B. W. Johnson. Equivalence of the arbiter, the synchronizer, the latch, and the inertial delay. *IEEE Transactions on Computers*, C-32(7):603–614, July 1983.

[4] Per Brinch Hansen. *Operating System Principles*. Prentice-Hall, Inc., Englewood Cliffs, New Jersey, 1973.

[5] E. W. Dijkstra. Solution of a problem in concurrent programming control. *Communications of the ACM*, 8(9):569, September 1965.

[6] E. W. Dijkstra. Cooperating sequential processes. In F. Genuys, editor, *Programming Languages*, pages 43–112. Academic Press, New York, 1968. Originally appeared as EWD123 (1965).

[7] Edsger W. Dijkstra. Self-stabilizing systems in spite of distributed control. *Communications of the ACM*, 17(11):643–644, November 1974.

[8] A. Holt and F. Commoner. Events and conditions. In *Record of the Project MAC Conference on Concurrent Systems and Parallel Computation*, pages 3–52. Project MAC, June 1970.

[9] Harris Hyman. Comments on a problem in concurrent programming control. *Communications of the ACM*, 9(1):45, January 1966.

[10] D. E. Knuth. Additional commments on a problem in concurrent program control. *Communications of the ACM*, 9(5):321–322, May 1966.

[11] Leslie Lamport. A new solution of Dijkstra's concurrent programming problem. *Communications of the ACM*, 17(8):453–455, August 1974.

[12] Leslie Lamport. Concurrent reading and writing. *Communications of the ACM*, 20(11):806–811, November 1977.

[13] Leslie Lamport. Time, clocks, and the ordering of events in a distributed system. *Communications of the ACM*, 21(7):558–565, July 1978.

[14] Leslie Lamport. A new approach to proving the correctness of multiprocess programs. *ACM Transactions on Programming Languages and Systems*, 1(1):84–97, July 1979.

[15] Leslie Lamport. The PlusCal algorithm language. In Martin Leucker and Carroll Morgan, editors, *Theoretical Aspects of Computing, ICTAC 2009*, volume 5684 of *Lecture Notes in Computer Science*, pages 36–60. Springer-Verlag, 2009.

[16] R. Milner. *A Calculus of Communicating Systems*, volume 92 of *Lecture Notes in Computer Science*. Springer-Verlag, Berlin, Heidelberg, New York, 1980.

[17] H. Minkowski. Space and time. In *The Principle of Relativity*, pages 73–91. Dover, 1952.

[18] C. A. Petri. Fundamentals of a theory of asynchronous information flow. In Cicely M. Popplewell, editor, *Information Processing 1962, Proceedings of IFIP Congress 62*, pages 386–390. North-Holland, 1962.

[19] Amir Pnueli. The temporal logic of programs. In *Proceedings of the 18th Annual Symposium on the Foundations of Computer Science*, pages 46–57. IEEE, November 1977.

[20] B. Randell, P. A. Lee, and P.C. Treleaven. Reliability issues in computing system design. *Computing Surveys*, 10(2):123–165, June 1978.

[21] Brian A. Rudolph. Self-assessment procedure xxi. *Communications of the ACM*, 33(5):563–575, May 1990.

TECHNICAL PERSPECTIVES ON LAMPORT'S WORK

Leslie Lamport skiing in Norway in 2002. (Photo by Dag Johansen)

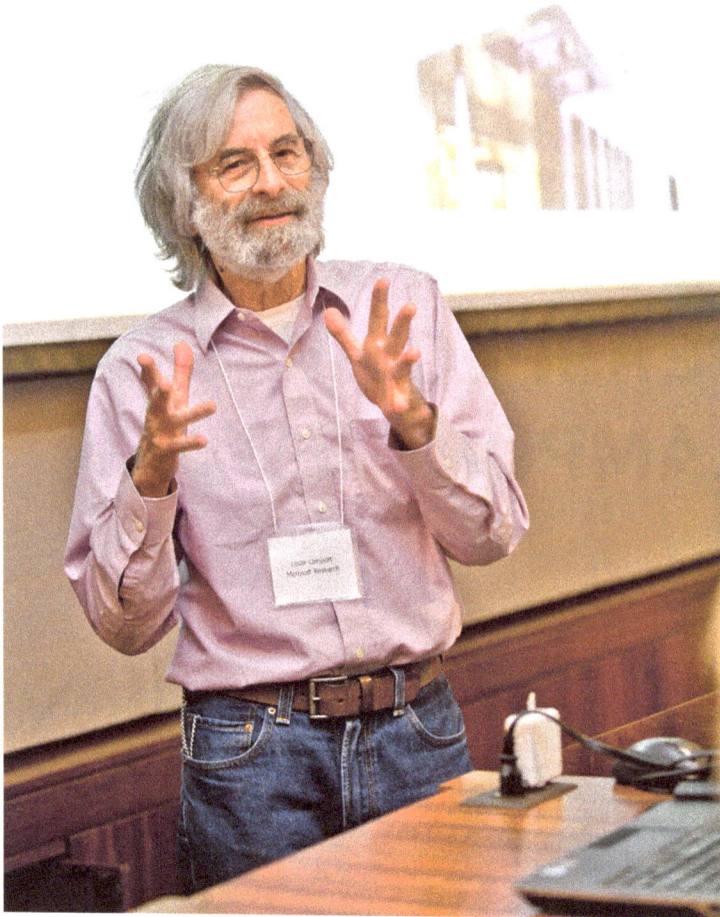

Leslie Lamport lecturing at Cornell University, Ithaca, NY, December 2, 2013.

Shared Memory and the Bakery Algorithm

Hagit Attiya, Jennifer L. Welch

1.1 Introduction

Starting in the early 1970s, Lamport was intrigued by the question of how to achieve synchronization and exclusion for multiprocessor computer systems in software, even when the hardware does not provide such facilities. This study of shared memory marked Lamport's first venture into distributed algorithms [Lamport 2019].

A multiprocessor consists of a set of sequential processes that communicate with each other through shared memory modules, which support fetch and store requests from the processes to read and write shared memory registers. *Mutual exclusion* is a fundamental problem in multiprocessors in which each process may occasionally request exclusive access to some resource for some finite period of time. A solution to the problem should ensure that each request is eventually granted.

Previous algorithms proposed for this problem suffered from several drawbacks that Lamport noticed. One drawback was that the algorithms were not fault tolerant: if a process crashed at an inopportune time, then the entire system would halt. Lamport [1974a] presented the Bakery algorithm for mutual exclusion, which avoids this problem. We present this algorithm in Section 1.2.

Another drawback was that previous work had assumed the shared memory was atomic, meaning that the reads and writes appeared to occur instantaneously and in some sequential order. But this is a strong assumption. A remarkable aspect of the Bakery algorithm is that its correctness does not depend on this assumption! It is still correct even if the shared memory satisfies much weaker properties.

To capture the weaker types of shared memory, Lamport introduced a new formalism [Lamport 1986c, 1986d]. Unlike most prior work, this formalism is not based on atomic actions. Instead, a system execution is modeled as a set of operation executions together with two precedence relations on the operation executions: "precedes" and "can affect". Different types of shared memory are captured by increasingly stronger sets of axioms these relations must satisfy. This formalism is then used to show how various types of shared memory can be simulated by one another. We present these simulations and their informal proofs in Section 1.3 and an overview of the formalism and its applications in Section 1.4.

Even earlier, Lamport introduced a shared memory consistency condition called *sequential consistency* [Lamport 1979b]. Although a similar notion was used previously [Dijkstra 1971, Lamport 1977a, Owicki and Gries 1976], this paper was the first to coin the term *sequential consistency*. The paper presents necessary and sufficient conditions for implementing sequential consistency in a multiprocessor. We discuss these results in Section 1.5.

1.2 Flavors of the Bakery Algorithm

The section describes the *Bakery algorithm* [Lamport 1974a], a mutual exclusion algorithm, as a vehicle to explain different types of shared memory. Unlike prior mutual exclusion algorithms, the Bakery algorithm tolerates crash failures of participating processes.

We first describe the algorithm assuming intuitive, atomic registers are used. We prove its correctness. Then we introduce weaker forms of shared memory, namely, regular and safe registers, and argue that the Bakery algorithm is still correct. For safe registers, shared variables used in the algorithm can increase arbitrarily, but we describe a fix for this undesirable behavior [Lamport 1977].

1.2.1 The Mutual Exclusion Problem

The *mutual exclusion problem* concerns a group of processes that occasionally need access to some resource that cannot be used simultaneously by more than a single process; for example, some output device. Each process may need to execute a code segment called a *critical section* such that, informally speaking, at any time, at most one process is in the critical section (*mutual exclusion*), and if one or more processes try to enter the critical section, then one of them eventually succeeds as long as no process stays in the critical section forever (*no deadlock*).

The above properties do not provide any guarantee on an individual basis because a process may try to enter the critical section and yet fail because it is always bypassed by other processes. A stronger property, which implies no deadlock, is *no lockout*: If a process wishes to enter the critical section, then it will eventually succeed as long as no process stays in the critical section forever. (This property is sometimes called *no starvation*.) Later we will see an even stronger property that limits the number of times a process might be bypassed while trying to enter the critical section.

Original solutions to the mutual exclusion problem relied on special synchronization support, such as semaphores and monitors. Here we focus on *distributed* software solutions using ordinary shared variables.

Each process executes some additional code before and after the critical section to ensure the above properties; we assume the program of a process is partitioned into the following sections:

Entry (trying). The code executed in preparation for entering the critical section.

Critical. The code to be protected from concurrent execution.

Exit. The code executed on leaving the critical section.

Remainder. The rest of the code.

Each process cycles through these sections in the order remainder, entry, critical, and exit. If a process wants to enter the critical section, it first executes the entry section; after that, the process enters the critical section; then the process releases the critical section by executing the exit section and returning to the remainder section.

A mutual exclusion algorithm consists of code for the entry and exit sections and should work no matter what goes in the critical and remainder sections. In particular, a process may transition from the remainder section to the entry section any number of times, either finite or infinite. We assume that the variables, both shared and local, accessed in the entry and exit sections are *not* accessed in the critical and remainder sections. We also assume that no process stays in the critical section forever.

To capture these requirements, we make the following assumptions in the formal model. If a process takes a step while in the remainder (resp., critical) section, it immediately enters the entry (resp., exit) section. The definition of admissible execution is changed to allow a process to stop in the remainder section. Thus an execution is *admissible* if for every process p_i, either p_i takes an infinite number of steps or p_i ends in the remainder section.

More formally, an algorithm for a shared memory system solves the mutual exclusion problem with no deadlock (or no lockout) if the following hold:

Mutual exclusion. In every configuration of every execution, at most one process is in the critical section.

No deadlock. In every admissible execution, if some process is in the entry section in a configuration, then there is a later configuration in which some process is in the critical section.

No lockout. In every admissible execution, if some process is in the entry section in a configuration, then there is a later configuration in which *that same* process is in the critical section.

We also require that in an admissible execution, no process is ever stuck in the exit section; this is called the *unobstructed exit* condition. In all the algorithms presented in this chapter, the exit sections are straight-line code (i.e., no loops), and thus the condition obviously holds.

Note that the mutual exclusion condition is required to hold in every execution, not just admissible ones.

1.2.2 The Bakery Algorithm

In this section, we describe the Bakery algorithm for mutual exclusion among n processes; the algorithm provides mutual exclusion and no lockout.

The main idea is to consider processes wishing to enter the critical section as customers in a bakery. Each customer arriving at the bakery gets a number, and the one with the smallest number is the next to be served. The number of a customer who is not standing in line is 0 (which does not count as the smallest ticket).

To make the bakery metaphor more concrete, we employ the following shared data structures: *Number* is an array of n integers that holds in its ith entry the number of p_i; *Choosing* is an array of n Boolean values such that *Choosing*[i] is true while p_i is in the process of obtaining its number.

Each process p_i wishing to enter the critical section tries to choose a number that is greater than all the numbers of the other processes and writes it to *Number*[i]. This is done by reading *Number*[0], . . . , *Number*[$n - 1$] and taking the maximum among them plus one. However, because several processes can read *Number* concurrently, it is possible for several processes to obtain the same number. To break symmetry, we define p_i's ticket to be the pair (*Number*[i], i). Clearly, the tickets held by processes wishing to enter the critical section are unique. We use the lexicographic order on pairs to define an ordering between tickets.

Algorithm 1.1 **The Bakery algorithm: code for process** p_i, $0 \le i \le n - 1$

Initially $Number[i] = 0$ and
$Choosing[i] =$ false, for i, $0 \le i \le n - 1$

$\langle Entry \rangle$:
1 $Choosing[i] :=$ true
2 $Number[i] := \max(Number[0], \dots , Number[n - 1]) + 1$
3 $Choosing[i] :=$ false
4 **for** $j := 0$ to $n - 1 \, (\ne i)$ **do**
5   wait until $Choosing[j] =$ false
6   wait until $Number[j] = 0$ or $(Number[j], j) > (Number[i], i)$
7 **end for**
$\langle Critical\ Section \rangle$
$\langle Exit \rangle$:
8 $Number[i] := 0$
$\langle Remainder \rangle$

After choosing its number, p_i waits until its ticket is minimal: For each other process p_j, p_i waits until p_j is not in the middle of choosing its number and then compares their tickets. If p_j's ticket is smaller, p_i waits until p_j executes the critical section and leaves it. The pseudocode appears in Algorithm 1.1.

We now prove the correctness of the Bakery algorithm. That is, we prove that the algorithm provides the three properties discussed above, mutual exclusion, no deadlock, and no lockout.

Fix an execution α of the algorithm. To show mutual exclusion, we first prove a property concerning the relation between tickets of processes.

Lemma 1.1 In every configuration C of α, if process p_i is in the critical section and for some $k \ne i$, $Number[k] \ne 0$, then $(Number[k], k) > (Number[i], i)$.

Proof Since p_i is in the critical section in configuration C, it finished the for loop, in particular the second wait statement (line 6), for $j = k$. There are two cases according to the two conditions in line 6:

Case 1: p_i read that $Number[k] = 0$. In this case, when p_i finished line 6 (the second wait statement) with $j = k$, p_k either was in the remainder or was not finished choosing its number (since $Number[k] = 0$). But p_i already finished line 5 (the first wait statement) with $j = k$ and observed $Choosing[k] =$ false. Thus p_k was not in the middle of choosing its number. Therefore, p_k started reading the $Number$ array after p_i wrote to $Number[i]$. Thus, in configuration C, $Number[i] < Number[k]$, which implies $(Number[i], i) < (Number[k], k)$.

Case 2: p_i read that $(Number[k], k) > (Number[i], i)$. In this case, the condition will clearly remain valid until p_i exits the critical section or as long as p_k does not choose another number. If p_k chooses a new number, the condition will still be satisfied since the new number will be greater than $Number[i]$ (as in case 1). ∎

The above lemma implies that a process that is in the critical section has the smallest ticket among the processes trying to enter the critical section. To apply this lemma, we need to prove that whenever a process is in the critical section its number is nonzero.

Lemma 1.2 If p_i is in the critical section, then $Number[i] > 0$.

Proof First, note that for any process p_i, $Number[i]$ is always nonnegative. This can be easily proved by induction on the number of assignments to $Number$ in the execution. The base case is obvious by the initialization. For the inductive step, each number is assigned either 0 (when exiting the critical section) or a number greater than the maximum current value, which is nonnegative by assumption.

Each process chooses a number before entering the critical section. This number is strictly greater than the maximum current number, which is nonnegative. Therefore, the value chosen is positive. ∎

To prove mutual exclusion, note that if two processes, p_i and p_j, are simultaneously in the critical section, then $Number[i] \neq 0$ and $Number[j] \neq 0$, by Lemma 1.2. Lemma 1.1 can then be applied (twice) to derive that $(Number[i], i) < (Number[j], j)$ and $(Number[i], i) > (Number[j], j)$, which is a contradiction. This implies

Theorem 1.1 Algorithm 1.1 provides mutual exclusion.

Finally, we show that each process wishing to enter the critical section eventually succeeds (no lockout). This also implies the no deadlock property.

Theorem 1.2 Algorithm 1.1 provides no lockout.

Proof Consider any admissible execution. Thus no process stays in the critical section forever. Assume, by way of contradiction, that there is a starved process that wishes to enter the critical section but does not succeed. Clearly, all processes wishing to enter the critical section eventually finish choosing a number, because there is no way to be blocked while choosing a number. Let p_i be the process with the smallest $(Number[i], i)$ that is starved.

All processes entering the entry section after p_i has chosen its number will choose greater numbers and therefore will not enter the critical section before p_i. All processes with smaller numbers will eventually enter the critical section (since by assumption they are not starved) and exit it (since no process stays in the critical section forever). At this point, p_i will pass all the tests in the for loop and enter the critical section, a contradiction. ∎

The numbers chosen by the processes can grow without bound during an execution. However, their values are upper bounded by approximately the number of requests to enter the critical section that have occurred so far in the execution.

The Bakery algorithm tolerates failures of the processes under the assumption that a process that crashes returns to its remainder section and eventually all the variables that it writes are reset to zero. Crashed processes that are repaired can start participating in the algorithm again. However, if a process continually fails and restarts, then it could cause other processes to deadlock, as other processes might always read a one from the *Choosing* variable of the faulty process.

Another pleasing feature of the Bakery algorithm is that, unlike some of the previous mutual exclusion algorithms, "turns" are not preassigned to processes. Instead, turns are assigned to processes in the order in which they contend for access to the critical section, and thus contending processes can make progress regardless of the speed of noncontending processes.

1.2.3 Weakening the Shared Variables

The analysis of the Bakery algorithm given above assumes that shared registers are atomic, so that operations appear to occur instantaneously. One pleasant feature of the Bakery algorithm is that such strong memory is not necessary for its correctness. As discussed in more detail in Section 1.3, Lamport introduced weaker forms of memory, regular and safe, which take into account the fact that reads and writes in reality are not instantaneous. Informally, a read of a *regular* register returns either the value of an overlapping write or the value of the latest write that ends before the read begins. A read of a *safe* register that overlaps a write can return any value in the range of the register, but if the read does not overlap a write, then it returns the value of the latest write that ends before the read begins.

As pointed out in Lamport [1974a], nothing in the analysis of the correctness of the Bakery algorithm relies on the shared variables being atomic, and in fact the algorithm is correct even if the shared variables only satisfy the safe property. The *Choosing* variables are binary and thus every read, even if it overlaps a write, gets either the old value or the new value. However, reading a *Number* variable while it is being written could return an arbitrary value, neither the old nor new one.

Consequently, with safe registers, as opposed to atomic or regular, the values of the *Number* variables are not guaranteed to have any relationship to the number of critical section entry requests that have occurred in the system. Lamport [1977] shows how to keep the *Number* variables incrementing by 1 instead of by arbitrary amounts. Replace each *Number* variable with a sequence of safe variables, each one holding one (nonnegative) digit of the number. To write a value to a *Number* variable, write the digits, in the separate safe variables, from right to left. To read a value from a *Number* variable, read the digits, in the separate safe variables, in the opposite direction, from left to right.

The idea of reading and writing data items in opposite orders is a common theme in Lamport [1977], where it is also applied to solve other distributed synchronization problems, including general readers-writers and producer-consumer. It is also used in an algorithm presented in Section 1.3.

1.3 A Plethora of Registers

Lamport [1986d] delved deeper into a study of the different kinds of registers mentioned in Section 1.2 and explored how stronger ones could be wait-free implemented out of weaker ones (the "base" registers). An implementation is *wait-free* if every execution of an operation on the simulated register completes within a finite number of operations on the base registers, regardless of the behavior of other processes. Wait-free implementations are desirable as they avoid any dependence on solving mutual exclusion or on timing assumptions. In addition to the consistency condition (safe, regular, or atomic), the main parameters of interest are the number of values that can be stored in the register (two or more) and the number of processes that can read the register (one or more). This paper did not consider the possibility of multiple writers accessing the same register.

1.3.1 Increasing the Number of Readers

Lamport [1986d] gave an intuitive algorithm for implementing an m-reader safe register out of a collection of m single-reader safe registers, in which each reader is assigned to one of the registers to read. In order to write the value v to the simulated register, the writer writes v into each of the m single-reader registers, one at a time. In order for the ith reader to read the simulated register, it reads the register to which it is assigned. The simulated register provides the same number of values as do the base registers.

The algorithm is wait-free, as each operation on the simulated register consists of a fixed finite number of operations on the base registers. The safe condition is guaranteed as any simulated read that does not overlap a simulated write returns the latest value written in its assigned base register, which is the value of the latest simulated write.

As noted in Lamport [1986d], the algorithm also works if the base registers are regular to simulate a regular multi-reader register. The only danger is if the base register read inside a simulated read is concurrent with a base register write inside a simulated write. But the base read is guaranteed to get either the old or new value of the base register, which is also the old or new value of the simulated register.

Unfortunately, if the building block registers are atomic, the algorithm does not ensure that the simulated register is atomic, as it is possible for two consecutive simulated reads that are concurrent with a simulated write to see first the new value and then the old value; this behavior is called a *new-old inversion*. However, subsequent work by Israeli and Shaham [1993] provided a more complicated algorithm to solve this problem. In this algorithm, the readers of the simulated register exchange information among themselves by writing information to shared base registers; this information includes sequence numbers, which grow without bound. A brief description of this algorithm follows.

To avoid new-old inversions, the readers write to each other through additional registers, creating an ordering among them. Before a reader returns from a read operation, it announces the value it has decided to return. A reader reads not only the value written for it by the writer but also the values announced by the other readers. It then chooses the most recent value among the values it has read. In order to decide which value is most recent, every value written is tagged with a sequence number i indicating that the current value is the ith value written by the writer.

With more effort (e.g., [Dwork and Waarts 1992, Singh et al. 1994, Dolev and Shavit 1997, Attiya and Welch 1998]), the sequence numbers can be bounded. However, the requirement for readers to write is provably necessary, as shown next.

Theorem 1.3 In any wait-free implementation of a single-writer multi-reader atomic register from single-writer single-reader atomic registers, at least one reader must write [Attiya and Welch 2004].

Proof Suppose in contradiction there is such an algorithm for two readers p_1 and p_2 in which no reader writes. Let 0 be the initial value of the simulated register. Since the base registers are single-reader, we can partition them into two sets: S_1, which are read by p_1, and S_2, which are read by p_2. Consider the execution in which the writer writes 1 to the simulated register. The write algorithm performs a series of writes $w_1, w_2, \ldots, w_k$ to the base registers. Let v_j^i be the value that would be returned if p_i were to read the simulated register immediately after w_j, where $i = 1, 2$ and $j = 1, \ldots, k$.

For each reader, the atomicity condition requires that there be a point when the writes to the base registers cause the value of the simulated register, as it would be observed by that reader, to "switch" from the old value 0 to the new value 1. Suppose it is after w_a for p_1 for some a; that is, $v_1^1 = v_2^1 = \ldots = v_{a-1}^1 = 0$ while $v_a^1 = v_{a+1}^1 = \ldots = v_k^2 = 1$. Similarly, it is after w_b for p_2 for some b. Since the base registers are single-reader, a cannot equal b, as w_a must write to a register in S_1 while w_b must write to a register in S_2.

Without loss of generality, assume $a < b$. Now suppose that between w_a and w_{a+1}, p_1 reads the simulated register and then p_2 reads the simulated register. The first read will return the new value 1 while the second read will return the old value 0, which is a new-old inversion and violates atomicity, a contradiction. ∎

1.3.2 Increasing the Number of Values

When considering safe registers, Lamport [1986d] shows that the standard binary representation of integers suffices for implementing a k-valued register using $\lceil \log_2 k \rceil$ binary registers: In order to write the value v to the simulated register, the writer writes the bits of v's binary representation into the base registers. In order to read the simulated register, the reader reads all the base registers and returns the represented value. Any number of readers can be supported as long as the base registers support the same number.

Unfortunately, the binary representation algorithm does not work for the regular condition. If a read overlaps multiple writes, it may observe an arbitrary sequence of bits representing a value that is neither the previously written value nor that of any overlapping write.

Lamport [1986d] described an algorithm for implementing a k-valued regular register using k binary regular registers based on the unary encoding of the value. Let $b_1, b_2, \ldots, b_k$ be the base registers. To write v, the writer writes 1 into b_v and then writes 0 into b_{v-1} down to b_1. To read, each reader reads the binary registers in order $b_1, b_2, \ldots$ until observing a 1, say, in b_v; then the reader returns v. Any number of readers can be supported by the simulated register as long as the base registers support the same number of readers.

The correctness of this algorithm is not obvious (and in fact is proved using the formalism discussed in Section 1.4). Part of the analysis shows that the reader is guaranteed to observe a 1 in some base register, and thus the reader will never read a 0 from b_k. Hence b_k is not necessary and the algorithm can be optimized to use only $k - 1$ base registers.

Lamport [1986d] does not consider the analogous problem for atomic registers, other than pointing out that the regular algorithm is subject to new-old inversions and thus does not work in the atomic case. However, Vidyasankar [1988] gave an algorithm for implementing a k-valued atomic register using binary atomic registers, where $k > 2$. Like the regular algorithm, it is based on the unary representation of the value and thus uses k base registers $b_1, b_2, \ldots, b_k$, but it has a new twist. The value i is represented by a 1 in b_i and 0 in all other base registers. To avoid new-old inversions, two changes are made to the regular algorithm. First, a write operation clears *only* the entries whose indices are smaller than the value it is writing. Second, a read operation does not stop when it finds the first 1 but makes sure there are still zeros in all lower indices. Specifically, the reader scans from the low values toward the high values until it finds the first 1; then it reverses direction and scans back down to the beginning, keeping track of the smallest index observed to contain a 1 during the downward scan. This is the value returned.

1.3.3 Strengthening the Consistency Condition

Implementing a regular binary register out of a safe binary register is easy [Lamport 1986d]. The only delicate point is that the writer should not write the safe register unless it is actually changing the value. Otherwise, reading and writing the simulated register is done simply by reading and writing the base register.

Using regular base registers to simulate an atomic register is rather involved. Lamport [1986d] presents an algorithm for one reader that implements a k-valued atomic register using two regular registers. One of the regular registers must hold $2k(k + 2)$ values and is written by the writer and read by the reader, while the other one is Boolean and is written by the reader and read by the writer. This algorithm also has a nontrivial correctness proof, which is done using the formalism discussed in Section 1.4.

Note that in the algorithm for implementing an atomic register out of regular registers, the reader and writer communicate with each other. It turns out that it is necessary for the reader to write for such algorithms [Lamport 1986d].

Theorem 1.4 In any algorithm that implements an atomic register using a finite number of regular registers, one of the regular registers must be written by a reader.

Proof Assume in contradiction that there is such an algorithm in which no reader writes to a base register. First note that without loss of generality, since there is only one writer, we can assume that there is only one base register and the writer writes to it just once. Similarly, we can argue that there is no point in a reader reading the base register more than once.

Suppose the initial value of the simulated register is 0. Consider an execution of the algorithm consisting of the following three consecutive operations on the simulated register: read 0, write 1, read 1. Each simulated operation consists of a single operation on the base register: first a read, then a write, and then a read. Let v_0 be the state of the base register before the write and v_1 be its state afterward. This execution implies that if the reader reads v_0 (resp., v_1) from the base register, then it must return 0 (resp., 1).

Now consider another execution in which two consecutive reads overlap a write of 1, and in particular, both reads of the base register overlap the write to the base register. Because the base register only satisfies regularity, it is possible for the first read to obtain v_1 and the second read to obtain v_0. Thus the first read returns 1 and the second read returns 0, which is a new-old inversion and violates atomicity. ∎

1.3.4   Increasing the Number of Writers

The case of multiple writers is not considered in Lamport [1986d] and has primarily been studied only for atomic registers, as generalizing the definitions of the safe and regular conditions for multiple writers is more involved. Vitányi and Awerbuch [1986] presented an algorithm for implementing a multi-writer atomic register out of single-writer atomic registers. In this algorithm, the writers communicate among themselves, and thus writers read; part of the information they exchange are sequence numbers that grow without bound.

A simplified version of the algorithm works as follows [Christian Cachin, personal communication, 2006]. Each writer is assigned one base register. All values written are tagged with a sequence number. To write the value v to the simulated register, a writer reads all the registers, chooses the largest sequence number that it observes, increments this sequence number by 1, and writes v together with the sequence number to its register. To read the simulated register, a reader reads all the registers and returns the value associated with the largest sequence number.

With more effort, the sequence numbers can be bounded (e.g., [Dwork and Waarts 1992, Dolev and Shavit 1997, Attiya and Welch 1998, Israeli 2005]). However, the requirement for readers to write is provably necessary, as shown next.

Theorem 1.5   In any wait-free implementation of a multi-writer atomic register from single-writer atomic registers, at least one writer must read.

Proof   Suppose in contradiction there is such an algorithm for two writers p_1 and p_2 in which no writer reads. Since the base registers are single-writer, we can partition them into two sets: S_1, which are written by p_1, and S_2, which are written by p_2. Consider the execution in which p_1 writes 1 to the simulated register, then p_2 writes 2 to the simulated register, and then a reader reads the simulated register; by atomicity the reader must obtain 2.

Since the writers do not read, each one is oblivious to the existence of other writers or readers and thus it always writes the same values to the same base registers, depending solely on its own local history. Also, since the writers write to disjoint sets of base registers, they cannot overwrite each other. As a result, the values of all the base registers in the two executions are the same after the two writes take place. Thus the reader observes the same values in the base registers in the second execution as it does in the first and returns 2, which is a new-old inversion and violates atomicity.   ∎

1.4 A New Model for Describing Concurrency

Many arguments about the correctness of shared memory algorithms were informal, and Lamport was interested in also having more formal proofs that could be used, for instance, in proving the register algorithms discussed in Section 1.3. Toward this goal, he presented a formalism in Lamport [1986c] for specifying concurrent systems that, unlike previous ones, did not assume that actions are atomic. For concreteness, imagine a system that implements operations on a shared object where the operations consist of lower-level actions and there is a global time model. Since the operations are not atomic, they might overlap in time. One operation execution A can "affect" another operation B if A either precedes or overlaps B. That is, some lower-level action inside A precedes some lower-level action inside B.

More formally, a *system execution* is a triple $\langle S, \longrightarrow, \dashrightarrow \rangle$, where S is a set of *operation executions* and $\longrightarrow$ and $\dashrightarrow$ are precedence relations on S satisfying

A1. $\longrightarrow$ is an irreflexive partial ordering.

A2. If $A \longrightarrow B$, then $A \dashrightarrow B$ and $B \not\longrightarrow B$. (If A precedes B, then A can affect B but B does not precede A.)

A3. If $A \longrightarrow B \dashrightarrow C$ or $A \dashrightarrow B \longrightarrow C$, then $A \longrightarrow C$. (If A precedes B and B can affect C, then A can affect C, and similarly if A can affect B and B precedes C.)

A4. If $A \longrightarrow B \dashrightarrow C \longrightarrow D$, then $A \longrightarrow D$. (If A precedes B, B can affect C, and C precedes D, then A precedes D.)

A5. For any A, the set of all B such that $A \not\longrightarrow B$ is finite. (Only a finite number of operation executions precede or overlap A.)

Lamport's experience is that "proofs based upon these axioms are simpler and more instructive than ones that involve modeling operation executions as sets of events" [Lamport 1986c]. See below for an example of a correctness proof using this formalism.

This formalism facilitates specifying and reasoning about hierarchical systems. Suppose $\langle S, \longrightarrow, --\rightarrow \rangle$ is a system execution. Let $\mathcal{H}$ be a set whose elements are sets of operation executions from S; the elements of $\mathcal{H}$ are called *higher-level operation executions*. An intuitive interpretation is that each higher-level operation in $\mathcal{H}$ is executed via a set of (lower-level) operation executions in S.

More formally, suppose G and H are in $\mathcal{H}$. Define $G \xrightarrow{\ *\ } H$ to mean that for all $A \in G$ and for all $B \in H$, $A \longrightarrow B$; i.e., G precedes H if every lower-level operation in G precedes every lower-level operation in H. Define $G --\overset{*}{\dashrightarrow} H$ to mean there exists $A \in G$ and there exists $B \in H$ such that $A --\rightarrow B$ or $A = B$; i.e., G can affect H if there exists a lower-level operation in A that either can affect or is equal to some lower-level operation in B.

The triple $\langle \mathcal{H}, \xrightarrow{\ *\ }, --\overset{*}{\dashrightarrow} \rangle$ satisfies Axioms A1–A4 because $\langle S, \longrightarrow, --\rightarrow \rangle$ does. In order to ensure that $\langle \mathcal{H}, \xrightarrow{\ *\ }, --\overset{*}{\dashrightarrow} \rangle$ is a system execution, it remains to add the following requirement that ensures Axiom A5: Each element of $\mathcal{H}$ is a finite, nonempty subset of S, and each element of S belongs to at least one element of $\mathcal{H}$ (but only a finite number). If $\mathcal{H}$ satisfies this condition, then $\mathcal{H}$ is called a *higher-level view* of S.

A system execution $\langle S, \longrightarrow, --\rightarrow \rangle$ *implements* a system execution $\langle \mathcal{H}, \xrightarrow{\ \mathcal{H}\ }, --\overset{\mathcal{H}}{\dashrightarrow} \rangle$ if $\mathcal{H}$ is a higher-level view of S and for all G and H in $\mathcal{H}$, if $G \xrightarrow{\ *\ } H$, then $G \xrightarrow{\ \mathcal{H}\ } H$.

A *system* is defined to be a set of system executions. A system **S** *implements* a system **H** if there is a mapping $\iota: \mathbf{S} \mapsto \mathbf{H}$ such that for every system execution $\langle S, \longrightarrow, --\rightarrow \rangle$ in **S**, $\langle S, \longrightarrow, --\rightarrow \rangle$ implements $\iota(\langle S, \longrightarrow, --\rightarrow \rangle)$.

Lamport [1986d] refines the formalism from [1986c] specifically for analyzing register implementations (cf. Section 1.3). The following additional axioms that must be satisfied by system executions are stated for a single register:

B0. The set of write operations is $\{V^{[0]}, V^{[1]}, \ldots\}$ with $V^{[0]} \longrightarrow V^{[1]} \longrightarrow \ldots$, where $V^{[i]}$ writes the value $v^{[i]}$, and for each read R, $V^{[0]} \longrightarrow R$. That is, all the writes are totally ordered, as there is only one writer, and there is an initial write that precedes every read.

B1. For each read R and write W, either $R --\rightarrow W$ or $W --\rightarrow R$. That is, there must be some causal connection between the reads and writes.

B2. Each read obtains one of the values that may be written to the register.

The axioms for safe, regular, and atomic registers rely on the following definition: A read R is said to *see* $v^{[i,j]}$, where i is the maximum k such that $R --\overset{}{\not\dashrightarrow} V^{[k]}$ and j is the maximum k such that $V^{[k]} \dashrightarrow R$. That is, R can see traces of the values written by the writes between $V^{[i]}$ and $V^{[j]}$.

B3. A read that sees $v^{[i,i]}$ obtains the value $v^{[i]}$. That is, a read that does not overlap any writes returns the value of the latest preceding write.

B4. A read that sees $v^{[i,j]}$ obtains the value $v^{[k]}$, for some k with $i \leq k \leq j$. That is, a read returns the value of an overlapping write or the latest preceding write.

B5. If a read sees $v^{[i,j]}$, then $i = j$. That is, a read does not (appear to) overlap any write.

A safe register satisfies B0–B3, a regular register satisfies B0–B4, and an atomic register satisfies B0–B5.

Consider the algorithm discussed in Section 1.3.1 for implementing an m-reader safe register out of m single-reader safe registers, denoted $v_1, \ldots, v_m$. Here is an outline of how the formalism is used to prove its correctness. The construction defines a system **S** that consists of all system executions $\langle \mathcal{S}, \longrightarrow, \dashrightarrow \rangle$ such that

- $\mathcal{S}$ consists of reads and writes of the v_i registers.

- Each v_i, $1 \leq i \leq m$, is written by the same writer and is read only by the ith reader.

- For each i and j, $1 \leq i, j \leq m$, if the write $V_i^{[k]}$ occurs, then $V_j^{[k]}$ also occurs and $V_i^{[k-1]} \longrightarrow V_j^{[k]}$. That is, a high-level write consists of writing all the v_i's and one high-level write finishes before the next begins.

- Each v_i is a safe register, i.e., satisfies B0–B3.

The target system **H** consists of all system executions $\langle \mathcal{H}, \xrightarrow{\mathcal{H}}, \dashxrightarrow{\mathcal{H}} \rangle$ that consist of reads and writes to an m-reader safe register. To show that **S** implements **H**, it must be shown there is a mapping $\iota : \mathbf{S} \mapsto \mathbf{H}$ such that for every system execution $\langle \mathcal{S}, \longrightarrow, \dashrightarrow \rangle$ in **S**, $\langle \mathcal{S}, \longrightarrow, \dashrightarrow \rangle$ implements some system execution $\iota(\langle \mathcal{S}, \longrightarrow, \dashrightarrow \rangle)$ in $\mathcal{H}$. Given $\langle \mathcal{S}, \longrightarrow, \dashrightarrow \rangle$, the mapping ι is defined as follows. The set of high-level operation executions, denoted $\iota(\mathcal{S})$, is created by having each set of low-level writes $\{V_1^{[k]}, \ldots V_m^{[k]}\}$ form a high-level write $V^{[k]}$ and having each low-level read form a high-level read. Then define $\xrightarrow{\mathcal{H}}$ to be $\xrightarrow{*}$ and $\dashxrightarrow{\mathcal{H}}$ to be $\dashxrightarrow{*}$. To finish the proof, it must be shown that $\langle \iota(\mathcal{S}), \xrightarrow{\mathcal{H}}, \dashxrightarrow{\mathcal{H}} \rangle$ is a system execution (satisfies A1–A5), $\langle \mathcal{S}, \longrightarrow, \dashrightarrow \rangle$ implements $\langle \iota(\mathcal{S}), \xrightarrow{\mathcal{H}}, \dashxrightarrow{\mathcal{H}} \rangle$, and $\langle \iota(\mathcal{S}), \xrightarrow{\mathcal{H}}, \dashxrightarrow{\mathcal{H}} \rangle$ is in **H** (satisfies B0–B3 for the simulated register).

1.5 Sequential Consistency

Lamport coined the term *sequentially consistent* for a multiprocessor that ensures that "the result of any execution is the same as if the operations of all the processes were executed in some sequential order, and the operations of each individual process appear in this sequence in the order specified by its program" [Lamport 1979b]. This correctness condition had been considered in previous work (e.g., [Dijkstra 1971, Owicki and Gries 1976, Lamport 1977]) but not under this name. As we explain below, sequentially consistent memory is weaker than atomic memory but is incomparable with regular and safe memory.

Even though a multiprocessor contains sequential processes, the sequential nature of the processes alone is not sufficient to ensure sequential consistency for the multiprocessor, since memory operations are not instantaneous. However, in Lamport [1979b], two necessary and sufficient conditions are given to ensure that the multiprocessor is sequentially consistent.

The first condition, R1, is that each process must issue its memory fetch and store requests in the order of its program. This is fairly intuitive, but does rule out some optimizations that are benign in the single-process situation.

The second condition, R2, is that all memory requests to the same memory module (or cell) must be serviced in the order in which the requests are made. In other words, there is a single FIFO queue for each memory module into which requests are put. Here's an example execution showing that without R2, sequential consistency is violated. Suppose there are two shared variables, a and b, both initially 0, and two processes, p_1 and p_2. Let p_1's sequential program consist of writing 1 to a and then reading b, while p_2's sequential program consists of writing 1 to b and then reading a. Consider the execution in which p_1 sends a request to write 1 to a to memory module 1, which is currently busy and thus puts the request in a queue, and then p_1 sends a request to read b to memory module 2, which immediately services the request. Then suppose p_2 sends a request to write 1 to b to memory module 2, which immediately services the request, and then p_2 sends a request to read a to memory module 1. If memory module 1 is still busy, then p_2's request is put in a queue, which is not the one containing p_1's request. Suppose memory module 1 eventually services p_2's read request before p_1's write request (see Figure 1.1). Then p_2's read of a gets the old value 0 instead of the new value 1. There is no sequentially consistent way to reconcile this behavior with the fact that p_1's read of b gets the old value 0.

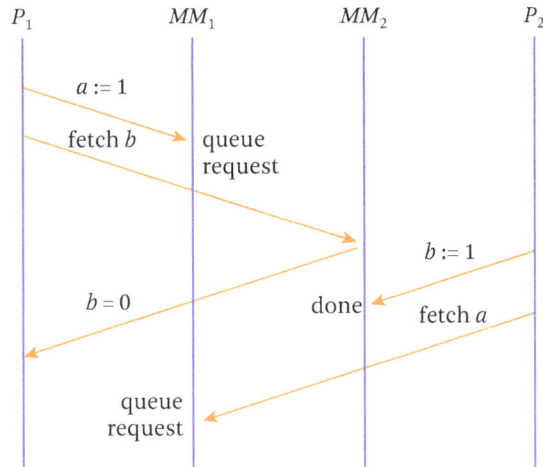

Figure 1.1   Diagram to justify the necessity of condition R2.

To prove the sufficiency of R1 and R2, first define a relation $\rightarrow$ on memory requests that orders requests by the same process in the order in which the process issues them and orders requests by different processes on the same memory module in the order in which the requests are enqueued. It is straightforward to see that $\rightarrow$ is a partial ordering. Then it can be shown that in any execution of the multiprocessor, each fetch and store operation has the same effect as if the operations were executed instantaneously in any total order that is consistent with the $\rightarrow$ partial order.

Tying back to the registers discussed in Section 1.3, sequential consistency is weaker than atomicity. Both conditions require a sequential ordering of the operations, but for atomic registers the ordering must reflect that of all non-overlapping operations, while for sequential consistency it is only for operations by the same process. Thus an execution in which one process writes a new value to the register and then later a second process reads the old value of the register may be sequentially consistent but not atomic. On the other hand, sequential consistency is incomparable with both regularity and safety, as the previous execution is not safe (and thus not regular), but the following execution is regular (and thus safe) but not sequentially consistent: the reader does two consecutive reads, both of which overlap with a write, where the first read returns the new value and the second read returns the old value.

A tremendous amount of work has been done on sequential consistency. A few (nonexhaustive) directions of interest include lower bounds on the latency of operations on sequentialy consistent memory (e.g., Lipton and Sandberg [1988]); performance differences between sequential consistency and other conditions (e.g., Attiya and Welch [1994]); identifying programming patterns that provide the illusion of sequential consistency on top of weaker conditions (e.g., Adve and Hill [1990], Gibbons et al. [1991]); determining whether a multiprocess actually provides sequential consistency (e.g., Gibbons [1997]); and understanding the complexity of deciding whether a protocol provides sequential consistency (e.g., Condon and Hu [2003]).

The Notions of Time and Global State in a Distributed System

Karolos Antoniadis, Rachid Guerraoui

2.1 Introduction

Our day-to-day life is filled with a smorgasbord of *events*: a child drops a ball, a phone rings, etc. Ordering such events by global time is simple. For example, if the phone rings at 2:00 PM and the child drops the ball at 5:00 PM, then we know that the phone rang *before* the child dropped the ball. But what if events occur very close to each other in time? It is still easy to order events if we are present when they occur. For instance, we can easily recognize that we received an email before our colleague coughed. Things get tricky if we want to order events occurring close to each other in different parts of the world. To give an example, Figure 2.1 depicts two persons, John and Alice, experiencing events. In this example, John buys a chocolate bar at time 10:59 PM based on his watch, while Alice gets the newspaper at time 11:00 PM based on her watch. But if Alice's watch is 3 minutes ahead then in reality, the purchase of the newspaper occurred before the purchase of the chocolate.

Nevertheless and as we will see later on, if the two persons interact in some way, then we can potentially infer the order of some events. For instance, if Alice throws a banana peel and then John passes by and slips on it, then we can infer that the throwing of the banana peel *happened before* the slip. In other words, we cannot really deduce whether the purchase of the chocolate or the newspaper took place first, but we can be certain that Alice first threw the banana peel and thereafter John slipped on it. We depict this "happens before" relation with an arrow between the

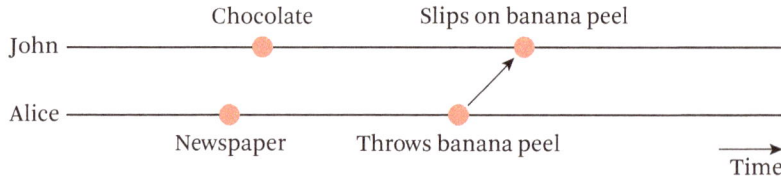

Figure 2.1 Two persons, John and Alice, experiencing events.

related events in Figure 2.1. Notice that in Figure 2.1, as well as all other figures in this chapter, time is depicted from left to right.

Similar to real life with different people, ordering events in distributed computing systems is a difficult issue. Distributed computing systems consist of a set of independent Turing machines (also called *processes* or *nodes*) that communicate with each other. Processes perform *events* that in a distributed system correspond to performing a computation, sending or delivering messages. We could try to introduce physical clocks to the processes to order events, but it would be difficult to keep them synchronized in order to extract meaningful information from them. It is natural for clocks to drift apart, so some clocks might move faster than others.

Lamport devised an approach to order events without resorting to physical time. His approach captures what he called *logical time*. Roughly speaking, logical time orders events based on *causality*: if some event possibly causes another event, then the first event *happens before* the other. We describe logical time in Section 2.2.

Lamport introduced his notion of logical time in 1978 in his celebrated paper "Time, Clocks, and the Ordering of Events in a Distributed System" [Lamport 1978b]. This paper is mostly known for defining logical time, as well as the concept of causality. However, of equal if not greater importance was the introduction (in the same paper) of a way to implement an arbitrary *state machine* in a distributed setting. In other words, he devised an approach that is based on a logical ordering of events and that can be used to implement in a distributed fashion every possible algorithm. We describe the distributed state machine abstraction idea and an algorithm to implement any algorithm in a distributed setting in Section 2.3.

Lastly, in Section 2.4 we describe the very concept of global state and how to retrieve it in a distributed system. This was first introduced in the influential paper by Chandy and Lamport [1985] titled "Distributed Snapshots: Determining Global States of Distributed Systems." This paper utilized ideas from logical time to capture the concept of *global state* in a distributed system.

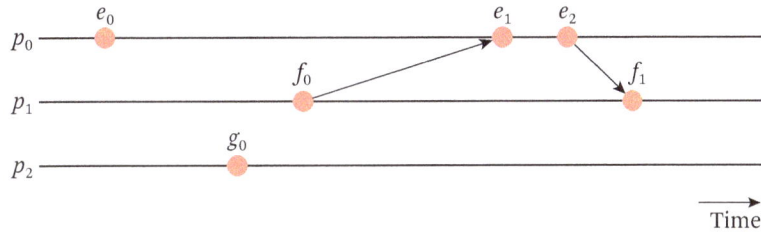

Figure 2.2   Three processes and their respective events.

2.2 The Notion of Logical Time

A distributed system consists of a set of independent processes (Turing machines) that communicate with each other, typically by exchanging messages[1] as depicted in Figure 2.2. Three types of events can take place in a distributed system from the perspective of every process: (i) perform some local computation, (ii) send a message, and (iii) deliver a message.

In Figure 2.2, we depict three processes p_0, p_1, and p_2 together with their respective events. Process p_0 performs some local computation (event e_0), then delivers a message (event e_1) and afterward sends a message (event e_2). Similarly, process p_1 sends a message (event f_0) and delivers a message (event f_1). Process p_2 performs a single computation (event g_0).

As we pointed out before, it is challenging to order events based on the actual physical time when the events occur. Sometimes, we are not even interested in which event took place first. For example, in Figure 2.2, whether e_0 took place before or after g_0 is perhaps unlikely to be of any consequence. Furthermore, even if we could augment each process with a physical clock, physical clocks could drift apart from each other, making it challenging to order events. Lamport realized that we can order events in a different but still useful way: based on *causality*. This way, if an event e possibly causes event f, then we can order these two events e and f and argue that e happened before f. For instance, if an event corresponds to a delivery of a message, this means that the event that sent this message preceded the delivery event. Knowledge of the order of events can be utilized to build distributed state machines. Knowing the order of events can also be useful in debugging distributed systems, garbage collecting old versions of data, etc. Lamport devised an algorithm

---

1. A multiprocessor can also be considered a distributed system. However, processes in a multiprocessor communicate by reading/writing to shared memory (see Chapter 1).

that captures what is called *logical time* and can express the possible causal order between events.

Remarks. Lamport's main inspiration for logical time was a report titled "The Maintenance of Duplicate Databases" by Johnson and Thomas [1975]. Johnson and Thomas introduced in this report the notion of timestamps in order to keep different copies of a database eventually consistent.[2] They used timestamps to order the operations issued to a distributed database. However, the timestamps they proposed were associated with clocks of processes and hence could get out of synchrony, thus violating causality. Furthermore, their work was specific to distributed databases. In contrast, logical time is applicable to every distributed system. As a side note, Johnson and Thomas pointed out in the same work that when a network partition occurs, either consistency is violated or we cannot provide availability. Eric Brewer made a similar observation 25 years later that is today known as the CAP theorem [Brewer 2000, Gilbert and Lynch 2002].

Another source of inspiration for logical time was Lamport's knowledge of special relativity. According to special relativity there is no fixed order on the exact time an event took place: different observers could experience the same event at different times. Lamport realized that the same principle applies to the events of a distributed system; however, we can still argue whether one event could have potentially caused another one.

2.2.1 Causality and Logical Time

Lamport's idea behind logical time is both simple and clever. Lamport realized that certain events in a distributed system are associated with each other through a "happens before" relation, while others are not. We cannot relate all events with regard to "happens before" since some events are concurrent (e.g., events e_0 and g_0 of Figure 2.2 are concurrent). Nevertheless, there are cases in which we can clearly state that one event happened before another event. For example, all the events that are occurring at a single process are ordered sequentially (e.g., a process first performed a computation, then the process sent a message, etc.). In other words, the "happens before" relation induces a partial order.

Given two events $e, f, e \rightarrow f$ denotes that an event e precedes another event f and we say that e "happens before" f. The $\rightarrow$ relation captures *causality* since it

---

2. *Eventually consistent* means that if processes stop performing updates to the database for enough time, then eventually all the copies of the database contain the exact same data.

means that e potentially caused f. We can infer whether an event e precedes an event f based on the following rules:

- If one process performs an event e before starting an event f, we can infer that e precedes f ($e \rightarrow f$).

- If e corresponds to the sending of a message from some process and f corresponds to the respective delivery of this message by some other process, then we can establish that $e \rightarrow f$.

- Naturally, transitivity applies and therefore if an event g exists such that $e \rightarrow g$ and $g \rightarrow f$, then $e \rightarrow f$.

Logical time refers to the fact that we can utilize the $\rightarrow$ relation to order events without knowing the actual physical time of the events.

2.2.2 An Algorithm to Capture Causality

A process in a distributed algorithm could utilize the notion of logical time to wait until something happens, before it proceeds to perform a computation. Therefore, capturing the aforementioned notion of causality algorithmically can prove useful. (We will see an example of the usefulness of capturing causality in the next section.)

To capture causality, Lamport devised a simple algorithm (see Algorithm 2.1). This algorithm can be used to augment other distributed algorithms and allow them to know if an event e precedes another event f. The algorithm operates as follows. Each process p is associated with a *logical clock* t_p that "ticks" at every event. In other words, each event is associated with a number (also known as *Lamport timestamp*) that is given by the logical clock. Each time a process p performs an event, p increments its clock t_p. Furthermore, each message is augmented with this clock value, so when a process p sends a message, p also includes the value of t_p. On the other end, when a process p receives a message, p sets its timestamp to the maximum between its local clock timestamp t_p and the received timestamp and then p increments t_p by one. Assuming the timestamp of each event is given by a function $C : events \rightarrow \mathbb{N}$, Algorithm 2.1 guarantees that for every two events e and f, if $e \rightarrow f$, then $C(e) < C(f)$. Figure 2.3 depicts the execution of Algorithm 2.1 and the timestamp assigned to each event.

Total Order.   We can extend the partial order of events to a total order by extending the timestamp with a unique identifier. This identifier could be, for example, the process identifier. For instance, an event in such a setting would be (e, id_e) where e is an event and id_e is an identifier. Then for any two events (e, id_e) and (f, id_f) we can say that $(e, id_e) < (f, id_f)$ if $e \rightarrow f$, or if $e \nrightarrow f$ and $f \nrightarrow e$ and $id_e < id_f$.

Algorithm 2.1   **Lamport's timestamps (for a process** p**)**

procedure ONCOMPUTATION()
  $t_p \leftarrow t_p + 1$
end procedure

procedure ONSEND (msg, p_k) ▷ send message *msg* to process p_k
  $t_p \leftarrow t_p + 1$
  $send([msg, t_p], p_k)$
end procedure

procedure ONRECEIVE()   ▷ on receiving some message
  $[m, t] \leftarrow receive()$
  $t_p \leftarrow \max(t, t_p) + 1$
end procedure

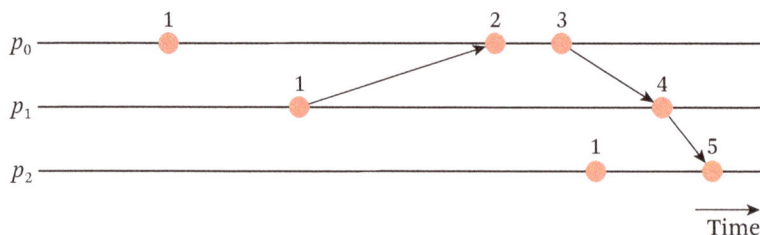

Figure 2.3   The timestamps assigned to events by using Algorithm 2.1.

By extending the partial order to a total order, we can utilize the total order to implement an arbitrary distributed state machine, as we show in the next section.

2.2.3   Impact of Logical Time

Lamport's work on logical time had an enormous impact in both theory research and practical systems.

An important extension emerging from Lamport's clocks is the notion of *vector clocks*. Vector clocks can capture the *lack* of causality while Lamport's clocks cannot. In other words, if $e \rightarrow f$, then $C(e) < C(f)$, but $C(e) < C(f)$ does not mean that $e \rightarrow f$. For example, in Figure 2.3, the first event of process p_2 has a smaller timestamp than the third event of process p_0; however, this does not mean that p_2's first event occurred before the third event of p_0. Vector clocks were developed independently in the late 1980s by Fidge [1988], Mattern [1989], and Schmuck [1988].

In practical systems, ideas based on logical time have been extensively used for replicating data (e.g., ISIS [Birman 1986, Birman et al. 1991]), debugging purposes (e.g., ShiViz [Beschastnikh et al. 2016]), garbage collection [Liskov and Ladin 1986, Terry et al. 1995], and reducing message communication (e.g., Bayou [Terry et al. 1995]). Among others, *version vectors* [Parker et al. 1983] that utilize logical time have been used in key-value stores, such as Dynamo [DeCandia et al. 2007], Riak [2019], and Voldemort [2019], as well as file systems (e.g., Coda [Satyanarayanan et al. 1990]) to handle write conflicts. Recently, causal consistency has gained attention. Causal consistency [Ahamad et al. 1995] is a consistency model inspired by causality and is the strongest consistency model that can tolerate network partitions [Attiya et al. 2015]. A multitude of recent distributed storage systems [Didona 2018, Du 2014, Lloyd et al. 2011, Lloyd et al. 2013, Zawirski et al. 2015] provide causal consistency.

2.3 The Distributed State Machine Abstraction

As with logical time, Lamport's inspiration behind the distributed machine abstraction was the Johnson and Thomas report [Johnson and Thomas 1975]. Johnson and Thomas tried to keep different copies (i.e., replicas) of a database eventually consistent, while allowing each replica to independently introduce updates. Lamport came up with a clean abstraction to solve this problem: the *distributed state machine abstraction*. Lamport's main insight behind the distributed state machine abstraction is that, by applying commands in the same order at all the replicas of a distributed system, we can obtain a universal approach for keeping the replicas consistent with each other.

Roughly speaking, Lamport's idea states that all the processes together simulate a state machine. This can be achieved if each process applies the exact same commands of the machine and in the same order as every other process. Specifically, this can be done with the following approach. Each process contains a local copy of the state machine. All processes initialize their state machine to the same initial state. Processes apply commands to their state machine such that each process applies the exact same commands in the same order.

The main difficulty of such an approach is ordering the commands, and this is where logical time comes into play. Although the approach seems simple, Lamport was the first one to conceptualize it, and it had an immense impact in practical systems.

We call an algorithm that implements a universal state machine in a distributed system by utilizing replication a *state machine replication* (SMR) algorithm. SMR algorithms are useful in practice in order to implement fault-tolerant systems. Implementing an SMR algorithm in a system where failures can occur (e.g., crashes) is a difficult problem [Lamport 1998a, Liskov and Cowling 2012, Ongaro and Ousterhout 2014].

To demonstrate the universality of the SMR approach, Lamport first presented a simple SMR algorithm that does not tolerate process failures. Equipped with the notions of logical time and SMR, the problem of keeping the replicas of a database consistent with each other is simply a matter of tracking the logical time of the updates that are separately generated and received by them. At the time there was no solution for keeping the copies of a database consistent.

Additionally, Lamport's SMR algorithm assumes that the communication links between processes are *perfect* and *FIFO* [Cachin et al. 2011]. By perfect we mean that if a process p sends a message m to a process q, then q eventually delivers m; and by FIFO we mean that if a process p sends a message m_1 before sending message m_2 to some process q, then q cannot deliver m_2 before having delivered m_1.

We continue by presenting Lamport's SMR algorithm that uses logical time. We conclude this section by discussing the impact Lamport's idea had in the theory of distributed computing, as well as in practical systems.

2.3.1   SMR Algorithm

We consider a state machine sm that serves commands $c_1, \ldots, c_k$, and we want to have a distributed algorithm in which each process simulates the execution of this state machine. In the following description we assume an *asynchronous* system with n processes $p_0, p_1, \ldots, p_{n-1}$. Each process has a state machine sm in an initial state. Additionally, each process contains a *log* of unexecuted (i.e., not yet applied) commands. Figure 2.4 depicts the data structures each process maintains locally, where the right box corresponds to the log of not yet applied commands (i.e., commands c_3 and c_{13} have not yet been applied to sm). Each entry in the log contains a Lamport timestamp, and the log is kept sorted according to timestamp order.

Finally, each process contains an array of n timestamps, the latest timestamp received from each other process. Process p_i maintains its own logical clock in *timestamps*[i]. Timestamps are maintained based on the Lamport timestamp algorithm presented in Section 2.2.2. In what follows, when we say that a message containing a timestamp t is being sent, this means that t corresponds to the timestamp given by the logical clock of the process for the "sending of the message" event.

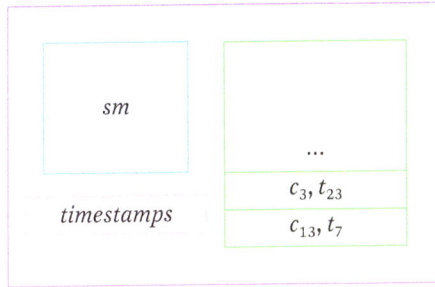

Figure 2.4   The data structures that a process maintains locally.

The main idea behind the SMR algorithm is that a process p can apply a command c by first broadcasting a message m that contains command c to all the other processes. Process p can apply command c to p's state machine when p receives from all the other processes at least one message carrying a higher timestamp than m.

Specifically, the SMR algorithm operates using the following simple rules:

- When a process p_i receives a message containing a timestamp t from another process p_j, p_i updates the *timestamps*[j] element of the array to contain t (recall that links are FIFO).

- To apply a command c_k, process p_i sends message $[c_k, t]$ to all the other processes where t is the timestamp of the message. Then, process p_i creates an entry $[c_k, t]$ and appends this entry to the log of not yet applied commands.

- When a process p_i receives a message $[c_k, t]$, process p_i appends the $[c_k, t]$ entry in its log of not yet applied commands and subsequently sends an acknowledgment message (i.e., $[ack, t']$) to every other process (i.e., broadcasts the message). Naturally, it is the case that $t' > t$. By sending an acknowledgment message, a process informs other processes that it has received the command.

- A process p_i applies a command c_k if the first (i.e., oldest) entry in p_i's log of not yet applied commands is $[c_k, t]$. However, p_i can only apply command c_k if p_i has received messages from every other process with timestamps greater than t (i.e., all the timestamps in the *timestamps* array contain values $> t$). If this is the case, p_i can apply c_k on its local state machine and remove the entry from its log.

Algorithm 2.2 presents the algorithm of process p_i.

Algorithm 2.2 **An SMR algorithm using logical time**

1   ▷ local variables
2   $sm_i \leftarrow init$ ▷ initial state machine
3   $log_i \leftarrow \emptyset$ ▷ log of not yet applied commands
4   $timestamps[n] \leftarrow \{0, \ldots, 0\}$

5   **procedure** APPLYCOMMAND(c_k)
6      $timestamps[i] \leftarrow timestamps[i] + 1$
7      $\forall p_j \neq p_i, send([c_k, timestamps[i]], p_j)$
8      $log_i.append([c_k, timestamps[i]])$
9   **end procedure**

10   **procedure** ONRECEIVE ()
11   ▷ p_i on receiving a message from process p_j
12      $msg \leftarrow receive()$
13   **if** $msg = [c_l, t_j]$ is a command message **then**
14          $log_i.append([c_l, t_j])$
15          $timestamps[i] \leftarrow \max(timestamps[i], t_j) + 1$
16          $timestamps[j] \leftarrow t_j$
17          $\forall p_j \neq p_i, send([ack, timestamps[i]], p_j)$
18   **else**   ▷ $msg = [ack, t_j]$ is an acknowledgment (*ack*) message
19          $timestamps[j] \leftarrow t_j$
20   **end if**
21   **end procedure**

22   **procedure** CONSTANTCHECK()
23   **while** *true* **do**
24          $[first\_command, first\_ts] \leftarrow log_i.peek()$
25          $can\_apply \leftarrow true$
26   **for** $j = 0; j < n; j = j + 1$ **do**
27   **if** $j \neq i$ **and** $first\_ts \geq timestamps[j]$ **then**
28                 $can\_apply \leftarrow false$
29   **break**
30   **end if**
31   **end for**
32   **if** can_apply **then**
33             $sm.apply(first\_command)$
34             $log_i.remove([first\_command, first\_ts])$
35   **end if**
36   **end while**
37   **end procedure**

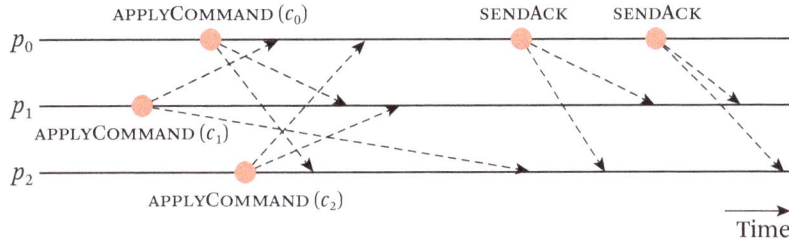

Figure 2.5 Execution of the SMR algorithm.

Procedure CONSTANTCHECK of Algorithm 2.2 runs in the background and checks (line 27) if there are entries from all processes in the log. In this case, the head of the log (i.e., the entry whose timestamp is the lowest) is applied.

The algorithm applies the exact same commands and in the same order at each process, since a process p applies a command c only if p has received messages with higher timestamps from all other processes. This guarantees that no command preceding c in the timestamp order exists, since p's communication with all other processes preserves FIFO order.

Figure 2.5 depicts an execution of Algorithm 2.2 in which three processes request to apply different commands concurrently. Although requests are issued concurrently, the processes apply the commands in the same order. Recall that logs are kept ordered by the global timestamp order. Assume that the timestamp ordering of the three commands in this scenario is c_0, c_1, c_2. For a process p to apply a command that is in its log, p needs to receive messages from all the other processes with greater timestamps. For instance, when process p_1 calls APPLYCOMMAND(c_1), p_1 just knows of its own command c_1. In order for p_1 to apply c_1, p_1 would need to receive messages with greater timestamps from processes p_0 and p_2. Since the communications links are FIFO, process p_0 would first send its command c_0 to p_1 and afterward the acknowledgment message to p_1. Therefore, p_1 would realize that it first needs to apply command c_0 of process p_0 before applying command c_1.

Remarks. The knowledgeable reader might think that if we assume a setting without failures, implementing an SMR algorithm can be easily done by using a leader-based approach. With a leader-based approach we can trivially achieve total ordering of the commands. For example, if we assume that a single process of the system acts as a *leader*, then it is easy to devise an SMR algorithm. Assuming that process p_0 is the leader, such an algorithm could operate as follows. Every process gets informed on what commands to apply and in which order by process p_0. Specifically, before a process applies a command, the process first sends the command to the leader p_0. Process p_0 can then order the commands it has received and dictate the execution order of these commands. Subsequently, p_0 can inform all the other processes about this execution order. Since there are no failures, we are guaranteed that p_0 is always up and running. However, the problem of implementing an SMR algorithm remains challenging if we exclude the trivial leader-based solution. Nevertheless, by utilizing logical time we can implement an SMR algorithm.

The reason Lamport proposed a non-leader-based SMR algorithm probably has to do with the fact that he was still thinking about the problem in the context of databases where we want to keep replicas consistent. Nevertheless, note that the SMR algorithm described in this section is quite effective as the basis for a fault-tolerant solution when clocks are synchronized. Lamport's first way of tackling fault tolerance was in fact to assume synchronized clocks (and separately to work on clock-synchronization protocols, which are mentioned in the next chapter).

2.3.2   Impact of the Distributed State Machine Abstraction

Although in retrospect the distributed state machine abstraction is conceptually simple, it had a tremendous impact on both theory and practice.

The distributed state machine abstraction appeared repeatedly in Lamport's subsequent work. After the "Time, Clocks, and the Ordering of Events in a Distributed System" [Lamport 1978b], Lamport proceeded to work on various SMR implementations. The culmination of Lamport's work led to SMR algorithms for both benign and Byzantine settings. See Chapters 3 and 4 for some of these algorithms.

In practice and with the surge of cloud computing, the SMR abstraction has been extensively used in practical systems. Major cloud infrastructure companies report using SMR in their data centers for lock services, data replication, and atomicity management. Likewise, major storage vendors are using it to manage data redundancy.

2.4   The Notion of Distributed Global State

A *distributed snapshot* refers to taking a "photograph" of a distributed system. This snapshot comprises the state of each process at the moment the snapshot is taken. The state of a process corresponds to the state of the local data structures of the process and what the process is executing (i.e., program counter). In other words, a snapshot captures the *global state* of the system. In this section, we describe an algorithm that is able to capture a distributed snapshot and discuss how it relates to the notion of the distributed global state. Before we start, we present the following analogy to better convey the meaning of a snapshot.

A parent had three children: Bob, Dan, and Tom. The parent wanted to instill financial awareness to his three sons and decided to give them an allowance of $20 each. Immediately after, the children started exchanging money with each other for toys, etc. One day, the father wanted to check on his children to see how much money each of them had. During that day, the father asked Bob, then Dan, and at the end Tom how much money they currently had. At the end of the day and based on the responses of the children, the father deduced that Bob, Dan, and Tom have $10, $30, and $50, respectively. Surprisingly, the children had $30 more than what they received from their father! The father quickly realized that the children did not magically become richer. Instead, what happened was that after asking Dan how much money he had and before asking Tom, Dan gave his $30 to Tom. Ideally, the father would want to get an instantaneous view of his sons' money boxes in which the total money is $60. In other words, the father wants to get a snapshot of his sons' money boxes.

In a distributed setting, the children are the processes and the father is an algorithm that takes a snapshot in order to perform some action. For example, instead of checking how much money each child had, we would like to find out the CPU utilization of each process when the snapshot is taken. However, compared with the aforementioned analogy, taking a snapshot in a distributed system is a more difficult problem. For instance, we cannot gather all the processes together in the same room and "ask" them what their current state is, something that the father could easily do. Such an approach would be analogous to having a synchronous system in which all processes provide their state at a specific point in time.

Here we consider an asynchronous system. In an asynchronous system, the notion of global state is elusive. For instance, it is challenging to define what a global state is, since we have no notion of global time. Ideally, we want to take a snapshot of a system while the system is executing a distributed algorithm, but without impeding the progress of the algorithm. In such a setting, it is hard to conceive what the global state of a system is, since the system is constantly in fluctuation (i.e., processes keep performing events).

Chandy and Lamport [1985] devised an algorithm to capture a snapshot in an asynchronous distributed system in their influential "Distributed Snapshots: Determining Global States of Distributed Systems." In that work, they managed to capture the notion of a distributed global state. We explain a simplified version of their algorithm in the next section. In Section 2.4.2 we describe the impact of their work.

Algorithm 2.3   **Snapshot algorithm (for process p_i)**

1 ▷ local variables
2 *stateRetrieved$_i$* ← *false*

3 **procedure** STARTSNAPSHOT()
4   *state$_i$* ← p_i.*getState*()
5   *stateRetrieved$_i$* ← *true*
6      $\forall j \neq i$, *send*(*marker*, p_j)
7 **end procedure**

8 **procedure** ONRECEIVEMARKER()
9   **if** *stateRetrieved$_i$* ≠ *true* **then**
10   *state$_i$* ← p_i.*getState*()
11   *stateRetrieved$_i$* ← *true*
12         $\forall j \neq i$, *send*(*marker*, p_j)
13   **end if**
14 **end procedure**

2.4.1   The Distributed Snapshot Algorithm

Similarly to Section 2.3, we consider an asynchronous system with no failures and with reliable and FIFO communication links. Furthermore, we assume that each process provides a *getState* function that can take a local snapshot of the local state (i.e., local data structures, program counter, etc.) of the process instantaneously. We present the algorithm for taking a distributed snapshot in Algorithm 2.3.

The algorithm works as follows: a *single* central process[3] p decides to take the snapshot and starts by executing STARTSNAPSHOT. Process p takes a snapshot of its local state (line 4), then sets the *stateRetrieved* variable to *true* (line 5) so that p does not retrieve its local state again at some later point in time (line 9), and then p sends a message that contains a *marker* (line 6) to every other process. The *marker* message is simply used to inform other processes to take a snapshot. When a process receives a *marker* message, it executes the ONRECEIVEMARKER function that retrieves the local state if it has not already retrieved it (line 9) and sends a *marker* message to all the other processes.

We remark that Algorithm 2.3 can augment a distributed algorithm in order to capture the global state of the system during the algorithm's execution without impeding the algorithm's progress (i.e., the distributed algorithm can keep

---

3. The central process can be assigned before the distributed system starts. Another way to decide on a central process can be by using the SMR algorithm of Section 2.3.

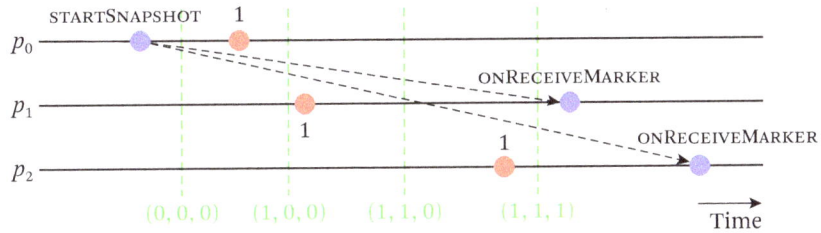

Figure 2.6   The distributed snapshot algorithm does not necessarily capture a global system state that actually occurred during an execution.

performing events while the snapshot is being taken). Additionally, note that Algorithm 2.3 describes when each process should take a snapshot of its local state but not how all the local states are assembled together to form the global state. This is beyond the scope of this section, but could be easily accomplished by having each process broadcast its local state after retrieving it.

Assume a distributed algorithm executing in a system with n processes that uses logical clocks to timestamp its events. Then we can think of a distributed snapshot taken by Algorithm 2.3 as a vector $(ts_0, ts_1, \ldots, ts_{n-1})$ of n elements (also known as a *cut*) where the local state of a process p_i is retrieved after an event e timestamped with ts_i and before the event immediately following e in process p_i. Figure 2.6 depicts the execution of an algorithm (red events at each process). Before process p_0 performs an event, p_0 starts capturing a snapshot of the system. The *marker* messages sent by p_0 are delivered to processes p_1 and p_2 after each of them has performed one event. The resulting distributed snapshot corresponds to the cut $(0, 1, 1)$. However, such a global state never existed in the system. The green-dashed vertical lines in Figure 2.6 show the global states that existed in the system. These global states correspond to the cuts $(0, 0, 0)$, $(1, 0, 0)$, $(1, 1, 0)$, and $(1, 1, 1)$. Surprisingly, the snapshot algorithm captures a global state that did not exist. It is challenging to capture a global state at a specific instant while processes keep performing events.

However, the snapshot algorithm satisfies two useful properties. The first property has to do with all the events that take place between the moment process p_0 invoked STARTSNAPSHOT and the moment all the processes have retrieved their local state (i.e., have called the *getState* function). We can reorder these events and execute the distributed algorithm based on this new order of events such that the snapshot returned by the snapshot algorithm corresponds to a global state during the distributed algorithm's execution. For instance, in Figure 2.6 if the events of processes p_1 and p_2 were ordered before the event of process p_0, then the cut $(0, 1, 1)$

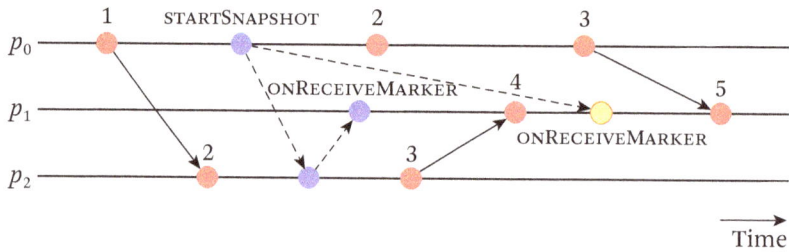

Figure 2.7 Taking a distributed snapshot during the execution of an algorithm.

would correspond to a global state during the execution of the system. The second property states that if the global state captured by the snapshot algorithm contains an event e in the local state of some process, then all the events that causally precede e are captured in the local states of some other processes that belong to the snapshot. In other words, the notion of a distributed global state is intertwined with causality.

In Figure 2.7 we present another example that depicts the execution of an algorithm while a distributed snapshot is being taken (blue and yellow events). In this example, p_0 is the process that initiates the snapshot by invoking STARTSNAPSHOT. By doing so, a *marker* message is sent to all the other processes. Process p_2 is the first process that receives the *marker*, so p_2 takes a snapshot of its local state and sends a *marker* to the other processes. Notice that since the communication links are FIFO the *marker* sent by p_2 reaches p_1 before the message that p_2 sent during the event with timestamp 3. When p_1 receives the *marker*, p_1 takes a snapshot of its local state and sends *marker* messages as well. For clarity and since each process has taken a snapshot of its local state, we omit the additional *marker* messages that are sent by the processes. Afterward, when p_1 receives the *marker* from p_0 (the yellow event), process p_1 does not perform anything since p_1 has already taken a snapshot of its local state.

Finally, in Figure 2.8 we present the same execution as in Figure 2.7 and show possible snapshots that can and cannot be returned by the algorithm. The red curved dashed lines correspond to snapshots that cannot be returned by the snapshot algorithm. For example, the snapshot that corresponds to the cut (2, 4, 2) cannot be returned by the algorithm, since p_1 includes the state of the process after the event with timestamp 4 has occurred but does not include the event with timestamp 3 of process p_2 that causally precedes p_1's event. Similarly, a snapshot that corresponds to the cut (2, 5, 3) cannot be returned by the algorithm since the

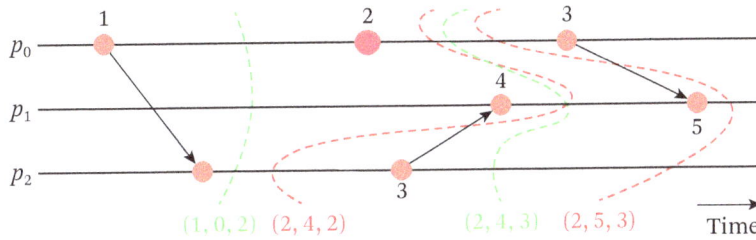

Figure 2.8 Valid (green) and invalid (red) snapshots based on causality. Algorithm 2.3 returns only valid snapshots.

cut does not capture causality. The green curved dashed lines correspond to cuts that can be returned by the snapshot algorithm, such as (1, 0, 2) and (2, 4, 3).

Remarks. Someone might think that we could take a distributed snapshot by utilizing an SMR algorithm. An idea would be for processes to just apply commands to the global (i.e., simulated) state machine. This way, if a process wants to get the global state of the system, the process just needs to retrieve the state of the global state machine. Such an approach is unsatisfactory since it does not really capture the state of the process, but instead captures the state of the global state machine. Additionally, such an approach is less practical since each possible event has to go through the SMR algorithm.

2.4.2   Impact of Distributed Global State

The distributed snapshot algorithm might take a snapshot of a global state of the system that never existed in reality. This raises the question whether such an algorithm is even useful.

However, as we mentioned before, the snapshot algorithm satisfies two useful properties. One of them states that there exists a reordering of the events that take place during the retrieval of the snapshot such that the returned global state exists in an execution corresponding to these reordered events. We present an example of this property in Figure 2.9, assuming that the snapshot algorithm returned a global state s_i'. Specifically, Figure 2.9(i) depicts the sequence of global states during the execution of the distributed algorithm. Note that state s_i' does not exist in the sequence of global states in Figure 2.9(i). Furthermore, global state s_{start} corresponds to the state where the snapshot algorithm is first invoked by process p_0, while s_{end} corresponds to the state where all processes have retrieved their local state. If we reorder the events that took place during the execution of the snapshot

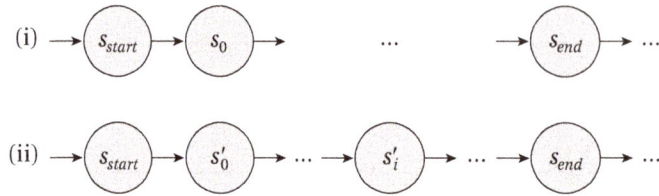

Figure 2.9 Sequence of global states (ii) corresponds to the states generated by an execution of the reordered events of execution (i).

algorithm, we get a possible different sequence of states (e.g., s_0 is different from s_0') that is depicted in Figure 2.9(ii) and in which state s_i' exists. The snapshot algorithm guarantees that immediately after the reordering of the events the system is in the same state as before the reordering; hence both sequences of states end with the state s_{end}. We refer the interested reader to the original paper [Chandy and Lamport 1985] for a formal proof for why the events-reordering property holds.

We can now see how the aforementioned property of the snapshot algorithm is useful in practice. The snapshot algorithm's property is useful in identifying whether a *stable property* of a system holds. A stable property is a property that if it holds in some state of the system, it holds in every subsequent state of the system. For instance, whether a deadlock has occurred is a stable property since if a deadlock occurs, the system remains forever deadlocked. We can use the distributed snapshot algorithm to detect a stable property by retrieving the global state and examining whether the stable property holds in the retrieved global state. If the stable property holds in the retrieved global state, then this means that the stable property holds in the system. For instance, if the stable property holds in the retrieved state s_i' in Figure 2.9(ii), this means that the stable property also holds in s_{end} and any subsequent state of s_{end} and hence the stable property holds in the system. To give an example, if we retrieve the global state and we detect a deadlock in this state, we can infer that the system is deadlocked. Detecting stable properties during the execution of an algorithm is extremely useful. Among others, such a detection mechanism can be used for checkpointing and failure recovery [Koo and Toueg 1987, Prakash and Singhal 1996].

To conclude, the notion of a global state in distributed computing had a huge impact in the last three decades, ranging from distributed [Mattern 1989] to concurrent [Afek et al. 1993, Jayanti 2005] systems.

2.5 Conclusion

After getting acquainted with the notions of time and global state in a distributed system, they become clear and might appear obvious in retrospect. This does not mean this was indeed the case. The work of Lamport successfully democratized these notions. Lamport's paper "Time, Clocks, and the Ordering of Events in a Distributed System" had tremendous impact on introducing the notion of time in a distributed system. Most importantly, the distributed state machine abstraction approach that stemmed from this paper spawned new research areas and has been widely implemented in various settings and deployed in a plethora of practical systems. Finally, the "Distributed Snapshots: Determining Global States of Distributed Systems" paper by Chandy and Lamport introduced the notion of a global state in a distributed system.

Byzantine Faults

Christian Cachin

3.1 Introduction

This chapter covers Lamport's most prominent works addressing attackers and malicious acts in distributed computing systems. One would think that dealing with adversaries lies in the domain of computer security and cryptography—both areas outside Lamport's core domain of *concurrency*, according to this book's title. But Lamport has initiated the study of distributed protocols in such adversarial settings through the formulation of the *Byzantine generals problem* and thereby founded a fruitful research program that has been vibrantly active for several decades. It is less widely known that he also made seminal contributions to cryptography and computer security in the early days of these fields.

In more detail, Lamport's work on the Byzantine generals problem [Lamport et al. 1982] has influenced generations of researchers and practitioners and represents one of his most important contributions. The intuitive story of the paper around the problem of reaching agreement, with all the connotations of the term *Byzantine*, has attracted and fascinated many people. However, the problem of reaching agreement in the presence of faults had already been the subject of two of his earlier papers that grew out of the NASA-sponsored Software Implemented Fault Tolerance (SIFT) project, whose goal was to build a resilient aircraft control system that tolerated faults of its components. Lamport's first research paper on SIFT appeared in 1978, with Wensley et al. [1978], and the second one in 1980, with Pease and Shostak [Pease et al. 1980]. But widespread interest in the problem arose only after the publication of the "The Byzantine Generals Problem" in 1982. Indeed, Lamport's intention behind writing this paper was to popularize the agreement problem. To use his own words [Lamport 2019]:

> I have long felt that, because it was posed as a cute problem about philosophers seated around a table, Dijkstra's dining philosopher's problem received

much more attention than it deserves. (For example, it has probably received more attention in the theory community than the readers/writers problem, which illustrates the same principles and has much more practical importance.) I believed that the problem introduced in [Lamport et al. 1982] was very important and deserved the attention of computer scientists. The popularity of the dining philosophers problem taught me that the best way to attract attention to a problem is to present it in terms of a story.

In order to reduce the problem to its most extreme case, the story of the Byzantine generals lets the faulty generals behave maliciously and adversarially. Lamport and coauthors originally did not think it was realistic to assume an attacker had actually gained access and was trying to create disruption from within, when their protocols would run in an industrial control system or even on an aircraft. This was rather chosen as a realistic and intuitive abstraction for covering all incorrect behavior that a protocol participant might exhibit. Much later only has the term *Byzantine fault tolerance* gained its current meaning of dealing with actually malicious parties and tolerating their actions.

Still, Lamport was very much aware of the need to secure distributed computer systems from attackers. In concurrent work addressing problems in security and cryptology, he introduced *one-time signatures* [Lamport 1979a], which are today known as *Lamport signatures* in cryptography, and a novel protocol for *password authentication using one-way functions* [Lamport 1981], which pioneered many others.

In the following, we highlight three prominent works of Lamport that deal with adversarial protocol participants: Byzantine agreement, clock synchronization in the presence of arbitrary faults, and digital signature schemes built from one-way functions.

3.2 Byzantine Agreement

The two papers by Lamport, Shostak, and Pease [Pease et al. 1980, Lamport et al. 1982] on Byzantine agreement address the same problem: Given n processes $p_1, \ldots, p_n$ with one input value each, how to synchronize them with a protocol that only uses point-to-point messages such that all processes agree on an output vector V of n values that correctly represent the inputs. During the protocol execution, an unknown set of t processes is *faulty* or *Byzantine* and the remaining $n - t$ processes are *correct*. The Byzantine processes may behave in arbitrary and adversarial ways, as if intending to prevent the correct processes from reaching agreement.

3.2.1 Definitions

The Byzantine agreement problem can be described in three slightly different ways, which are all equivalent to each other in the *synchronous* model considered by Lamport and coauthors. There are small and conceptually simple transformations to convert one variant to another. The three forms are called *interactive consistency*, the *Byzantine generals problem*, and *Byzantine agreement*. (In *asynchronous* systems, however, where no common clock exists, these three notions differ considerably; failure to distinguish these nuances has led to some confusion in the literature. We consider only synchronous systems in this chapter.)

Interactive Consistency. The agreement problem described in the paragraph above is called *interactive consistency*: Each process inputs a value, say, p_i inputs v_i, and each process outputs a vector V of such values. It satisfies these properties:

Agreement. Each correct process outputs the same vector of values.

Validity. If a correct process outputs V and a process p_i is correct and inputs v_i, then $V[i] = v_i$.

In the SIFT project building an aircraft controller, interactive consistency was intended to synchronize the different processes, where each process would supply its locally read sensor values as input. After reaching agreement on an output vector like this, each process would then derive its actions deterministically from the output. This ensures that the actions of all processes remain synchronized and safe.

Byzantine Generals Problem. The Byzantine generals problem [Lamport et al. 1982] is best understood as a *broadcast primitive*, where a designated *sender* process p_s starts with an input value v and all other processes have no input; at the end all processes output some value. The goal is that the sender conveys its input to all processes in a *reliable* way such that all processes output the same value. For this reason we call it *Byzantine broadcast* here, also because it is reminiscent of other notions for (Byzantine) reliable broadcast [Cachin et al. 2011].

In the Byzantine generals formulation, there is one *commander* acting as the sender p_s and all other processes are *lieutenants* that should obey the order of the commander. More abstractly, a protocol for the Byzantine generals problem or for Byzantine broadcast ensures

Agreement. Each correct process outputs the same value.

Validity. If the sender process, p_s, is correct and has input v, then every correct process also outputs v.

This notion was formalized by Lamport et al. [1982] and used to describe the impossibility results and several protocols. In the introduction of the paper, however, the story describes that "the multiple divisions of the Byzantine army are camped outside an enemy city, each division commanded by its own general" and that "they must decide upon a common plan of action." This is again the notion of interactive consistency.

The relation between the two primitives is straightforward, which is why Lamport et al. introduce the simplification. Namely, given a solution for Byzantine broadcast, interactive consistency can be achieved by running n separate instances of Byzantine broadcast in parallel, one for each process, and that process acts as the sender in its instance. In the other direction, the relation is already evident from the definition, as interactive consistency is the composition of n Byzantine broadcasts, one for each process as a sender. Lamport et al. [1982] explain all of this in the classic paper.

Byzantine Agreement. The notion of *Byzantine agreement* or *Byzantine consensus* stands between interactive consistency and the Byzantine generals problem. In this primitive, *every* process inputs a value and every process outputs again a *single* value. Formally, it satisfies

  Agreement. Each correct process outputs the same value.

  Validity. If all correct processes input the same value v, then every correct process outputs v.

Note that *validity* in Byzantine agreement may not be useful for practical applications since it says nothing about the situation where the correct processes start with diverging inputs. If not all processes supply the same input, then Byzantine agreement may choose a value that comes out of thin air; for example, it could be some default value $\perp$ to indicate that no agreement was reached or it could be something made up by the faulty processes. On the other hand, if all correct processes input the same value, they appear to "agree" already, so why should they run an agreement protocol? The answer is, clearly, that running the protocol helps them because they don't *know* that they agree a priori.

The validity notion of Byzantine agreement has many subtle aspects. One could simplify it by additionally requiring that the output value was input by a *correct* process. However, then the set from which those values are chosen starts to play a role [Fitzi and Garay 2003] and impacts the resilience of possible protocols (i.e., the relation between the number of faulty processes, t, and n). In other contexts, it has been suggested to *externalize* the decision on which agreement values are "valid" and permit any value to be output, as long as it satisfies some predicate known to each process [Ben-Or and El-Yaniv 2003, Cachin et al. 2001].

Despite these and other issues with validity in Byzantine agreement, this formulation of the agreement problem has become the preferred one of the three variants. This may also be because the equivalent notion of *consensus* in asynchronous systems, even if processes are only subject to crashes, plays a fundamental role in distributed computing [Herlihy and Wing 1990, Chandra and Toueg 1996].

To implement Byzantine agreement from interactive consistency, the processes first run interactive consistency to agree on an input value for each process. Then every process runs a deterministic procedure locally that selects the output according to the validity notion required by Byzantine agreement. Implementing Byzantine agreement from a primitive for Byzantine broadcast (i.e., a protocol for the Byzantine generals problem) works similarly.

To realize Byzantine broadcast for sender p_s from Byzantine agreement, process p_s first sends its value directly to each process in the system. Then all processes run Byzantine agreement once, whereby a correct process inputs the value received from p_s. This protocol can be extended to an implementation of interactive consistency as explained under the description of the Byzantine generals problem.

3.2.2   Implementations

Protocols for Byzantine agreement start from a model that makes authenticated point-to-point links available, such as provided by physical channels linking all pairs of processes or by using an open communication network and protecting the communication using a cryptographic message-authentication code (MAC) that prevents the Byzantine processes from tampering with messages among correct processes.

The necessary and sufficient conditions on t and n that make Byzantine agreement possible differ based on whether one considers *oral messages* or permits the use of *digital signatures*. With oral messages, the integrity of a statement made by one process and forwarded by a Byzantine process cannot be guaranteed, in the sense that the recipient process cannot determine whether the forwarding process has altered the statement. Digital signatures, on the other hand, provide data authentication based on a cryptographic public-key/private-key pair for each process.

Digital Signatures. A *digital signature scheme* provides two operations, $sign_i$ and $verify_i$. Every invocation of $sign_i(v)$ specifies the index i of a process, takes a bit string $v \in \{0, 1\}^*$ as input, and returns a signature $\sigma \in \{0, 1\}^*$ with the response. Only p_i may invoke $sign_i$. The operation $verify_i$ takes a bit string σ that should be verified and a bit string v as parameters. It returns a Boolean value with the response. Implementations of these methods satisfy that $verify_i(\sigma, v)$ returns TRUE for any $i \in \{1, \ldots, n\}$ and $v \in \{0, 1\}^*$ if and only if p_i has executed $sign_i(v)$ and obtained σ before; otherwise, $verify_i(\sigma, v)$ returns FALSE. Every process may invoke *verify*. Therefore, it is not possible for any Byzantine process to cook up a statement and a valid signature on it from a correct process.

Impossibility Results. The most fundamental impossibility result concerning Byzantine agreement states that Byzantine broadcast with oral messages (in the synchronous model) requires $n > 3t$. In other words, no protocol exists for $n \leq 3t$. To see why, consider the Byzantine broadcast problem for the special case $n = 3$ and $t = 1$ as follows [Lamport et al. 1982].

The commander C should send either *attack* or *retreat* to the two lieutenants, L_1 and L_2. The argument introduces two scenarios that are *indistinguishable* from each other by one of the correct participants (L_1) because it receives exactly the same information. In the first scenario, the sender C is correct and inputs *attack*. Then L_1 receives *attack* directly from C but L_2 is Byzantine and changes all protocol messages to L_1 as if C had input *retreat*. By the validity property, L_1 must output *attack*. However, in a second scenario, C is Byzantine and acts toward L_1 as if its input were *attack* and toward L_2 as if its input were *retreat*. Since L_2 is correct, it behaves toward L_1 as if C had input *retreat*. The correct L_1 observes the same information as in the first scenario and decides *attack*. A dual argument for the second scenario then implies also that L_2 decides *retreat*, since C acts toward L_2 with input *retreat*. Then the two correct lieutenants output different values, which violates the agreement condition and shows that no such protocol exists.

The result can be extended to arbitrary $n \leq 3t$ by considering groups of processes [Lamport et al. 1982]. Many subsequent results have used this proof method to establish impossibilities and lower bounds on the resilience of distributed protocols for other tasks and under different assumptions.

Intuitively, process L_1 cannot obtain the correct output in the example because there are only two other processes that interact with L_1, each one suggesting a different binary value. With one more process, L_1 could decide for the value that it learns from a majority and break the tie. The underlying problem is the same as in an error-correcting code for tolerating garbled symbols, specifically, in a repetition code that requires two correctly transmitted symbols for each corrupted symbol. The relation between agreement problems and error-correcting codes was explored in depth later, for example, by Friedman et al. [2007].

Table 3.1   **Bounds on the resilience of (synchronous, deterministic) Byzantine agreement problems**

Problem	Signed Messages	Oral Messages
Interactive consistency	$n > 2t$	$n > 3t$
Byzantine broadcast (Byzantine generals)	$n > t$	$n > 3t$
Byzantine agreement	$n > 2t$	$n > 3t$

The lower bound of $n > 3t$ extends in a straightforward way to the problems of interactive consistency and Byzantine agreement. Note that the argument exploits the mutability of oral messages. In fact, if digital signatures are available, then the Byzantine broadcast problem can be implemented for any $n > t$. Protocols for interactive consistency and for Byzantine agreement with signatures require $n > 2t$, however.

The difference arises, intuitively, because there is much less ambiguity about the output value in a Byzantine broadcast if signatures are available than about the decision in an agreement problem. Since the sender p_s may digitally sign its input, every process can recognize this value as correct from the signature. A typical protocol would spread around the signed input until every correct process is guaranteed to have it [Lamport et al. 1982, Sec. 4]. This mechanism also prevents disagreement among the receivers because if p_s were to sign multiple inputs, then the dissemination protocol ensures that every correct process would get all of them. The processes would then decide that the sender was faulty and output a default value.

In Byzantine broadcast without signatures, on the other hand, and in the other two variants (interactive consistency and Byzantine agreement), no such knowledge from a single sender exists. In these forms of the problem, *every* process has an input value or is free to echo what it heard directly from p_s in Byzantine broadcast. Hence digital signatures cannot "isolate" the correct output value in a Byzantine broadcast, and the protocols must resort to decisions among a correct majority.

Table 3.1 summarizes these bounds on the resilience of Byzantine agreement variants, with digitally signed messages and oral messages (and deterministic protocols in the synchronous model).

Protocols.   The most intuitive protocol for one of the Byzantine agreement problems in the two classic papers solves Byzantine broadcast. It uses digital signatures, takes $t + 1$ rounds, and incurs exponential communication cost in n.

Algorithm 3.1 **Byzantine broadcast using digital signatures for** p_i

1 $V \leftarrow \emptyset$
2 **on input** v **do**   ▷ Sender (commander) p_s only
3      $\sigma_s \leftarrow sign_s(\text{VALUE}\|v)$
4   send round-0 message $[v, 0; p_s; \sigma_s]$ to $p_1, \ldots, p_n$
5 **end on**
6 **for** $k \leftarrow 1, \ldots, t+1$ **do**
7   **on** receiving a round-$(k-1)$ message M from p_j **do**
8          $[v, m; p_s, p_{i_1}, \ldots, p_{i_m}; \sigma_s, \sigma_{i_1}, \ldots, \sigma_{i_m}] \leftarrow M$
9   **if** $m = k - 1 \wedge i_m = j \wedge validate(M) \wedge v \notin V$ **then**
10              $V \leftarrow V \cup \{v\}$ ▷ Collect all values in V
11              $\sigma_i \leftarrow sign_i(M)$
12              $M' \leftarrow [v, m+1; p_s, p_{i_1}, \ldots, p_{i_m}, p_i; \sigma_s, \sigma_{i_1}, \ldots, \sigma_{i_m}, \sigma_i]$
13   send round-k message M' to $p_\ell \in \{p_1, \ldots, p_n\} \setminus \{p_i, p_{i_1}, \ldots, p_{i_m}\}$
14   **end if**
15   **end on**
16 **end for**
17 **if** $V = \{w\}$ **then**
18   **output** w
19 **else**   ▷ $|V| > 1$
20   **output** $\perp$
21 **end if**

Recall that in a Byzantine broadcast (or the Byzantine generals problem), a designated sender p_s (the commander) conveys an order to the other processes (the lieutenants). Any t of the n processes may be Byzantine. The protocol introduced in the paper proceeds in $t+1$ synchronized rounds. Basically, the sender signs the value it wants to broadcast and sends it to all processes. Whenever a process receives a properly signed message, it remembers the value and signs the message again. Then the process appends its own signature to the message and forwards it to those processes that have not yet signed it. At the end, after $t+1$ rounds, a process examines its set of received values: if it contains exactly one entry, the process outputs this value as its decision, otherwise, it chooses a default value. The pseudocode is shown in Algorithm 3.1. As an optimization, in the last round ($k = t + 1$) a process can skip lines 11–13.

The function $validate(M)$ is defined on a message M as follows:

function *validate*(M)

    $[v, m; p_s, p_{i_1}, \ldots, p_{i_m}; \sigma_s, \sigma_{i_1}, \ldots, \sigma_{i_m}] \leftarrow M$

    if $m = 0$ **then**

        return $verify_s(\sigma_s, \text{VALUE}\|v)$

    else

        $M' \leftarrow [v, m - 1; p_s, p_{i_1}, \ldots, p_{i_{m-1}}; \sigma_s, \sigma_{i_1}, \ldots, \sigma_{i_{m-1}}])$

        return $verify_{i_m}(\sigma_{i_m}, M') \wedge validate(M')$

    end if

end function

To see why this algorithm is correct, let us first examine validity: If the sender p_s is correct and has input v, then no protocol message with a value different from v will be accepted by *validate*. Since p_s also sends v in its first protocol message to all processes, it follows that $V = \{v\}$ for each correct process when the protocol terminates. Hence every correct process outputs v. The *agreement* property requires that no two correct processes output different values. Since the function determining the output from variable V is deterministic, it is sufficient to show that all correct processes have the same V after round $t + 1$. Suppose some correct p_i adds v_i to its V in some round. Then we must show that another correct process p_j also adds v_i to its set V. There are two cases to consider: (1) If p_i receives v_i from p_1 in round 1, then it sends a round-1 message containing v_i to p_j and p_j adds v_i after receiving this. (2) If p_i receives v_i in round $k \geq 2$, then p_i has received a round-$(k - 1)$ message with k signatures. If p_j is one of the signers, then it already has added v_i to its set V according to the protocol. Otherwise, we consider again two cases: (2a) If $k \leq t$, then p_i forwards v_i to p_j in its round-k message; p_j receives this in round $k + 1$ and adds v_i to its V. Else (2b) we have $k = t + 1$ and among the $t + 1$ processes that issued the $t + 1$ signatures in the round-t message received by p_i, there must be at least one other correct process. This process has also forwarded v_i to p_j in a valid message and the set V at p_j therefore contains v_i. Hence the two processes output the same value.

This protocol incurs exponentially large communication cost and time complexity in n (for $t = O(n)$) because, in the worst case, each process p_i may receive a round-k message signed by a set of $k + 1$ processes for each one of the $(k + 1)!$ possible paths across the process set that such a message from the sender may have taken until it reached p_i. In fact, all Byzantine agreement protocols in the early papers of Lamport, Shostak, and Pease [Pease et al. 1980, Lamport et al. 1982] used this protocol structure, which has also been called *exponential information gathering* [Lynch 1996].

In the model with oral messages, a variant of this protocol is described by Lamport et al. [1982], also implementing Byzantine broadcast. Informally, the modification introduces a step of choosing a value among multiple ones that a process receives from others. This provides an example of how a *majority decision* ensures safety in an agreement algorithm.

Soon after the pioneering papers appeared, Byzantine agreement protocols with polynomial cost were developed for the models with signatures and without, first by Dolev and Strong [1982, 1983]. The same authors also showed formally that $t + 1$ rounds are required for deterministic synchronous Byzantine agreement [Dolev and Strong 1983].

Many more protocols for Byzantine agreement were developed later; their number is so large that one cannot even start with most important ones here. The longest-lasting open problem posed directly by Lamport in the two early papers was closed only about 15 years later, when Garay and Moses [1998] described the first efficient (polynomial-time) protocol with oral messages that achieves optimal resilience $n > 3t$ and an optimal latency of $t + 1$ rounds.

The following section further examines distributed agreement protocols in asynchronous and partially synchronous networks. These algorithms use slightly different approaches. Protocols that completely disregard synchrony also introduce randomization as a fundamental mechanism to relax the deterministic models discussed here.

3.3   Byzantine Clock Synchronization

In order to achieve the synchrony necessary to operate a distributed system, early works by Lamport focused on the problem of synchronizing the clocks of a group of processes. In a classic paper Lamport and Melliar-Smith [1985] formalized this problem for the first time and initiated a long series of works that extended and refined their ideas.

Their model assumes that each process has an associated clock; this clock can be read by all processes in the system as in a shared-memory multiprocessor computer. This assumption stands in contrast to models used later, where each process has exclusive access to its own clock. However, this variation does not lead to a fundamental change in the ideas used by the respective clock synchronization protocols. Faulty clocks and processes may be Byzantine and subject to arbitrary faults.

To formalize the problem, Lamport and Melliar-Smith assume that all clocks are initially synchronized and that the clocks of correct processes run at approximately the same rate, that is, their differences are bounded by some small value δ per unit of real time. The second assumption they introduce concerns the message-transmission times: the processes must know how fast they can convey information to each other. In particular, a correct process can obtain the difference between its own clock and that of another correct process within a time interval bounded by ϵ.

Synchronizing the clocks means (1) that the clock values at the correct processes are approximately the same at each instant, and (2) that the clock at every correct process differs at most by a bounded value from real time. In their pioneering paper, Lamport and Melliar-Smith introduce two fundamental methods for addressing clock synchronization.

The first algorithm is based on *averaging* the time values read from other processes. Very informally speaking, this means that each process periodically reports its clock reading to all others; each process then sets its own clock to the average of the reported clock values. Unreasonably large differences between a reported value and the clock of the receiver process are discarded. This can be done safely, assuming that bounds are placed on the message transmission times and on the difference between the clocks among the correct processes. The protocol itself uses a simple structure with direct messages among the processes, only conveying clock readings to each other.

The second algorithm introduces the idea of setting the clock of a process to the *median* among reported values; this reduces the influence of outliers compared to the average and ensures that, with n processes and at most $t < n/3$ faulty ones, the derived clock value always lies between the real clock value of two correct processes. Processes use in this solution a subprotocol for interactive consistency, as in the earlier papers on agreement, in order to exchange clock values. The subprotocol is extended by measures that take into account the time spent executing the protocols.

3.4 Digital Signatures

Around the same time as he was working on distributed agreement and replication, Lamport developed an interest in the nascent field of *public-key cryptography*. Modern cryptography was born in 1976 with the paper "New Directions in

Cryptography" by Diffie and Hellman [1976], which introduced the field of public-key cryptography with the novel concepts of trapdoor one-way functions, public-key cryptosystems, and digital signatures. Although the paper postulated that all these primitives could be realized from computationally hard problems that arise in number theory and discrete mathematics, it did not provide concrete realizations except for the interactive key-agreement protocol that now bears the name of the paper's authors.

Digital signatures were envisaged by Diffie and Hellman to have applications to authenticating digital documents, securing messages sent over a network from tampering, and protecting remote logins to multiuser computers. (All these predictions, and many more, have come true.) And while the key-agreement protocol of Diffie and Hellman had been closely related to public-key cryptosystems, and therefore a candidate implementation seemed feasible, there was no similar construction for a digital signature anywhere on the horizon.

However, Lamport had developed such a primitive from more traditional cryptographic building blocks soon after hearing about the invention of public-key cryptography. The scheme is actually contained in the paper of Diffie and Hellman and is attributed there to Lamport [Diffie and Hellman 1976, Sec. IV], but he actually never published it himself. Lamport devised a related signature scheme later and described it in a technical report [Lamport 1979a].

Cryptographic Definition of Digital Signatures. Recall the notion of a *digital signature scheme* from Section 3.2.2, with two operations, *sign* and *verify*. This is an idealized formulation (in the sense of Dolev and Yao [1983]) made for studying protocols because it omits the key material, but not suitable for describing and analyzing actual constructions. Here we redefine a signature scheme, as in modern cryptography, to consist of a triple (*keygen*, *sign*, *verify*) of efficient algorithms. The *key generation* algorithm *keygen* outputs a public-key/private-key pair (*pk*, *sk*). The signing algorithm *sign* takes as input the private key and a message $m \in \{0, 1\}^*$, and produces a signature $\sigma \in \{0, 1\}^*$. The verification algorithm *verify* takes the public key, a message m, and a putative signature σ, and outputs a Boolean value (TRUE or FALSE) that indicates whether it accepts or rejects the signature. The signature is *valid* for the message when *verify* accepts. All signatures produced by the signing algorithm must be valid.

A digital signature scheme is secure against *existential forgery* if no efficient adversary $\mathcal{A}$ can output any message together with a valid signature that was not produced by the legitimate signer. More formally, $\mathcal{A}$ is given *pk* and is allowed to request and obtain signatures on a sequence of messages of its choice, where any message may depend on previously observed signatures. If $\mathcal{A}$ can output a valid signature on a message whose signature it never obtained, then the adversary has successfully *forged* a signature. A signature scheme is *secure* if any efficient $\mathcal{A}$ can forge a signature only with negligible probability. (Formally, *efficient* means with running time polynomial in a security parameter κ of the scheme, and *negligible* is smaller than any polynomial fraction of κ.)

Lamport Signatures. Lamport's signature scheme from 1976 is based on a generic cryptographic *one-way function*. This is a function $F : \{0, 1\}^k \to \{0, 1\}^k$ that is efficiently computable but hard to invert on average. More precisely, this means for $x \in_R \{0, 1\}^k$, i.e., a random, uniformly chosen k-bit string, and $y = F(x)$, and any efficient adversary $\mathcal{A}$ that is given y, the probability that $\mathcal{A}(y)$ outputs x is negligible. In practice, a one-way function is often implemented by a collision-free hash function, such as SHA-2 or SHA-3, or constructed from a block cipher like AES.

Key generation for a Lamport signature on ℓ-bit messages first selects 2ℓ random bit strings of length k each, which together form the private key

$$sk = (x_1[0], x_1[1], \ldots, x_\ell[0], x_\ell[1]).$$

Then the one-way function F is applied to each $x_j[b]$ to compute

$$y_j[b] = F(x_j[b]), \quad \text{for } j = 1, \ldots, \ell \text{ and } b \in \{0, 1\}.$$

The public key is the list of 2ℓ such bit strings of length k each,

$$pk = (y_1[0], y_1[1], \ldots, y_\ell[0], y_\ell[1]).$$

To sign an ℓ-bit message $m = (m_1, \ldots, m_\ell)$, algorithm $sign(sk, m)$ returns

$$\sigma = (x_1[m_1], \ldots, x_\ell[m_\ell]),$$

i.e., one preimage under F as prepared during key generation for each message position, selected by the bit value in that position.

For validating a signature $\sigma = (\sigma_1, \ldots, \sigma_\ell)$ on m, algorithm $verify(pk, m, \sigma)$ applies F itself to the bit strings in the signature and checks if all of them match pk, as determined by the bits in the message, according to

$$y_j[m_j] \overset{?}{=} F(\sigma_j), \quad \text{for } j = 1, \ldots, \ell.$$

Discussion. The signature scheme exploits a simple but powerful idea, which is to reveal secrets selectively determined by a protocol input. The fixed length is not a drawback. In practice, messages of arbitrary length are first compressed with a collision-free cryptographic hash function to the ℓ-bit inputs of the signature scheme.

Still, the public key and the secret key each have size $2\ell k$, which is not practical. Merkle [1980] reduced the public-key size to one k-bit string by constructing a tree, with all 2ℓ strings in the private key at the leaves. Each node in this tree, which now bears Merkle's name, is the output of a cryptographic hash function applied to its children. During a *sign* operation, extra values in the tree are added and allow *verify* to establish the same integrity properties as in Lamport's scheme. In particular, for authenticating a leaf node, Merkle's scheme considers the path from a leaf node to the root and adds the values of all sibling nodes along the path to the signature.

In contrast to the general notion of a public-key digital signature, however, Lamport's scheme can be used *only once* for a given key pair. Namely, if any index $j^* \in \{1, \ldots, \ell\}$ would be reused by different *sign* operations for messages m' and m'' that differ in position j^* and also elsewhere, then the adversary could exploit this and forge a valid signature on a message m^* that has never been signed. Such an m^* can be obtained, for instance, by flipping bit j^* in m'.

For this reason, Lamport signatures are also called *one-time signatures*. Even if a larger key is prepared to sign multiple messages, this will be exhausted in linear time, proportional to the number of signing operations. If multiple uses are foreseen, then the signing operation must keep state—a further drawback that is problematic in practice compared to generic public-key signatures.

To see why the scheme satisfies the definition of a cryptographic signature scheme, observe first that for every signature produced by *sign*, algorithm *verify* returns TRUE. For the unforgeability property, assume that no index in the key is used twice. Toward a contradiction, suppose adversary A has produced a forgery in terms of a message m^* and a signature σ^* such that $verify(pk, m^*, \sigma^*) = $ TRUE. Since no index in σ^* has been used before, A has successfully inverted F on the bit strings in pk. However, this is not possible if F is one-way.

The RSA cryptosystem [Rivest et al. 1978] provided the first practical realization of digital signatures that fully matched the concept proposed by Diffie and Hellman. Many other constructions based on trapdoor one-way functions built from number-theoretic primitives followed. Lamport's one-time signatures, on the other hand, were not developed much further due to their impracticality with large keys and the state to be kept by the signer.

Revival. Around 1990, surprising results by Naor and Yung [1989] and Rompel [1990] showed that, in principle, one-way functions were sufficient to build cryptographically secure digital signatures (instead of trapdoor one-way functions as postulated by Diffie and Hellman). These constructions rely at their core on Lamport's one-time scheme, but they had no impact on the practice of cryptography.

Lamport's and Merkle's signature schemes were largely neglected until around 2005–2010 when the approach was rediscovered for practical use due to the threat that quantum computers pose to number-theoretic cryptographic primitives. All cryptographic digital signature schemes used in practice today (2019) rely on the hardness of factoring, the RSA problem, or the difficulty of computing discrete logarithms. However, a working quantum computer would make it possible to break these assumptions, as has been known since the 1990s. For these reasons, research on *quantum-safe* or *post-quantum* cryptosystems has grown tremendously in the last 15 years and become an important and successful development in cryptography.

As the security of ordinary cryptographic hash functions is not threatened, in principle, by quantum computers, research into signature schemes based on hash functions has resumed and led to many new schemes, such as XMSS [Buchmann et al. 2011], which introduced forward security to hash-based signatures. The SPHINCS scheme of Bernstein et al. [2015] was the first practical scheme of this kind that removed the need for the signer to store state. It relies on algorithmic advances, which can be seen to improve the efficiency of earlier theoretical constructions of suitable Merkle trees, and on a modern interpretation of what is considered to be "practical." Due to advances in computer hardware, the signature size of SPHINCS, which amounts to some dozen kilobytes, is no longer prohibitive.

A multiyear standardization process for post-quantum cryptography has been initiated by NIST, the US National Institute of Standards and Technology [NIST 2018]; it received more than 80 submissions in late 2017. The newly proposed constructions rely on lattices, multivariate polynomials, error-correcting codes, and other primitives. Two stateless hash-based signature constructions have also been submitted, both of which extend SPHINCS. The agreement and process driven by NIST will proceed in multiple rounds and is expected to conclude with draft standards around 2022–2024.

Through these surprising developments, Lamport's work on digital signatures may also gain a lasting impact on the cryptography that secures communications over the Internet.

State Machine Replication with Benign Failures

Robbert van Renesse

Lamport's interest in replication emerged in an era when it was conjectured that no solution can keep the copies of a database synchronized, but nothing had been proved or disproved.

The earliest known examples of replication are for databases in the early 1970s (for example, Mullery [1971]). RFC 677 by Johnson and Thomas [1975] listed increasing reliability and ensuring efficiency of data access as primary motivations for replication. The RFC presented a replication technique using local timestamps, ties broken by replica identifiers, where "the latest update wins." It may be the first example of an "eventually consistent" database, which as a concept became very popular at the beginning of the cloud computing era [Vogels 2009]. Interestingly, RFC 677 concluded that "the probability of seemingly strange behavior can be made very small. However, the distributed nature of the system dictates that this probability can never be zero."

In 1976, Alsberg and Day [1976] presented a technique that goes a long way toward proving this assertion wrong, but not quite. Often claimed to be the first description of a primary-backup protocol, the basic technique involves a primary server and a backup server. Clients send update requests to the primary server, which orders and applies all incoming updates and forwards them to the backup server. The backup server also applies the updates, in the order set by the primary server, and sends acknowledgments back to the client. The paper gives no information on how to perform read commands and has only vague descriptions of how to deal with network partitions or how to generalize to multiple backups. But for the two-server case the protocol can perhaps be claimed as the first instantiation of a replication protocol that provides sequential consistency. The protocol does not deal with mistaken failure suspicions due to, say, network partitions. Moreover, reading from the primary can lead to incorrect results. An inefficient workaround is to treat read commands the same as updates. A better solution, suggested by van Renesse and Schneider [2004] in a variant called *chain replication*, is to have only the backup server respond to read commands.

In 1977, Clarence Ellis of Xerox PARC developed techniques for maintaining multiple copies of a database complete with a formal specification and verification based on Petri nets [Ellis 1977]. The techniques provide eventual consistency similar to RFC 677. Again, the techniques do not address query commands, and although fault tolerance is claimed as a useful property, the solutions presented do not appear to offer it by today's understanding of fault tolerance. Specifically, for liveness the techniques require that each crashed replica is eventually restarted, and from the state at which it crashed.

Lamport's seminal 1978 "Time, Clocks, and the Ordering of Events" paper is the first to present *state machine replication* (SMR), although not by that name, as a general principle for keeping copies of a deterministic state machine synchronized, although only focusing on the failure-free case. Lamport later writes that RFC 677 inspired this paper. Indeed, Lamport proves the assertion in the conclusion of RFC 677 wrong. (As pointed out in Chapter 2, the problem with RFC 677 timestamps is that they do not capture causality.) The SMR technique is presented almost as a side note, noting its generality but developing it for the specific case of distributed mutual exclusion. However, it should be recognized as a groundbreaking result, demonstrating that, at least in the absence of failures, strong consistency (single-copy semantics) and replication can coexist.

In the same year, Lamport published "The Implementation of Reliable Distributed Multiprocess Systems" in *Computer Networks* [Lamport 1978] (first published as a Massachusetts Computer Associates Technical Report in 1977), which demonstrates protocols for SMR for synchronous networks: one for fail-stop failures and one for Byzantine failures. This may be the first paper that describes a fault-tolerant SMR protocol providing strong consistency and the first paper that describes Byzantine failures (although again not by that name).

These two Lamport papers started a cottage industry of SMR papers that continues to this day, over 40 years later. This chapter focuses on the SMR model in the face of so-called benign process failures. "Benign" is a misnomer, but it indicates that a process follows its specification until it stops altogether. In particular, a process will not execute steps that are not according to its specification, but a faulty process may stop performing steps that are in its specification.

4.1 Active versus Passive Replication

In the literature, we find a distinction between active and passive replication protocols. Informally, in active replication protocols each replica is a copy of the original state machine, starting in the same state, and each (surviving) replica is presented with the same commands in the same order. In passive replication, at any time there is only a single copy of the state machine, the primary, while the remaining replicas, the backups, only maintain state. Clients send commands to the primary. Commands that cause a state change result in the primary broadcasting "state update commands" to the backups. Such state update commands simply request overwriting part of the state kept on the backups with a specific new value. Should the primary fail, one of the backups is promoted to be primary. Note that, under this definition, the Alsberg and Day [1976] protocol, while often claimed to be the first passive replication protocol, is actually an active replication protocol, as all replicas are "active," maintaining the full state machine and applying client commands in the same order.

Both active and passive replication are generic approaches to making a state machine fault tolerant. Passive replication appears more efficient as on average the replicas do less work, but failure recovery takes time; in contrast, active replication masks failures. However, a slight refactoring of function reveals that they are both instantiations of the SMR approach. In passive replication, client update requests are preprocessed and turned into state update commands. After that, all state update commands are applied to all replicas in the same order. Note that because state update commands may write overlapping parts of the state, the order is important. So for the purposes of this chapter, we do not equate active replication and SMR, but consider both active and passive replication instantiations of the SMR approach.

4.2 A Brief Review of State Machine Replication

The objective of SMR is to provide the illusion of a single "state machine," however one that is particularly reliable and responsive in the face of various types of failures. Consider a state machine (SM) to be a process that receives a sequence of commands and produces a sequence of output values. Most importantly, the entire sequence of output values generated by an SM is completely determined by the sequence of commands the SM has processed. This appears to require that an SM is purely sequential and deterministic. Fortunately, there exist deterministic parallelism techniques that still allow an SM to leverage concurrency

[Bocchino et al. 2009]. In addition, nondeterministic choices such as reading a clock or generating a random number can be modeled as inputs to a deterministic SM.

The output values of the SM are tagged with their intended destination, often clients who send request commands to the SM. We do not, however, require that clients and SMs follow a client-server or RPC-style communication pattern. For example, one client can send a command to the SM, and the SM in response can produce multiple different output values intended for multiple other destination processes.

Both SMs and clients are instances of processes. Consistent with the end-to-end model of communication [Saltzer et al. 1984], we assume that the network that connects these processes can lose, reorder, and duplicate messages. We assume that messages have checksums so that garbled messages can be equated with lost messages. Finally, we assume that the network is fair, meaning that if a message is continuously retransmitted from a correct sending process to a correct destination process, then eventually the destination process will receive and process at least one copy of the message. (A *correct process* is a process that never crashes.) Using sequence numbers and retransmission, it is then possible to implement reliable transmission between correct processes while filtering out duplicates. We therefore assume that communication between correct processes is reliable and ordered, although it will not always be necessary to make it so. We also assume that if a process p receives a message, then some process sent that message to p.

Processes can crash, and in particular a single SM fails if the process that runs the SM crashes. To improve fault tolerance of an SM, a *replicated state machine* consists of a set of copies of an SM, aka replicas, with the following properties:

Same Initial State. The replicas start in the same state.

Agreement. If replica R_1 has processed a sequence of commands S_1, and replica R_2 has processed a sequence of commands S_2, then S_1 is a prefix of S_2 or vice versa.

Completion. At least one replica is correct and eventually processes all commands sent to the SM by correct clients.

For more details, we refer to Schneider's "Implementing Fault-Tolerant Services Using the State-Machine Approach" [Schneider 1990]. It is up to a specific SMR protocol to ensure that these properties hold. Given that they do, it is easy to see that the SMR produces the same output values that an unreplicated SM would have. Moreover, the duplication of output messages produced due to having multiple replicas is filtered out by the destination processes by the very same sequence numbers used to ensure reliable end-to-end communication channels.

4.3 Benign System Models

Before we delve into SMR protocols, it is useful to look more carefully at timing properties and process failure properties. These are assumptions that one makes about the system, and it should be carefully considered that every assumption made is a potential weakness. The two extreme timing models are *synchrony* and *asynchrony:*

Synchrony. There is a known upper bound on message latencies, the time for a process to handle a command and produce zero or more output values, the drift of the clock of a process (the rate at which the clock of a process differs from real time), as well as the maximum skew (difference) between clock values of different processes at the same time.

Asynchrony. There are no assumptions on timing whatsoever.

In between, there are useful so-called semi-synchronous models. We use the following semi-synchronous model below:

Almost-Asynchrony. (aka *partial synchrony*) There is an unknown upper bound on message latencies, message handling (processing step) latencies, and clock drift.

We note that this almost-asynchronous assumption makes very weak timing assumptions. For example, it includes systems where a message between correct processes is delivered within a million years, and clocks drift by a factor of 1000 (1000 times slower or faster than real time), although processes do not actually know what these bounds are. But, from a theoretical point of view, the distinction from asynchrony is significant, as we shall soon see.

In addition, we will be more precise about various classes of benign process failures. We distinguish the following two types of assumptions about process failures:

Crash Failures. Processes follow their specification in that they do not take any steps that deviate from the specification. However, if a process crashes, then the process stops making steps indefinitely. Note that crash failures are a stronger assumption than Byzantine failures. Also note that in a synchronous environment crash failures can be detected accurately with a pinging protocol, while no such protocol is possible in an asynchronous environment. Even the almost-asynchronous environment does not support accurate failure detection because processes do not know the timing bounds in the system.

Fail-Stop Failures. These are like crash failures, except that we assume that failures can be detected accurately by a *failure detection oracle* or simply *failure detector*. In particular, we assume that the crash of a process is eventually detected by all correct processes, while no correct process is ever suspected of having crashed. Note that fail-stop failures are essentially a synchrony assumption in disguise—in a synchronous environment we do not need to make a distinction between crash failures and fail-stop failures. But in an almost-asynchronous or asynchronous environment, fail-stop failures are a stronger assumption than crash failures.

A process that keeps its state on disk can survive power failures, but not disk failures. In fact, in an asynchronous or almost-asynchronous environment, a power failure is not a failure at all unless it persists. Thus while in practice keeping state on disk can be helpful, from a theoretical perspective it does not have much influence on the design of the protocol.

4.4 SMR Protocol Basics

An SMR protocol implements the SMR properties above given a certain set of system assumptions. There are two general—and essentially equivalent—approaches, both involving a group of participants:

Total Ordering Protocols. A total ordering protocol is a protocol in which processes broadcast messages to one another, satisfying the following properties:

> **T-Completion.** A message sent or delivered by a correct process is eventually delivered to all correct processes.

> **T-Validity.** If a process delivers a message, it was sent by some process.

> **T-Agreement.** If two processes deliver the same two messages, they deliver them in the same order.

Consensus Protocols. A consensus protocol is a protocol in which processes in the group can each propose a value. The properties are then as follows:

> **C-Completion.** If a correct process proposes or decides a value, all correct processes eventually decide a value.

C-Validity. If a process decides a value, then that value was proposed by some process.

C-Agreement. If two processes decide a value, they decide the same value.

A total ordering protocol only needs to be instantiated once per SMR. Instead, a consensus protocol is instantiated for each "slot" in the sequence of commands to an SMR. The processes can be the same set of processes that run the replicas of the SMR or a separate set of processes that relate their decisions to the replicas. It is straightforward to see that one can build a total ordering protocol out of a consensus protocol and vice versa.

The aforementioned paper "The Implementation of Reliable Distributed Multiprocess Systems" by Lamport demonstrates what is possibly the first total ordering protocol for a synchronous environment with process failures. The conceptual idea is to assign a unique timestamp (ties broken by source identifier) to each message sent, and then flood the message to all other processes so all messages are delivered within a maximum amount of time that can be computed from the network topology. After this time, a message can be delivered in order of its timestamp, knowing that all prior messages must have been received as well.

The synchronous model, while simplifying the SMR problem significantly, is unfortunately rarely realistic in today's computing environments. On the other hand, Fischer et al. [1985] show that in an asynchronous environment it is impossible to solve consensus in the presence of crash failures. Most protocols therefore provide only Agreement in purely asynchronous settings, and make one of the following trade-offs for Completion:

- Completion guaranteed only if the environment is almost-asynchronous.
- Completion guaranteed with probability 1 (aka Almost Surely). That is, Completion is ensured with the same probability as the probability of heads coming up when a coin is flipped indefinitely.

Both of these are eminently practical trade-offs, and thus for the remainder of this chapter we will ignore synchronous SMR protocols as well as protocols that assume fail-stop failures. Also, we will mostly cover consensus protocols rather than totally ordered broadcast protocols, because most of both the early and more recent work on SMRs has focused on the problem of consensus.

Asynchronous consensus protocols with crash failures require at least $2f + 1$ participants. To see why this is so, consider a fictitious protocol that survives f crash failures but requires only $2f$ processes. Split the processes into two groups of f processes, one in which all processes propose some proposal Red and another in which all processes propose some proposal Blue. Consider the following three scenarios:

1. All the processes that proposed Red crash before sending any messages. The processes that proposed Blue cannot discover if the other processes proposed Red or Blue. Thus they have no choice but to decide eventually (C-Completion), and they must decide Blue (C-Validity). Assume that they do so by some time T_b.

2. Same but vice versa: The Red processes decide Red by some time T_r.

3. All processes are correct. Let T be the maximum of T_b and T_r, and assume that until time T there exists a network partition in which processes in different groups cannot exchange messages. Because the network is fair, the network partition cannot persist indefinitely. Unfortunately, to the Red and Blue processes this situation is indistinguishable from the first two scenarios, and thus they decide before T inconsistently, violating C-Agreement.

4.5 Early Asynchronous Consensus Protocols

Working up to Lamport's seminal Paxos protocol, we now review two works that precede Paxos but that illustrate various important concepts in asynchronous consensus protocols, including *rounds*, *phases*, *majority voting*, and *leaders*.

4.5.1 Ben-Or

In 1983, Michael Ben-Or published an extended abstract in the Proceedings of the ACM Symposium on Principles of Distributed Computing (PODC) called "Another Advantage of Free Choice: Completely Asynchronous Agreement Protocols" [Ben-Or 1983]. The consensus protocol (which we will name after Ben-Or) is intended for an asynchronous environment with crash failures and guarantees both C-Validity and C-Agreement, and C-Completion with probability 1.

The protocol is binary in that there are only two possible proposals, which we call Red and Blue. Nonetheless, the protocol illustrates important concepts that most asynchronous and almost-asynchronous consensus protocols share. Assume there are N processes total, $N > 2f$. Figure 4.1 shows the protocol that each process p runs (slightly modified from its original to be more consistent with the protocols that follow in this chapter).

The protocol is an excellent illustration of Lamport's lessons on "Time, Clocks, and the Ordering of Events" in practice. In the asynchronous model, there is no

0. Initially, set estimate e_p to p's proposal and round number $r_p = 1$.

1. Phase P1:
   (a) Broadcast message $\langle phase = P1, round = r_p, estimate = e_p \rangle$.
   (b) Wait for messages of the form $\langle phase = P1, round = r_p, estimate = * \rangle$ from $> N/2$ different processes.
   (c) If all contain the same estimate e, then set $v_p = e$. Otherwise set $v_p = \perp$.

2. Phase P2:
   (a) Broadcast message $\langle phase = P2, round = r_p, estimate = v_p \rangle$.
   (b) Wait for messages of the form $\langle phase = P2, round = r_p, estimate = * \rangle$ from $> N/2$ different processes.
   (c) (i) If all messages contain the same non-$\perp$ estimate e, then **decide** e.
       (ii) If one of the messages contains a non-$\perp$ estimate e, then **accept** e by setting $e_p = e$. Otherwise **accept** a random estimate by setting e_p to Red or Blue uniformly at random.

3. Increment r_p and go to Step 1.

Figure 4.1 A variant of the Ben-Or consensus protocol.

concept of time or clocks. The round number r_p simulates a local clock for p. However, note that there is no bound on the difference between the round numbers of two different processes, nor on the rate at which the round number of a process increases. Process p only considers messages for the round r_p that it is in; it ignores messages for prior rounds and buffers messages for future rounds. Doing so, the processes can pretend that together they run one round at a time, but in reality their execution may be arbitrarily skewed and different rounds will typically overlap in real time.

Each process p maintains an estimate e_p. A process can accept as well as decide an estimate in the second phase of a round. Accepting an estimate simply means that a process updates its own estimate. (Accepting is also referred to as *voting*, but we use Lamport's terminology here.) It is guaranteed that if a process decides estimate e, it also accepts e.

Define an estimate e to be *safe* in round r if the following two properties hold:

1. Some process proposed e as its initial estimate in step 0; and

2. No process decides or has decided a different estimate in round r' where $r' \leq r$.

An important invariant to keep in mind in this consensus protocol is that at any time and for any process p, any estimate that p accepts is safe in round r_p. A similar invariant usually holds in other asynchronous consensus protocols. Because a process never decides an estimate that it does not accept in the same round, C-Validity and C-Agreement follow trivially from this invariant.

The protocol subdivides a round into two subrounds or *phases,* P1 and P2. Each phase consists of each correct process p performing three actions:

(a) p broadcasts a message (sent to all processes including self);

(b) p waits for more than $N/2$ messages (but no more than $N - f$) from peers (including self);

(c) p updates its local state based on its current state and the messages that p has received.

Inductively, it is easy to show that each phase, and therefore each round, eventually terminates. After all, given that no more than f processes crash and $N > 2f$, each process is guaranteed to receive $N - f$ $(N - f > N/2)$ messages in each phase.

An invariant of the Ben-Or protocol is that the estimates of all processes going into phase P1 (either from step 0 or from step 3) of round r are safe in round $r - 1$. It is clear that this is true for the initial estimates (all estimates are safe in round 0 as no proposal has been decided yet), and we will informally argue that it also holds for later rounds while explaining the protocol.

The purpose of phase P1 in the Ben-Or protocol is to reduce the number of estimates that are eligible for decision in phase P2 to at most a single one. To win, each process p computes a value v_p that is either a proposal (Red or Blue) or $\bot$ in step 1c after having received a majority of estimates. Because it is not possible that there exist two different majorities, one in which all processes have sent estimate Red and another in which all processes have sent estimate Blue, it must be the case that if two processes p and q compute non-$\bot$ values v_p and v_q, then $v_p = v_q$. It is also important to note that, if all processes that broadcast an estimate in step 1a broadcast the same estimate e, then all processes p that set v_p in step 1c set $v_p = e$.

The purpose of phase P2 is for each process p to possibly decide an estimate and in any case accept an estimate that is safe in round r_p. A process p decides an estimate e in round r_p if it receives that estimate from more than a majority of processes in phase P2 of round r_p.

First assume this is the case. Because all other processes wait for P2 messages from a majority of processes, it follows that all other processes that reach step 2c in the same round must receive at least one P2 message with the same estimate

e. Moreover, as we saw above, it is not possible that processes receive a non-$\perp$ estimate other than e. Thus all processes that reach step 2c of round r will accept (and possibly decide) e in round r. Moreover, as e was safe in round $r - 1$ and no estimate other than e could have been decided before round r, e must still be safe. In this case, all processes that enter the next round $r + 1$ enter with their estimate set to e, satisfying the invariant.

Perhaps the more interesting case is what happens when no process decides in some round r because no process received a non-$\perp$ estimate from a majority. Note that if some estimate e had been decided before round r, then only that estimate would have been safe in round $r - 1$ and all processes would have received e in step 1c. Since this is not the case, we may conclude that no estimate was decided before round r. Because no process decides in round r either, both Red and Blue are safe estimates in round r.

In this case, some processes may still receive a non-$\perp$ estimate in step 2b. Recall that all such processes are guaranteed to receive the same estimate e and thus will set their estimate to e in step 2c.ii. The remaining processes accept a random estimate in step 2c.ii. By accepting a random estimate if only $\perp$ messages are received in phase P2, there is a chance, even if small, that all processes doing so happen to accept the same estimate e in step 2c.ii. And this in turn would cause all correct processes to decide e in the next round. Thus each round (except possibly the first) has a nonzero chance of deciding. Given that the number of rounds is unbounded, the Ben-Or protocol satisfies C-Completion with probability 1, just like the probability of heads coming up is 1 if a coin is flipped an unbounded number of times. This convergence can be sped up dramatically if the processes use a so-called shared coin, that is, a pseudorandom coin that comes up the same at all processes in the same round.

Note that although the protocol as described continues to run even after all correct processes have decided, it is easy to see that a process that decides can stop running the protocol after finishing just one more round, as all correct processes are guaranteed to have decided by then.

The reader may wonder why it is necessary to have two phases, rather than just one. In fact, it is easy to design a consensus protocol that has only one phase. However, the minimal number of participants for such a protocol has to be $3f + 1$ in order to tolerate f failures [Brasileiro et al. 2001]. By reducing the number of eligible proposals to at most one in phase P1 of the Ben-Or protocol, a simple majority vote in phase P2 is sufficient to decide. Replicas are expensive, and two phases allow asynchronous consensus protocols to meet the $2f + 1$ lower bound on the number of replicas.

4.5.2 Dwork, Lynch, and Stockmeyer

In 1984, one year after the publication of the Ben-Or consensus protocol, Cynthia Dwork, Nancy Lynch, and Larry Stockmeyer published a preliminary version of their "Consensus in the Presence of Partial Synchrony" paper [Dwork et al. 1988] about a consensus protocol (referred to here as the DLS protocol after its authors) for the almost-synchronous model that illustrates two other important concepts. The first is the concept of using a leader, and the second is demonstrating that consensus can satisfy C-Completion in the almost-asynchronous model.

As pointed out above, asynchronous consensus protocols that meet the lower bound on the number of replicas need two phases, the first of which reduces the number of proposals eligible for decision and acceptance to at most one. For the Ben-Or protocol, this was accomplished by a majority vote in the first phase. A simpler approach is to assign to each round a leader and have that leader select a safe estimate for that round. Should the leader crash, then the next round, with another leader, can still make progress.

We will not reproduce the entire DLS protocol here. Instead, we modify the Ben-Or protocol to use a leader in phase P1. We call the resulting protocol *Franken consensus*. Let the leader of a round r be the participating process $r \mod N$. Figure 4.2 shows the steps that each process p executes.

There are three important differences from the Ben-Or protocol:

1. The Franken protocol uses a timeout parameter T_p, which is initialized to a nonzero value and increased for each round (doubling is not essential, as long as T_p increases by a nontrivial amount on each round).

2. Phase P1 of the protocol has a leader proposing a particular estimate instead of the processes determining one by majority vote. Note that the number of messages that cross the network in phase P1 is reduced from $N(N-1)$ to $N-1$. If a process times out waiting for the estimate from the leader of the current round, it continues with the $\perp$ value.

3. In step 2c.ii, if a process receives only messages containing $\perp$ estimates, then it accepts its current estimate, rather than accepting a random estimate.

Phase P1 of Ben-Or consensus and Franken consensus are different implementations but serve exactly the same purpose: to select at most one of the estimates that are safe in round $r-1$ for acceptance by the processes in round r. Initially, all processes may time out, but eventually parameter T_p will grow sufficiently large so that other processes will not time out waiting for messages from a correct leader, guaranteeing C-Completion. However, until then it is possible that all processes do

0. Initially, set estimate e_p to p's proposal, round number r_p to 1, and T_p to some initial value > 0.

1. Phase P1:
    (a) If p is leader of r_p, broadcast $\langle phase = P1, round = r_p, estimate = e_p \rangle$.
    (b) Leader or not:
        (i) Wait for a message of the form $\langle phase = P1, round = r_p, estimate = e \rangle$ from the leader of r_p, up to T_p ticks measured on p's clock.
        (ii) Upon receipt set $v_p = e$. On timeout, set $v_p = \bot$.

2. Phase P2:
    (a) Broadcast $\langle phase = P2, round = r_p, estimate = v_p \rangle$.
    (b) Wait for messages of the form $\langle phase = P2, round = r_p, estimate = * \rangle$ from $> N/2$ different processes.
    (c) (i) If all messages contain the same non-$\bot$ estimate e, then **decide** e.
        (ii) If one of the messages contains a non-$\bot$ estimate e, then **accept** e by setting $e_p = e$. Otherwise **accept** e_p (i.e., leave e_p unchanged).

3. Increment r_p, double T_p, and go to step 1.

Figure 4.2   The Franken consensus protocol.

timeout waiting for a correct leader *even if all estimates started out the same.* Thus, unlike in the Ben-Or protocol, a process may not decide in phase P2 if all estimates going into phase P1 are the same, and in particular, a process may not decide in round r if some estimate was decided in a round prior to r.

In step 2c, it would not be safe for a process to accept a random estimate if it received only $\bot$ estimates. Instead, a process accepts its current estimate. To see why this estimate is safe, consider the following. As in the Ben-Or protocol, if a process decides an estimate e in a round r, all correct processes are guaranteed to accept (and possibly decide) e in round r. Moreover, going into round $r + 1$ the only estimate left in play is estimate e because processes running the Franken protocol accept no random values.

If the initial timeout parameter of each process is chosen reasonably well and crash failures are rare, Franken consensus is a significant improvement in practice over Ben-Or consensus. In this sometimes called "normal case," all correct participants in the Franken consensus protocol will decide the leader's estimate in a single round, even if all processes start with different proposals. Also note that, unlike the Ben-Or protocol, Franken consensus supports more than two different proposals.

The published DLS protocol, while different, shares all these advantages with the Franken protocol. Unfortunately, the DLS protocol remained a theoretical curiosity, and SMR protocols at the time only existed in the form of primary-backup protocols. Such protocols assume fail-stop failures and can violate Agreement when there are latency anomalies either in the network or in a process itself violating the fail-stop assumption.

4.6 Paxos

Lamport discovered the Paxos protocol in the late 1980s while investigating the fault tolerance of the Echo file system being developed at Digital's Systems Research Center [Hisgen et al. 1989]. Paxos made SMR for almost-asynchronous environments significantly more practical. Described in his seminal "The Part-Time Parliament" paper [Lamport 1998a], its underlying consensus protocol (known as the Synod protocol, but these days most use Paxos to refer to both the SMR protocol and the underlying consensus algorithm) has two important improvements over prior protocols:

1. Like other protocols that meet the $2f + 1$ lower bound, Paxos uses two phases per round (called *ballots* in Paxos), but both phases P1 and P2 only use $O(N)$ messages instead of $O(N^2)$ messages. Hence a round only uses $O(N)$ messages.

2. In the "normal case" in which failures and failure suspicions are rare, the leader of a round can make a series of decisions, requiring running only phase P2 for each command executed by the SMR.

As in the original Paxos paper, we develop the protocol in two steps: first reducing the message complexity, and then eliminating the first phase except in case a leader is suspected of having failed. For the first protocol, we reuse the structure of the Franken protocol, in the hope that the intuitions about consensus in the almost-asynchronous model learned above help with understanding the Paxos protocol. However, each phase consists of two subphases:

(a) The leader broadcasts a message to the processes, called *acceptors* in Paxos. Upon receipt, an acceptor updates its state;

(b) Each acceptor that received a message responds to the leader. The leader awaits responses from a majority of acceptors and updates its state.

Figure 4.3 shows the steps that each process p executes in a variant of Lamport's "single-decree Synod protocol."

0. Initially, set estimate $e_p = \perp$, round number $r_p = 1$, and T_p to some initial value > 0.

1. Phase P1:

   (a) (i) If p is leader of r_p, broadcast $\langle phase = P1a, round = r_p \rangle$.

       (ii) Leader or not:
   - Wait for a message of the form $\langle phase = P1a, round = r \rangle$ such that $r \geq r_p$.
   - Set $r_p = r$.

   (b) (i) Send $\langle phase = P1b, round = r, estimate = e_p \rangle$ to the leader of r.

       (ii) If p is leader of r_p, then:
   - Wait for messages of the form $\langle phase = P1b, round = r_p, estimate = * \rangle$ from $> N/2$ different processes.
   - If some estimates are non-$\perp$, set v_p to the proposal in the highest numbered estimate. If instead all estimates are $\perp$, then set v_p to the initial proposal of p.

2. Phase P2:

   (a) (i) If p is leader of r_p, broadcast $\langle phase = P2a, round = r_p, estimate = \langle r_p, v_p \rangle \rangle$.

       (ii) Leader or not:
   - Wait for a message of the form $\langle phase = P2a, round = r_p, estimate = e \rangle$ from the leader of r_p.
   - **Accept** e by setting estimate $e_p = e$.

   (b) (i) Send $\langle phase = P2b, round = r_p \rangle$ to the leader of r_p.

       (ii) If p is leader of r_p, then:
   - Wait for messages of the form $\langle phase = P2b, round = r_p \rangle$ from $> N/2$ different processes.
   - **Decide** the proposal in e_p and broadcast decision to all replicas.

3. If p is not leader of round r_p, then upon timeout waiting for a message from the leader of round r_p:
   - Increase r_p to the next round for which p is leader.
   - Double T_p and go to step 1.

Figure 4.3   A variant of the single-decree Paxos protocol.

While the protocol resembles the Franken protocol, there are some important differences to note:

- Estimate e_p is no longer a proposal, but initially $\perp$ and later assigned to be a $\langle round\ number, proposal \rangle$ pair. There cannot be two different estimates with the same round number (as the leader of a round only generates at most one).

Estimates are ordered by round number, with $\perp$ representing the smallest possible estimate.

- In the Franken protocol, all estimates going into phase 1 of round r are safe in round $r - 1$. Not so in Paxos. In phase P1, the leader of round r does not distribute its estimate, because it may not be safe. Instead, it announces only its round number and collects the estimates of its peers, who promise not to accept more estimates in rounds less than r. After hearing back from a majority, the leader determines the highest estimate among them. If this is $\perp$, the leader learns that no proposal was decided in rounds lower than r. In this case, it will use as a safe estimate $\langle r, \textit{leader's own proposal} \rangle$. Otherwise, the highest estimate is safe in round r.

- In phase P2, instead of an N^2 communication pattern, the leader broadcasts its estimate. If still acceptable given the peer's round number, the peer accepts the estimate and responds to the leader. If the leader hears back from a majority, it knows that any future leader that might take over will learn about this estimate, and therefore it can decide the proposal in the estimate.

- A process p no longer simply runs one round at a time. Instead, it can *skip* to any future round when it receives a P1a message from the leader of such a round. When doing this, its stored estimate in e_p may no longer be safe in the new round. This is why eligible estimates are determined at the end of phase P1, rather than at the beginning.

- A leader may crash, and therefore each wait on a message from the leader has a timeout of T_p time units. When timing out on a leader, a process tries to become the leader itself by initiating a new round, as specified in step 3.

If all this sounds complicated, there is a reason for that: it is difficult for anyone but a computer to understand an operational description of a protocol. The beauty of the "Part-Time Parliament" paper is that it starts out with demonstrating what principles a consensus protocol must satisfy in order for it to satisfy C-Validity and C-Agreement. (The paper does not address C-Completion.) As a result, the paper describes a family of consensus protocols that satisfy C-Validity and C-Agreement by construction. We will not even attempt to duplicate the beautiful presentation of the "Part-Time Parliament" paper here (or its "simpler cousin" [Lamport 2001]), for the simple reason that there is no need to.

The "Part-Time Parliament" goes on to describe an important improvement by allowing the same leader to decide a sequence of proposals rather than just a single one. This way, execution of phase P1 can be avoided unless the leader is suspected of having crashed. This advance is made possible because a leader does not propose a value until the end of phase P1. The leader can continue to extend the sequence of decided proposals until (after a timeout causing the leader to be suspected of having crashed) a majority of acceptors have moved on with a larger round number. The resulting protocol is these days often called Multi-Paxos [Chandra et al. 2007].

4.6.1   Read-Only Commands

In many workloads, read commands are much more frequent than update commands, and thus their efficiency is important to the overall practicality of SMR. If clients were to read from any replica, they may well read from a stale one, violating one-copy semantics. Performing read commands just like update commands is inefficient, particularly if Paxos state is kept on disk. Reading from all replicas and selecting the most recent one would not be fault tolerant and intolerably slow even if all replicas were up. It is possible to read from a quorum of replicas, but obtaining the state this way is tricky to get right and still inefficient compared to reading off a single replica.

To solve the problem, the "Part-Time Parliament" paper proposes to appoint primary replicas for specific intervals of real time. This is akin to leases [Gray and Cheriton 1989]. Only one replica can have a lease at a time. Only a replica with a valid lease can produce output messages, and only that replica can respond to queries. The time intervals assigned to leases should be short so that, should the lease holder crash, it will not be long before another replica can take over. This elegant solution has approximately the same read efficiency as an unreplicated SM, but note that it requires that processor clocks are tightly synchronized. While it is possible to allow for a known bounded skew between clocks, or even just to rely on a known bounded drift of clocks, these assumptions are still stronger than the almost-asynchronous model. In practice, however, it is easy to have access today to clocks with bounded skew and/or drift, while message latencies and processing times are still hard to bound.

4.6.2   Discussion

While it is often claimed that viewstamped replication (VR) by Oki and Liskov [1988] bears a resemblance to Multi-Paxos (and indeed, VR can be considered a protocol in the Paxos family of consensus protocols), the VR protocol is a specific implementation of a consensus protocol for passive replication. The VR protocol is a significant advance, but the paper gives only an operational description of the VR protocol and contains no clear expression of principles nor a proof of the protocol's correctness. The "Part-Time Parliament" paper thus represents an important contribution to the science of fault-tolerant asynchronous distributed systems even if an example of a protocol in the Paxos family had been demonstrated previously.

Paxos was first deployed in the Petal distributed storage system [Lee and Thekkath 1996]. In time, Paxos has become probably the best-known replication protocol and variants of it have been widely deployed, including in systems such as Google's Chubby system [Burrows 2006] and Microsoft's NoSQL Azure Cosmos database, and in countless open source projects such as Yahoo!/Apache ZooKeeper [Hunt et al. 2010], Facebook Cassandra [Lakshman and Malik 2009], Ceph [Weil et al. 2006], and Raft [Ongaro and Ousterhout 2014].

Disk Paxos [Gafni and Lamport 2003] replaces acceptor processes with disks that support only read block and write block operations and can therefore be considered a "shared memory" version of Paxos. It was originally developed in 1998 for an interesting scenario at Digital Equipment Corporation's storage group, in which there were only two processors. Two processors are generally not enough to tolerate a crash failure in an asynchronous environment, but it turns out it can be done if there are at least three independent disks that can be accessed by both processors. In general, Disk Paxos requires $m > f$ processors and $n > 2f$ disks to tolerate f processor and f disk failures.

The protocol still resembles the original Paxos. There are m leaders, one on each processor. Each leader has a block on each disk that only that leader can write, but all leaders can read all blocks. Thus there are a total of $n \times m$ blocks. To start a new round, a leader remotely writes a P1a message to its block on at least a majority of the disks, simulating a broadcast to the acceptors. The leader then tries to read all m blocks from each of a majority of disks to see if some other leader initiated a higher round. If not, the leader moves on to phase P2, which proceeds similarly.

4.7 Dynamic Reconfiguration

Being able to replace replicas is important for fault-tolerant services that must remain up 24/7 and cannot be taken down temporarily for maintenance operations, such as replacing failed replicas or performing hardware upgrades. Lamport described how to do this in synchronous environments in his 1984 paper "Using Time Instead of Timeout for Fault-Tolerant Distributed Systems." The basic idea is to introduce a reconfiguration command that replaces the set of replicas. The "Part-Time Parliament" paper adopts the same approach, but using slot numbers (indexes into the message input stream to the SMR) instead of time. So slot i could contain a reconfiguration command that specifies what the configuration is starting at slot $i + \alpha$. While α could be as small as 1, this would require that one cannot know the configuration for slot $i + 1$ until after a command is decided for slot i. Hence no concurrency would be possible. For $\alpha > 1$, the current configuration of replicas can be deciding α commands (slots i through $i + \alpha - 1$) in parallel, which can improve throughput.

While perhaps sounding simple enough, dealing with reconfiguration has been an Achilles' heel for practical Paxos deployments. The dynamic reconfiguration approach described above has complicated implementation corner cases. For example, clients have to deal with the fact that multiple configurations may be simultaneously active, while replicas have to deal with the fact that decisions may come out of order, both within a configuration and across configurations. Also, as multiple (α) decisions may be outstanding at any time, a single configuration can, in theory, decide on multiple future configurations.

Much work in the last couple of decades has gone into refining failure handling and recovery for practical, large-scale deployments of Paxos. An early approach, Cheap Paxos [Lamport and Massa 2004], looks at reducing cost in the normal case while still being able to reconfigure the replicas should the need arise. Instead of using $2f + 1$ or more acceptors, Cheap Paxos uses only $f + 1$ acceptors combined with f "auxiliary" acceptors that are idle during normal execution but play an important role in failure recovery. The optimization is based on the observation that during normal operation Paxos only needs a majority of processes to participate in the protocol. However, if one of those processes becomes unresponsive, some of the auxiliary acceptors are necessary to run phase P1 of the protocol. The reconfiguration protocol of Paxos can then be used to replace the unresponsive acceptors with new ones, restoring the fault tolerance of the system.

Vertical Paxos [Lamport et al. 2009a] takes this idea a step further, fixing the round number and leader during normal operation, similar to primary-backup protocols. When a failure occurs, an auxiliary "configuration master" decides on what the new configuration will be. The new leader then accesses the state of the processes in the old configuration to obtain the old state and informs the configuration master. This old state can then be used to create a new configuration that is a consistent continuation of the old one. A similar technique is used for recovery in the Google File System [Ghemawat et al. 2003] and the chain replication protocol [van Renesse and Schneider 2004]. In order to be fault tolerant, the configuration master itself must be replicated and may also require dynamic reconfiguration.

An alternative approach to dynamic reconfiguration is to, in a single reconfiguration operation, terminate the old configuration and create a new one. This approach takes inspiration from so-called view changes in group communication protocols such as Isis [Birman et al. 1991]. For example, in Stoppable Paxos [Lamport et al. 2010], a special STOP reconfiguration command has the simplifying property that if some configuration decides a STOP command in slot i, then that configuration can no longer decide commands in slots after i (while still allowing concurrency). In Lamport et al. [2010], Lamport, Malkhi, and Zhou discuss advantages and disadvantages of various SMR reconfiguration methods.

Formal Specification and Verification

Stephan Merz

5.1 Introduction

Beyond his seminal contributions to the theory and the design of concurrent and distributed algorithms, Leslie Lamport has throughout his career worked on methods and formalisms for rigorously establishing the correctness of algorithms. Commenting on his first article about a method for proving the correctness of multiprocess programs [Lamport 1977a] on the website providing access to his collected writings [Lamport 2019], Lamport recalls that this interest originated in his submitting a flawed mutual exclusion algorithm in the early 1970s. As a trained mathematician, Lamport is perfectly familiar with mathematical set theory, the standard formal foundation of classical mathematics. His career in industrial research environments and the fact that his main interest has been in algorithms, not formalisms, has certainly contributed to his designing reasoning methods that combine pragmatism and mathematical elegance. The methods that he designed have always been grounded in the semantics of programs and their executions rather than being driven by the syntax in which these programs are expressed, in contrast to many methods advocated by "pure" computer scientists.

The famous "Time/Clocks" paper [Lamport 1978b] describes executions of distributed state machines and introduces the happened-before or causality relation, a partial order on the events occurring in runs. The "philosophically correct" way for reasoning about distributed executions would thus appear to be based on a partial ordering between operations. Indeed, Lamport explored this idea and proposed a method based on two relations called *precedes* and *may affect* [Lamport 1979c]. This method can notably be applied to algorithms that involve nonatomic operations, such as the Bakery algorithm. However, Lamport felt that the method did not scale well, unlike assertional reasoning about global states of systems that can be visible to an idealized external observer, even if no single process can observe them. This style of reasoning considers linearizations of distributed executions, and it generally requires algorithms to be described in terms of their atomic operations (an exception being [Lamport 1990]). The notion of an overall system invariant that is preserved by every operation plays a central role in this approach: such an invariant explains why the algorithm is correct. Assertional proofs have since been demonstrated to be completely rigorous, to be amenable to mechanized checking, and to scale well.

Lamport realized that there are two fundamental classes of correctness properties that arise in the verification of concurrent algorithms, for which he coined the terms *safety* and *liveness* properties [Lamport 1977a]. Generalizing, respectively, partial correctness and termination of sequential programs, safety properties assert that "nothing bad ever happens" and liveness properties require that "something good happens eventually." These intuitive concepts were later formalized by Alpern and Schneider [1985], who showed that any property of runs can be expressed as the intersection of a safety property and a liveness property. Although proofs of liveness properties generally rely on auxiliary invariants, the basic principles for proving safety and liveness properties are different, and the two are therefore best considered separately.

Lamport advocates describing algorithms in terms of state machines whose operations are atomic. Invariants, and more generally safety properties, are then established by induction: the invariant holds in all possible initial states and is preserved by every operation of the state machine. The proof of liveness properties usually relies on associating a measure with the states of the algorithm and showing that the measure decreases with every step as long as the "good state" has not been reached. This argument is made formal through the use of well-founded orderings, which do not admit infinite decreasing chains. A direct application of that proof principle would require fixing a scheduler that governs the execution of different processes—an undesirable requirement since one wants to establish the correctness of the algorithm for any "reasonable" scheduler. A useful generalization requires that as long as the target state has not been reached, no step of the algorithm increases the measure, "helpful" steps decrease the measure, and some helpful step will eventually be executed. In order to justify the latter (which in itself is a liveness property!), one invokes fairness assumptions [Attie et al. 1993, Lamport 2000] that assert that executable operations will not be neglected forever, fixing the precise understanding of a "reasonable" scheduler for the particular application.

Another fundamental concept underlying the rigorous development and proof of concurrent algorithms advocated by Lamport is that of *refinement*. It allows a designer to describe the fundamental correctness properties using a high-level (possibly centralized) state machine and then prove that another state machine whose description is given at a lower level of abstraction faithfully implements the high-level description. For example, a high-level state machine describing a consensus algorithm [Lamport et al. 1982] could have a variable *chosen* holding a set of values, initialized to the empty set, a *Choose* operation that assigns *chosen* to the singleton set {v} for some value v among the proposed values, and *Decide* operations that set the decision values of each process to that chosen value. A lower-level refinement would then describe the actual algorithm in terms of exchanged messages and votes. A technical complication in that approach is that the lower-level state machine will have operations that modify only low-level variables, i.e., variables that do not exist at the higher level of abstraction. These operations cannot be mapped to operations of the high-level state machine. For example, operations that send messages in the putative consensus algorithm have no meaning in the high-level specification. Lamport advocates that formalisms for describing executions of state machines should be insensitive to *stuttering steps* that leave unchanged the state visible to the specification.

The remainder of this chapter focuses on the Temporal Logic of Actions (TLA) and the specification language TLA$^+$. These are Lamport's contributions to the formal specification and verification of algorithms that have had the greatest impact in the academic community and in industry, and their design was guided by the principles that have been outlined above.

5.2 The Temporal Logic of Actions

Temporal logic [Prior 1967] is a branch of modal logic in which the accessibility relation corresponds to temporal succession. During the 1970s, several authors [Burstall 1974, Kröger 1977] suggested adopting temporal logic as a basis for proving programs correct. Pnueli's influential paper [Pnueli 1977] provided the insight that temporal logic was most useful for specifying and reasoning about *reactive systems*, which include concurrent and distributed systems. A generalization of Pnueli's logic that is based on the "next" and "until" connectives remains the standard variant of linear-time temporal logic used in computer science to this day.

5.2.1 The Genesis of TLA

In 1977, Lamport proposed a method for proving the correctness of concurrent programs [Lamport 1977a]. It used invariant reasoning (based on Floyd's method [Floyd 1967]) for establishing safety properties and lattices of leads-to properties for proving liveness. The method relied on a fixed progress assumption for each process in order to establish elementary leads-to properties.

Lamport was introduced to temporal logic in the late 1970s during a seminar organized by Susan Owicki at Stanford University. At that time, the distinction between linear-time and branching-time temporal logics was not yet clearly established in computer science. Lamport clarified this difference [Lamport 1980] and showed that the expressive powers of LTL and CTL are incomparable. He quickly realized that temporal logic was a convenient language for expressing and reasoning about fairness and liveness properties. For example, weak and strong fairness of executions with respect to an action α, representing an operation of a process in a concurrent system, can be written as

$$\Box(\Box\, en(\alpha) \Rightarrow \Diamond\, exec(\alpha)) \quad \text{and} \quad \Box(\Box \Diamond\, en(\alpha) \Rightarrow \Diamond\, exec(\alpha)).$$

In these formulas, the predicate $en(\alpha)$ characterizes those states in which α is enabled (may be executed), $exec(\alpha)$ is true when action α has been executed, and $\Box$ and $\Diamond$ are the "always" and "eventually" operators of LTL. Weak fairness requires that an action cannot remain perpetually enabled without eventually being executed. Strong fairness requires that even an action that is infinitely often (but perhaps not perpetually) enabled must eventually be executed. Using such formulas, more general fairness hypotheses than uniform progress of processes considered in Lamport [1977a] can be expressed unambiguously. Moreover, the principles of reasoning about leads-to lattices could be derived from the general proof rules of temporal logic. A joint paper with Owicki [Owicki and Lamport 1982] develops these ideas into a full-fledged method for proving the correctness of concurrent programs. In the introduction to this paper, the authors write:

> While we hope that logicians will find this work interesting, our goal is to define a method that programmers will find useful.

This motto describes well Lamport's approach to formalisms for specification and verification.

Whereas standard LTL was clearly useful for expressing fairness and liveness properties, Lamport felt that it was not convenient for writing complete specifications of actual systems. His intuition was confirmed when he observed colleagues at SRI struggling with specifying a FIFO queue in Pnueli's temporal logic. (It was later proved that this was actually impossible unless one assumes that the values presented to the queue are unique.) This observation led his colleagues to introduce a more expressive temporal logic based on intervals [Schwartz et al. 1984]. In contrast, Lamport concluded that the fundamental problem was the "property-oriented" style of specifications as a list (conjunction) of properties observed at the interface of a system, such as the inputs and outputs of the queue, but excluding any reference to internal system states. He designed TLA as a logic geared toward specifying and reasoning about state machines, based on a few orthogonal and simple concepts that provide a higher level of abstraction (and elegance!) than the use of a pseudo-programming language, as in the earlier paper with Owicki [Owicki and Lamport 1982].

5.2.2 The Logic TLA

Lamport designed TLA around 1990 [Lamport 1991, 1994c]. TLA formulas are built from *constants*, whose values are fixed throughout an execution, and (state) *variables*. We use x, y, z to denote constants and u, v, w to denote variables. A *state* is a mapping from variables to values. TLA distinguishes three levels of expressions:

- The syntax of state functions and state predicates is that of standard terms and formulas of first-order logic. Concrete examples of state predicates are $v \geq 0$ or $\exists x : x \in u \wedge x \notin v$. Semantically, they are interpreted over individual states.[1]

- Transition functions and transition predicates, also called *actions*, are first-order terms and formulas that may contain both standard (unprimed) variables u, v, w and primed variables u', v', w'. Example formulas are $u' \in v$ or $\exists x : u' + x = v$. Semantically, transition formulas are interpreted over pairs $\langle s, t \rangle$ of states, with unprimed variables being interpreted in state s and primed variables in t.

- Temporal formulas are built from state and transition formulas by applying operators of temporal logic according to the rules given below. They are interpreted over *behaviors*, i.e., sequences $\sigma = \langle s_0, s_1, \ldots \rangle$ of states.

Whereas standard LTL builds temporal formulas solely from state formulas, the introduction of transition formulas as a primitive building block is fundamental to specifying state machines. For example, the LTL equivalent to the TLA action $u' \in v$ would be

$$\exists x : x \in v \wedge \circ(u = x)$$

---

1. We could distinguish a level of constant formulas that do not contain any variables, but we will consider such formulas to be state formulas.

where ∘ denotes LTL's next-time operator. Rather than using a pseudo-programming notation as in Owicki and Lamport [1982], actions are just first-order formulas over primed and unprimed variables. One reasons about them using ordinary mathematical logic, rather than introducing special principles for reasoning about programs. At the temporal level, any formula can in principle be considered as a system specification or as a property. There is no formal distinction between the two, and reasoning about them relies on the same fundamental principles of temporal logic.

TLA introduces several notations at the levels of state and transition formulas. Given a state formula e, the transition formula e' is obtained by replacing all (free) occurrences of state variables by their primed counterparts. Semantically, e' denotes the value of e at the second state of the pair of states at which e' is evaluated. The action UNCHANGED e is shorthand for $e' = e$. For an action A and a state formula e, the actions $[A]_e$ and $\langle A \rangle_e$ stand for $A \vee e' = e$ and $A \wedge e' \neq e$, respectively. The action formula $[A]_e$ represents closure of A under stuttering (with respect to e); in particular, it is true of a pair of states $\langle s, t \rangle$ if A is true or if $s = t$. Dually, $\langle A \rangle_e$ requires A to be true and the step from state s to state t to be observable through a change of e. Finally, the state predicate ENABLED A is obtained by existential quantification over all primed state variables that occur in the action A. For example,[2]

$$\text{if } A \triangleq v > 0 \wedge v' = v - 1 \wedge w' = w$$

$$\text{then} \quad \text{ENABLED } A \triangleq \exists v', w' : v > 0 \wedge v' = v - 1 \wedge w' = w$$

It is easy to see that for this example, ENABLED A is logically equivalent to the predicate $v > 0$. In general, ENABLED A is true at state s if there exists some state t such that A holds for the pair $\langle s, t \rangle$.

Formulas at all three levels are closed under Boolean operators ($\neg, \wedge, \vee, \Rightarrow, \equiv$) and first-order quantifiers ($\forall, \exists$). The rules for forming temporal formulas are as follows:

- Every state predicate is a temporal formula.
- If A is an action and e is a state formula, then $\Box[A]_e$ is a temporal formula.
- If φ is a temporal formula, then so is $\Box \varphi$.
- If φ is a temporal formula, x is a constant, and v is a variable, then $\exists x : \varphi$ and $\exists v : \varphi$ are temporal formulas.

---

2. The symbol $\triangleq$ denotes "is defined as."

The formulas $\diamond \varphi$ and $\diamond \langle A \rangle_e$ are shorthand for $\neg \square \neg \varphi$ and $\neg \square [\neg A]_e$, respectively. Also, $\varphi \rightsquigarrow \psi$ ("φ leadsto ψ") abbreviates $\square(\varphi \Rightarrow \diamond \psi)$. Observe in particular that if A is an action formula, $\square A$ is in general not well formed: actions need to be "protected" by square or angle brackets inside temporal formulas.

The operators $\square$ and $\diamond$ are the familar "always" and "eventually" operators of LTL: $\square \varphi$ is true of σ if φ is true of every suffix of σ. The formula $\square[A]_e$ is true of $\sigma = \langle s_0, s_1, \ldots \rangle$ if, for all $n \in \mathbb{N}$, the action A holds for the state pair $\langle s_n, s_{n+1} \rangle$ or the state formula e evaluates to the same value in s_n and s_{n+1}, and the interpretation of $\diamond \langle A \rangle_e$ is dual. The syntactic restriction of allowing action formulas to appear only inside brackets ensures that all temporal formulas φ of TLA are insensitive to finite stuttering: if two state sequences σ and τ agree up to insertions or removals of finite repetitions of states, then φ is true of σ if and only if φ is true of τ. The formula $\exists v : \varphi$ is true of $\sigma = \langle s_0, s_1, \ldots \rangle$ if φ is true of a sequence $\tau = \langle t_0, t_1, \ldots \rangle$ such that, for all n, s_n and t_n agree on the values of all variables except possibly v. The formal definition is somewhat more complicated in order to preserve invariance under stuttering [Lamport 1994c].

The notion of validity of TLA formulas is standard. In particular, a temporal formula φ is valid if it is true of all behaviors. Lamport also provides a set of proof rules for TLA. In particular, he states that the proof rules reproduced in Figure 5.1, plus ordinary first-order reasoning, are sufficient (in the sense of relative completeness [Apt 1981]) for reasoning about algorithms specified in TLA without quantification over state variables. These rules should be read as asserting that if the hypotheses are valid, then so is the conclusion. For example, rule STL1 is the

STL1. $\dfrac{\varphi}{\square \varphi}$ STL4. $\dfrac{\varphi \Rightarrow \psi}{\square \varphi \Rightarrow \square \psi}$

STL2. $\square \varphi \Rightarrow \varphi$ STL5. $\square(\varphi \wedge \psi) \equiv \square \varphi \wedge \square \psi$

STL3. $\square \square \varphi \equiv \square \varphi$ STL6. $\diamond \square(\varphi \wedge \psi) \equiv \diamond \square \varphi \wedge \diamond \square \psi$

TLA1. $\dfrac{P \wedge e' = e \Rightarrow P'}{\square P \equiv P \wedge \square[P \Rightarrow P']_e}$ TLA2. $\dfrac{P \wedge [A]_e \Rightarrow Q \wedge [B]_f}{\square P \wedge \square[A]_e \Rightarrow \square Q \wedge \square[B]_f}$

Lattice. $\dfrac{\begin{array}{c}(S, \prec) \text{ is a well-founded ordering} \\ \forall x \in S : \varphi(x) \rightsquigarrow (\psi \wedge \exists y \in S : y \prec x \wedge \varphi(y))\end{array}}{(\exists x \in S : \varphi(x)) \rightsquigarrow \psi}$

Figure 5.1 Proof rules for simple TLA.

well-known necessitation rule of modal logic, and it is justified because any suffix of a behavior is again a behavior, of which φ is true by the hypothesis of the rule. Of course, the implication $\varphi \Rightarrow \Box \varphi$ is not valid in general. From the elementary rules of Figure 5.1, further useful verification rules can be derived, such as the following rule for proving that a state predicate P is an invariant of a system specification:

$$\text{INV1.} \quad \frac{P \wedge [A]_e \Rightarrow P'}{P \wedge \Box[A]_e \Rightarrow \Box P.}$$

This rule, like most other rules for system verification in TLA, establishes a conclusion expressed in temporal logic from nontemporal (action-level) hypotheses. In this way, reasoning at the temporal level is confined to the top levels of a TLA proof and typically represents less than 5% of the proof steps. In particular, reasoning about safety properties does not involve temporal logic.

Lamport's rules are intended for the verification of algorithms. In contrast, providing a proof system for—even propositional—TLA that is complete in the standard sense of formal logic (i.e., that allows all valid formulas to be derived as theorems) is more delicate. In particular, whereas INV1 is sufficient for proving invariants of systems, the general induction axiom of LTL

$$\Box(\varphi \Rightarrow \circ\varphi) \;\Rightarrow\; (\varphi \Rightarrow \Box \varphi)$$

cannot be expressed in TLA because there is no next-time operator that could be applied to temporal formulas. A generalization of TLA, together with a system of rules that is complete for the propositional fragment of that logic, appears in Merz [1999].

5.2.3   Refinement, Hiding, and Composition

We mentioned above that TLA does not formally distinguish between system specifications and their properties: both are represented as temporal formulas. In practice, specifications of state machines are usually written in the form

$$Init \wedge \Box[\, Next \,]_v \wedge L \tag{5.1}$$

where the state predicate *Init* specifies the possible initial states of the system, the action *Next* represents its next-state relation, v is the tuple of all state variables used in the specification, and L expresses fairness conditions. Typically, *Next* is a disjunction of actions A_i that describe atomic transitions of the system or of its environment, and L is a conjunction of strong or weak fairness conditions on (some of) the actions A_i.

Refinement of Specifications.   Perhaps influenced by ideas on program refinement developed by Back [1981] and Morgan [1990], ultimately inspired by Dijkstra [1976], Lamport [1983d] already observes that "temporal logic supports hierarchical specification and reasoning in a simple, natural way." He also notes that the essential ingredient for this to be possible is the invariance of temporal logic formulas under stuttering, ensured by the absence of a next-time operator. The idea is that a refinement R of a high-level specification S introduces implementation detail, represented by additional state variables. Newly introduced actions that modify solely these new variables correspond to stuttering steps at the level of S and cannot invalidate S. Actions that modify the variables present in S must do so in ways that are allowed by (the next-state relation of) S. Whereas R may have fewer behaviors (when projected to the state space of S), the fairness conditions in S must be preserved: if a high-level action A_i for which S states a fairness condition is sufficiently often enabled in a run, R must ensure that some action whose effect corresponds to the occurrence of A_i will eventually occur in that run.

Summing up, R refines S if and only if the implication $R \Rightarrow S$ is valid. Assuming that R and S are specified using formulas of shape (5.1) (with superscripts R and S), refinement is proved by finding a state predicate I such that all of the following implications hold:

$$Init^R \Rightarrow I \wedge Init^S$$

$$I \wedge [Next^R]_{v^R} \Rightarrow I' \wedge [Next^S]_{v^S}$$

$$\Box\, I \wedge \Box[Next^R]_{v^R} \wedge L^R \Rightarrow L^S$$

In words, I is an invariant of the low-level specification R that is strong enough to prove that every transition according to R's next-state relation is also a possible transition for S, possibly stuttering, and to show that R implies the liveness hypotheses asserted by S. The first two proof obligations establish the safety part of the refinement and do not involve temporal logic; the third one concerns liveness and requires temporal reasoning.

Hiding of Internal State.   The standard form (5.1) of specifications is useful for describing a system as a state machine, but it does not distinguish between variables that are visible at the interface and those that represent the internal state of the machine. This distinction is, however, important in the sense that the "contract" between the implementation of a system and its users should only constrain the interface, not the internal state. For example, a high-level specification S_{set} of a key-value store may represent the current content of the store in a variable *store* holding a set of pairs (k, v), but the implementer should be free to choose another suitable data structure, such as a hash table. Because the operations of the lower-level specification S_{tbl} update a hash table instead of a set of pairs, the implication $S_{tbl} \Rightarrow S_{set}$ cannot be proved. Indeed, the internal variable *store* (and the set of values that it holds) is not part of the interface of the system, which consists solely of the input and output channels through which the system corresponds with its environment. Lamport realized that this form of *information hiding* corresponds to existential quantification: the actual high-level specification of our system is not S_{set}, but rather $\exists\, store : S_{set}$, which asserts that the system behaves as if it contained a store represented as a set of key-value pairs. Similarly, the lower-level specification is $\exists\, store : S_{tbl}$,[3] and in order to establish refinement, we have to prove the implication

$$(\exists\, store : S_{tbl}) \Rightarrow (\exists\, store : S_{set}). \tag{5.2}$$

Applying standard quantifier rules, that proof can be reduced to proving the implication

$$S_{tbl} \Rightarrow (\exists\, store : S_{set})$$

where the internal state of the lower-level specification has been exposed. It now suffices to find a suitable state function s that provides a witness term for the internal state of the higher-level specification, i.e., such that the implication

$$S_{tbl} \Rightarrow (S_{set} \text{ WITH } store \leftarrow s) \tag{5.3}$$

is provable. (The notation used here for substituting the variable *store* by the expression s is not part of TLA.) In our example, a suitable witness s is provided by the contents of the hash table.

State functions that serve as witness terms for refinement proofs are known as *refinement mappings*. They serve to reconstruct the value of an internal state variable used in the high-level specification from the corresponding lower-level state. Semantically, showing an implication of the form (5.2) requires exhibiting an infinite sequence of values for the quantified variable on the right-hand side, given a sequence of values for the variable on the left. In contrast, a refinement mapping

---

3. Of course, it is immaterial if the names of the bound variables in the two specifications are the same or not.

as in (5.3) computes values state by state, which is clearly weaker: one cannot refer to previous or future values in the sequence of values satisfying the left-hand specification. Indeed, in general a suitable refinement mapping need not exist even if (5.2) holds. Abadi and Lamport [1991] suggested that for the proof of refinement, the low-level specification may be augmented by *auxiliary variables*. The augmented specification is semantically equivalent to the original one, but the additional variables help in defining a refinement mapping. In particular, Abadi and Lamport defined principles for augmenting specifications by *history* and *prophecy* variables, and they provided sufficient conditions for these principles to be complete for proving refinement. The constructions were presented in a semantic framework independent of TLA. Proof rules for introducing auxiliary variables in TLA appear in Lamport and Merz [2017].

Representing Parallel Composition.   The above discussion has shown that refinement and hiding can be represented in TLA using implication and quantification, and therefore standard principles of logical deduction can be applied to reason about these concepts. Now consider two components, specified by TLA formulas Φ and Ψ, that are intended to operate in parallel. In order for both parallel components to adhere to their specifications, the variables of the first component must evolve as prescribed by Φ, and similarly for the second component. In particular, any steps that change a variable shared by both components must be permitted by both Φ and Ψ. Transitions that exclusively modify variables from one specification appear as stuttering steps to the other one and are trivially allowed by that specification, whereas variables shared between Φ and Ψ synchronize transitions of the two specifications. It follows that the formula $\Phi \wedge \Psi$ characterizes the parallel composition of the two specifications. (We see in Section 5.3.3 that for some computational models, it may be useful to adopt a stronger specification $\Phi \wedge \Psi \wedge \Xi$, where Ξ expresses extra synchronization hypotheses embodied in the computational model.)

Expressing composition as conjunction corresponds to the overall philosophy of TLA that structural concepts are expressed by logical operators. Although the conjunction of two specifications Φ and Ψ written in the standard form of (5.1) is not itself in standard form, it can easily be transformed into standard form by applying the equivalence

$$\Box[A]_u \wedge \Box[B]_v \equiv \Box\big[[A]_u \wedge [B]_v\big]_{\langle u,v \rangle}$$

Specifying Open or Closed Systems.   When specifying a component, one invariably has to describe not just the component itself but also the environment that the component is going to operate in. A closed-system specification of a component describes the most general environment that is acceptable, together with the component itself. In particular, the specification's next-state relation will be a disjunction of actions that describe the component's transitions and of actions that describe steps of the environment. Although this style works well in practice, it does not yield the most general specification of the overall system. Instead of constraining the environment, we may want to write a specification that allows the environment to behave arbitrarily, but that leaves the behavior of the component unconstrained after a step occurs that is disallowed by the assumptions on the environment. Abadi and Lamport considered ways of writing specifications that separate the environment assumptions E and the component guarantees C. The implication $E \Rightarrow C$ is a natural way for expressing such an assumption-guarantee specification, and this form is explored in Abadi and Lamport [1993]. However, the implication holds of behaviors in which first the component violates C, and later the environment violates E. In later work, Abadi and Lamport [1994, 1995] introduced the stronger operator $\xrightarrow{+}$ such that $E \xrightarrow{+} C$ requires that (the safety part of) C may be violated only if (the safety part of) E was violated strictly earlier.[4] Given two components described through assume-guarantee specifications, one may wish to prove that their composition refines a higher-level specification of the composed system. This is expressed in TLA as a proof obligation of the form

$$(E_1 \xrightarrow{+} C_1) \wedge (E_2 \xrightarrow{+} C_2) \;\Rightarrow\; (E \xrightarrow{+} C)$$

In order to establish the overall system guarantee C from the component guarantees C_1 and C_2, one will need to show that the environment assumptions E_1 and E_2 hold true. Now, the environment of each component consists of the overall environment (assumptions on which are expressed by E) and the other component, so one will want to use both E and C_2 for establishing E_1, and similarly for the other component. Despite the apparent circularity of this reasoning chain, Abadi and Lamport [1995] give rules that support this approach in a sound way, based on a form of computational induction that is embodied in the definition of the $\xrightarrow{+}$ operator.

---

4. $\xrightarrow{+}$ can actually be expressed in TLA, but it is useful to consider it as a separate operator.

5.3   The Specification Language TLA$^+$

Lamport designed TLA as a variant of linear-time temporal logic that is particularly appropriate for specifying executions of fair state machines. Stuttering invariance is key for representing composition as conjunction of specifications, and refinement as validity of implication. Quantification over state variables adds significant expressive power and is useful notably for distinguishing the state visible at the interface of a component from the internal state used for its implementation.

However, TLA is not a full specification language: it does not fix the interpretation of elementary function and predicate symbols such as $+$ and $\in$. These symbols are provided by an underlying mathematical language based on first-order or higher-order logic. In particular, nontemporal proof obligations that arise during the verification of a system property or during a refinement proof should then be discharged using a (possibly mechanized) proof system associated with that host language.

5.3.1   Overall Design of TLA$^+$

Starting in the early 1990s and encouraged by successful experiments with TLP [Engberg et al. 1992], a prototype proof system for TLA based on the Larch Prover, Lamport developed the specification language TLA$^+$. The language is described in the book *Specifying Systems* [Lamport 2002]; the Hyperbook and Lamport's video series [Lamport 2015, 2018] provide excellent tutorial introductions, whereas the description of TLA$^+$ in Merz [2008] focuses on the semantics of the language.

TLA$^+$ is based on a variant of Zermelo-Fraenkel set theory with choice (ZFC) for describing the data manipulated by an algorithm. ZFC is widely accepted by mathematicians as the basis for formalizing mathematical theories. In order to emphasize the expressiveness of ZFC, Lamport shows that a formal definition of the Riemann integral can be given in just 15 lines starting from a standard module defining the real numbers with ordinary arithmetical operators [Lamport 1992]. When writing high-level specifications of algorithms, it is useful to model data in terms of concepts such as sets and functions rather than using low-level data types provided by programming languages and their libraries. In this respect, TLA$^+$ adopts a similar approach to the specification languages Z and (Event-)B [Abrial 1996, Abrial 2010, Spivey 1992]. However, the latter languages impose a typing discipline on set theory, whereas TLA$^+$ is untyped. Again, Lamport follows classical mathematical practice and, for example, considers that the set $\{2, 4, 6, \ldots\}$ of positive even numbers can be viewed as a type just like the set of all integers. He maintains that imposing a decidable type system on a specification language leads to unacceptable restrictions of the expressiveness of that language. Also, embedding partial operations in a typed language often leads to objectionable choices. For example, declaring integer division as a binary operation with integer arguments and result asserts that division by 0 returns an integer, whereas implementations naturally raise an exception.[5] Although TLA⁺ is untyped and handles partial operators by underspecification [Gries and Schneider 1995], this does not preclude tools for TLA⁺ from contructing types when this is convenient for their analyses. An article by Lamport and Paulson [1999] contains an interesting discussion of these questions.

5.3.2   A Glimpse of TLA⁺

TLA⁺ specifications are organized in *modules*. A module can extend other modules; semantically, this is equivalent to copying the content of the extended modules (with duplicates removed) into the extending module.

A module may declare constant and variable parameters. Any symbol that occurs in an expression in the module must be either a built-in symbol of TLA⁺, a parameter in the context in which the expression appears, or a symbol that was previously defined or declared.

Modules may assert properties of constant parameters in the form of assumptions or axioms, both of which express hypotheses of the module.[6] Modules may also state theorems that can be proved using TLAPS, the TLA⁺ Proof System.

The bulk of the contents of a typical TLA⁺ module consists of definitions of operators, used to build up more complex expressions. An operator may take zero or more arguments, including operator arguments (whose arity must be specified). For example, the definition

$$Symmetric(R(\_,\_), S) \triangleq \forall x, y \in S : R(x, y) \equiv R(y, x)$$

introduces an operator characterizing a symmetric binary relation R over a set S. Besides the ordinary operators of first-order set theory, TLA⁺ also borrows a few constructions from programming languages, such as conditional expressions (including n-ary case distinctions) and local definitions introduced through LET-bindings.

---

5. Some proof assistants such as Isabelle/HOL go even further and define n div $0 = 0$, which is unlikely to hold in an implementation and may actually mask errors.

6. TLC will verify that an assumption evaluates to true for the concrete values substituted for the module parameters, but it will not evaluate axioms.

─────────────────── MODULE *FIFO* ───────────────────

EXTENDS *Sequences*
CONSTANTS *Data*, *null*
ASSUME *null* $\notin$ *Data*
VARIABLES *in*, *q*, *out*

───

TypeOK $\triangleq$ *in* $\in$ (*Data* $\cup$ {*null*}) $\wedge$ *out* $\in$ (*Data* $\cup$ {*null*}) $\wedge$ *q* $\in$ *Seq*(*Data*)
Init $\triangleq$ *in* = *null* $\wedge$ *out* = *null* $\wedge$ *q* = $\langle\,\rangle$
Enq $\triangleq$ $\wedge$ *in'* $\in$ (*Data* $\cup$ {*null*}) \ {*in*}
          $\wedge$ *q'* = IF *in'* $\in$ *Data* THEN *Append*(*q*, *in'*) ELSE *q*
          $\wedge$ *out'* = *out*
Deq $\triangleq$ $\wedge$ $\vee$ *q* = $\langle\,\rangle$ $\wedge$ *out'* = *null* $\wedge$ *q'* = *q*
          $\vee$ *q* $\neq$ $\langle\,\rangle$ $\wedge$ *out'* = *Head*(*q*) $\wedge$ *q'* = *Tail*(*q*)
       $\wedge$ *in'* = *in*
vars $\triangleq$ $\langle$*in*, *q*, *out*$\rangle$
FIFO $\triangleq$ *Init* $\wedge$ $\Box$[*Enq* $\vee$ *Deq*]$_{vars}$ $\wedge$ WF$_{vars}$(*Deq*)

───

THEOREM *FIFOType* $\triangleq$ *FIFO* $\Rightarrow$ $\Box$ *TypeOK*
THEOREM *InOut* $\triangleq$ *FIFO* $\Rightarrow$ $\Box$[*in'* = *in* $\vee$ *out'* = *out*]$_{vars}$
THEOREM *Liveness* $\triangleq$ *FIFO* $\Rightarrow$ $\forall$ *x* $\in$ *Data*: (*in* = *x*) $\rightsquigarrow$ (*out* = *x*)

───

Figure 5.2   TLA$^+$ specification of a FIFO queue.

A module containing a system specification usually defines operators corresponding to the initial condition, the next-state relation, the overall specification, and properties to be verified. As a concrete example, Figure 5.2 contains a TLA$^+$ specification of a FIFO queue. It extends the library module *Sequences*, which defines the set *Seq*(*S*) of finite sequences that contain elements of *S* and operations such as *Head* and *Tail* to access the first element and the remaining elements of a sequence. Module *FIFO* then declares two constants *Data* and *null* that correspond to the data to be stored in the queue and a "null" element representing the absence of data. The module also declares the variables *in*, *out*, and *q* that are used for specifying the state machine describing the behavior of the FIFO queue. Concretely, *in* and *out* represent the channels for data input and output, whereas *q* contains the current contents of the queue.

Again, TLA$^+$ is untyped, and consequently one does not declare types for constant or variable parameters. Because TLA$^+$ is based on set theory, there is no need to assert that *Data* is a set. In fact, semantically all values are sets, although it is more useful to think of the elements of set *Data* ∪ {*null*}, as well as of numbers or strings, as atomic values.

The second block of the module contains operator definitions.[7] The first operator corresponds to the (intended) type invariant of the specification. The definitions of the operators *Init*, *Enq*, and *Deq* introduce the initial condition and the enqueue and dequeue actions of the queue. The initial predicate simply requires that the input and output channels contain the *null* value and that the queue is empty. The enqueue action models a change of value at the input channel. If a data value is sent over the channel, it is appended to the current contents of the queue. Otherwise (i.e., if a null value appears on the channel), the queue remains unchanged. The output value of the queue remains unchanged during an enqueue operation. Symmetrically, a dequeue operation does not modify the input channel. It puts *null* on the output channel and leaves the queue unchanged if the queue is empty and otherwise sends *Head*(*q*) on the output channel and removes that element from the queue. Formula *FIFO* represents the overall queue specification. Its next-state relation is the disjunction of the enqueue and dequeue actions. The fairness conjunct requires dequeue actions to happen eventually so that the queue must eventually output the values it stores.

The third block of the module states three theorems. The first theorem asserts that the type correctness predicate holds throughout any execution. The second theorem states that the values of the input and output channels never change simultaneously, and the third theorem asserts that every data value that appears on the input channel will eventually be output by the queue. We see in Section 5.5 how these properties can be verified using the TLA+ tools.

5.3.3 Composing Modules

Beyond module extension, TLA+ offers *instantiation* as a second way for composing modules. An instance conceptually creates a copy of the original module in which the constant and variable parameters can be instantiated by (constant and state) expressions. This construction is useful for composing specifications. For example, module *TwoFIFO* of Figure 5.3 declares the composition of two FIFO queues by creating two instances *Left* and *Right* of the *FIFO* module of Figure 5.2. Instance *Left* uses variables *q1* and *mid* for the internal queue and the output channel; all other parameters are instantiated by the parameters of the same name declared in module *TwoFIFO*. Similarly, instance *Right* uses *mid* and *q2* for *in* and *q*. The conjunction of the two instantiated specifications *Left*!*FIFO* and *Right*!*FIFO* describes the com-

---

7. The horizontal bars are decorative and have no semantic meaning.

─────────────────── MODULE *TwoFIFO* ───────────────────

EXTENDS *Sequences*

CONSTANTS *Data*, *null*

ASSUME *null* $\notin$ *Data*

VARIABLES *in*, *q1*, *mid*, *q2*, *out*

───

Left $\triangleq$ INSTANCE *FIFO* WITH $q \leftarrow q1$, $out \leftarrow mid$

Right $\triangleq$ INSTANCE *FIFO* WITH $in \leftarrow mid$, $q \leftarrow q2$

Conc $\triangleq$ INSTANCE *FIFO* WITH $q \leftarrow q2 \circ q1$

Interleave $\triangleq$ $in' = in \lor out' = out$

TwoFIFO $\triangleq$ *Left*!*FIFO* $\land$ *Right*!*FIFO* $\land$ $\square[Interleave]_{in,out}$

───

THEOREM *Implementation* $\triangleq$ *TwoFIFO* $\Rightarrow$ *Conc*!*FIFO*

───

Figure 5.3   Composition of two FIFO queues.

position of two FIFO queues that communicate through the shared communication channel *mid*. We would like to assert that the conjunction of these specifications behaves like a FIFO whose internal queue is given by the concatenation of the internal queues of the two components. The instance *Conc* represents this "longer" FIFO queue with input channel *in* and output channel *out*, and we would therefore like to assert the theorem

$$Left!FIFO \land Right!FIFO \Rightarrow Conc!FIFO.$$

However, this implication is not valid: the conjunction on the left-hand side allows an enqueue action of the left FIFO queue and a dequeue action of the right FIFO queue to happen simultaneously (observe that both actions leave the shared variable *mid* unchanged). In this case, the values of the channels *in* and *out* change simultaneously, and this is not allowed by specification *Conc*!*FIFO*. Indeed, we wrote our specification according to an interleaving model, where enqueue and dequeue actions do not happen simultaneously. We have to explicitly enforce this interleaving assumption for the composition of the two FIFO queues, as expressed in the specification *TwoFIFO*, in order to obtain the theorem *Implementation* stated at the end of the module.

5.4 PLUSCAL: An Algorithm Language

Due to its expressiveness and high level of abstraction, TLA$^+$ is a very powerful language for specifying high-level designs of concurrent algorithms and systems.

However, it may feel unfamiliar to programmers, in particular due to the syntax based on mathematical logic and to the absence of explicit control flow in the specification of systems and algorithms. Lamport designed PLUSCAL [Lamport 2009] as a language for describing algorithms that combines the look and feel of pseudocode and the precision of TLA$^+$. It uses primitives that are familiar from imperative programming languages for describing the control flow of an algorithm. In contrast, the data manipulated by the algorithm is represented by TLA$^+$ expressions, letting the algorithm designer benefit from the abstraction afforded by set theory without being constrained by concerns of how to concretely implement data structures.

A PLUSCAL algorithm is embedded as a comment within a TLA$^+$ module and has access to all operators available at that point of the module (whether defined in extended modules or locally). The PLUSCAL translator converts the algorithm into a TLA$^+$ specification that is inserted into the module. The user then states properties in terms of the TLA$^+$ translation and verifies them just as for any other TLA$^+$ specification, using the tools described in Section 5.5.

A PLUSCAL algorithm may declare several process templates for parallel execution, and each template can have a fixed number of instances.[8] Variables can be declared globally, representing shared state (including the communication network of a distributed system), or locally for each process. The control flow of each process is described using standard primitives of imperative languages (sequencing, conditional statements, loops, procedure calls, etc.). In addition, the two primitives

$$\textbf{either } \{ \dots \} \qquad \text{and} \qquad \textbf{with}(x \in S)\{ \dots \}$$
$$\textbf{or } \{ \dots \}$$

are available for modeling nondeterminism. The first construct can be used to introduce a fixed number of alternatives; the second one executes a block of code for some value that is chosen nondeterministically from the set S. Synchronization among processes is modeled using the instruction **await** P that blocks until the predicate P becomes true.

An important aspect for the specification of concurrent algorithms is to identify the "grain of atomicity," i.e., which blocks of statements should be executed without interference from other processes. Rather than imposing an arbitrary fixed level of atomicity, PLUSCAL uses labels to identify yield points at which processes may be interrupted. A group of statements between two labels is assumed to be executed atomically. This allows the designer to choose the degree of atomicity appropriate for the specification and to compare algorithms described at different degrees

---

8. PLUSCAL does not support dynamic spawning of processes.

```
─────────────────────────── MODULE ProducerConsumer ───────────────────────────
EXTENDS Naturals, Sequences
CONSTANTS Data, maxCapacity
ASSUME maxCapacity ∈ Nat\{0}
(*
–algorithm ProducerConsumer {
    variable q = ⟨⟩;
    define {
        nonempty ≜ Len(q) > 0
        nonfull ≜ Len(q) < maxCapacity
    }
    process (Producer = "p") {
    p: while (TRUE) {
        await nonfull;
        with (item ∈ Data) {
            q := Append(q, item)
    } } }
    fair process (Consumer = "c")
        variable rcvd; {
    c:  while (TRUE) {
            await nonempty;
            rcvd := Head(q);
            q := Tail(q)
    } }
}
*)
```

Figure 5.4 A specification of a producer-consumer system in PLUSCAL.

of atomicity.[9] In order to ensure liveness of PLUSCAL algorithms, fairness conditions may be attached to labels or to entire processes. These ensure that the group of statements following the label (respectively, the entire process) will eventually execute if it is enabled sufficiently often.

As an example, a PLUSCAL algorithm modeling a simple producer-consumer system appears in Figure 5.4. It declares two process templates for the producer and

---

9. Some rules govern where labels must or cannot be placed, essentially to ensure that PLUSCAL algorithms are easy to translate into TLA$^+$ specifications.

the consumer, each of which is instantiated once for process identities "*p*" and "*c*." The two processes communicate using a shared FIFO queue of bounded capacity *maxCapacity*. Each process has an infinite loop: the producer repeatedly adds new data to the queue, while the consumer retrieves the data from the queue. By declaring a (weak) fairness condition for the consumer process, we ensure that every data item that is present in the queue will eventually be consumed. In this specification of the algorithm, the bodies of the while loops execute atomically; nonatomic execution would be modeled by inserting additional labels. The operations *Len*, *Append*, *Head*, and *Tail* that appear in the presentation of the algorithm are defined in the standard module *Sequences* that is extended by module *ProducerConsumer*.

Invoking the PLUSCAL translator on module *ProducerConsumer* generates a TLA$^+$ specification corresponding to the algorithm. In particular, the translator generates declarations of TLA$^+$ variables corresponding to the global and local variables of the PLUSCAL algorithm, and it derives the initial condition from the initializations of the PLUSCAL variables.[10] The essential step of the translation is to generate a TLA$^+$ action for each group of statements between two consecutive labels. For example, the single group of statements contained in the producer process of Figure 5.4 is represented by the action

$$Producer \triangleq \wedge nonfull$$
$$\wedge \exists \, item \in Data: q' = Append(q, item)$$
$$\wedge rcvd' = rcvd$$

For more complicated algorithms, the translator adds a variable *pc* that represents the current point of control of each process. When a process type has several instances, their local variables are represented using arrays (i.e., TLA$^+$ functions).

Because the translation from PLUSCAL to TLA$^+$ is fairly direct, the generated TLA$^+$ specification is usually quite readable. This is important because correctness properties of the algorithm are written in TLA$^+$ rather than in PLUSCAL. For our producer-consumer example, we may want to verify the invariant *BoundedQueue* and the temporal property *Liveness*, defined as

$$BoundedQueue \triangleq q \in Seq(Data) \wedge Len(q) \leq maxCapacity$$
$$Liveness \triangleq \forall \, d \in Data: (\exists \, i \in 1..Len(q): q[i] = d) \rightsquigarrow rcvd = d$$

that express type correctness and eventual reception of every data item contained in the queue.

---

10. For PLUSCAL variables that are not initialized, such as *rcvd* in our example, the translator adds a default initialization, which is necessary for model checking using TLC.

5.5 Tool Support

5.5.1 The Model Checker TLC

Lamport originally designed TLA$^+$ as a precise and expressive language for specifying algorithms and for (deductively) reasoning about their properties. It was used in the second half of the 1990s by hardware designers at Digital Equipment Corporation, in particular for describing cache coherence protocols of multiprocessors [Joshi et al. 2003]. They wrote rigorous, informal proofs for key invariants maintained by these protocols. Yuan Yu then recognized that it was possible to support this type of reasoning using model checking. Lamport reports that originally he was very skeptical of this idea. Input languages for model checkers such as Spin [Holzmann 2003], SMV [McMillan 1993], or Murphi [Dill et al. 1992] are based on low-level primitives carefully chosen to support efficient verification of finite-state systems, whereas TLA$^+$ uses the full power of ZF set theory and is intended for modeling systems of arbitrary size. It is not possible in general to systematically enumerate all behaviors that satisfy a given TLA$^+$ formula.

TLC, the TLA$^+$ model checker, accepts a subset of TLA$^+$ specifications written in standard form (5.1). It is an explicit-state model checker, intended for verifying finite instances of specifications. In addition to the specification, the user has to provide the model checker with a *model* that describes a finite instance by fixing specific values for constant parameters. For the queue specification of Figure 5.2, one could, for example, fix parameter values $Data = \{1, 2, 3\}$ and $null = 0$. TLC then interprets the specification, restricted to this model, by decomposing the next-state relation into disjuncts (bounded existential quantification over finite sets is expanded into an explicit disjunction) and evaluating each disjunct from left to right. The first occurrence of a primed variable v' has to be of the form $v' = e$ or $v' \in e$ for an expression e that TLC can evaluate; in the second form, e must evaluate to a finite set. The first form is interpreted as an assignment of (the value denoted by) e to v in the successor state. The second form leads to the generation of one successor state per element of e, with v assigned to that element. Subsequent occurrences of v' are interpreted by the value assigned to v in the successor state in this way. For example, the conjunct

$$in' \in (Data \cup \{null\}) \setminus \{in\}$$

of the action *Enq* of Figure 5.2 generates one successor state for each element of $Data \cup \{null\}$, except for the current value of *in*. The occurrences of in' in the second conjunct of *Enq* then refer to the value chosen for that successor state. The initial predicate is evaluated in a similar way. TLC aborts with an error message if the initial predicate or some subaction of the next-state relation does not assign a value to some of the variables declared in the module.

When evaluating set-theoretic expressions, TLC will generally enumerate the elements, but it will apply some optimizations. For example, in evaluating the predicate $e \in Nat$ that may occur in a typing invariant, TLC simply checks if (the value denoted by) e is a natural number. TLC disallows unbounded quantification, and it will signal an error when it would have to enumerate an infinite set.

Using the strategy outlined above, TLC enumerates all reachable states in a breadth-first manner, and it checks the invariant predicates provided by the user during this state enumeration. When an invariant evaluates to false, the run is aborted and a counterexample is displayed. (Due to breadth-first search, that counterexample will be of minimal length.) Liveness properties are evaluated over the state graph computed during state enumeration, based on the tableau algorithm of Lichtenstein and Pnueli [1985]. TLC parallelizes state enumeration on multicore machines and provides a distributed implementation for running in a cluster or cloud environment. States may be stored to disk so that state exploration is not memory bound, and TLC regularly performs checkpoints so that model checking can be resumed in case of a crash. In order to limit the explored state space, the user can impose state constraints. For example, the FIFO queue of Figure 5.2 generates an unbounded state space even for a fixed finite set *Data* because the length of the queue can grow without bound, and the user can choose not to explore successors of states in which $Len(q)$ exceeds some fixed value. TLC also implements symmetry reduction in order to explore only a quotient of the state space with respect to an equivalence relation. In the queue example, the user may choose to declare *Data* (or more precisely, the set that the parameter *Data* is instantiated with in the concrete model) as a symmetry set because all operations are insensitive to particular values in that set.

Although TLC imposes certain restrictions on the specifications that it can check, most specifications that are written in practice adhere to those restrictions or can easily be rewritten so that they do. (The fact that TLC has been the main analysis tool for TLA+ specifications has also contributed to disciplining users so that they respect those restrictions.) In particular, TLA+ specifications obtained from translating PlusCal algorithms can be checked using TLC. The different properties asserted in the modules of the previous sections can be verified by TLC for concrete instances of parameters, including the theorems of Figures 5.2 and 5.3, as well as the properties of the producer-consumer system given at the end of Section 5.4.[11]

---

11. The specification *TwoFIFO* of Figure 5.3 needs to be rewritten in standard form so that TLC can verify it.

Like most model checkers, TLC is most useful when a counterexample to a putative property is discovered. A positive verdict only means that the checked properties hold for the particular model that TLC checked, and it requires sound engineering judgment to determine if this gives enough confidence in the correctness of the properties for arbitrary instances of the specification.

5.5.2 The TLA⁺ Proof System

TLAPS, the TLA⁺ Proof System [Cousineau et al. 2012], is a proof assistant for checking proofs written in TLA⁺. For this purpose, TLA⁺ was extended to include a language for writing hierarchical proofs based on a format that Lamport had proposed earlier [Lamport 1995] for writing rigorous pencil-and-paper proofs. For example, the proof of type correctness for the FIFO queue of Figure 5.2 can be written as follows.

$$\text{THEOREM } FIFOType \triangleq FIFO \Rightarrow \Box\, TypeOK$$

$$\langle 1\rangle 1.\ Init \Rightarrow TypeOK$$

$$\text{BY DEF } Init, TypeOK$$

$$\langle 1\rangle 2.\ TypeOK \wedge [Enq \vee Deq]_{vars} \Rightarrow TypeOK'$$

$$\text{BY DEF } Enq, Deq, vars, TypeOK$$

$$\langle 1\rangle 3.\ \text{QED}$$

$$\text{BY } \langle 1\rangle 1, \langle 1\rangle 2, \text{PTL DEF } FIFO$$

Following a standard pattern for invariance proofs (cf. rule INV1 of Section 5.2.2), the first two steps of the proof establish that the initial predicate of the *FIFO* specification implies predicate *TypeOK*, and that the predicate is preserved by every step allowed by the next-state relation. The third step concludes the proof of the theorem. The justifications for each step are indicated following the keyword BY. For the first two steps, it suffices to expand the relevant definitions and then apply built-in automatic proof back-ends that mechanize standard mathematical reasoning. The justification of the third step uses the assertions of the two preceding steps and propositional temporal logic; it also expands the definition of *FIFO* in order to expose its initial and next-state predicates. Because the proof is so simple, we only need one level of proof: all step names have the form $\langle 1\rangle n$. The steps of more complicated proofs can be decomposed into lower-level proof steps until TLAPS can prove the leaf steps of the proof automatically.

Figure 5.5 schematizes the architecture of TLAPS. The central component is the proof manager that interprets the proof language, maintains the context of

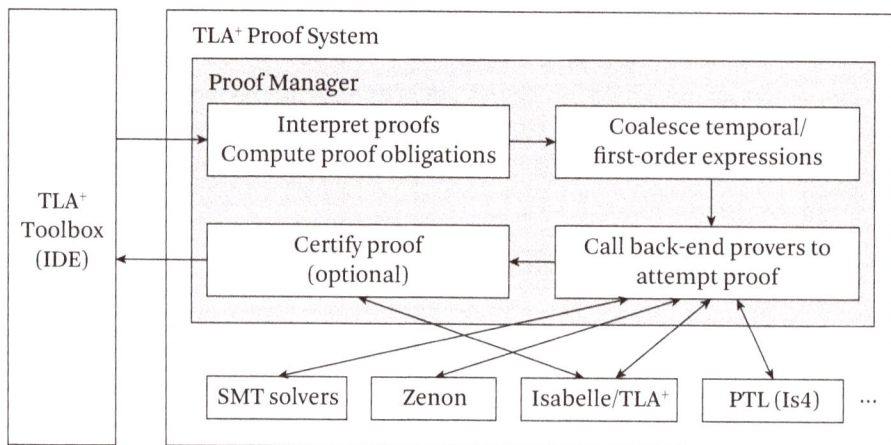

Figure 5.5 Architecture of the TLA$^+$ Proof System.

each proof step (i.e., the visible identifiers, assumptions, and definitions) and computes the corresponding proof obligations. In a nontemporal step (such as the first two steps in the above example), primes are pushed inside complex expressions, and then primed symbols are replaced by fresh identifiers. Similarly, any temporal expressions appearing in the context are abstracted by fresh predicate symbols. Similarly, in a temporal step (such as the QED step above), any first-order formulas are abstracted by propositional variables. This transformation is called *coalescing* [Doligez et al. 2014]; it is necessary so that back-end provers see the proof obligation either as a standard formula of mathematical set theory or as a propositional temporal logic formula. The proof manager then calls back-end provers to attempt and prove the proof obligation. Currently, TLAPS supports SMT solvers (via a translation to the SMT-LIB2 language [Barrett and Tinelli 2018]), the tableau prover Zenon [Bonichon et al. 2007], and an encoding of TLA$^+$'s mathematical set theory as an object logic in the logical framework Isabelle [Paulson 1994] for proving nontemporal steps. It also comes with a decision procedure for propositional temporal logic [Suda and Weidenbach 2012] for proving temporal proof obligations. The architecture is open for supporting additional back-end provers through suitable translations of proof obligations into their input language. For increased confidence in the correctness of TLAPS proofs, when a back-end prover finds a proof it may return a justification to the proof manager for checking by the trusted kernel of Isabelle. This certification step is optional and currently only available for proofs found by Zenon.

TLAPS is currently restricted to proving safety properties. The planned extension to liveness properties requires support for handling ENABLED predicates and for first-order temporal logic reasoning, for example, for mechanizing the Lattice rule of Section 5.2.2. TLAPS has been used for verifying several distributed algorithms, including variants of Paxos [Lamport 2011, Chand et al. 2016] and a version of the Pastry distributed hash table [Azmy et al. 2018].

5.5.3 The TLA$^+$ Toolbox

Editing and analyzing TLA$^+$ specifications is facilitated by the TLA$^+$ Toolbox, an Eclipse application that provides an IDE (integrated development environment) for TLA$^+$. It provides support for editing TLA$^+$ specifications and proofs, such as looking up operator definitions, properly indenting TLA$^+$ specifications, renumbering proof steps, and hiding subproofs that are irrelevant for the current branch. The Toolbox is integrated with the TLA$^+$ tools, including SANY, the TLA$^+$ syntactic and semantic analyzer, the TLATEX pretty printer, TLC, and TLAPS. In particular, the user interface to TLC provided by the Toolbox greatly simplifies the definition of finite-state models to be verified, the analysis of counterexamples, and the evaluation of TLA$^+$ expressions.

All TLA$^+$ tools are released as open-source software under licenses for use in industry or academia.

5.6 Impact

The concepts that Lamport introduced for the formal specification and verification of algorithms have deeply influenced the research community. The notions of safety, liveness, and fairness are universally recognized for their fundamental importance. The concept of stuttering invariance is valuable in contexts other than those strictly related to refinement and composition; in particular, it plays an important role in partial-order reductions used for model checking distributed systems [Godefroid and Wolper 1994, Valmari 1990]. The idea of writing system specifications in terms of state machines is widely accepted [Abrial 2010, Gurevich 1995]. The specification language TLA$^+$ is taught at universities around the world, and PLUSCAL is starting to be used as a vehicle for teaching courses on distributed algorithms.

The first significant use of TLA$^+$ in industry was for specifying and verifying cache coherence protocols by the group of hardware engineers that designed Digital Equipment Corporation's Alpha processors [Joshi et al. 2003]. Members of that group subsequently moved to Intel and continued to use TLA$^+$, although little is publicly known about the impact of that work. Work at Microsoft using TLA$^+$ started around 2003 with the specification of the Web Services Atomic Transaction protocol [Johnson et al. 2007]. This experience was considered successful, and engineers at Microsoft continued to use TLA$^+$. Reportedly, use of TLA$^+$ contributed to identifying a serious error in the XBox 360 memory system that would have been difficult to debug using conventional techniques. The Farsite project [Bolosky et al. 2007] at Microsoft Research developed a scalable, serverless, and location-transparent distributed file system that could tolerate nodes being unavailable, as well as malicious participants. The designers used TLA$^+$ for specifying the distributed directory service and refined a centralized functional specification into the formal description of a distributed protocol. They report that the main benefit of using formal specification and verification was to understand the invariants that the system must maintain through different levels of refinement. They consider that it would have been far more costly to iterate through several designs at the implementation level where aspects related to the distributed protocol would have been mixed with low-level coding details. In contrast, they found that developing an implementation from the protocol specification was rather straightforward because only sequential code had to be written, without a need for thinking about aspects related to distributed execution. In the later IronFleet project [Hawblitzel et al. 2015, 2017], researchers at Microsoft pushed this idea even further. Combining a TLA-style approach to state machine specification and refinement with a Floyd-Hoare style of reasoning about imperative programs provided by Dafny [Leino 2010], they obtained a mechanized framework for designing, implementing, and verifying distributed systems from high-level (centralized) specifications to distributed protocols and further to executable code that exhibited competitive performance. Based on an embedding of TLA and its proof rules in Dafny, they could prove not only safety but even liveness properties in a unified framework. The approach was used to develop a replicated state machine library and a sharded key-value store.

An interesting account of the use of TLA$^+$ in industry was provided by a group around Chris Newcombe working at Amazon Web Services [Newcombe et al. 2015]. They reported that not only have TLA$^+$ specifications contributed to finding subtle bugs in high-level designs of distributed protocols, but the understanding and confidence obtained from formal specification and verification allowed them to make aggressive performance optimizations without sacrificing correctness. Several other companies developing web and cloud services, including the groups working on Azure at Microsoft, actively use TLA$^+$ and TLC for describing and verifying the protocols they design. The TLA$^+$ Google group[12] and regular in-person community meetings provide forums for the members of the TLA$^+$ community to exchange and help each other in case of problems.

TLA$^+$ is intended as a formalism for modeling and verifying high-level designs of algorithms and systems. Doing so does not prevent coding errors from creeping into implementations of verified algorithms: such errors can be caught using techniques of program verification. However, the implementation of a buggy design is virtually guaranteed to contain the design errors, and finding and fixing these issues at the level of executable code is much more difficult and costly than doing so at an early stage of development, using specifications written at the appropriate level of abstraction.

---

12. https://groups.google.com/forum/#!forum/tlaplus

Biography

Roy Levin

6.1 Early Years

Leslie Lamport was born in 1941, the year the United States entered World War II. Computers were specialized and primitive. Computing, as a discipline, didn't exist. Vannevar Bush's famous essay *As We May Think* [Bush 1945], which foresaw the modern computing world of interconnected computers on which Lamport would have enormous impact, wouldn't appear for another four years.

Lamport grew up in New York City. His interest in mathematics began in elementary school, and he recalls that his mother taught him long division years before he heard about it in the classroom, which would normally have been around age 9. Learning arithmetic at home was perhaps more common in the years before computers became commonplace, as the focus of grade-school mathematics education was to teach "shopkeeper math," which most parents had learned themselves in the same way. Now, of course, many parents can't do division without a calculator.

The atmosphere of Lamport's childhood home wasn't math- or science-oriented, though his father had prepared for medical school as a college undergraduate, premed being a three-year, nondegree program then. Lamport's father never went to medical school (it was the Great Depression), but he had a scientific turn of mind, and colleagues at his workplace called him "Doc" [Lamport 2018b]. Lamport recalls taking long walks with his father, during which his father told him things that stimulated an interest in physics. (Recalling those walks, Lamport wondered "if that's why I've always had the habit of getting up and walking (or pacing) when I was thinking" [ibid.].)

In 1954 at age 13, Lamport began the tenth grade at the famed Bronx High School of Science, having skipped two grades previously. He doesn't recall any interest in computers before entering high school, even though they had acquired broad public awareness through television in 1952 when a UNIVAC computer predicted a landslide win for Dwight Eisenhower in the US presidential election.[1] Lamport's family, however, didn't acquire a television until 1954 (to see the Army-McCarthy hearings). But he did become aware of computers—more precisely, the mathematics behind the circuits out of which they were built—from a book on Boolean algebra, probably in his junior year. He also thinks he probably saw them in the movies [ibid.].

During high school, Lamport also tried to build a computer with a friend. He visited IBM in New York City and acquired some functional used vacuum tubes. (Maintenance procedures of the day dictated that tubes be replaced on a schedule rather than waiting for them to fail.) Lamport and his friend got as far as building a working four-bit counter: quite a way from a complete computer but enough to impress interviewers at MIT when Lamport later applied for admission there [Lamport and Levin 2016a, page 3].

These first explorations of computing, however, didn't rival Lamport's earlier interest in mathematics.[2] It was in his senior year of high school that he first entertained the idea of a career as a mathematician, though he freely confesses that he probably had no idea what that entailed [ibid.]. He showed the first signs of mathematical creativity in that year, when he published his first paper, "Braid Theory," in the *Mathematics Bulletin of the Bronx High School of Science* [Lamport 1957]. Today, he downplays its significance, saying it "shows I was not a prodigy" [Lamport 2019, comment 1]. But it shows that, even as a 16-year-old, Lamport wanted to communicate his ideas effectively. The same publication contains the companion article "An Introduction to Group Theory" by his classmate Alison Lord, which Lamport's paper references in its opening sentence as "essential" background. Evidently, the teacher responsible for the publication saw sufficient merit in Lamport's work to provide readers with the context needed to understand it.

---

1. This was the first use of computers for election prediction, and the CBS television network executives suppressed the prediction, believing it to be wrong since it differed sharply from conventional polling. When it proved accurate, CBS was forced to eat crow [Wikipedia 2018d].

2. Recalling his grade-school years more than a half century later, Lamport opined: "I suspect that I was attracted to math because of its simple certainty, which was in stark contrast to the unpredictable behavior of human beings. I see no point in trying to psychoanalyze that" [Lamport 2018b].

6.2 Education and Early Employment

6.2
After graduating from high school, Lamport worked for a summer at Consolidated Edison (Con Ed), the electric utility company in New York City. He began doing what he characterized as "very boring stuff" [Lamport and Levin 2016a, page 3] but managed to get transferred to the computer center where there was an IBM 705, a relatively sophisticated computer for 1957.[3] Though Lamport's job was to be a classic "glass house" computer operator—mounting/dismounting tapes and running card-deck jobs—he and the computer had enough spare time that he learned to program it. Of course, he used assembly language, as FORTRAN was just coming into existence [Backus et al. 1957]. Lamport recalls that his first program computed e to around 125 digits, that number being chosen because it matched the size of the 705's accumulator, thereby sparing him the need to do multiple-precision arithmetic [Lamport and Levin 2016a, page 3].

After his first summer at Con Ed, Lamport began his undergraduate years at MIT. He initially planned to major in physics but switched to mathematics when he discovered that it was the only major that didn't require an undergraduate thesis [ibid.]. Nevertheless, he continued to study physics as well, and supported himself by writing programs: during the academic year for a professor in the business school and during the summer at Con Ed. The summer job offered him a different kind of intellectual stimulation than math or physics. As Lamport recalled it [Lamport and Levin 2016a, page 11, edited]:

> I had a manager who became sort of a mentor to me, and he would give me these problems. In those days, programs were on punch cards, and you would load the punch cards into the hopper, and you'd press a button on the console. The computer would read the first card and then put that card in memory and execute that piece of memory as a program. So, the first card would usually be something that had just enough of a program in it to load a few more cards, so you'd have a decent-sized program that you would then execute to load your program and start that program executing. I remember he posed the problem to me to write a loader that worked all on a single card. And I worked on that problem and I would present him the solution and he'd say, "Yeah, that's good. Now make your loader also have this other property," and we went through a few iterations like that. I just loved those puzzles.

---

3. Readers unfamiliar with computers of the era will find the technical marketing document educational [IBM 1955]. In particular, the main memory capacity (magnetic cores) was trumpeted as 20,000 *characters*.

Lamport's later focus on concurrency began with the same love of puzzles, though more than 15 years would elapse before he found the opportunity to apply his knowledge of physics to those problems. During his undergraduate years, he pursued interests in math, physics, and computing, but they were "completely separate worlds" [Lamport and Levin 2016a, page 4] to him at the time. He certainly didn't think of computing as a career, for as a math major, "the only thing I knew that mathematicians did was teach math, so I suppose my career goal was to be a professor of mathematics" [ibid.].

He undertook his graduate education in mathematics, at Brandeis University, with that objective, earning his M.S. in 1963 and his Ph.D. in 1972. During those years, computing continued to be a part-time livelihood. He worked as a programmer at MITRE Corporation (1962–65), a government contractor, then beginning in 1970 at Massachusetts Computer Associates (COMPASS), a software contracting company, on the recommendation of a Brandeis faculty member. In between, he taught undergraduate mathematics at Marlboro College (1965–69) and authored an unpublished calculus text.

As he approached his Ph.D. dissertation, Lamport initially planned to work in mathematical physics, combining his two undergraduate foci, but he instead settled on a topic in analytic partial differential equations. He characterizes his thesis as "a small, solid piece of very classical math" and adds, "I learned nothing about analytic partial differential equations except what was needed for my thesis research, and I have never looked at them since then" [Lamport 2019, comment 7].

6.3 The COMPASS Years (1970–1977)

When Lamport finished his Ph.D. in 1972, he planned to leave Boston after 15 years of education and become a professor at the University of Colorado in Colorado Springs. But he had been working part-time at COMPASS for two years and they offered him a staff position . . . in California. They had no office there, but anticipated setting one up and said that he could work for them until the office was in place. So, he turned down the academic job in Colorado and began working full-time in the computer industry, where he remained throughout his career.

COMPASS's main business was building FORTRAN compilers, something that nearly every computer sold in the 1970s needed to have. Scientific computation, for which FORTRAN was intended, often involves matrices whose elements can be operated upon in parallel if the computer has the hardware to do so and if the software can take advantage of it. But FORTRAN was conceived before parallel computation was a reality, so FORTRAN programs on matrices were customarily written as loops, often nested, obscuring the inherent parallelism.[4] In the early 1970s, the University of Illinois tried to build an array processing computer, the ILLIAC IV, for which COMPASS had contracted to create a FORTRAN compiler that rediscovered the parallelism in these loops.[5] This compiler was terra incognita for COMPASS, and they turned to Lamport for help.

Lamport proposed that he work on the problem while spending a month or two with a friend in New Mexico. COMPASS agreed. Lamport worked out the theory (based on linear algebra), which he characterized as "pretty straightforward," and created the algorithms based on the theory [Lamport 2019, comment 9]. To communicate both clearly to his colleagues, he wrote a substantial document. Such a thing was unheard of in the software industry at the time, but it had the desired effect. Lamport said, "I learned later from observation that this tome . . . was practically a sacred text that people studied, and they did use it to build the compiler" [Lamport and Levin 2016a, page 6].

In retrospect, this episode represents a significant first in Lamport's career, for several reasons. It was the first setting in which he created a software specification with a firm mathematical foundation. It was his first substantive piece of work to appear in the prestigious *Communications of the ACM* (*CACM*) [Lamport 1974b], other than a short note earlier commenting on another's work [Lamport 1970]. Perhaps most significantly, it established his ability to operate as an independent researcher in a corporate context, for on the strength of the parallelizing compiler work, COMPASS agreed to send him to California before their office existed. As things transpired, the office never materialized, but Lamport moved to the San Francisco Bay Area and worked independently for COMPASS, supported by various government contracts while carrying out self-directed research that sometimes had little immediate relevance to those contracts. As Lamport put it, the parallelizing compiler work "reassured the people at COMPASS that I could go off by myself without supervision and actually do something useful" [Lamport and Levin 2016a, page 6]. He continued to do so, visiting the COMPASS office in Massachusetts for about a month annually, for another five years. During those years he created two

---

4. FORTRAN was already well established as the de facto standard language for scientific computation, despite its unsuitability for expressing matrix computations. Better alternatives existed, such as Iverson's APL [Iverson 1962], a language in which arrays are the only data structure. APL was commercially available on IBM S/360 computers in 1966. However, it was implemented as a time-shared, multiuser interpreter, making it unsuitable for many workloads. Despite its power and elegance, it never achieved widespread use.

5. ILLIAC IV's design had four CPUs and 256 FPUs, but only one "quadrant" of the machine was built, effectively creating a single-processor machine with 64 arithmetic units [Wikipedia 2019c].

of his seminal works—the Bakery algorithm and the Time/Clocks paper—though their significance would not be recognized for many years.

Lamport's algorithms for the parallelizing FORTRAN compiler used a specialized kind of concurrent computation matched to the architecture of ILLIAC IV: a single thread of control that operates synchronously in parallel on arrays distributed across multiple processing units.[6] By contrast, the Bakery algorithm and essentially all of Lamport's subsequent work in concurrency use multiple communicating processes, the kind of parallelism that has become ubiquitous in modern computing. Lamport described how the algorithm came about [Lamport and Levin 2016a, pages 7–8, edited]:

> In 1972, I became a member of the ACM. One of the first *CACM* issues that I received contained a mutual exclusion algorithm.[7] I looked at that, and it seemed to me that that was awfully complicated: there should be a simpler solution. I decided, "Oh. Here's a very simple solution for two processors." I wrote it up, I sent it to ACM, and the editor sent it back saying, "Here is the bug in your algorithm." That taught me something! It taught me that concurrency was a difficult problem and that it was essential to have proofs of correctness of any algorithm that I wrote. Well, of course, it got me mad at myself for being such an idiot. I determined to solve the problem, and in attempting to solve it, I came up with the Bakery algorithm.

Mutual exclusion of parallel processes accessing shared data is a central problem in concurrent computation. It was not new when Lamport conceived the Bakery algorithm, having received considerable attention in publications going back at least seven years earlier. Chapter 1 defines the problem and explains how Lamport's Bakery algorithm addresses it. Lamport didn't mention either bakeries or mutual exclusion in the title of his paper: "A New Solution of Dijkstra's Concurrent Programming Problem" [Lamport 1974a]. Indeed, the analogy with bakeries doesn't appear until nearly halfway through the concise paper. As noted in Lamport and Levin [2016a, page 7], though the paper presents a concrete algorithm, it couldn't

---

6. Lamport had earlier used another specialized form of concurrency when he designed a file system for a computer being built by Foxboro Computers (again, COMPASS had the software contract for the machine). This system used interrupts, a low-level form of concurrency requiring careful discipline to program correctly [Lamport and Levin 2016a, page 5]. Much of the early research in concurrency sought to create better-behaved mechanisms to replace interrupts.

7. In the early decades of computing, the *Communications of the ACM* had a monthly algorithms section.

appear in *CACM*'s algorithms section, since publication there required working code and, at the time, there were no working general multiprocessors! Despite its brevity, the paper contains several notable features beyond its technical innovation. It prominently includes a proof of the algorithm's correctness—a direct consequence of Lamport's experience quoted above. It points the way to a major area of Lamport's future work, fault tolerance, with a single concluding sentence: "Since [the algorithm] does not depend upon any form of central control, it is less sensitive to component failure than previous solutions." It devotes three paragraphs to characterizing a practical problem in implementing the algorithm: the potentially unbounded values of counters and the implications for storing them in fixed-length registers. (Lamport subsequently worked on this problem as well; see the discussion in Chapter 1.) The paper also contains the first appearance of some techniques that Lamport would employ regularly in subsequent work, such as the use of a counter as a timestamp. In fact, this kind of timestamp plays an essential role in the other seminal work of Lamport's COMPASS years, the Time/Clocks paper.

The Bakery algorithm paper of 1974 documents Lamport's first significant research result—one in which he takes pride [Lamport and Levin 2016a, page 11, edited]:

> I think in other things that I've done, I can look back and see: "This idea developed from something else." Sometimes it would lead back to a previous idea of mine, very often it would lead to something somebody else had done. But the Bakery algorithm just seemed to come out of thin air to me. There was nothing like it that preceded it, so perhaps that's why I'm proudest of it.

"Time, Clocks and the Ordering of Events in a Distributed System" [Lamport 1978b]—generally shortened to the Time/Clocks paper—grew out of a working paper by Paul Johnson and Robert Thomas entitled "The Maintenance of Duplicate Databases" [Johnson and Thomas 1975], published as an RFC in 1975.[8] Lamport received a copy of the paper, probably in 1975, and realized that the algorithm it proposed for keeping replicated databases in synchrony wasn't quite right because "it permitted a system to do things that, in ways, seemed to violate causality"[Lamport and Levin 2016a, page 20]. Lamport believes that his physics background enabled

---

8. The acronym RFC (Request for Comments) in this context refers to the mechanism of technical communication created as part of the ARPANET project, one of the inspirations for the Internet. RFCs, which were hand-produced in days before computer-based word processing, ran the gamut from working papers to specifications of standards.

him both to recognize the deficiency and to correct it; specifically, he could directly apply special relativity and the space-time view of Minkowski's seminal 1908 paper [Minkowski 2017]. "I realized that the problems in distributed systems are very much analogous to what's going on in relativity because in relativity there's no notion of a total ordering of events: to different observers, events will appear to happen in different orders. But there is a notion of causality, and I realized that there's an obvious analog of that in distributed systems" [Lamport and Levin 2016a, page 20, edited].

To order the events in their replicated databases paper, Johnson and Thomas used timestamps, and Lamport's solution does as well. Lamport has frequently pointed this out when people mistakenly credit him with inventing the use of timestamps for this purpose. Perhaps the fame that this paper enjoyed for its real innovations led readers to believe that everything in it was novel. Since Lamport's paper was not an explicit response to Johnson and Thomas—their paper served as the initial stimulus for Lamport's thinking—many readers were doubtless unaware of the earlier work, which did not receive the wide circulation of Lamport's *CACM* paper. Whatever the reason, it is ironic that many people consider the causal ordering of events via timestamps, and the algorithm that Lamport chose to implement it, as the key innovations of the paper. In Lamport's words [Lamport and Levin 2016a, page 21, edited]:

I realized that this algorithm was applicable not just to distributed databases, but to anything, and the way to express "anything" is a state machine. What I introduced in this paper was the notion of describing a system by a state machine. . . . What I said in the paper was: what any system is supposed to do can be described as a state machine, and you can implement any state machine with this algorithm, so you can solve any problem. The simplest example I could think of was a distributed mutual exclusion algorithm, and since distributed computing was a very new idea, this was the first distributed mutual exclusion algorithm, but I never took that seriously as an algorithm. Nor do I take the Time/Clocks paper's algorithm as the solution to all problems, because although in principle you can solve any problem this way, it didn't deal with failures. It's not clear that the solution would be efficient, and there could be better solutions. In fact, I never thought that my distributed mutual exclusion algorithm would in any sense be an efficient way of doing mutual exclusion. Well, the result of publishing the paper was that some people thought that it was about the partial ordering of the events, some people thought it was about distributed mutual exclusion, and almost nobody thought it was about state machines! And as a matter of fact, on two separate occasions, when I was discussing that paper with somebody and I said, "the really important thing is state machines," they said to me, "There's nothing about state machines in that paper." I had to go back and look at the paper to convince myself that I wasn't going crazy and that I really did mention state machines in that paper![9]

Chapter 2 includes an overview of the Time/Clocks paper. Whether or not the field remembers the paper's key insight about the generality of state machines for building distributed systems, the state machine approach caught on. A few months after the paper appeared, Fred Schneider, then a first-year assistant professor at Cornell University, mailed Lamport a draft of a paper [Schneider 1982] that built on the Time/Clocks paper. Schneider's paper considered failures, which Lamport's had not, and that first interaction led to a highly productive multidecade collaboration and a half-dozen papers exploring how to reason about concurrent programs. Inspired by the Time/Clocks paper, Schneider later produced a tutorial on state machines that became the essential reference on the state machine approach [Schneider 1990].

A great deal of Lamport's subsequent work in concurrency can be traced back to these two seminal papers of his COMPASS years that address fundamental issues in distributed systems: mutual exclusion (Bakery algorithm) and causality (Time/Clocks). Remarkably, at that time distributed systems played a relatively small and isolated role in the computing universe. Why, then, did Lamport work on them? He said: "I don't want to give the impression that I was drawn to concurrency by fundamental problems. The fact of the matter is that they were just really cool puzzles. Concurrency added a whole new dimension of complexity, and so even the simplest problem became complicated" [Lamport and Levin 2016a, pages 11–12, edited].

But the computing universe was rapidly changing. By the time the Time/Clocks paper appeared, Lamport had moved to a new employer, and he quickly became engaged in a project with a very real distributed system.

6.4 The SRI Years (1977–1985)

In 1977, COMPASS decided not to continue Lamport's remote working arrangement. Lamport wanted to remain in California, so he interviewed with two well-known research labs: Xerox PARC in Palo Alto and SRI International in neighboring Menlo Park.

---

9. As Butler Lampson put it: "The paper is quite famous, but hardly anyone (including myself, until Leslie pointed it out to me) has noticed that it introduced replicated state machines; everyone has focused on the fact that it introduced logical clocks, a much less important idea" [Lampson 2018].

Xerox PARC had pioneered personal distributed computing in the early 1970s. Its Computer Science Lab (CSL) created what became the archetype of personal computing: the Alto workstation, the Ethernet, and essential network services for file storage and printing. In retrospect, it seems a natural fit for someone doing pioneering work in distributed systems, but at the time, Lamport didn't strike the leaders as sufficiently practically minded, so he didn't receive a job offer [Lampson 2018].

SRI was a different sort of research lab. Originally a part of Stanford University, SRI had become an independent entity doing contract research, much of it for the US government. When Lamport interviewed, they had a multiyear contract to build an airplane flight control system with stringent fault tolerance requirements, and they hired him to join that effort.

The SIFT project (software-implemented fault tolerance) originated indirectly in the so-called Arab Oil Crisis of 1973, in which an embargo on the export of oil from the Middle East caused prices to skyrocket in much of the world [Wikipedia 2019a]. Conservation efforts ensued, including research into techniques for making aircraft significantly lighter. To do so required active control of the flight surfaces, implying the need for automation to effect small adjustments many times per second. While computers performed a variety of functions in aircraft in the 1970s, those functions weren't critical, and the human crew could take over in the event of a failure. For aircraft requiring continuous adjustments to continue flying, a computer system became essential and obviously required high reliability, which could only be achieved through replication of critical components and software to manage those components coherently. NASA contracted with SRI to build that software. The contract specified a probability of system failure of less than 10^{-9} per hour, comparable with manned spacecraft systems [Wensley et al. 1978].

When Lamport arrived at SRI, much of the work on SIFT had been done, including the solution of a central problem: how to get a set of processors to agree on something in the presence of faults. Marshall Pease had proved that $3t + 1$ processors are necessary and sufficient to tolerate t faulty processors under customary communication assumptions.[10] Lamport observed that the result could be significantly improved by the use of communication involving digital signatures, reaching back to some work he had done at COMPASS before digital signatures were generally known in the field. (They became known through Diffie and Hellman's landmark cryptography paper [Diffie and Hellman 1976], which appeared in

---

10. Pease was inspired by the work of his colleague down the hall, Robert Shostak, who had proved the result for $t = 1$, the case of practical interest for SIFT [Shostak 2018].

1976 but mentions Lamport's earlier digital signature work.[11]) But Lamport says his main contribution to the paper describing the fault tolerance results [Pease et al. 1980] was getting Shostak and Pease to write the paper in the first place [Lamport 2019, comment 41], as publication generally wasn't (and generally still isn't) a priority for researchers in industry.

Lamport continued to refine the fault tolerance algorithm (and its description), which led to a second paper with Shostak and Pease. The first paper eventually came to be recognized as a foundational result—it received the 2005 Edsger W. Dijkstra Prize in Distributed Computing—but the second paper gave the problem of agreement in the presence of arbitrary faults the name that has stuck. Lamport recalls being inspired by Jim Gray, who had earlier described a problem that he coined the "two generals paradox." The problem involves two generals who want to coordinate an attack that cannot succeed unless both of their armies participate. The generals communicate only through messengers sent between them. The problem: Since any messenger may fail to arrive, how can the generals ever be certain that they have reached agreement to attack? The similarity with the fault tolerance problem of the SIFT project led Lamport to seek a similar catchy name [Lamport and Levin 2016a, page 34, edited]:

> I decided on a story of a bunch of generals who had to reach agreement on something and they could only send messengers and stuff like that. I originally called it the Albanian Generals, because at that time Albania was the most communist country in the world; it was a black hole, and I figured nobody in Albania is ever going object to that. Fortunately, Jack Goldberg, who was my boss at SRI said, "You really should think of something else because, you know, there <u>are</u> Albanians in the world." So, I thought . . . and suddenly: Byzantine Generals! Of course, with the connotation of intrigue, that was the perfect name.

The Byzantine generals paper [Lamport et al. 1982] overlapped significantly with the earlier paper containing the central $3t + 1$ result. Lamport freely admits that "the main reason for writing this paper was to assign the new name to the problem" [Lamport 2019, comment 46]. However, he reformulated the algorithm in a simpler way, since Pease's original algorithm, which Lamport characterized as "an amazing piece of work" [Lamport and Levin 2016a, page 13], was difficult to

---

11. Diffie had been working on the digital signature problem in the mid-1970s. He met with Lamport in a coffeehouse in Berkeley and told him about the problem. Lamport recalls that he "thought a minute and literally on a napkin I wrote out a solution involving one-way functions" [Lamport and Levin 2016a, page 14].

follow and the proof was even more so. As Lamport recognized, names matter, so while the earlier paper with the core result justly received the Dijkstra Prize, that result indelibly bears the name from the later one: Byzantine agreement. During his SRI years, Lamport continued to work on fault tolerance, incorporating the state machine formulation he introduced in the Time/Clocks paper. Chapter 3 discusses the original Byzantine generals result and subsequent ones.

Lamport's work at SRI extended well beyond fault tolerance. Much as at COM-PASS, Lamport nominally worked on a variety of contracts, but actually carried out a largely self-directed research program, pursuing threads that reached back to earlier work and would continue well into the future. One such thread involved the arbiter problem, sometimes more colloquially named "the glitch," in which Lamport became interested some years earlier when it was noted that the Bakery algorithm required an arbiter. The problem arises from trying to decide between discrete outcomes—say, having a circuit output a zero or a one—in a bounded time interval. Engineers were familiar with the problem, though many did not accept that it was unsolvable. Lamport and Richard Palais, his former de jure thesis adviser, found a mathematical formulation using a carefully chosen topology that, coupled with theorems about continuity, produced a proof of impossibility. Their paper, submitted for publication in 1976, was rejected because, Lamport believes, the mathematics was foreign to the reviewers [Lamport and Levin 2016a, pages 24–25]. It is possible, however, that (in the spirit of "the impossible takes a little longer") they were reluctant to accept the conclusion. Lamport quotes a related story [Lamport 2019, comment 60]:

> Charles Molnar, one of the pioneers in the study of the problem, reported the following in a lecture given on February 11, 1992, at HP Corporate Engineering in Palo Alto, California: "One reviewer made a marvelous comment in rejecting one of the early papers, saying that if this problem really existed it would be so important that everybody knowledgeable in the field would have to know about it, and 'I'm an expert and I don't know about it, so therefore it must not exist.' "

Lamport and Palais's paper was never published, but Lamport wrote a less formal treatment under the title "Buridan's Principle." Surprisingly, though it described the arbiter problem for a general scientific audience, neither *Science* nor *Nature* wanted to publish it. Eventually, in 2012, it found acceptance in *Foundations of Physics* [Lamport 2012], perhaps because that discipline was more comfortable with the mathematical ideas and with the sometimes unintuitive consequences of formalizing the behavior of physical systems.

During his SRI years, Lamport explored concurrency well beyond the arbiter problem. He contributed to an influential paper on concurrent garbage collection by Edsger Dijkstra in 1978. The paper was ahead of its time because, in the late 1970s, programming languages generally didn't depend on garbage collection and rarely ran on computer systems offering true concurrency. (Lamport considered his contribution minor, but Dijkstra thought it significant enough to make him a co-author.) In this area, as in others, Lamport foresaw practical problems and devised their solutions decades before most of the field recognized their need or importance. Other noteworthy papers by Lamport during this time include his work with Mani Chandy on distributed snapshots [Chandy and Lamport 1985] (see Chapter 2) and his paper on cache coherence [Lamport 1979b], which gives a precise definition of sequential consistency (see Chapter 1). As the size of programs increased, spurred on by the exponential growth of computing capacity characterized by Moore's law, many researchers sought techniques to verify program correctness. Since Lamport had worried about proving correctness at least since his COMPASS days, he naturally contributed to this area, focusing on suitable formalisms and techniques for verification of concurrent programs. He published several papers in this area while at SRI, including one that used arrows in a way reminiscent of the causality relation in the Time/Clocks paper, and others that represent initial forays into the use of temporal logic, which would become part of the methodology he ultimately adopted for specification and verification (see Chapter 5).

Aside from his Ph.D. thesis and a paper derived from it, Lamport never published a mathematical paper. But during his time at SRI, he published something that had a huge impact on the field of mathematics, as well as computer science: the LaTeX system.

When Lamport began writing papers, computers provided only limited tools to assist authors of technical communications. Simple computer-based text processing systems had existed since the 1960s, but until the mid-1970s mechanical typesetting remained the technology for creating books and journals, even if the manuscript to be published had been prepared on a computer. Lamport himself did not begin using computer-based document production systems until around the time he arrived at SRI in 1977. What is now known as word processing was then in its infancy, appearing in experimental systems such as Butler Lampson and Charles Simonyi's Bravo [Wikipedia 2018a] and Brian Reid's Scribe [Wikipedia 2018c]. Coupled with computer-driven laser printing, these systems enabled authors to produce immediately publishable versions of technical documents, without going through an intermediary that typeset their content. These new systems featured multiple fonts and text styles, hierarchical sectioning, footnotes, bibiliographic citations, cross-referencing, and the like.[12] Lamport began using Scribe soon after it was available, around 1978 [Lamport 2018].

These early systems adopted an essentially linear document model that worked adequately for ordinary prose but could not accommodate the two-dimensional typesetting requirements of mathematics. Seeking to marry the benefits of an author-controlled technical document production system with the printing quality achievable in professional typesetting, Donald Knuth digressed from his ambitious book project, *The Art of Computer Programming*, to create a system capable of creating aesthetically pleasing documents with mathematical content.[13] He named that system TeX [Wikipedia 2019d].

TeX made two-dimensional layout a first-class notion, which distinguished it not only from its contemporaries like Scribe and Bravo but also from most of their successors, which tend to treat formulas and other two-dimensional structures as a separate kind of object, like a picture or table, to be dropped into an otherwise linear text stream. Knuth also created the necessary fonts of mathematical symbols for formula construction.[14] Finally, and crucially, Knuth wanted great flexibility in the typesetting, so he avoided building in assumptions about document structure. Instead, he gave TeX a macro capability, enabling users to build structures for different purposes.

"If you build it, they will come." The users came, and they built and exchanged macro packages, and TeX quickly found adherents within the computer science and mathematics communities.[15] Lamport began using it around 1979 for his papers. Knuth soon began working on a second version, which would come to be called TeX82. Around the same time, Lamport began working on a book and decided that the available macro packages for something of that size were unsuitable, so he set

12. This was a classic example of technologists innovating to solve a problem they personally experienced: the cumbersome and error-prone publication cycle of manuscripts, galleys, and page proofs.

13. Knuth begin this long-running book project in 1962. It was originally conceived as a single book of 12 chapters, then of 7 volumes, some of which now (in 2018) have several subvolumes.

14. Some mathematical symbols could be incorporated in documents produced in Bravo through its flexible font capability. Scribe could handle multiple fonts too, but in its early days it often ran in computing environments with printers of limited capability. Lamport recalls trying to create acceptable-looking mathematical symbols for dot-matrix printers and expoiting Scribe's font capabilities to print them [Lamport 2018].

15. Other disciplines, including physics and statistics, came along later.

out to develop his own macros and thought, "I might as well make them usable for others" [Lamport 2018]. LaTeX was born.[16]

LaTeX combined the power of TeX's 2D typesetting with Scribe's notion of a document *style*. Scribe was one of the first document systems to provide a flexible and intuitive way of compartmentalizing detailed decisions about a document's structure and appearance, a feature that Lamport wanted for his book project.[17] Unsurprisingly, that proved a winning combination with many authors, and after a first version and manual became available around 1983, the system spread rapidly through the computer science community.[18] The manual was later published by Addison-Wesley [Lamport 1994b]; the software itself has always been free.

Over the next few years, LaTeX became the de facto standard way to create computer science papers and books, accelerating as personal computer workstations became more common. But with success comes support, and by the end of the 1980s a group of volunteers [LaTeX Project 2019] had assumed responsibility for the evolution of LaTeX, and Lamport ceased to be directly involved. (As of this writing (mid 2019), LaTeX 2_ϵ, with a manual from 1995, is the current version. Version 3 is a long-running research project.) Three decades later, writers of computing papers with mathematical content, including Lamport, still use LaTeX as their document production system of choice, though other systems, such as Microsoft Word, have caught up for other classes of papers.[19]

The book for which Lamport conceived LaTeX, which he self-mockingly calls "The Great American Concurrency Book," remains incomplete, though parts have

---

16. The Wikipedia article on TeX [Wikipedia 2019d] explains its pronunication (properly the final letter is pronounced as in Bach but often has the sound of a "k"). LaTeX, Lamport's system, is variously pronounced with a long or short "a". Wikipedia doesn't indicate which is preferred, but in ordinary conversation its creator generally says "lay-tek" [Lamport 2018].

17. In the first edition of the LaTeX manual, Lamport freely acknowledged Scribe's influence, quoting a sentiment attributed to Igor Stravinsky (among others): "Lesser artists borrow; great artists steal."

18. The American Mathematical Society, which naturally embraced TeX, initially standardized on a different set of macros called AMS-TeX [American Mathematical Society 2019b], which existed in an early version when Lamport began work on LaTeX. However, it did not include the larger-scale document structuring capabilities of LaTeX. Subsequently, it harmonized the two in AMS-LaTeX [American Mathematical Society 2019a].

19. In 2000 [Ziegler 2000], Lamport said: "I don't think TeX and LaTeX would have become popular had they not been free. Indeed, I think most users would have been happier with Scribe. Had Scribe been free and had it continued to be supported, I suspect it would have won out over TeX. On the other hand, I think it would have been supplanted more quickly by [Microsoft] Word than TeX has been."

been written more than once. There may be a parallel here with Knuth's *The Art of Computer Programming*.

6.5 The DEC/Compaq Years (1985–2001)

In 1985, Lamport went looking for another job. SRI had changed its management in a way that he felt introduced unnecessary structure, which often impedes research activity. As he looked for job opportunities, he sought a situation in which research would be stimulated by real-world problems, much as he had experienced while working on SIFT. He gravitated toward corporate research labs rather than academia for that reason, as professors in that era worked largely on self-defined problems supported by government funding agencies that took a more expansive view of research than they did a decade or two later [Lamport and Levin 2016a, pages 18–19]. Digital Equipment Corporation (DEC), a high-flying computer company in the 1970s and early 1980s, had recently opened a new lab in Palo Alto, the Systems Research Center (SRC), at which Lamport interviewed and was offered a position. Comparing SRC with SRI, he recalled [ibid., pages 17–18, edited]:

> There was more community. At SRI, we said "Grant proposals are our most important product."[20] The people who started SRC were the people who came from Xerox PARC, where they had just created personal computing, so there was very much a sense that the lab would continue to create the computing of the future. SRC had a qualitative feel that was different from SRI. That had a lot to do with Bob Taylor, the lab director and founder, who was just a wonderful manager."

Despite being young, SRC was already as large—about 15 researchers—as the group that Lamport had left at SRI, and within a year it had become considerably larger. Ultimately, it grew to about 60 researchers while retaining a completely flat management structure, one of Bob Taylor's many unconventional management practices.[21] The absence of hierarchy made it easy for researchers to share research questions and to introduce each other to problems originating elsewhere in the company. In fact, as Lamport noted in retrospect, more of the problems on which

---

20. A parody of a contemporary General Electric slogan: "Progress is our most important product."

21. Taylor came to DEC from Xerox PARC, where he had been the director of CSL. His disagreements there with his superiors over research management practices precipitated his departure and the founding of DEC/SRC.

he worked came from outside the lab, including especially from the rest of DEC
[ibid., page 19].

By the early 1980s, the march of Moore's law had created single-chip micro-
processors sufficiently powerful to be used for general-purpose computation. They
were modest in performance but a great deal cheaper that the multichip CPUs
that preceded them. The idea of using a multiprocessor to get affordable desktop
computing power took hold in the research world. In 1984, as SRC was staffing
up, DEC introduced its MicroVAX line, which used DEC's first single-chip CPU
that implemented the (non-floating-point) VAX instruction set. Researchers at SRC
launched a project to design a multiprocessor machine—the Firefly—around the
anticipated second chip in the family.[22] Since no standard operating system yet
existed for multiprocessors, they launched a concurrent project to create one to
work in harmony with Unix, which already was well established on the VAX line in
addition to DEC's flagship operating system, VMS. Just down the street from SRC
in Palo Alto, the Western Research Lab, a sibling DEC laboratory, was building another multiprocessor—the MultiTitan [DEC WRL 2018]—with a CPU chip based on
WRL's earlier Titan [Nielsen 2018]. Both multiprocessor projects involved Lamport,
though in different ways.

The hardware of a multiprocessor mediates access by the processors to the
shared memory. This mediation depends on mutual exclusion, a topic that had
engaged Lamport since his days at COMPASS. Shortly after Lamport came to DEC,
the MultiTitan designers sought his help to create a mutual exclusion algorithm,
using only reads and writes, that would be fast in the absence of contention. No one
had considered this problem before multiprocessing became practical. Lamport
created an algorithm and proved it was optimal [Lamport 1987].

Lamport's involvement in the Firefly project was less direct, though what he
created would prove much more significant. SRC's network of Firefly workstations
was to serve as a computing base for the researchers, many of whom had come
from PARC. As such, it would consolidate what they had learned about building
a practical, general-purpose, distributed computing environment. That environment would include scalable global naming, replicated fault-tolerant storage, and

---

22. This chip was colloquially called the MicroVAX II or Mayflower, though strictly speaking these
names referred to the DEC product machine built around the 78032 CPU chip (and its companion
78132 floating-point unit).

network security; the project that put together those capabilities was the Echo Distributed File System [Birrell 1993]. Echo caught Lamport's attention, for its fault tolerance approach seemed to violate an impossibility result published a few years earlier [Fischer et al. 1985].[23] He recalled that "I sat down to try to prove that it couldn't be done. And, instead of coming up with the proof, I came up with an algorithm. . . . It's an algorithm that guarantees consistency,[24] and it gets termination if you're lucky" [Lamport and Levin 2016a, page 36]. That algorithm would come to be known as Paxos, and it was destined to become one of Lamport's most important inventions.

Lamport completed his writeup of the Paxos algorithm and its correctness proof in 1990 in a draft paper called "The Part-Time Parliament," though by then Echo was already in service using a different consensus algorithm to achieve consistency. (See Chapter 4 for a technical description of the Paxos algorithm.) The significance of Paxos was not widely recognized at the time. Lamport recalled [Lamport 2019, comment 122]:

> Inspired by my success at popularizing the consensus problem by describing it with Byzantine generals, I decided to cast the algorithm in terms of a parliament on an ancient Greek island. Leo Guibas suggested the name *Paxos* for the island. I gave the Greek legislators the names of computer scientists working in the field, transliterated with Guibas's help into a bogus Greek dialect. (Peter Ladkin suggested the title.) Writing about a lost civilization allowed me to eliminate uninteresting details and indicate generalizations by saying that some details of the parliamentary protocol had been lost. To carry the image further, I gave a few lectures in the persona of an Indiana-Jones-style archaeologist, replete with Stetson hat and hip flask. My attempt at inserting some humor into the subject was a dismal failure. People who attended my lecture remembered Indiana Jones, but not the algorithm. People reading the paper apparently got so distracted by the Greek parable that they didn't understand the algorithm.

---

23. Lamport said, "The FLP result, as it is generally known, says that, while you may have an algorithm in which multiple processes agree on a value, the algorithm cannot guarantee that such a value will eventually be chosen" [Lamport and Levin 2016a, page 36, edited]. He also characterized it as "one of the most, if not the most, important papers on distributed systems ever written" [ibid.].

24. The consistency guarantee means that the algorithm "can tolerate the failure of any number of its processes (possibly all of them) without losing consistency, and that will resume normal behavior when more than half the processes are again working properly" [Lamport 2019, comment 122].

When Lamport submitted the paper for publication, the reviewers wanted the Paxos story removed. Annoyed, Lamport put the paper aside.[25] Had it been taken more seriously, a reviewer might have noticed a strong similarity between the Paxos algorithm and one called viewstamped replication that appeared in Brian Oki's 1988 Ph.D. thesis [Oki and Liskov 1988]—a case of independent invention of which Lamport became aware only years later: "I looked in Brian's thesis and there, indeed, was very clearly, the same algorithm. But I don't feel guilty about it being called Paxos, rather than Timestamp [sic] Replication, because [Oki and Barbara Liskov, his adviser] never published a proof. And as far as I'm concerned, an algorithm without a proof is a conjecture" [Lamport and Levin 2016a, page 37].

Meanwhile, the problem of maintaining consistency in replicated systems grew more important as networking and inter-networking became more widespread in the 1990s. At SRC, Ed Lee and Chandu Thekkath wanted to build a distributed system that provided replicated virtual disks, which they called Petal [Lee and Thekkath 1996]. They therefore needed a consistency protocol, and another SRC colleague, Mike Schroeder, directed them to the unpublished Paxos paper. They produced an implementation for Petal, apparently unhindered by the lost Greek civilization story. Subsequently, with SRC colleague Tim Mann, they built a scalable distributed file system called Frangipani on top of Petal, which used a different Paxos implementation for its distributed lock server.[26] With Paxos thus in use, in the mid-1990s Lamport was again motivated to try to publish his paper.[27] The revised version retained the storytelling of the original but added some annotations on related work from the intervening years, which were provided by Lamport's colleague Keith Marzullo in a way that continued the parable. "The Part-Time

---

25. The anonymous reviewer wasn't the only person who found the Paxos story problematic. Butler Lampson recalls: "When Leslie wrote the first paper about Paxos, it was pretty incomprehensible. . . . I had to read the paper about 6 times before I could figure it out, but then it was clear to me that it was really important." Lampson tried unsuccessfully to convince Lamport to revise the paper [Lampson 2018].

26. The Petal and Frangipani implementations of the Paxos algorithm were partial; fuller implementations of the Paxos algorithm are discussed later in this chapter.

27. Butler Lampson recalls an additional motivation: "Leslie . . . refused to make any changes, so for eight years the paper remained unpublished. . . . I believe that what broke this logjam was that I wrote a description of the algorithm that Leslie hated" [Lampson 2018].

Parliament" finally appeared in 1998, nearly a decade after the invention of the Paxos algorithm.[28]

During the years between the invention of Paxos and the eventual publication of the paper, Lamport continued to pursue three interrelated threads of research that had engaged him for more than a decade. The first, of course, was concurrent algorithms, including mutual exclusion, interprocess communication, and fault tolerance.[29] The other two topics—precise specification of system behavior and formal verification of program properties—had also prominently figured in his work, motivated initially by the experience that led to his discovery of the Bakery algorithm (recounted in Section 6.3). He published papers on the specification and verification of concurrent programs beginning in 1977 [Lamport 1977a], and by the time he came to SRC, he had published at least a dozen papers more. Much of this work sought to create practical methods that didn't collapse under the weight of real-world algorithmic problems.

By the time he invented Paxos, Lamport had created the temporal logic of actions (TLA), a formal logic for specifying the behavior of a state machine and proving invariance properties about it. He had been evolving toward this formalism since he introduced the state machine model in the Time/Clocks paper, and he had used invariance to characterize the meanings of programs even earlier at COMPASS in his work on parallelizing FORTRAN.

Lamport developed TLA at a time when many other researchers wanted to specify program behavior within a programming language. Lamport disagreed; he regarded mathematics as the correct vehicle. Accordingly, a specification in TLA could use mathematical objects not generally found in a programming language (such as sets), thereby freeing the specification from the clutter of implementation details

---

28. There is evidence that the original journal editor's objection to the style of the paper had some validity. Lamport reports [Lamport 2019, comment 129] and Lampson confirms [Lampson 2018] that distributed systems specialists had difficulty understanding the algorithm. He then relented and published *Paxos Made Simple* [Lamport 2001] with a one-sentence abstract: "The Paxos algorithm, when presented in plain English, is very simple." At least one commercial implementation of Paxos took advantage of this paper [Burrows 2019], even though Lamport's web page warns against implementing from this informal description.

29. Around the time that Lamport joined SRC, he completed two two-part papers on mutual exclusion [Lamport 1986a, 1986b] and interprocess communication [Lamport 1986c, 1986d] that consolidated much of his work over the preceding decade or so. See Chapter 1. Considerably earlier, in a 1979 paper [Lamport 1979b], he had also considered the problem of multiprocessor cache coherence, a topic in mutual exclusion directly relevant to the Firefly.

extraneous to an algorithm's essence. In short, TLA directly supported *abstraction*, an essential technique for managing the complexity of describing and verifying real-world systems. (See Chapter 5 for more background and details about TLA.)

TLA provided a formal way to state properties of programs, but proving those properties was another matter. Lamport knew the pitfalls of informal verification, and he recognized that for TLA to be useful for anything other than small examples, it would need to be supported by a mechanical proof system. Building a full-scale theorem prover was and is a substantial and daunting undertaking, so Lamport initiated a project to build a system to translate TLA formulas into the input of an existing theorem prover with which he and SRC colleagues had experience: LP, the Larch prover [Garland and Guttag 1988]. Armed with this tool—later developed further by Urban Engberg and dubbed TLP [Engberg 1996]—one could write a proof in TLA, translate it into the language of LP, and have LP check it.

However, TLA with TLP was an incomplete solution for Lamport's purposes.[30] TLP demonstrated the feasibility of mechanically verifying a TLA specification, but it handled only a limited subset of what TLA could express. It was a step along the road, but many more would be required.

By 1993, Lamport had enough experience with TLA to begin using it in published work, introducing it first in a workshop paper [Lamport 1993] and then in a journal paper the next year [Lamport 1994c]. TLA figured prominently in most of his published papers over the next several years. Then, in 1996, TLA had its first opportunity to affect a DEC product.

By the time the initial version of TLP was showing promise, multiprocessing had moved from the research labs to the DEC product stream. During the 1980s, the "RISC versus CISC" controversy raged in the field, sparked by the work on Reduced Instruction Set Computers (RISC) at UC Berkeley (although similar architectures had existed earlier). Most commercial computers of the era were of the non-RISC type, at that time dubbed "CISC," a back-formation for Complex (or Comprehensive) Instruction Set Computer. DEC's flagship VAX architecture was CISC, but several influential engineers believed that the company's survival depended on using a RISC design for the VAX's successor. That architecture was eventually named

---

30. The initial work on TLP occurred around 1991, but the real-world test did not come until several years later when Georges Gonthier carried out a mechanical proof of a concurrent garbage collector for his Ph.D. thesis. Lamport wrote: "Gonthier estimated that using TLP instead of working directly in LP reduced the amount of time it took him to do the proof by about a factor of five" [Lamport 2019, comment 96].

Alpha [Wikipedia 2019b]. In the same spirit as the VAX and the IBM S/360/370 architectures, the Alpha design was intended to last 25 years, being implemented in different but functionally compatible ways as technology evolved. This meant, of course, that the Alpha architecture had to accommodate multiprocessor implementations and that the designers of each implementation would need to verify that it satisfied a common specification. That specification was the *Alpha Architecture Reference Manual*. It contained a major section on the Alpha memory model, which had been formally specified by three DEC researchers: Kourosh Gharachorloo at WRL and Jim Saxe and Yuan Yu at SRC.

In 1996, a DEC product team had designed a multiprocessor system called Wildfire that utilized a complicated Alpha processor with out-of-order execution, internally called EV6. The cache coherence protocol to support this processor was extremely complex. The protocol designers contacted Gharachorloo to inquire if he or perhaps other researchers would be interested in verifying that the protocol satisfied the Alpha memory model. Gharachorloo in turn contacted Yu and Saxe to see if they would participate. Yu forwarded the invitation to Lamport, who soon became involved [Lamport 2018c], along with Mark Tuttle of the DEC Cambridge (Massachusetts) Research Lab.

Yu and Lamport brought complementary skills to the EV6 protocol verification project. Yu's Ph.D. dissertation at UT Austin involved verification of low-level code and had been supervised by J Moore, one of the legends of mechanical theorem-proving. Lamport, in addition to his nearly two decades of experience with precise specification and correctness proofs, had by this time created TLA$^+$, an extension of TLA with capabilities to support large formulas,[31] as well as a methodology for organizing large proofs hierarchically [Lamport 1995], both of which would be essential for the EV6 verification effort.

Essential, yes, but barely sufficient. TLA$^+$ lacked tools to support writing or checking specifications, so the work was entirely manual. Lamport, Tuttle, and Yu began by studying the EV6 documents, consulting the hardware engineers in the product team when necessary to understand the protocol's detailed workings. They wrote in TLA$^+$ both an invariant describing the Alpha memory system and an abstraction of the protocol that EV6 used to implement it, then proved that the protocol indeed preserved the invariant.

---

31. The definition of TLA$^+$ didn't appear in broadly available form until 2002 [Lamport 2002], though an earlier version of part of that book appeared in 1999 in course notes for a summer school [Lamport 1999]. See Section 5.3 for an overview of TLA$^+$.

Of course, it wasn't nearly that simple; the process was highly iterative and took most of a year. Yu had no experience in formulating invariants of this kind. He recalled that they spent most of the time in Lamport's office, proposing abstractions and invariants and trying to prove that one implied the other. Usually, an invariant was either wrong or too weak, so the proof couldn't be completed. Even when it could be, they would often discover later it was flawed, since they had no tools to check it rigorously [Yu 2018]. To carry out a complete proof by hand would have been much too time consuming so, as they wrote [Lamport et al. 2002]:

> We selected two conjuncts, each about 150 lines long, as the part of the invariant most likely to reveal an error. We completed the proof for one of the conjuncts; it was about 2000 lines long and 13 levels deep. The proof of the second conjunct would have been about twice as long, but we stopped about halfway through because we decided that the likelihood of its discovering an error was too small to justify further effort. We spent about seven months on these two proofs. We also wrote an informal higher-level proof of one crucial aspect of the protocol. It was about 550 lines long and had a maximum depth of 10 levels.

While it was now evident that TLA⁺ was equal to the task of specifying a real-world memory system, neither Yu nor Lamport cared to attempt another such project without tools. Yu began working on a model checker for (a subset of) TLA⁺, though Lamport was skeptical that it could be done and even tried to talk Yu out of it. Yu persevered and within about three months had a working proof-of-concept model checker. Lamport was immediately convinced and became a strong supporter of TLC, as the model checker for TLA⁺ came to be called. (See Section 5.5.1.) Other than a simple syntax checker, TLC was the first real tool supporting the production of TLA⁺ specifications.[32] It was none too soon, for a few months later, Lamport and Yu would undertake the verification of EV7, the next chip in the Alpha line.

The EV7 verification began in early 1998. "This time, the specification was written by [a DEC product] engineer who received a few hours' instruction on TLA⁺. (At the time, there was no language manual.) His specification was about 1800 lines long" [ibid.]. Though no fanfare accompanied it, this marked the first use of TLA⁺

---

32. A model checker is not a theorem prover. A theorem prover, when it succeeds, demonstrates that a theorem is correct, but often gives little guidance when the "theorem" is wrong. By contrast, a model checker examines a purported theorem in a specific, concrete instance (e.g., for a memory system, the case of exactly two processors) and looks exhaustively for a counterexample. Model checking is far more useful during the development and debugging of a specification, when it is nearly always wrong, since the model checker pinpoints each error.

by someone outside a research organization. The product group put TLC to work and it paid off [Lamport et al. 2002]:

> As soon as we started using TLC, we found many errors in the TLA$^+$ specification. Not counting simple mistakes that were easily corrected, we found about 70 errors. About 90% of them were discovered by TLC; the rest were found by a human reading the specification. Most of the errors were introduced when translating from the informal specification; they demonstrate the ambiguity inherent in such specifications. Five design/implementation errors were discovered—one directly by TLC, the other four by using TLC error traces to generate simulator input.

The Alpha product engineers were pleased with the outcome. They planned to use TLA$^+$ and TLC for EV8, the next processor in the Alpha line, and to replace the English version of the cache coherence protocol specification with the TLA$^+$ one. But though TLA$^+$ was in the ascendant, DEC and the Alpha were not. Compaq acquired DEC in 1998 and had no use for Alpha. The architecture that was intended to last 25 years was sold to Intel in 2001, and DEC engineers went with it. Among them were some who continued to use the TLA$^+$ approach to specification, marking the first use of TLA$^+$ without Lamport as an in-house consultant.

In the several years preceding the EV6 verification project, Lamport had developed a style of proof well suited to the theorems that arise in formal verification. As the preceding quotations indicate, these formulas are large—the specification for the EV6 and EV7 cache coherence protocols each amounted to about 1800 lines. The conventional proof style favored by mathematicians, being informal and essentially linear, cannot cope with such complexity. As Lamport observed, "The structure of mathematical proofs has not changed in 300 years. The proofs in Newton's *Principia* differ in style from those of a modern textbook only by being written in Latin. Proofs are still written like essays, in a stilted form of ordinary prose" [Lamport 1995].

Conquering that complexity required a methodological tool that Lamport knew well from his background as a programmer: hierarchical decomposition. Lamport would repeatedly divide the steps of a proof into smaller and smaller statements to be proved, essentially in the style of a formal deduction of a statement in mathematical logic, familiar to anyone who has taken a first-year symbolic logic course. How far should that iterative decomposition go? Lamport wrote: "My own rule of thumb is to expand the proof until the lowest level statements are obvious, and then continue for one more level. This requires discipline" [ibid.]. The extent of that discipline required for the EV6 verification is evident from looking back at the numbers quoted above.

Discipline in carrying out a hand proof is a good thing, but relying on proof automation is better still. "Structured hand proofs are much more reliable than conventional mathematical proofs, but not as reliable as mechanically checked ones" [Ladkin et al. 1999]. For TLA$^+$ to be more broadly adopted, Lamport would need to provide it with tools that reduce the amount of discipline required.[33] That would be a priority in the next phase of his career.

6.6 The Microsoft Years (2001–)

In early 1996, Bob Taylor retired as the director of SRC, unhappy with management changes that occurred as DEC attempted to adapt to the Internet age. Roy Levin took over as director of SRC. Within two years, Compaq Computer Company, which had established itself as a leader in the so-called IBM PC clone business, acquired DEC, but was unable to capitalize on DEC's technical and market strengths. As support for research eroded, Levin and Assistant Director Mike Schroeder approached Rick Rashid, founder and head of Microsoft Research, with the offer to create a lab in Silicon Valley. Rashid was supportive, and in August the lab opened. By the end of 2001, a few researchers from DEC/Compaq had joined, and Lamport was among them.

Before moving to Microsoft, Lamport had been devoting much of his attention to TLA$^+$ and its associated tools. The DEC engineers who moved to Intel with the sale of the Alpha in 2001 wanted to continue using TLA$^+$, and therefore wanted a license agreement to use Compaq's intellectual property. The sale of Alpha had been a symptom of Compaq's decline, and in September 2001, HP announced that it would acquire Compaq.[34] Shortly before that announcement, Compaq released TLA$^+$ code under a BSD-style license, which enabled Lamport to continue to evolve it at Microsoft and to share the results broadly.

Lamport wanted to continue the TLA$^+$ collaboration with the now Intel engineers, but he also saw opportunities for TLA$^+$ within his new employer. DEC had been chiefly a hardware company, even though it did significant software development. Microsoft had been a software company since day one and had a vast array

---

33. Indeed, the need for hierarchical proof structure accompanied by mechanical verification had already been noted in the first use of TLA with the TLP prover, described earlier.

34. 2001 was also the year that Dell moved ahead of Compaq as the biggest supplier of PCs, a fact that certainly influenced HP's decision to acquire Compaq [Wikipedia 2018b]. The HP acquisition of Compaq was completed in mid-2002.

of software systems, both products and internal services. Many of these systems were just beginning to come to grips with distributed computing environments and the problems of concurrency in which Lamport was an expert. An outside observer might have thought it an ideal marriage of skills and needs.

Nevertheless, the relationship progressed slowly. A new research laboratory with ten or twenty researchers needs time to find its way in a corporation with tens of thousands of software developers, despite the well-established mechanisms within Microsoft Research for engaging with product organizations. The Silicon Valley lab sat on a satellite campus, and as most of Microsoft's development work occurred in the corporate center in Redmond, Washington, product organizations and researchers had to learn how to build relationships at a distance. The ex-SRC researchers knew all about this, since DEC's central development sites had been across the country in Massachusetts, but it was a new way of working for product developers accustomed to having researchers a few blocks away. Even though the new lab was in the same time zone—an advantage that SRC researchers hadn't had—it took some time before product groups became comfortable with remote collaboration. Unsurprisingly, researchers at the new lab established initial ties to product groups on the satellite campus in Mountain View where the new lab resided. However, none of these connections provided a natural outlet for Lamport's expertise.

Once the TLC model checker had demonstrated its value in hardware verification, Lamport knew that TLA$^+$ now could reach a wider user audience. Writing formal specifications without tools required dedication that only Lamport and his closest disciples could muster; with tools, the methodology could be adopted by practitioners and taught to a new generation of engineers. At DEC, Lamport had begun to promulgate the TLA$^+$ approach—he had begun writing a book on concurrency before the Compaq acquisition and had used portions of it in a course in 1998 [Lamport 1999]. At Microsoft, he completed the book *Specifying Systems* and published it in 2002 [Lamport 2002]. By this time, the TLA$^+$ toolset comprised the TLC model checker, the syntactic analyzer that parses specifications and checks for errors, and the TLATEX typesetter that renders the plaintext specifications accepted by other tools more readable using established publication conventions for mathematical works.[35] Lamport explicitly described *Specifying Systems* as the reference manual for TLA$^+$ and its tools, and much of it is devoted to extensive, varied examples that illustrate Lamport's approach to formal specification. To reduce the

---

35. Leveraging Lamport's own LaTeX, of course.

adoption barrier further (and with the notable support of his publisher, Addison-Wesley), Lamport made the book freely available online for noncommercial use.

With this material now readily available, Lamport pursued a two-pronged strategy for TLA$^+$: engage with product organizations to help them understand how TLA$^+$ can benefit them and enhance the toolset to make TLA$^+$ more robust and more attractive to practitioners. He was under no illusions about how difficult the first of these would be. In 2002, he published an experience paper [Lamport et al. 2002] with coauthors who had joined him on specification/verification projects at DEC. In it they wrote [page 4]:

> An important lesson we have learned is that moving formal methods from the research community to the engineering community requires patience and perseverance. Engineers are under severe constraints when designing a system. Speed is of the essence, and they never have as many people as they can use. Engineers must be convinced that formal methods will help before they will risk using them.

They also noted that, although there is "no fundamental difference between hardware and software" when dealing at the specification level, hardware engineers are both more accustomed and more inclined to use formal methods for specification, in part because of the higher, more immediate cost of errors in hardware design. They further noted:

> TLA$^+$, which has proven useful for hardware, should be just as useful for software. However, there does seem to be a cultural difference between hardware and software engineers. Software engineers do not have the same tradition of relying on specifications that hardware engineers do.

Now that Lamport worked in a software company, he knew he faced a challenging path to get TLA$^+$ adopted for specifying software systems.

By late 2002, when *Specifying Systems* appeared, the so-called dot-com boom had ended rather abruptly, and the industry, perhaps somewhat chastened, began regrouping. The term "Web 2.0" became popular, loosely referring to web-based behavior beyond the first generation of static web pages. Rather than being a specific technical idea, Web 2.0 was a philosophy of interaction between users and services that emphasized the more dynamic behavior now familiar in such ubiquitous capabilities as online shopping and forums. Such a world required communication capabilities and standards beyond the basic HTTP protocol of the early web.

Microsoft, originally successful as a packaged software company, was rapidly retooling itself to address this new distributed world. It had several organizations focused on "web services." Lamport and a visiting academic colleague, Friedrich "Fritz" Vogt, met two key architects in Redmond, James Johnson and David Langworthy, who liked the idea of creating formal specifications for web services protocols for which they had informal descriptions. Lamport summarized the resulting collaboration to write a specification for a web services atomic transaction protocol [Lamport 2019, comment 150]:

> Fritz and I spent part of our time for a couple of months writing it, with a lot of help from Jim and Dave in understanding the protocol. . . . This was a routine exercise for me, as it would have been for anyone with a moderate amount of experience specifying concurrent systems. Using TLA$^+$ for the first time was a learning experience for Fritz. It was a brand new world for Jim and Dave, who had never been exposed to formal methods before. They were happy with the results. Dave began writing specifications by himself, and has become something of a TLA$^+$ guru for the Microsoft networking group.

The experience paper reporting on this project appeared in 2004, by which time Lamport's other efforts toward TLA$^+$ adoption within Microsoft had begun to pay off. Notably, he was no longer the only person using TLA$^+$ within the research organization: Tom Rodeheffer, a local colleague, was engaged with another product group designing a protocol, and two researchers in Microsoft's Redmond lab were using TLA$^+$ to specify the protocol for a distributed storage project. Dave Langworthy's initial enthusiasm had matured into advocacy, noting that "[My team and Lamport] spent a day working on replication and discussed several other topics. . . . Above the specific interactions, Leslie has improved the way we think about building distributed systems" [Langworthy 2005].

Any builder of software knows that, regardless of how well developed the concept behind a system is, its users always ask for more. So, as Lamport pursued the second prong of his TLA$^+$ strategy—growing the toolset—he enhanced the system in response to his users' experience and requests. Yuan Yu, who had built the original TLC, reimplemented it more robustly and with somewhat expanded capabilities. But though the model checker made specifications easier to debug, it didn't help with writing them in the first place.

One frequent obstacle for engineers encountering TLA$^+$ was its grounding in mathematical logic, a subject superficially related to programming but essentially different. This difference created a wide gulf between the way engineers think about algorithms and the way they are specified in TLA$^+$. To bridge that gulf, Keith Marzullo suggested creating a form of pseudocode, which engineers often use to sketch algorithms, that could be mechanically translated into a TLA$^+$ specification. Lamport and Marzullo built the translator and called their pseudocode language PlusCal (initially, +Cal), a nod to Pascal, which had often been used as a basis for informal pseudocode[36] [Lamport 2009, 2006c]. (See Section 5.4 for an overview of PlusCal.)

Even with the addition of PlusCal, the TLA$^+$ Toolbox, as it was now called, still lacked an important capability: mechanical proof. TLC, the model checker, had made it practical to find errors in specifications, but as Edsger Dijkstra famously observed, "Program testing can be used very effectively to show the presence of bugs but never to show their absence" [Dijkstra 1971]. Since the experiments with TLP in the early 1990s (see Section 6.5), Lamport had wanted a theorem prover for TLA$^+$. In 2006, he found a way to get one. Microsoft Research and INRIA had recently launched a joint research lab in Paris, and several of Lamport's former collaborators began working there. He organized a project to create a modern theorem prover for TLA$^+$. Despite advances in the theorem-proving technology and vastly more powerful hardware on which to run it, the project faced considerable challenges in producing a usable tool. In 2010, the first release of TLAPS, the TLA$^+$ Proof System, joined the TLA$^+$ Toolbox [Microsoft Research 2019]. (See Section 5.5.2 for an overview of TLAPS.)

The arrival of the theorem prover amplified the efforts of Lamport's colleagues who were trying to use TLA$^+$ for their own research. Chief among them was Tom Rodeheffer, who had been intrepid enough to use TLA$^+$ even before the model checker was available. Now Rodeheffer was able to apply TLA$^+$ to a partial replication system, a distributed atomic memory system, and a data-center network built out of configurable switches. Rodeheffer sat two offices away from Lamport and was the source of many suggestions for enhancement of the tool suite.

The last component of the Toolbox differed in character from its predecessors. The word "toolbox" suggests something holds all the tools, which perform their individual functions. Indeed, from the outset, the individual TLA$^+$ tools had been

36. Lamport has often written about the way in which programming languages limit software developers' thinking, and he repeatedly resisted (indeed, railed against) adding language-like features, such as types, to TLA$^+$. PlusCal doesn't do that; it provides a thin layer of surface syntax over TLA$^+$ to help those who, Lamport might say, are afflicted with "Whorfian syndrome," which he defines as confusing language (programming) with reality (mathematics) [Lamport and Levin 2016a, page 22].

built in the conventional command-line style. While natural enough in the previous century, in the present one the lack of tool integration was a bit quaint. Developers had increasingly become accustomed to using a programming environment in which the tools were tightly integrated, so that program editors, compilers, debuggers, performance analyzers, and the like seamlessly shared an understanding of the program under development and could display its various aspects simultaneously in a collection of interrelated display windows. TLA$^+$ needed a similar interactive development environment (IDE).

To build the IDE for TLA$^+$, Lamport turned to Simon Zambrovski, who spent a postdoctoral year working with Lamport at Microsoft. He built it on Eclipse, a widely available open-source platform used chiefly for Java, in which the original TLA$^+$ tools had been written. The IDE, first released in 2010, received subsequent improvements from Markus Kuppe (who as an intern with Lamport had built a distributed version of TLC that enabled it to check specifications on larger cases) and Daniel Ricketts. By 2013, TLA$^+$ had an integrated, comprehensive Toolbox available to the computing community [Lamport 2019]. (See Section 5.5.3 for an overview of the Toolbox.)

Finally, more than two decades after the creation of TLA, Lamport could see the fruits of his efforts. TLA$^+$ and its toolset had taken root in Microsoft product organizations and in other companies. Brannon Batson, a former DEC engineer on the Alpha team that went to Intel, characterized TLA$^+$ around 2006 as follows [Merz 2008]:

> The next big frontier in computer engineering is algorithmic complexity. In order to tackle this increasingly complex world, we need tools and languages which augment human thought, not supplant it. TLA$^+$ is a language which connects engineers to the underlying mathematics of their design—providing insight which they otherwise wouldn't have.

Later, Chris Newcombe, a former principal engineer at Amazon, wrote on a TLA$^+$ discussion group [Newcombe 2012]:

> TLA$^+$ is the most valuable thing that I've learned in my professional career. It has changed how I work, by giving me an immensely powerful tool to find subtle flaws in system designs. It has changed how I think, by giving me a framework for constructing new kinds of mental-models, by revealing the precise relationship between correctness properties and system designs, and by allowing me to move from "plausible prose" to precise statements much earlier in the software development process.

By 2012, TLA$^+$ was in regular use at Amazon, with the distributed model checker running on hundreds of computers [ibid.]. Lamport believes that Amazon's experience, reported in Newcombe et al. [2015], was influential in stimulating use of TLA$^+$ within Microsoft's Azure team.

Much of Lamport's effort on TLA$^+$ in his Microsoft years could be called the unglamorous part of research: taking an idea that has had a successful proof of concept and pushing it forward into a practical system that others can and want to use. The effort required to do this in a research environment should not be underestimated, as the innovator cannot usually bring an idea to fruition alone and colleagues with the right skills and temperament for this kind of work are rare. Lamport was very fortunate to find such colleagues in the research labs at DEC, Microsoft, and INRIA.[37] Nevertheless, getting TLA$^+$ adopted for precise, verifiable specification of algorithms remains one of Lamport's long-term projects.

While maintaining a steady pressure to advance TLA$^+$ and its toolset, Lamport also pursued other research interests. During the same years in which the TLA$^+$ Toolbox was expanding, Lamport continued to work on the problem of agreement protocols that had inspired his Paxos work in the 1990s. Even before the Paxos paper appeared in 1998, a product effort at DEC to build a replicated storage system had led Lamport and colleague Eli Gafni to create Disk Paxos [Gafni and Lamport 2003]. Within a few years, the explosion of Internet-based services led various groups at Yahoo, Google, Microsoft, Facebook, and elsewhere to build and deploy systems that used Paxos (see Section 4.6.2). However, these systems did not use the full generality of the algorithm.

Lamport's insights into the fundamental behavior of distributed systems had led him, in Paxos, to specify a very general algorithm that intertwined the solutions to two problems: replication of state to achieve robustness and reconfiguration to maintain system availability. In practice, this intertwining posed many implementation challenges, which is why Paxos implementations from Petal onward used Paxos's state machine replication but invented alternative, simpler mechanisms for availability. In the mid-2000s, Lamport worked on variants of Paxos that improved its performance by reducing the number of replicas (Cheap Paxos [Lamport and Massa 2004], inspired by Microsoft product engineer and coauthor Mike Massa) or messages required for the protocol (Fast Paxos [Lamport 2006b]), but these

---

37. In an interview in 2002, Lamport was asked: "To what extent do you consider research fun versus hard work?" He replied: "Hard work is hauling bales of hay or cleaning sewers. Scientists and engineers should be grateful that society is willing to pay us to have fun" [Milojicic 2002].

enhancements did not directly address the complexity of implementing reconfiguration. Eventually, however, colleague Dahlia Malkhi persuaded Lamport that the separation of replication and reconfiguration, which occurred in all known Paxos implementations, needed a principled foundation. At the end of the decade, Lamport, Malkhi, and their colleague Lidong Zhou published Vertical Paxos [Lamport et al. 2009a] and two related papers [Lamport et al. 2009b, Lamport et al. 2010] that established that foundation (see Section 4.7).[38]

During these years of Paxos evolution, Lamport also continued to explore the relationships between Paxos and other agreement protocols, including a paper with Jim Gray showing that classic two-phase commit is a special case of Paxos [Gray and Lamport 2006] and a paper showing the Castro-Liskov algorithm for handling Byzantine faults is a refinement of Paxos [Lamport 2011]. The latter paper notably exploited the TLA$^+$ Proof System, TLAPS, to formally verify the relationship.

By 2012—more than two decades after Lamport invented the Paxos algorithm—its importance for creating practical, large-scale, fault-tolerant distributed systems had been widely recognized, and "The Part-time Parliament"—a paper that almost was never published—won the SIGOPS Hall of Fame Award.[39]

As of this writing (mid 2019), Lamport continues his research at Microsoft. Though Microsoft Research Silicon Valley was closed in 2014, he collaborates with colleagues at INRIA and elsewhere. For someone who has spent his entire career in industry rather than academia, Lamport invests very considerable effort in education through both frequent lectures and papers. Indeed, roughly a tenth of his papers could be viewed as efforts to teach others what he has learned through his research rather than as reports of that research. Unsurprisingly, the fraction of such papers has increased in recent years; after nearly half a century of carrying out and reflecting on research, he increasingly tries to distill in writing the insights he has gained. He believes in the power of writing; in *Specifying Systems*, he opens with a favorite quote, from cartoonist Dick Guindon: "Writing is nature's way of letting you know how sloppy your thinking is." Some examples of Lamport's own pithy observations:

---

38. Vertical Paxos provided a jumping-off spot for researchers other than Lamport to explore further evolution of the algorithm, notably Howard, Malkhi, and Spiegelman's Flexible Paxos [Howard et al. 2016].

39. Somewhat analogously, a paper by Butler Lampson and Howard Sturgis, "Crash Recovery in a Distributed Data Storage System," also won a SIGOPS Hall of Fame Award, but was never published [Lampson and Sturgis 1979]. For years, it was informally referred to as an "underground classic."

- On using mathematics rather than natural language for specifications: "Mathematics is nature's way of letting you know how sloppy your writing is" [Lamport 2002, page 2].

- On the indispensability of proof: "Never believe anything that is obvious until you have a proof of it" [Lamport and Levin 2016a, page 33].

- On using structured rather than prose proofs: "A proof should not be great literature; it should be beautiful mathematics. Its beauty lies in its logical structure, not its prose" [Lamport 2012, page 19].

- On distributed systems: "A distributed system is one in which the failure of a computer you didn't even know existed can render your own computer unusable" [Lamport 1987]. This is probably his most frequently quoted aphorism, written in an email in 1987.

6.7 Honors

Lamport's work has been extensively recognized:

- National Academy of Engineering (1991)
- PODC Influential Paper Award (2000) (for [Lamport 1978b])
- Honorary doctorate, University of Rennes (2003)
- Honorary doctorate, Christian Albrechts University, Kiel (2003)
- Honorary doctorate, École Polytechnique Fédérale de Lausanne (2004)
- IEEE Piore Award (2004)
- Edsger W. Dijkstra Prize in Distributed Computing (2005) (for [Pease et al. 1980])
- Honorary doctorate, Università della Svizzera Italiana, Lugano (2006)
- ACM SIGOPS Hall of Fame Award (2007) (for [Lamport 1978b])
- Honorary doctorate, Université Henri Poincaré, Nancy (2007)
- LICS 1988 Test of Time Award (2008) (for [Abadi and Lamport 1991])
- IEEE John von Neumann Medal (2008)
- National Academy of Sciences (2011)
- ACM SIGOPS Hall of Fame Award (2012) (for [Lamport 1998a])
- Jean-Claude Laprie Award in Dependable Computing (2013) (for [Lamport et al. 1982])

- ACM SIGOPS Hall of Fame Award (2013) (for [Chandy and Lamport 1985])
- 2013 ACM A. M. Turing Award (2014)
- American Academy of Arts and Sciences (2014)
- Jean-Claude Laprie Award in Dependable Computing (2014) (for [Wensley et al. 1978])
- Edsger W. Dijkstra Prize in Distributed Computing (2014) (for [Chandy and Lamport 1985])
- Honorary doctorate, Brandeis University (2017)
- Fellow, Computer History Museum (2019)

It is noteworthy that the first of these honors—membership in the National Academy of Engineering—is one more customarily awarded considerably later in an individual's career, after other honors have brought them to prominence. One would also be hard pressed to identify another computer scientist with as many honorary doctorates, even among those in the elite category of Turing Award recipients.

Several awards Lamport received recognize work that has stood the "test of time." While such awards inherently occur years after the work they recognize, in Lamport's case recognition occurred after uncharacteristically long intervals. The Time/Clocks paper [Lamport 1978b] appeared in 1978; it was recognized in 2000 and 2007. The Byzantine generals work appeared in papers in 1980 and 1982; it was recognized in 2005 and 2013. The Paxos paper, published in 1998 but embodying work done nearly a decade before, was recognized in 2012. And the Distributed Snapshots paper [Chandy and Lamport 1985] that Lamport wrote with Mani Chandy, another luminary in the field of distributed systems, appeared in 1985 and was recognized in 2013 and 2014.[40] These intervals, averaging roughly 20 years, suggest how far-sighted some of Lamport's most important works have been and how long it took the field to fully appreciate them, since for most awards the "test of time" is a decade. (To be fair, some of the awards only came into existence in the 21st century, though Lamport's seminal works weren't always recognized in their inaugural year.)

Lamport received the ACM A. M. Turing Award, generally considered the equivalent of the Nobel Prize in computing, for 2013. It recognizes a body of work "for major contributions of lasting importance to computing." Lamport's award citation reads: "For fundamental contributions to the theory and practice of distributed

---

40. Surprisingly, this was the only paper these two distributed computing experts ever wrote together.

and concurrent systems, notably the invention of concepts such as causality and logical clocks, safety and liveness, replicated state machines, and sequential consistency." While the specific concepts listed occupied much of Lamport's attention in the 1970s and 1980s, the first portion of the citation embraces his work on Paxos and fault tolerance as well.

6.8 Collegial Influences

As of this writing, Lamport's "My Writings" web page [Lamport 2019] lists 184 works.[41] Fewer than a third of them (59) have coauthors, a fraction that would be unusual for any computer scientist. Some people attribute this to prickliness, claiming Lamport is hard to work with. Obviously, those who have succeeded view the matter differently, painting instead a picture of a serious and uncompromising yet supportive collaborator. Their experiences in working with Lamport, related below with minor editing for readability, also provide additional insight into Lamport's modus operandi and its impact on his colleagues.

Lidong Zhou [Zhou 2018]

Working with Leslie serves as a constant reminder of what scientific research is all about. Leslie has always been a role model who demonstrates how a scientist is driven by curiosity, stays insulated and focused in the pursuit of truth and perfection, and sticks to the core principles of research, which are often forgotten as too many of us constantly rush to get papers published in top conferences or journals as a means to gain personal fame.

Mani Chandy [Chandy 2018]

Leslie is a master at identifying and specifying core problems that abstract the essence of a myriad of practical situations that appear to be different.

You can see the nuggets, and their impact across a spectrum of applications, throughout Leslie's career. Leslie specified the key idea formally, using mathematics; however, the path to get to the key idea used anthropomorphisms and analogies. A lesson from Leslie's career for future generations of computer scientists is the importance of identifying core problems and specifying them clearly. Identifying the nugget is as important as finding the solution.

---

41. Nearly all these publications pertain to computing, but two show another side of Lamport as a scientist: "On Hair Color in France" [Gilkerson and Lamport 2004] and "Measuring Celebrity" [Lamport 2006]. Both appear in the *Annals of Improbable Research*.

Yuan Yu [Yu 2018]

All of Leslie's work is derived from practical systems. His ability to gain insight into the system problems and be able to abstract them out—I haven't seen anyone else who can do this.

My ten months of work with him on TLC was like an intensive training camp. Unfortunately, not everyone can have this kind of experience! He was not treating the EV6 specification as tutoring—we were partners, working on a project.

I don't think I mastered the ability to abstract problems. Leslie is still the master, but I got part of it, and that's very valuable to me. Later on, in all the systems I was involved in building, I was thinking about them in terms of state and the inductive invariants. I'm not sure that this is the only way, but this is clearly one very productive way of thinking about systems.

Some people say Leslie is hard to work with, but obviously I didn't have that experience. He tolerated my inexperience; I'm very grateful. He does have a very low tolerance of nonsense. . . . If you talk about something that he thinks is clearly nonsense and you have an argument with him, that's when he's going to show his anger.

Fred Schneider [Schneider 2018]

Lamport and I first met in person at the December 1979 SOSP conference at Asilomar. We got along, which is not something you can ever explain—simply a matter of personal chemistry. I would observe that we both grew up in New York City in working-class Jewish families (though neither of us was religious). Not only did we both have interest in fault tolerance, but we both were interested in reasoning about concurrent programs, which is quite a separate subject with a disjoint community of researchers. Most importantly, though, I think we both were less interested in building artifacts than in identifying principles.

Writing our first joint paper ("The Hoare Logic of CSP, and All That") was quite the education for me. He sat at a terminal; I sat next to him. He'd type a sentence, I'd read it, and we fought about wording. And notation. And formatting. I learned a good deal about writing technical papers from this experience, though at times it did get tiresome. Lamport had a strong idea about where the paper was headed, and he had developed the precursor to the programming logic we were developing as we wrote. I understood neither very deeply. But this meant that Lamport, sitting there, got to see "in real time" how a naive reader might misunderstand the points he wanted to make and the exact wording, especially since I was viewing things through the lens of the Owicki-Gries method, which was the defining characteristic of our target audience. . . . I don't recall how many visits I made to the West Coast, but the paper was written in these five-day sessions of sitting side by side. (Two of) our subsequent . . . papers were written in this way too. Needless to say, finishing a paper took quite some time, but the prose was well exercised.

Butler Lampson [Lampson 2018]

When Howard Sturgis and I wrote our paper on crash recovery in a distributed storage system [Lampson and Sturgis 1979], we never published it because we couldn't figure out how to prove the correctness of the algorithm, so it became known only in samizdat.

Like almost everyone else who does it seriously, I learned how to do proofs of concurrent systems from Leslie.

Stephan Merz [Merz 2018]

Leslie tends to be initially skeptical of ideas he hasn't come up with, but he is quick to realize a good idea, adopt it, and develop it further. Several years ago, I had a student who worked on a variant of the PlusCal language and suggested some extensions that would allow more elaborate algorithms to be modeled in it. Among the extensions was what we considered to be a minor suggestion for adding fairness annotations to processes and to labels within processes. When Leslie heard about this work, he was furious because we had dubbed the language "PlusCal 2" for lack of a better name. When we explained that this was just an internal moniker, he agreed to discuss the proposed extensions during a visit to Paris. He considered that most of our proposed additions were irrelevant or contrary to the spirit of PlusCal. However, he told us that he would steal the fairness annotations—except that prefixing a label by "fair" or "strong fair" (as we had done) was too heavy a notation, and he would rather affix a single character to the label. This is now part of PlusCal. Of course, our extended language is long forgotten. Incidentally, this anecdote shows Leslie's strong ideas about notation that permeate his work.

Tom Rodeheffer [Rodeheffer 2018]

I had a couple of trips to Paris (to theorem-proving conferences). I was there once visiting the INRIA lab and Leslie was there at the same time. He had me over for lunch at his apartment there and that was pretty cool because we just walked to his apartment and had a simple lunch of bread and cheese. The cheese was the best I had ever had so I asked about it. Leslie described the cheese and then told me all about the French cheese stores that I had never known to exist! He's a very personable guy, and here I am—this random person that's just using his tools, and he was very friendly.

Dahlia Malkhi [Malkhi 2018]

I am awed when I look back at the ten years at Microsoft Research Silicon Valley (MSR SVC) during which I had the pleasure of working with and alongside Leslie.

For me—despite him having strong opinions and strong wills, and the fact that when you work with him you always feel inferior because he's so good—I love working with him. Whenever he had the availability to work with me, he was my top choice, no question. I don't say this vacuously: There are people who are difficult to work with, and you don't care how smart or good they are, you just don't want to work with them—it's not worth it. That's not Leslie. Everything he argues about comes from a completely technical point of view—there's nothing personal.

I believe that his personal influence on people in the MSR SVC lab and beyond is priceless. Many of the SVC researchers whom I talked to received life advice and wisdom from him beyond whatever technical matters they discussed with him. They really appreciated him as a role model and got advice from him on how to think about a problem, what to look for in the problems that you work on, and how to think about your career as an industrial researcher. He used to tell us: "Go to engineers and see what problems they are tackling—this is the best source of questions." His confidence is something that I think rubbed off on all of us, that sticking to our inner (scientific) truth and was more important than getting papers published. Beyond the lab, his personal web page and all the stories about rejected papers are an inspiration and an encouragement to every graduate student.

I was at Lamport's Turing Award lecture at PODC in France. He came on stage, was introduced, and got, as you would expect, a standing ovation. Unexpectedly, the ovation did not last 10 seconds—it lasted a solid few minutes. The audience just didn't stop—completely spontaneously. He was stunned and really humbled that people loved him that much.

Roy Levin

I never collaborated with Lamport on a technical matter, though during my years as a researcher I did once seek his guidance on a formal specification for a complex system. However, as the director of SRC and subsequently as director of Microsoft Research Silicon Valley, I frequently sought his wisdom on hiring researchers. Everyone in the lab participated in hiring decisions, and we shared a view of what qualities were essential in our researchers. Lamport regularly reminded us of the importance of focusing on those qualities when considering a candidate. In our lab-wide hiring discussions, Lamport often did not feel the need to speak up, but when he did (as in the old E. F. Hutton ads), people listened. Lamport interviewed many candidates whose expertise didn't overlap with his own; nevertheless, he accurately assessed their overall technical strength, and when the lab found itself uncertain about the correct decision, he could bring the question into sharp focus. Years later, I can clearly remember several cases in which he made the key characterization of a candidate that cleared away the clouds obscuring the correct hiring decision. We considered that choosing our colleagues was the most important thing the lab did, and Lamport's incisive contributions to that process were therefore invaluable.

It is appropriate in a biography to let the subject have the last words. Here are Lamport's [Lamport and Levin 2016b, page 31]:

> One effect that winning the [Turing] award had on me is that it got me to look back at my career in ways that I hadn't, and I think it made me realize the debt that I owed to other computer scientists that I hadn't realized before. For example, when I look back at Dijkstra's mutual exclusion paper now—I've recognized for decades what an amazing paper that was in terms of the insight that he showed, both in recognizing the problem and in stating it so precisely and so accurately— one thing that I didn't realize, I think, until fairly recently, is how much of the whole way of looking at the idea of proving something about an algorithm was new in that paper. He was assuming an underlying model of computation that I somehow accepted as being quite natural. I don't think I understood until recently how much he created that, and I think there are some other instances like that where I absorbed things from other people without realizing it. One of the reasons for that may be that I never had a computer science mentor. . . . I never got that in school really—I never had a one-on-one relationship with any professor. So, the whole concept of mentoring is somewhat alien to me. I hope that, in the couple of occasions where I've been in a position to mentor others, I didn't do too bad a job, but I have no idea whether I did or not. But my mentors have been my colleagues and I learned a lot from them by osmosis that, in retrospect, I'm very grateful for, but I was unaware at the time.

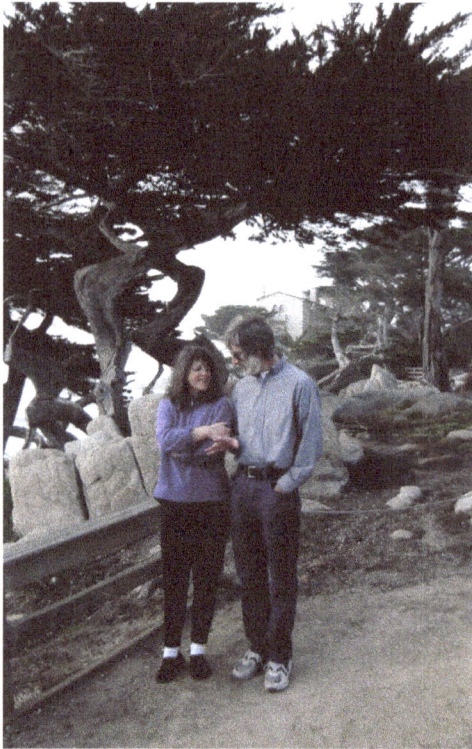

Leslie Lamport and wife Ellen Gilkerson near
Monteray, CA, January 24, 2003.

Leslie Lamport and friends at a winery in Napa or Sonoma
in 2001. Left to right: Lamport, Ellen Gilkerson, Mimi
Bussan, Fred Schneider, Susan Armstrong. (Photo by
Keith Marzullo)

SELECTED PAPERS

Richard Palais and Leslie Lamport at a lunch in celebration of Palais's 80th birthday in 2011.

Leslie says: "Its significance is that he was my de jure thesis adviser and was the most influential post-high school teacher I had. (It's impossible for me to compare his influence with that of earlier teachers who taught me at a more impressionable age.) He showed me that real math could be made completely rigorous."

Leslie Lamport receives his first honorary doctorate in Rennes, France, in 2003.

Leslie Lamport receives an honorary degree in Nancy. He is standing next to Dominque Mery.

A New Solution of Dijkstra's Concurrent Programming Problem

Leslie Lamport (Massachusetts Computer Associates, Inc.)

A simple solution to the mutual exclusion problem is presented which allows the system to continue to operate despite the failure of any individual component.

Key Words and Phrases: critical section, concurrent programming, multiprocessing, semaphores

CR Categories: 4.32

Introduction

Knuth [1], deBruijn [2], and Eisenberg and McGuire [3] have given solutions to a concurrent programming problem originally proposed and solved by Dijkstra [4]. A simpler solution using semaphores has also been implemented [5]. These solutions have one drawback for use in a true multicomputer system (rather than a time-shared multiprocessor system): the failure of a single unit will halt the entire system. We present a simple solution which allows the system to continue to operate despite the failure of any individual component.

This research was supported by the Advanced Research Projects Agency of the Department of Defense and was monitored by U.S. Army Research Office–Durham, under Contract No. DAHC04-70-C-0023. Author's address: Massachusetts Computer Associates, Inc., Lakeside Office Park, Wakefield, MA 01880.
Paper originally published in *Communications of the ACM* 17(8), August 1974.

The Algorithm

Consider N asynchronous computers communicating with each other only via shared memory. Each computer runs a cyclic program with two parts—a *critical section* and a *noncritical section.* Dijkstra's problem, as extended by Knuth, is to write the programs so that the following conditions are satisfied:

1. At any time, at most one computer may be in its critical section.

2. Each computer must eventually be able to enter its critical section (unless it halts).

3. Any computer may halt in its noncritical section.

Moreover, no assumptions can be made about the running speeds of the computers.

The solutions of [1–4] had all N processors set and test the value of a single variable k. Failure of the memory unit containing k would halt the system. The use of semaphores also implies reliance upon a single hardware component.

Our solution assumes N processors, each containing its own memory unit. A processor may read from any other processor's memory, but it need only write into its own memory. The algorithm has the remarkable property that if a read and a write operation to a single memory location occur simultaneously, then only the write operation must be performed correctly. The read may return *any* arbitrary value!

A processor may fail at any time. We assume that when it fails, it immediately goes to its noncritical section and halts. There may then be a period when reading from its memory gives arbitrary values. Eventually, any read from its memory must give a value of zero. (In practice, a failed computer might be detected by its failure to respond to a read request within a specified length of time.)

Unlike the solutions of [1–4], ours is a first-come-first-served method in the following sense. When a processor wants to enter its critical section, it first executes a loop-free block of code—i.e. one with a fixed number of execution steps. It is then guaranteed to enter its critical section before any other processor which later requests service.

The algorithm is quite simple. It is based upon one commonly used in bakeries, in which a customer receives a number upon entering the store. The holder of the lowest number is the next one served. In our algorithm, each processor chooses its own number. The processors are named $1, \ldots, N$. If two processors choose the same number, then the one with the lowest name goes first.

The common store consists of

integer array *choosing*[1 : *N*], *number*[1 : *N*]

Words *choosing*(*i*) and *number*[*i*] are in the memory of processor *i*, and are initially zero. The range of value of *number*[*i*] is unbounded. This will be discussed below.

The following is the program for processor *i*. Execution must begin inside the noncritical section. The arguments of the maximum function can be read in any order. The relation "less than" on ordered pairs of integers is defined by $(a, b) < (c.d)$ if $a < c$, or if $a = c$ and $b < d$.

```
begin integer j;
    L1:    choosing[i] := 1;
           number[i] := 1 + maximum(number[1], . . . , number[N]);
           choosing[i] := 0;
           for j = 1 step 1 until N do
               begin
                   L2:    if choosing[j] ≠ 0 then goto L2;
                   L3:    if number[j] ≠ 0 and (number[j], j) < (number[i], i)
                              then goto L3;
               end;
           critical section;
           number[i] := 0;
           noncritical section;
           goto L1;
    end
```

We allow process *i* to fail at any time, and then to be restarted in its noncritical sections (with *choosing*[*i*] = *number*[*i*] = 0). However, if a processor keeps failing and restarting, then it can deadlock the system.

Proof of Correctness

To prove the correctness of the algorithm, we first make the following definitions. Processor *i* is said to be *in the doorway* while *choosing*[*i*] = 1. It is said to be *in the bakery* from the time it resets *choosing*(*i*) to zero until it either fails or leaves its critical section. The correctness of the algorithm is deduced from the following assertions. Note that the proofs make no assumptions about the value read during an overlapping read and write to the same memory location.

Assertion 1   If processor i and k are in the bakery and i entered the bakery before k entered the doorway, then $number[i] < number[k]$.

Proof   By hypothesis, $number[i]$ had its current value while k was choosing the current value of $number[k]$. Hence, k must have chosen $number \geq 1 + number[i]$. ∎

Assertion 2   If processor i is in its critical section, processor k is in the bakery, and $k \neq i$, then $(number[i], i) < (number[k], k)$.

Proof   Since $choosing[k]$ has essentially just two values—zero and nonzero—we can assume that from processor i's point of view, reading or writing it is done instantaneously, and a simultaneous read and write does not occur. For example, if $choosing[k]$ is being changed from zero to one while it is also being read by processor i, then the read is considered to happen first if it obtains a value of zero; otherwise the write is said to happen first. All times defined in the proof are from processor i's viewpoint.

Let t_{L2} be the time at which processor i read $choosing[k]$ during its last execution of $L2$ for $j = k$, and let t_{L3} be the time at which i began its last execution of $L3$ for $j = k$, so $t_{L2} < t_{L3}$. When processor k was choosing its current value of $number[k]$, let t_e be the time at which it entered the doorway, t_w the time at which it finished writing the value of $number[k]$, and t_c the time at which it left the doorway. Then $t_e < t_w < t_c$.

Since $choosing[k]$ was equal to zero at time t_{L2}, we have either (a) $t_{L2} < t_e$ or (b) $t_c < t_{L2}$. In case (a), Assertion 1 implies that $number[i] < number[k]$, so the assertion holds.

In case (b), we have $t_w < t_c < t_{L2} < t_{L3}$, so $t_w < t_{L3}$. Hence, during the execution of statement $L3$ begun at time t_{L3}, processor i read the current value of $number[k]$. Since i did not execute $L3$ again for $j = k$, it must have found $(number[i], i) < (number[k], k)$. Hence, the assertion holds in this case, too. ∎

Assertion 3   Assume that only a bounded number of processor failures may occur. If no processor is in its critical section and there is a processor in the bakery which does not fail, then some processor must eventually enter its critical section.

Proof   Assume that no processor ever enters its critical section. Then there will be some time after which no more processors enter or leave the bakery. At this time, assume that processor i has the minimum value of $(number[i], i)$ among all processors in the bakery. Then processor i must eventually complete the **for** loop and enter its critical section. This is the required contradiction. ∎

Assertion 2 implies that at most one processor can be in its critical section at any time. Assertions 1 and 2 prove that processors enter their critical sections on a first-come-first-served basis. Hence, an individual processor cannot be blocked unless the entire system is deadlocked. Assertion 3 implies that the system can only be deadlocked by a processor halting in its critical section, or by an unbounded sequence of processor failures and re-entries. The latter can tie up the system as follows. If processor j continually fails and restarts, then with bad luck processor i could always find $choosing[j] = 1$, and loop forever at $L2$.

Further Remarks

If there is always at least one processor in the bakery, then the value of $number[i]$ can become arbitrarily large. This problem cannot be solved by any simple scheme of cycling through a finite set of integers. For example, given any numbers r and s, if $N \geq 4$, then it is possible to have simultaneously $number(i) = r$ and $number(j) = s$ for some i and j.

Fortunately, practical considerations will place an upper bound on the value of $number[i]$ in any real application. For example, if processors enter the doorway at the rate of at most one per msec, then after a year of operation we will have $number[i] < 2^{35}$—assuming that a read of $number[i]$ can never obtain a value larger than one which has been written there.

The unboundedness of $number[i]$ does raise an interesting theoretical question: can one find an algorithm for finite processors such that processors enter their critical sections on a first-come-first-served basis, and no processor may write into another processor's memory? The answer is not known.[1]

The algorithm can be generalized in two ways: (i) under certain circumstances, to allow two processors simultaneously to be in their critical sections; and (ii) to modify the first-come-first-served property so that higher priority processors are served first. This will be described in a future paper.

Conclusion

Our algorithm provides a new, simple solution ot the mutual exclusion problem. Since it does not depend upon any form of central control, it is less sensitive to component failure than previous solutions.

Received September 1973; revised January 1974

---

1. We have recently found such an algorithm, but it is quite complicated.

References

[1] Knuth, D.E. Additional comments on a problem in concurrent programming control. *Comm. ACM 9,* 5 (May 1966), 321–322.

[2] deBruijn, N.G. Additional comments on a problem in concurrent programming control. *Comm. ACM 10,* 3 (Mar. 1967), 137–138.

[3] Eisenberg, M.A., and McGuire, M.R. Further comments on Dijkstra's concurrent programming control problem. *Comm. ACM 15,* 11 (Nov. 1972), 999.

[4] Dijkstra, E.W. Solution of a problem in concurrent programming control. *Comm. ACM 8,* 9 (Sept. 1965), 569.

[5] Dijstra, E.W. The structure of THE multiprogramming system. *Comm. ACM 11,* 5 (May 1968), 341–346.

Time, Clocks, and the Ordering of Events in a Distributed System

Leslie Lamport (Massachusetts Computer Associates, Inc.)

The concept of one event happening before another in a distributed system is examined, and is shown to define a partial ordering of the events. A distributed algorithm is given for synchronizing a system of logical clocks which can be used to totally order the events. The use of the total ordering is illustrated with a method for solving synchronization problems. The algorithm is then specialized for synchronizing physical clocks, and a bound is derived on how far out of synchrony the clocks can become.

Key Words and Phrases: distributed systems, computer networks, clock synchronization, multiprocess systems

CR Categories: 4.32, 5.29

This work was supported by the Advanced Research Projects Agency of the Department of Defense and Rome Air Development Center. It was monitored by Rome Air Development Center under contract number F 30602-76-C-0094.
Author's address: Computer Science Laboratory, SRI International, 333 Ravenswood Ave., Menlo Park CA 94025.
Paper originally published in *Communications of the ACM* 21(7), July 1978.

Introduction

The concept of time is fundamental to our way of thinking. It is derived from the more basic concept of the order in which events occur. We say that something happened at 3:15 if it occurred *after* our clock read 3:15 and before it read 3:16. The concept of the temporal ordering of events pervades our thinking about systems. For example, in an airline reservation system we specify that a request for a reservation should be granted if it is made *before* the flight is filled. However, we will see that this concept must be carefully reexamined when considering events in a distributed system.

A distributed system consists of a collection of distinct processes which are spatially separated, and which communicate with one another by exchanging messages. A network of interconnected computers, such as the ARPA net, is a distributed system. A single computer can also be viewed as a distributed system in which the central control unit, the memory units, and the input-output channels are separate processes. A system is distributed if the message transmission delay is not negligible compared to the time between events in a single process.

We will concern ourselves primarily with systems of spatially separated computers. However, many of our remarks will apply more generally. In particular, a multiprocessing system on a single computer involves problems similar to those of a distributed system because of the unpredictable order in which certain events can occur.

In a distributed system, it is sometimes impossible to say that one of two events occurred first. The relation "happened before" is therefore only a partial ordering of the events in the system. We have found that problems often arise because people are not fully aware of this fact and its implications.

In this paper, we discuss the partial ordering defined by the "happened before" relation, and give a distributed algorithm for extending it to a consistent total ordering of all the events. This algorithm can provide a useful mechanism for implementing a distributed system. We illustrate its use with a simple method for solving synchronization problems. Unexpected, anomalous behavior can occur if the ordering obtained by this algorithm differs from that perceived by the user. This can be avoided by introducing real, physical clocks. We describe a simple method for synchronizing these clocks, and derive an upper bound on how far out of synchrony they can drift.

The Partial Ordering

Most people would probably say that an event a happened before an event b if a happened at an earlier time than b. They might justify this definition in terms of physical theories of time. However, if a system is to meet a specification correctly, then that specification must be given in terms of events observable within the system. If the specification is in terms of physical time, then the system must contain real clocks. Even if it does contain real clocks, there is still the problem that such clocks are not perfectly accurate and do not keep precise physical time. We will therefore define the "happened before" relation without using physical clocks.

We begin by defining our system more precisely. We assume that the system is composed of a collection of processes. Each process consists of a sequence of events. Depending upon the application, the execution of a subprogram on a computer could be one event, or the execution of a single machine instruction could be one event. We are assuming that the events of a process form a sequence, where a occurs before b in this sequence if a happens before b. In other words, a single process is defined to be a set of events with an a priori total ordering. This seems to be what is generally meant by a process.[1] It would be trivial to extend our definition to allow a process to split into distinct subprocesses, but we will not bother to do so.

We assume that sending or receiving a message is an event in a process. We can then define the "happened before" relation, denoted by "$\rightarrow$", as follows.

Definition   The relation "$\rightarrow$" on the set of events of a system is the smallest relation satisfying the following three conditions: (1) If a and b are events in the same process, and a comes before b, then $a \rightarrow b$. (2) If a is the sending of a message by one process and b is the receipt of the same message by another process, then $a \rightarrow b$. (3) If $a \rightarrow b$ and $b \rightarrow c$ then $a \rightarrow c$. Two distinct events a and b are said to be *concurrent* if $a \nrightarrow b$ and $b \nrightarrow a$.

We assume that $a \nrightarrow a$ for any event a. (Systems in which an event can happen before itself do not seem to be physically meaningful.) This implies that $\rightarrow$ is an irreflexive partial ordering on the set of all events in the system.

It is helpful to view this definition in terms of a "space-time diagram" such as Figure 1. The horizontal direction represents space, and the vertical direction represents time—later times being higher than earlier ones. The dots denote events, the vertical lines denote processes, and the wavy lines denote messages.[2] It is easy

---

1. The choice of what constitutes an event affects the ordering of events in a process. For example, the receipt of a message might denote the setting of an interrupt bit in a computer, or the execution of a subprogram to handle that interrupt. Since interrupts need not be handled in the order that they occur, this choice will affect the ordering of a process' message-receiving events.

2. Observe that messages may be received out of order. We allow the sending of several messages to be a single event, but for convenience we will assume that the receipt of a single message does not coincide with the sending or receipt of any other message.

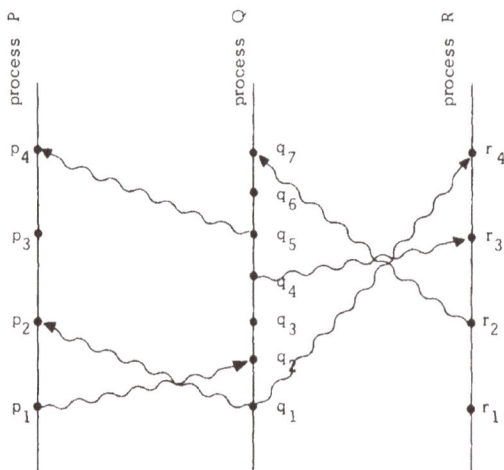

Figure 1

to see that $a \rightarrow b$ means that one can go from a to b in the diagram by moving forward in time along process and message lines. For example, we have $p_1 \rightarrow r_4$ in Figure 1.

Another way of viewing the definition is to say that $a \rightarrow b$ means that it is possible for event a to causally affect event b. Two events are concurrent if neither can causally affect the other. For example, events p_3 and q_3 of Figure l are concurrent. Even though we have drawn the diagram to imply that q_3 occurs at an earlier physical time than p_3, process P cannot know what process Q did at q_3 until it receives the message at p_4. (Before event p_4, P could at most know what Q was *planning* to do at q_3.)

This definition will appear quite natural to the reader familiar with the invariant space-time formulation of special relativity, as described for example in [1] or the first chapter of [2]. In relativity, the ordering of events is defined in terms of messages that *could* be sent. However, we have taken the more pragmatic approach of only considering messages that actually *are* sent. We should be able to determine if a system performed correctly by knowing only those events which *did* occur, without knowing which events *could* have occurred.

Logical Clocks

We now introduce clocks into the system. We begin with an abstract point of view in which a clock is just a way of assigning a number to an event, where the number is thought of as the time at which the event occurred. More precisely, we define a clock C_i for each process P_i to be a function which assigns a number $C_i\langle a\rangle$ to any event a in that process. The entire system of clocks is represented by the function C which assigns to any event b the number $C\langle b\rangle$, where $C\langle b\rangle = C_j\langle b\rangle$ if b is an event in process P_j. For now, we make no assumption about the relation of the numbers $C_i\langle a\rangle$ to physical time, so we can think of the clocks C_i as logical rather than physical clocks. They may be implemented by counters with no actual timing mechanism.

We now consider what it means for such a system of clocks to be correct. We cannot base our definition of correctness on physical time, since that would require introducing clocks which keep physical time. Our definition must be based on the order in which events occur. The strongest reasonable condition is that if an event a occurs before another event b, then a should happen at an earlier time than b. We state this condition more formally as follows.

Clock Condition For any events a, b: if $a \to b$ then $C\langle a\rangle < C\langle b\rangle$.

Note that we cannot expect the converse condition to hold as well, since that would imply that any two concurrent events must occur at the same time. In Figure 1, p_2 and p_3 are both concurrent with q_3, so this would mean that they both must occur at the same time as q_3, which would contradict the Clock Condition because $p_2 \to p_3$.

It is easy to see from our definition of the relation "$\to$" that the Clock Condition is satisfied if the following two conditions hold.

C1 If a and b are events in process P_i, and a comes before b, then $C_i\langle a\rangle < C_i\langle b\rangle$.

C2 If a is the sending of a message by process P_i and b is the receipt of that message by process P_j, then $C_i\langle a\rangle < C_j\langle b\rangle$.

Let us consider the clocks in terms of a space-time diagram. We imagine that a process' clock "ticks" through every number, with the ticks occurring between the process' events. For example, if a and b are consecutive events in process P_i with $C_i\langle a\rangle = 4$ and $C_i\langle b\rangle = 7$, then clock ticks 5, 6, and 7 occur between the two events. We draw a dashed "tick line" through all the like-numbered ticks of the different processes. The space-time diagram of Figure 1 might then yield the picture in Figure 2. Condition C1 means that there must be a tick line between any two events on a process line, and condition C2 means that every message line must cross a tick line. From the pictorial meaning of $\to$, it is easy to see why these two conditions imply the Clock Condition.

We can consider the tick lines to be the time coordinate lines of some Cartesian coordinate system on space-time. We can redraw Figure 2 to straighten these

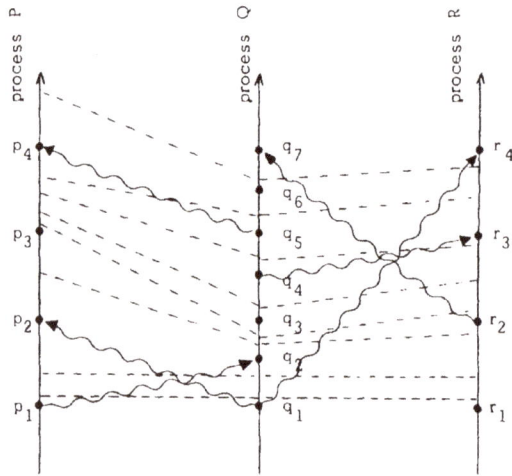

Figure 2

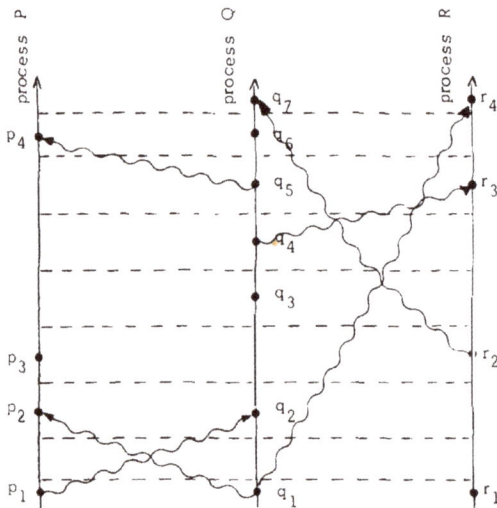

Figure 3

coordinate lines, thus obtaining Figure 3. Figure 3 is a valid alternate way of representing the same system of events as Figure 2. Without introducing the concept of
physical time into the system (which requires introducing physical clocks), there is
no way to decide which of these pictures is a better representation.

The reader may find it helpful to visualize a two-dimensional spatial network of processes, which yields a three-dimensional space-time diagram. Processes and messages are still represented by lines, but tick lines become two-dimensional surfaces.

Let us now assume that the processes are algorithms, and the events represent certain actions during their execution. We will show how to introduce clocks into the processes which satisfy the Clock Condition. Process P_i's clock is represented by a register C_i, so that $C_i\langle a\rangle$ is the value contained by C_i during the event a. The value of C_i will change between events, so changing C_i does not itself constitute an event.

To guarantee that the system of clocks satisfies the Clock Condition, we will insure that it satisfies conditions C1 and C2. Condition C1 is simple; the processes need only obey the following implementation rule:

IR1   Each process P_i increments C_i between any two successive events.

To meet condition C2, we require that each message m contain a *timestamp* T_m which equals the time at which the message was sent. Upon receiving a message timestamped T_m, a process must advance its clock to be later than T_m. More precisely, we have the following rule.

IR2   (a) If event a is the sending of a message m by process P_i, then the message m contains a timestamp $T_m = C_i\langle a\rangle$. (b) Upon receiving a message m, process P_j sets C_j greater than or equal to its present value and greater than T_m.

In IR2(b) we consider the event which represents the receipt of the message m to occur after the setting of C_j. (This is just a notational nuisance, and is irrelevant in any actual implementation.) Obviously, IR2 insures that C2 is satisfied. Hence, the simple implementation rules IR1 and IR2 imply that the Clock Condition is satisfied, so they guarantee a correct system of logical clocks.

Ordering the Events Totally

We can use a system of clocks satisfying the Clock Condition to place a total ordering on the set of all system events. We simply order the events by the times at which they occur. To break ties, we use any arbitrary total ordering $\prec$ of the processes. More precisely, we define a relation $\Rightarrow$ as follows: if a is an event in process P_i and b is an event in process P_j, then $a \Rightarrow b$ if and only if either (i) $C_i\langle a\rangle < C_j\langle b\rangle$ or (ii) $C_i\langle a\rangle = C_j\langle b\rangle$ and $P_i \prec P_j$. It is easy to see that this defines a total ordering, and that the Clock Condition implies that if $a \rightarrow b$ then $a \Rightarrow b$. In other words, the relation $\Rightarrow$ is a way of completing the "happened before" partial ordering to a total ordering.[3]

The ordering $\Rightarrow$ depends upon the system of clocks C_i, and is not unique. Different choices of clocks which satisfy the Clock Condition yield different relations $\Rightarrow$. Given any total ordering relation $\Rightarrow$ which extends $\rightarrow$, there is a system of clocks satisfying the Clock Condition which yields that relation. It is only the partial ordering $\rightarrow$ which is uniquely determined by the system of events.

Being able to totally order the events can be very useful in implementing a distributed system. In fact, the reason for implementing a correct system of logical clocks is to obtain such a total ordering. We will illustrate the use of this total ordering of events by solving the following version of the mutual exclusion problem. Consider a system composed of a fixed collection of processes which share a single resource. Only one process can use the resource at a time, so the processes must synchronize themselves to avoid conflict. We wish to find an algorithm for granting the resource to a process which satisfies the following three conditions: (I) A process which has been granted the resource must release it before it can be granted to another process. (II) Different requests for the resource must be granted in the order in which they are made. (III) If every process which is granted the resource eventually releases it, then every request is eventually granted.

We assume that the resource is initially granted to exactly one process.

These are perfectly natural requirements. They precisely specify what it means for a solution to be correct.[4] Observe how the conditions involve the ordering of events. Condition II says nothing about which of two concurrently issued requests should be granted first.

It is important to realize that this is a nontrivial problem. Using a central scheduling process which grants requests in the order they are received will not work, unless additional assumptions are made. To see this, let P_0 be the scheduling process. Suppose P_1 sends a request to P_0 and then sends a message to P_2. Upon receiving the latter message, P_2 sends a request to P_0. It is possible for P_2's request to reach P_0 before P_1's request does. Condition II is then violated if P_2's request is granted first.

To solve the problem, we implement a system of clocks with rules IR1 and IR2, and use them to define a total ordering $\Rightarrow$ of all events. This provides a total

---

3. The ordering $\prec$ establishes a priority among the processes. If a "fairer" method is desired, then $\prec$ can be made a function of the clock value. For example, if $C_i \langle a \rangle = C_j \langle b \rangle$ and $j < i$, then we can let $a \Rightarrow b$ if $j < C_i \langle a \rangle \bmod N \leq i$, and $b \Rightarrow a$ otherwise; where N is the total number of processes.
4. The term "eventually" should be made precise, but that would require too long a diversion from our main topic.

ordering of all request and release operations. With this ordering, finding a solution becomes a straightforward exercise. It just involves making sure that each process learns about all other processes' operations.

To simplify the problem, we make some assumptions. They are not essential, but they are introduced to avoid distracting implementation details. We assume first of all that for any two processes P_i and P_j, the messages sent from P_i to P_j are received in the same order as they are sent. Moreover, we assume that every message is eventually received. (These assumptions can be avoided by introducing message numbers and message acknowledgment protocols.) We also assume that a process can send messages directly to every other process.

Each process maintains its own *request queue* which is never seen by any other process. We assume that the request queues initially contain the single message T_0: P_0 *requests resource*, where P_0 is the process initially granted the resource and T_0 is less than the initial value of any clock.

The algorithm is then defined by the following five rules. For convenience, the actions defined by each rule are assumed to form a single event.

1. To request the resource, process P_i sends the message T_m: P_i *requests resource* to every other process, and puts that message on its request queue, where T_m is the timestamp of the message.

2. When process P_j receives the message T_m: P_i *requests resource*, it places it on its request queue and sends a (timestamped) acknowledgment message to P_i.[5]

3. To release the resource, process P_i removes any T_m: P_i *requests resource* message from its request queue and sends a (timestamped) P_i *releases resource* message to every other process.

4. When process P_j receives a P_i *releases resource* message, it removes any T_m: P_i *requests resource* message from its request queue.

5. Process P_i is granted the resource when the following two conditions are satisfied: (i) There is a T_m: P_i *requests resource* message in its request queue which is ordered before any other request in its queue by the relation $\Rightarrow$. (To define the relation "$\Rightarrow$" for messages, we identify a message with the event of sending it.) (ii) P_i has received a message from every other process timestamped later than T_m.[6]

---

5. This acknowledgment message need not be sent if P_j has already sent a message to P_i timestamped later than T_m.

6. If $P_i \prec P_j$, then P_i need only have received a message timestamped $\geq T_m$ from P_j.

Note that conditions (i) and (ii) of rule 5 are tested locally by P_i.

It is easy to verify that the algorithm defined by these rules satisfies conditions I–III. First of all, observe that condition (ii) of rule 5, together with the assumption that messages are received in order, guarantees that P_i has learned about all requests which preceded its current request. Since rules 3 and 4 are the only ones which delete messages from the request queue, it is then easy to see that condition I holds. Condition II follows from the fact that the total ordering $\Rightarrow$ extends the partial ordering $\rightarrow$. Rule 2 guarantees that after P_i requests the resource, condition (ii) of rule 5 will eventually hold. Rules 3 and 4 imply that if each process which is granted the resource eventually releases it, then condition (i) of rule 5 will eventually hold, thus proving condition III.

This is a distributed algorithm. Each process independently follows these rules, and there is no central synchronizing process or central storage. This approach can be generalized to implement any desired synchronization for such a distributed multiprocess system. The synchronization is specified in terms of a *State Machine*, consisting of a set $\mathbf{C}$ of possible commands, a set $\mathbf{S}$ of possible states, and a function $\mathbf{e}: \mathbf{C} \times \mathbf{S} \rightarrow \mathbf{S}$. The relation $\mathbf{e}(C, S) = S'$ means that executing the command C with the machine in state S causes the machine state to change to S'. In our example, the set $\mathbf{C}$ consists of all the commands P_i *requests resource* and P_i *releases resource*, and the state consists of a queue of waiting request commands, where the request at the head of the queue is the currently granted one. Executing a *request* command adds the request to the tail of the queue, and executing a *release* command removes a command from the queue.[7]

Each process independently simulates the execution of the State Machine, using the commands issued by all the processes. Synchronization is achieved because all processes order the commands according to their timestamps (using the relation $\Rightarrow$), so each process uses the same sequence of commands. A process can execute a command timestamped T when it has learned of all commands issued by all other processes with timestamps less than or equal to T. The precise algorithm is straightforward, and we will not bother to describe it.

This method allows one to implement any desired form of multiprocess synchronization in a distributed system. However, the resulting algorithm requires the active participation of all the processes. A process must know all the commands issued by other processes, so that the failure of a single process will make it impos-

---

7. If each process does not strictly alternate request and release commands, then executing a *release* command could delete zero, one, or more than one request from the queue.

sible for any other process to execute State Machine commands, thereby halting the system.

The problem of failure is a difficult one, and it is beyond the scope of this paper to discuss it in any detail. We will just observe that the entire concept of failure is only meaningful in the context of physical time. Without physical time, there is no way to distinguish a failed process from one which is just pausing between events. A user can tell that a system has "crashed" only because he has been waiting too long for a response. A method which works despite the failure of individual processes or communication lines is described in [3].

Anomalous Behavior

Our resource scheduling algorithm ordered the requests according to the total ordering $\Rightarrow$. This permits the following type of "anomalous behavior." Consider a nationwide system of interconnected computers. Suppose a person issues a request A on a computer A, and then telephones a friend in another city to have him issue a request B on a different computer B. It is quite possible for request B to receive a lower timestamp and be ordered before request A. This can happen because the system has no way of knowing that A actually preceded B, since that precedence information is based on messages external to the system.

Let us examine the source of the problem more closely. Let $\mathcal{S}$ be the set of all system events. Let us introduce a set of events which contains the events in $\mathcal{S}$ together with all other relevant external events, such as the phone calls in our example. Let $\rightarrow$ denote the "happened before" relation for $\underline{\mathcal{S}}$. In our example, we had A $\rightarrow$ B, but A $\nrightarrow$ B. It is obvious that no algorithm based entirely upon events in $\mathcal{S}$, and which does not relate those events in any way with the other events in $\underline{\mathcal{S}}$, can guarantee that request A is ordered before request B.

There are two possible ways to avoid such anomalous behavior. The first way is to explicitly introduce into the system the necessary information about the ordering $\rightarrow$. In our example, the person issuing request A could receive the timestamp T_A of that request from the system. When issuing request B, his friend could specify that B be given a timestamp later than T_A. This gives the user the responsibility for avoiding anomalous behavior.

The second approach is to construct a system of clocks which satisfies the following condition.

Strong Clock Condition   For any events a, b in $\mathcal{S}$: if $a \rightarrow b$ then $C \langle a \rangle < C \langle b \rangle$.

This is stronger than the ordinary Clock Condition because $\Rightarrow$ is a stronger relation than $\rightarrow$. It is not in general satisfied by our logical clocks.

Let us identify $\underline{S}$ with some set of "real" events in physical space-time, and let $\rightarrow$ be the partial ordering of events defined by special relativity. One of the mysteries of the universe is that it is possible to construct a system of physical clocks which, running quite independently of one another, will satisfy the Strong Clock Condition. We can therefore use physical clocks to eliminate anomalous behavior. We now turn our attention to such clocks.

Physical Clocks

Let us introduce a physical time coordinate into our space-time picture, and let $C_i(t)$ denote the reading of the clock C_i at physical time t.[8] For mathematical convenience, we assume that the clocks run continuously rather than in discrete "ticks." (A discrete clock can be thought of as a continuous one in which there is an error of up to $1/2$ "tick" in reading it.) More precisely, we assume that $C_i(t)$ is a continuous, differentiable function of t except for isolated jump discontinuities where the clock is reset. Then $dC_i(t)/dt$ represents the rate at which the clock is running at time t.

In order for the clock C_i to be a true physical clock, it must run at approximately the correct rate. That is, we must have $dC_i(t)/dt \approx 1$ for all t. More precisely, we will assume that the following condition is satisfied:

PC1   There exists a constant $\kappa \ll 1$ such that for all i: $|dC_i(t)/dt - 1| < \kappa$.

For typical crystal controlled clocks, $\kappa \leq 10^{-6}$.

It is not enough for the clocks individually to run at approximately the correct rate. They must be synchronized so that $C_i(t) \approx C_j(t)$ for all i, j, and t. More precisely, there must be a sufficiently small constant ϵ so that the following condition holds:

PC2   For all i, j: $|C_i(t) - C_j(t)| < \epsilon$.

If we consider vertical distance in Figure 2 to represent physical time, then PC2 states that the variation in height of a single tick line is less than ϵ.

Since two different clocks will never run at exactly the same rate, they will tend to drift further and further apart. We must therefore devise an algorithm to insure

---

8. We will assume a Newtonian space-time. If the relative motion of the clocks or gravitational effects are not negligible, then $C_i(t)$ must be deduced from the actual clock reading by transforming from proper time to the arbitrarily chosen time coordinate.

that PC2 always holds. First, however, let us examine how small κ and ϵ must be to prevent anomalous behavior. We must insure that the system $\underline{S}$ of relevant physical events satisfies the Strong Clock Condition. We assume that our clocks satisfy the ordinary Clock Condition, so we need only require that the Strong Clock Condition holds when a and b are events in $\underline{S}$ with $a \not\rightarrow b$. Hence, we need only consider events occurring in different processes.

Let μ be a number such that if event a occurs at physical time t and event b in another process satisfies $a \rightarrow b$, then b occurs later than physical time $t + \mu$. In other words, μ is less than the shortest transmission time for interprocess messages. We can always choose μ equal to the shortest distance between processes divided by the speed of light. However, depending upon how messages in $\underline{S}$ are transmitted, μ could be significantly larger.

To avoid anomalous behavior, we must make sure that for any i, j, and t: $C_i(t + \mu) - C_j(t) > 0$. Combining this with PC1 and 2 allows us to relate the required smallness of κ and ϵ to the value of μ as follows. We assume that when a clock is reset, it is always set forward and never back. (Setting it back could cause C1 to be violated.) PC1 then implies that $C_i(t + \mu) - C_i(t) > (1 - \kappa)\mu$. Using PC2, it is then easy to deduce that $C_i(t + \mu) - C_j(t) > 0$ if the following inequality holds:

$$\epsilon/(1 - \kappa) \leq \mu.$$

This inequality together with PC1 and PC2 implies that anomalous behavior is impossible.

We now describe our algorithm for insuring that PC2 holds. Let m be a message which is sent at physical time t and received at time t'. We define $\nu_m = t' - t$ to be the *total delay* of the message m. This delay will, of course, not be known to the process which receives m. However, we assume that the receiving process knows some *minimum delay* $\mu_m \geq 0$ such that $\mu_m \leq \nu_m$. We call $\xi_m = \nu_m - \mu_m$ the *unpredictable delay* of the message.

We now specialize rules IR1 and 2 for our physical clocks as follows:

IR1'   For each i, if P_i does not receive a message at physical time t, then C_1 is differentiable at t and $dC_i(t)/dt > 0$.

IR2'   (a) If P_i sends a message m at physical time t, then m contains a timestamp $T_m = C_i(t)$. (b) Upon receiving a message m at time t', process P_j sets $C_j(t')$ equal to maximum$(C_j(t' - 0), T_m + \mu_m)$.[9]

---

9. $C_j(t' - 0) = \lim_{\delta \rightarrow 0} C_j(t' - |\delta|)$.

Although the rules are formally specified in terms of the physical time parameter, a process only needs to know its own clock reading and the timestamps of messages it receives. For mathematical convenience, we are assuming that each event occurs at a precise instant of physical time, and different events in the same process occur at different times. These rules are then specializations of rules IR1 and IR2, so our system of clocks satisfies the Clock Condition. The fact that real events have a finite duration causes no difficulty in implementing the algorithm. The only real concern in the implementation is making sure that the discrete clock ticks are frequent enough so C1 is maintained.

We now show that this clock synchronizing algorithm can be used to satisfy condition PC2. We assume that the system of processes is described by a directed graph in which an arc from process P_i to process P_j represents a communication line over which messages are sent directly from P_I to P_j. We say that a message is sent over this arc every τ seconds if for any t, P_i sends at least one message to P_j between physical times t and $t + \tau$. The *diameter* of the directed graph is the smallest number d such that for any pair of distinct processes P_j, P_k, there is a path from P_j to P_k having at most d arcs.

In addition to establishing PC2, the following theorem bounds the length of time it can take the clocks to become synchronized when the system is first started.

Theorem   Assume a strongly connected graph of processes with diameter d which always obeys rules IR1$'$ and IR2$'$. Assume that for any message m, $\mu_m \leq \mu$ for some constant μ, and that for all $t \geq t_0$: (a) PC1 holds. (b) There are constants τ and ξ such that every τ seconds a message with an unpredictable delay less than ξ is sent over every arc. Then PC2 is satisfied with $\epsilon \approx d(2\kappa\tau + \xi)$ for all $t \gtrsim t_0 + \tau d$, where the approximations assume $\mu + \xi \ll \tau$.

The proof of this theorem is surprisingly difficult, and is given in the Appendix. There has been a great deal of work done on the problem of synchronizing physical clocks. We refer the reader to [4] for an introduction to the subject. The methods described in the literature are useful for estimating the message delays μ_m and for adjusting the clock frequencies dC_i/dt (for clocks which permit such an adjustment). However, the requirement that clocks are never set backwards seems to distinguish our situation from ones previously studied, and we believe this theorem to be a new result.

Conclusion

We have seen that the concept of "happening before" defines an invariant partial ordering of the events in a distributed multiprocess system. We described an algorithm for extending that partial ordering to a somewhat arbitrary total ordering, and showed how this total ordering can be used to solve a simple synchronization problem. A future paper will show how this approach can be extended to solve any synchronization problem.

The total ordering defined by the algorithm is somewhat arbitrary. It can produce anomalous behavior if it disagrees with the ordering perceived by the system's users. This can be prevented by the use of properly synchronized physical clocks. Our theorem showed how closely the clocks can be synchronized.

In a distributed system, it is important to realize that the order in which events occur is only a partial ordering. We believe that this idea is useful in understanding any multiprocess system. It should help one to understand the basic problems of multiprocessing independently of the mechanisms used to solve them.

Appendix

Proof of the Theorem For any i and t, let us define C_i^t to be a clock which is set equal to C_i at time t and runs at the same rate as C_i, but is never reset. In other words,

$$C_i^t(t') = C_i(t) + \int_t^{t'} [dC_i(t)/dt]dt \tag{1}$$

for all $t' \geq t$. Note that

$$C_i(t') \geq C_i^t(t') \quad \text{for all } t' \geq t. \tag{2}$$

Suppose process P_1 at time t_1 sends a message to process P_2 which is received at time t_2 with an unpredictable delay $\leq \xi$, where $t_0 \leq t_1 \leq t_2$. Then for all $t \geq t_2$ we have:

$$
\begin{aligned}
C_2^{t_2}(t) &\geq C_2^{t_2}(t_2) + (1-\kappa)(t-t_2) && \text{[by (1) and PC1]} \\
&\geq C_1(t_1) + \mu_m + (1-\kappa)(t-t_2) && \text{[by IR2$'$(b)]} \\
&= C_1(t_1) + (1-\kappa)(t-t_1) - [(t_2 - t_1) - \mu_m] + \kappa(t_2 - t_1) \\
&\geq C_1(t_1) + (1-\kappa)(t-t_1) - \xi.
\end{aligned}
$$

Hence, with these assumptions, for all $t \geq t_2$ we have:

$$C_2^{t_2}(t) \geq C_1(t_1) + (1-\kappa)(t-t_1) - \xi. \tag{3}$$

Now suppose that for $i = 1, \ldots, n$ we have $t_i \leq t_i' < t_{i+1}, t_0 \leq t_1$, and that at time t_i' process P_i sends a message to process P_{i+1} which is received at time t_{i+1} with an unpredictable delay less than ξ. Then repeated application of the inequality (3) yields the following result for $t \geq t_{n+1}$.

$$C_{n+1}^{t_{n+1}}(t) \geq C_1(t_1') + (1-\kappa)(t - t_1') - n\xi. \tag{4}$$

From PC1, IRI$'$ and 2$'$ we deduce that

$$C_1(t_1') \geq C_1(t_1) + (1-\kappa)(t_1' - t_1).$$

Combining this with (4) and using (2), we get

$$C_{n+1}(t) \geq C_1(t_1) + (1-\kappa)(t - t_1) - n\xi \tag{5}$$

for $t \geq t_{n+1}$.

For any two processes P and P$'$, we can find a sequence of processes P $=$ $P_0, P_1, \ldots, P_{n+1} = P'$, $n \leq d$, with communication arcs from each P_i to P_{i+1}. By hypothesis (b) we can find times t_i, t_i' with $t_i' - t_i \leq \tau$ and $t_{i+1} - t_i' \leq \nu$, where $\nu = \mu + \xi$. Hence, an inequality of the form (5) holds with $n \leq d$ whenever $t \geq t_1 + d(\tau + \nu)$. For any i, j and any t, t_1 with $t_1 \geq t_0$ and $t \geq t_1 + d(\tau + \nu)$ we therefore have:

$$C_i(t) \geq C_j(t_1) + (1-\kappa)(t - t_1) - d\xi. \tag{6}$$

Now let m be any message timestamped T_m, and suppose it is sent at time t and received at time t'. We pretend that m has a clock C_m which runs at a constant rate such that $C_m(t) = t_m$ and $C_m(t') = t_m + \mu_m$. Then $\mu_m \leq t' - t$ implies that $dC_m/dt \leq 1$. Rule IR2$'$(b) simply sets $C_j(t')$ to $maximum(C_j(t'-0), C_m(t'))$. Hence, clocks are reset only by setting them equal to other clocks.

For any time $t_x \geq t_0 + \mu/(1-\kappa)$, let C_x be the clock having the largest value at time t_x. Since all clocks run at a rate less than $1 + \kappa$, we have for all i and all $t \geq t_x$:

$$C_i(t) \leq C_x(t_x) + (1+\kappa)(t - t_x). \tag{7}$$

We now consider the following two cases: (i) C_x is the clock C_q of process P_q. (ii) C_x is the clock C_m of a message sent at time t_1 by process P_q. In case (i), (7) simply becomes

$$C_i(t) \leq C_q(t_x) + (1+\kappa)(t - t_x). \tag{8i}$$

In case (ii), since $C_m(t_1) = C_q(t_1)$ and $dC_m/dt \leq 1$, we have

$$C_x(t_x) \leq C_q(t_1) + (t_x - t_1).$$

Hence, (7) yields

$$C_i(t) \leq C_q(t_1) + (1+\kappa)(t - t_1). \tag{8ii}$$

Since $t_x \geq t_0 + \mu/(1 - \kappa)$, we get

$$C_q(t_x - \mu/(1 - \kappa)) \leq C_q(t_x) - \mu \qquad \text{[by PC1]}$$

$$\leq C_m(t_x) - \mu \qquad \text{[by choice of } m]$$

$$\leq C_m(t_x) - (t_x - t_1)\mu_m/\nu_m \qquad [\mu_m \leq \mu, t_x - t_1 \leq \nu_m]$$

$$= T_m \qquad \text{[by definition of } C_m]$$

$$= C_q(t_1) \qquad \text{[by IR2}'\text{(a)]}$$

Hence, $C_q(t_x - \mu/(1 - \kappa)) \leq C_q(t_1)$, so $t_x - t_1 \leq \mu/(1 - \kappa)$ and thus $t_1 \geq t_0$.

Letting $t_1 = t_x$ in case (i), we can combine (8i) and (8ii) to deduce that for any t, t_x, with $t \geq t_x \geq t_0 + \mu/(1 - \kappa)$ there is a process P_q and a time t_1 with $t_x - \mu/(1 - \kappa) \leq t_1 \leq t_x$ such that for all i:

$$C_i(t) \leq C_q(t_1) + (1 + \kappa)(t - t_1). \tag{9}$$

Choosing t and t_x with $t \geq t_x + d(\tau + \nu)$, we can combine (6) and (9) to conclude that there exists a t_1 and a process P_q such that for all i:

$$C_q(t_1) + (1 - \kappa)(t - t_1) - d\xi \leq C_i(t)$$
$$\leq C_q(t_1) + (1 + \kappa)(t - t_1) \tag{10}$$

Letting $t = t_x + d(\tau + \nu)$, we get

$$d(\tau + \nu) \leq t - t_1 \leq d(\tau + \nu) + \mu/(1 - \kappa).$$

Combining this with (10), we get

$$C_q(t_1) + (t - t_1) - \kappa d(\tau + \nu) - d\xi \leq C_i(t) C_q(t_1)$$
$$+ (t - t_1) + \kappa[d(\tau + \nu) + \mu/(1 - \kappa)] \tag{11}$$

Using the hypothesis that $\kappa \ll 1$ and $\mu \leq \nu \ll \tau$, we can rewrite (11) as the following approximate inequality.

$$C_q(t_1) + (t - t_1) - d(\kappa\tau + \xi) \lesssim C_i(t)$$
$$\lesssim C_q(t_1) + (t - t_1) + d\kappa\tau. \tag{12}$$

Since this holds for all i, we get

$$|C_i(t) - C_j(t)| \lesssim d(2\kappa\tau + \xi),$$

and this holds for all $t \gtrsim t_0 + dt$.

Note that relation (11) of the proof yields an exact upper bound for $|C_i(t) - C_j(t)|$ in case the assumption $\mu + \xi \ll \tau$ is invalid. An examination of the proof suggests a simple method for rapidly initializing the clocks, or resynchronizing them if they should go out of synchrony for any reason. Each process sends a message which is relayed to every other process. The procedure can be initiated by any process, and requires less than $2d(\mu + \xi)$ seconds to effect the synchronization, assuming each of the messages has an unpredictable delay less than ξ.

Acknowledgment. The use of timestamps to order operations, and the concept of anomalous behavior are due to Paul Johnson and Robert Thomas.

Received March 1976; revised October 1977

References

[1] Schwartz, J.T. *Relativity in Illustrations.* New York U. Press, New York, 1962.

[2] Taylor, E.F., and Wheeler, J.A. *Space-Time Physics*, W.H. Freeman, San Francisco, 1966.

[3] Lamport, L. The implementation of reliable distributed multiprocess systems. To appear in *Computer Networks.*

[4] Ellingson, C., and Kulpinski, R.J. Dissemination of system-time. *IEEE Trans. Comm. Com-23,* 5 (May 1973), 605–624.

How to Make a Multiprocessor Computer That Correctly Executes Multiprocess Programs

Leslie Lamport

Abstract—Many large sequential computers execute operations in a different order than is specified by the program. A correct execution is achieved if the results produced are the same as would be produced by executing the program steps in order. For a multiprocessor computer, such a correct execution by each processor does not guarantee the correct execution of the entire program. Additional conditions are given which do guarantee that a computer correctly executes multiprocess programs.

Index Terms—Computer design, concurrent computing, hardware correctness, multiprocessing, parallel processing.

A high-speed processor may execute operations in a different order than is specified by the program. The correctness of the execution is guaranteed if the processor satisfies the following condition: the result of an execution is the same as if the operations had been executed in the order specified by the program. A processor satisfying this condition will be called *sequential*. Consider a computer composed of several such processors accessing a common memory. The customary approach to designing and proving the correctness of multiprocess algorithms [1]–[3] for

Manuscript received September 28, 1977; revised May 8, 1979.

The author is with the Computer Science Laboratory, SRI International, Menlo Park, CA 94025.

Paper originally published in *IEEE Transactions on Computers* C-28(9), September 1979, pp. 690–691.

such a computer assumes that the following condition is satisfied: the result of any execution is the same as if the operations of all the processors were executed in some sequential order, and the operations of each individual processor appear in this sequence in the order specified by its program. A multiprocessor satisfying this condition will be called *sequentially consistent.* The sequentiality of each individual processor does not guarantee that the multiprocessor computer is sequentially consistent. In this brief note, we describe a method of interconnecting sequential processors with memory modules that insures the sequential consistency of the resulting multiprocessor.

We assume that the computer consists of a collection of processors and memory modules, and that the processors communicate with one another only through the memory modules. (Any special communication registers may be regarded as separate memory modules.) The only processor operations that concern us are the operations of sending fetch and store requests to memory modules. We assume that each processor issues a sequence of such requests. (It must sometimes wait for requests to be executed, but that does not concern us.)

We illustrate the problem by considering a simple two-process mutual exclusion protocol. Each process contains a *critical section,* and the purpose of the protocol is to insure that only one process may be executing its critical section at any time. The protocol is as follows.

<u>process 1</u>
   a := 1;
  <u>if</u> b = 0 <u>then</u> critical section;
             a := 0
       else ... <u>fi</u>

<u>process 2</u>
   b := 1;
  if a = 0 <u>then</u> critical section;
             b := 0
      <u>else</u> ... <u>fi</u>

The <u>else</u> clauses contain some mechanism for guaranteeing eventual access to the critical section, but that is irrelevant to the discussion. It is easy to prove that this protocol guarantees mutually exclusive access to the critical sections. (Devising a proof provides a nice exercise in using the assertional techniques of [2] and [3], and is left to the reader.) Hence, when this two-process program is executed by a sequentially consistent multiprocessor computer, the two processors cannot both be executing their critical sections at the same time.

We first observe that a sequential processor could execute the "b := 1" and "fetch b" operations of process 1 in either order. (When process 1's program is considered by itself, it does not matter in which order these two operations are performed.) However, it is easy to see that executing the "fetch b" operation first can lead to an error—both processes could then execue their critical sections at the same time. This immediately suggests our first requirement for a multiprocessor computer.

Requirement R1 Each processor issues memory requests in the order specified by its program.

Satisfying Requirement R1 is complicated by the fact that storing a value is possible only after the value has been computed. A processor will often be ready to issue a memory fetch request before it knows the value to be stored by a preceding store request. To minimize waiting, the processor can issue the store request to the memory module without specifying the value to be stored. Of course, the store request cannot actually be executed by the memory module until it receives the value to be stored.

Requirement R1 is not sufficient to guarantee correct execution. To see this, suppose that each memory module has several ports, and each port services one processor (or I/O channel). Let the values of "a" and "b" be stored in separate memory modules, and consider the following sequence of events.

1. Processor 1 sends the "a := 1" request to its port in memory module 1. The module is currently busy executing an operation for some other processor (or I/O channel).

2. Processor 1 sends the "fetch b" request to its port in memory module 2. The module is free, and execution is begun.

3. Processor 2 sends its "b := 1" request to memory module 2. This request will be executed after processor 1's "fetch b" request is completed.

4. Processor 2 sends its "fetch a" request to its port in memory module 1. The module is still busy.

There are now two operations waiting to be performed by memory module 1. If processor 2's "fetch a" operation is performed first, then both processes can enter their critical sections at the same time, and the protocol fails. This could happen if the memory module uses a round robin scheduling discipline in servicing its ports.

In this situation, an error occurs only if the two requests to memory module 1 are not executed in the same order in which they were received. This suggests the following requirement.

Requirement R2   Memory requests from all processors issued to an individual memory module are serviced from a single FIFO queue. Issuing a memory request consists of entering the request on this queue.

Condition R1 implies that a processor may not issue any further memory requests until after its current request has been entered on the queue. Hence, it must wait if the queue is full. If two or more processors are trying to enter requests in the queue at the same time, then it does not matter in which order they are serviced.

Note   If a fetch requests the contents of a memory location for which there is already a write request on the queue, then the fetch need not be entered on the queue. It may simply return the value from the last such write request on the queue.

Requirements R1 and R2 insure that if the individual processors are sequential, then the entire multiprocessor computer is sequentially consistent. To demonstrate this, one first introduces a relation $\rightarrow$ on memory requests as follows. Define $A \rightarrow B$ if and only if 1) A and B are issued by the same processor and A is issued before B, or 2) A and B are issued to the same memory module, and A is entered in the queue before B (and is thus executed before B). It is easy to see that R1 and R2 imply that $\rightarrow$ is a partial ordering on the set of memory requests. Using the sequentiality of each processor, one can then prove the following result: each fetch and store operation fetches or stores the same value as if all the operations were executed sequentially in any order such that $A \rightarrow B$ implies that A is executed before B. This in turn proves the sequential consistency of the multiprocessor computer.

Requirement R2 states that a memory module's request queue must be serviced in a FIFO order. This implies that the memory module must remain idle if the request at the head of its queue is a store request for which the value to be stored has not yet been received. Condition R2 can be weakened to allow the memory module to service other requests in this situation. We need only require that all requests *to the same memory cell* be serviced in the order that they appear in the queue. Requests to different memory cells may be serviced out of order. Sequential consistency is preserved because such a service policy is logically equivalent to considering each memory cell to be a separate memory module with its own request queue. (The fact that these modules may share some hardware affects the rate at which they service requests and the capacity of their queues, but it does not affect the logical property of sequential consistency.)

The requirements needed to guarantee consistency rule out some techniques which can be used to speed up individual sequential processors. For some applications, achieving sequential consistency may not be worth the price of slowing down the processors. In this case, one must be aware that conventional methods for designing multiprocess algorithms cannot be relied upon to produce correctly executing programs. Protocols for synchronizing the processors must be designed at the lowest level of the machine instruction code, and verifying their correctness becomes a monumental task.

References

[1] E. W. Dijkstra, "Hierarchical ordering of sequential processes," *Acta Informatica,* vol. 1, pp. 115–138, 1971.

[2] L. Lamport, "Proving the correctness of multiprocess programs," *IEEE Trans. Software Eng.*, vol. SE-3, pp. 125–143, Mar. 1977.

[3] S. Owicki and D. Gries, "Verifying properties of parallel programs: an axiomatic approach," *Commun. Assoc. Comput. Mach.*, vol. 19, pp. 279–285, May 1976.

The Byzantine Generals Problem

Leslie Lamport (SRI International),
Robert Shostak (SRI International),
Marshall Pease (SRI International)

Reliable computer systems must handle malfunctioning components that give conflicting information to different parts of the system. This situation can be expressed abstractly in terms of a group of generals of the Byzantine army camped with their troops around an enemy city. Communicating only by messenger, the generals must agree upon a common battle plan. However, one or more of them may be traitors who will try to confuse the others. The problem is to find an algorithm to ensure that the loyal generals will reach agreement. It is shown that, using only oral messages, this problem is solvable if and only if more than two-thirds of the generals are loyal; so a single traitor can confound two loyal generals. With unforgeable written messages, the problem is solvable for any number of

This research was supported in part by the National Aeronautics and Space Administration under contract NAS1-15428 Mod. 3, the Ballistic Missile Defense Systems Command under contract DASG60-78-C-0046, and the Army Research Office under contract DAAG29-79-C-0102.

Authors' address: Computer Science Laboratory, SRI International, 333 Ravenswood Avenue, Menlo Park, CA 94025.

Paper originally published in *Transactions on Programming Languages and Systems*, 4(3), July 1982, pp. 382–401.

generals and possible traitors. Applications of the solutions to reliable computer systems are then discussed.

Categories and Subject Descriptors: C.2.4. [**Computer-Communication Networks**]: Distributed Systems—*network operating systems;* D.4.4 [**Operating Systems**]: Communications Management—*network communication;* D.4.5 [**Operating Systems**]: Reliability—*fault tolerance*

General Terms: Algorithms, Reliability

Additional Key Words and Phrases: Interactive consistency

1 Introduction

A reliable computer system must be able to cope with the failure of one or more of its components. A failed component may exhibit a type of behavior that is often overlooked—namely, sending conflicting information to different parts of the system. The problem of coping with this type of failure is expressed abstractly as the Byzantine Generals Problem. We devote the major part of the paper to a discussion of this abstract problem and conclude by indicating how our solutions can be used in implementing a reliable computer system.

We imagine that several divisions of the Byzantine army are camped outside an enemy city, each division commanded by its own general. The generals can communicate with one another only by messenger. After observing the enemy, they must decide upon a common plan of action. However, some of the generals may be traitors, trying to prevent the loyal generals from reaching agreement. The generals must have an algorithm to guarantee that

A   All loyal generals decide upon the same plan of action.

The loyal generals will all do what the algorithm says they should, but the traitors may do anything they wish. The algorithm must guarantee condition A regardless of what the traitors do.

The loyal generals should not only reach agreement, but should agree upon a reasonable plan. We therefore also want to insure that

B   A small number of traitors cannot cause the loyal generals to adopt a bad plan.

Condition B is hard to formalize, since it requires saying precisely what a bad plan is, and we do not attempt to do so. Instead, we consider how the generals reach a decision. Each general observes the enemy and communicates his observations to the others. Let $v(i)$ be the information communicated by the ith general. Each general uses some method for combining the values $v(1), \ldots, v(n)$ into a single plan of action, where n is the number of generals. Condition A is achieved by having all generals use the same method for combining the information, and Condition B is achieved by using a robust method. For example, if the only decision to be made is whether to attack or retreat, then $v(i)$ can be General i's opinion of which option is best, and the final decision can be based upon a majority vote among them. A small number of traitors can affect the decision only if the loyal generals were almost equally divided between the two possibilities, in which case neither decision could be called bad.

While this approach may not be the only way to satisfy conditions A and B, it is the only one we know of. It assumes a method by which the generals communicate their values $v(i)$ to one another. The obvious method is for the ith general to send $v(i)$ by messenger to each other general. However, this does not work, because satisfying condition A requires that every loyal general obtain the same values $v(1), \ldots, v(n)$, and a traitorous general may send different values to different generals. For condition A to be satisfied, the following must be true:

1. Every loyal general must obtain the same information $v(1), \ldots, v(n)$.

Condition 1 implies that a general cannot necessarily use a value of $v(i)$ obtained directly from the ith general, since a traitorous ith general may send different values to different generals. This means that unless we are careful, in meeting condition 1 we might introduce the possibility that the generals use a value of $v(i)$ different from the one sent by the ith general—even though the ith general is loyal. We must not allow this to happen if condition B is to be met. For example, we cannot permit a few traitors to cause the loyal generals to base their decision upon the values "retreat", $\ldots$, "retreat" if every loyal general sent the value "attack". We therefore have the following requirement for each i:

2. If the ith general is loyal, then the value that he sends must be used by every loyal general as the value of $v(i)$.

We can rewrite condition 1 as the condition that for every i (whether or not the ith general is loyal),

1. Any two loyal generals use the same value of $v(i)$.

Conditions 1' and 2 are both conditions on the single value sent by the ith general. We can therefore restrict our consideration to the problem of how a single general sends his value to the others. We phrase this in terms of a commanding general sending an order to his lieutenants, obtaining the following problem.

Byzantine Generals A commanding general must send an order to his $n - 1$ lieutenant generals such that

IC1   All loyal lieutenants obey the same order.

IC2   If the commanding general is loyal, then every loyal lieutenant obeys the order he sends.

Conditions IC1 and IC2 are called the interactive consistency conditions. Note that if the commander is loyal, then IC1 follows from IC2. However, the commander need not be loyal.

To solve our original problem, the ith general sends his value of $v(i)$ by using a solution to the Byzantine Generals Problem to send the order "use $v(i)$ as my value," with the other generals acting as the lieutenants.

2 Impossibility Results

The Byzantine Generals Problem seems deceptively simple. Its difficulty is indicated by the surprising fact that if the generals can send only oral messages, then no solution will work unless more than two-thirds of the generals are loyal. In particular, with only three generals, no solution can work in the presence of a single traitor. An oral message is one whose contents are completely under the control of the sender, so a traitorous sender can transmit any possible message. Such a message corresponds to the type of message that computers normally send to one another. In Section 4 we consider signed, written messages, for which this is not true.

We now show that with oral messages no solution for three generals can handle a single traitor. For simplicity, we consider the case in which the only possible decisions are "attack" or "retreat". Let us first examine the scenario pictured in Figure 1 in which the commander is loyal and sends an "attack" order, but Lieutenant 2 is a traitor and reports to Lieutenant 1 that he received a "retreat" order. For IC2 to be satisfied, Lieutenant 1 must obey the order to attack.

Now consider another scenario, shown in Figure 2, in which the commander is a traitor and sends an "attack" order to Lieutenant 1 and a "retreat" order to Lieutenant 2. Lieutenant 1 does not know who the traitor is, and he cannot tell what message the commander actually sent to Lieutenant 2. Hence, the scenarios in these two pictures appear exactly the same to Lieutenant 1. If the traitor lies consistently, then there is no way for Lieutenant 1 to distinguish between these two situations, so he must obey the "attack" order in both of them. Hence, whenever Lieutenant 1 receives an "attack" order from the commander, he must obey it.

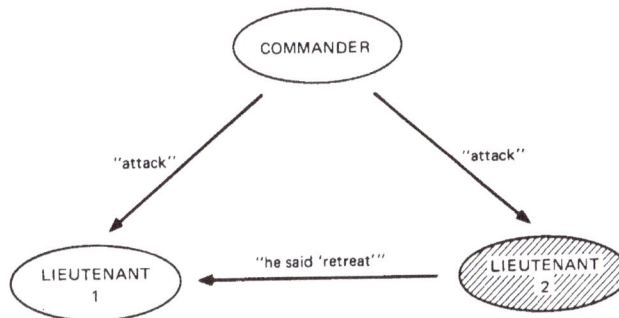

Figure 1   Lieutentant 2 a traitor.

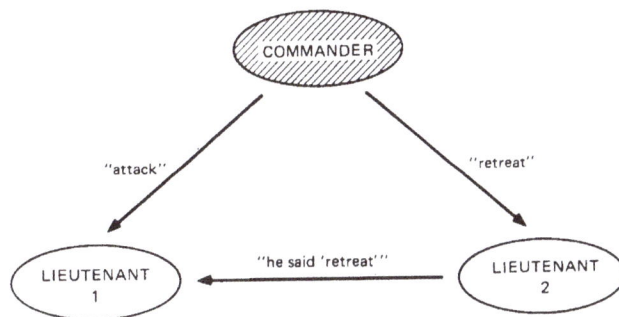

Figure 2   The commander a traitor.

However, a similar argument shows that if Lieutenant 2 receives a "retreat" order from the commander then he must obey it even if Lieutenant 1 tells him that the commander said "attack". Therefore, in the scenario of Figure 2, Lieutenant 2 must obey the "retreat" order while Lieutenant 1 obeys the "attack" order, thereby violating condition IC1. Hence, no solution exists for three generals that works in the presence of a single traitor.

This argument may appear convincing, but we strongly advise the reader to be very suspicious of such nonrigorous reasoning. Although this result is indeed correct, we have seen equally plausible "proofs" of invalid results. We know of no area in computer science or mathematics in which informal reasoning is more likely to lead to errors than in the study of this type of algorithm. For a rigorous proof of the impossibility of a three-general solution that can handle a single traitor, we refer the reader to [3].

Using this result, we can show that no solution with fewer than $3m + 1$ generals can cope with m traitors.[1] The proof is by contradiction—we assume such a solution for a group of $3m$ or fewer and use it to construct a three-general solution to the Byzantine Generals Problem that works with one traitor, which we know to be impossible. To avoid confusion between the two algorithms, we call the generals of the assumed solution Albanian generals, and those of the constructed solution Byzantine generals. Thus, starting from an algorithm that allows $3m$ or fewer Albanian generals to cope with m traitors, we construct a solution that allows three Byzantine generals to handle a single traitor.

The three-general solution is obtained by having each of the Byzantine generals simulate approximately one-third of the Albanian generals, so that each Byzantine general is simulating at most m Albanian generals. The Byzantine commander simulates the Albanian commander plus at most $m - 1$ Albanian lieutenants, and each of the two Byzantine lieutenants simulates at most m Albanian lieutenants. Since only one Byzantine general can be a traitor, and he simulates at most m Albanians, at most m of the Albanian generals are traitors. Hence, the assumed solution guarantees that IC1 and IC2 hold for the Albanian generals. By IC1, all the Albanian lieutenants being simulated by a loyal Byzantine lieutenant obey the same order, which is the order he is to obey. It is easy to check that conditions IC1 and IC2 of the Albanian generals solution imply the corresponding conditions for the Byzantine generals, so we have constructed the required impossible solution.

One might think that the difficulty in solving the Byzantine Generals Problem stems from the requirement of reaching exact agreement. We now demonstrate that this is not the case by showing that reaching approximate agreement is just as hard as reaching exact agreement. Let us assume that instead of trying to agree on a precise battle plan, the generals must agree only upon an approximate time of attack. More precisely, we assume that the commander orders the time of the attack, and we require the following two conditions to hold:

IC1   All loyal lieutenants attack within 10 minutes of one another.

IC2   If the commanding general is loyal, then every loyal lieutenant attacks within 10 minutes of the time given in the commander's order.

---

1. More precisely, no such solution exists for three or more generals, since the problem is trivial for two generals.

2 Impossibility Results **209**

(We assume that the orders are given and processed the day before the attack and that the time at which an order is received is irrelevant—only the attack time given in the order matters.)

Like the Byzantine Generals Problem, this problem is unsolvable unless more than two-thirds of the generals are loyal. We prove this by first showing that if there were a solution for three generals that coped with one traitor, then we could construct a three-general solution to the Byzantine Generals Problem that also worked in the presence of one traitor. Suppose the commander wishes to send an "attack" or "retreat" order. He orders an attack by sending an attack time of 1:00 and orders a retreat by sending an attack time of 2:00, using the assumed algorithm. Each lieutenant uses the following procedure to obtain his order.

1. After receiving the attack time from the commander, a lieutenant does one of the following:
   (a) If the time is 1:10 or earlier, then attack.
   (b) If the time is 1:50 or later, then retreat.
   (c) Otherwise, continue to step (2).

2. Ask the other lieutenant what decision he reached in step (1).
   (a) If the other lieutenant reached a decision, then make the same decision he did.
   (b) Otherwise, retreat.

It follows from IC2′ that if the commander is loyal, then a loyal lieutenant will obtain the correct order in step (1), so IC2 is satisfied. If the commander is loyal, then IC1 follows from IC2, so we need only prove IC1 under the assumption that the commander is a traitor. Since there is at most one traitor, this means that both lieutenants are loyal. It follows from ICI′ that if one lieutenant decides to attack in step (1), then the other cannot decide to retreat in step (1). Hence, either they will both come to the same decision in step (1) or at least one of them will defer his decision until step (2). In this case, it is easy to see that they both arrive at the same decision, so IC1 is satisfied. We have therefore constructed a three-general solution to the Byzantine Generals Problem that handles one traitor, which is impossible. Hence, we cannot have a three-general algorithm that maintains ICI′ and IC2′ in the presence of a traitor.

The method of having one general simulate m others can now be used to prove that no solution with fewer than $3m + 1$ generals can cope with m traitors. The proof is similar to the one for the original Byzantine Generals Problem and is left to the reader.

3 A Solution with Oral Messages

We showed above that for a solution to the Byzantine Generals Problem using oral messages to cope with m traitors, there must be at least $3m + 1$ generals. We now give a solution that works for $3m + 1$ or more generals. However, we first specify exactly what we mean by "oral messages". Each general is supposed to execute some algorithm that involves sending messages to the other generals, and we assume that a loyal general correctly executes his algorithm. The definition of an oral message is embodied in the following assumptions which we make for the generals' message system:

A1   Every message that is sent is delivered correctly.

A2   The receiver of a message knows who sent it.

A3   The absence of a message can be detected.

Assumptions A1 and A2 prevent a traitor from interfering with the communication between two other generals, since by A1 he cannot interfere with the messages they do send, and by A2 he cannot confuse their intercourse by introducing spurious messages. Assumption A3 will foil a traitor who tries to prevent a decision by simply not sending messages. The practical implementation of these assumptions is discussed in Section 6.

The algorithms in this section and in the following one require that each general be able to send messages directly to every other general. In Section 5, we describe algorithms which do not have this requirement.

A traitorous commander may decide not to send any order. Since the lieutenants must obey some order, they need some default order to obey in this case. We let RETREAT be this default order.

We inductively define the Oral Message algorithms OM(m), for all nonnegative integers m, by which a commander sends an order to $n - 1$ lieutenants. We show that OM(m) solves the Byzantine Generals Problem for $3m + 1$ or more generals in the presence of at most m traitors. We find it more convenient to describe this algorithm in terms of the lieutenants "obtaining a value" rather than "obeying an order".

The algorithm assumes a function *majority* with the property that if a majority of the values v_i equal v, then $majority(v_1, \ldots, v_{n-1})$ equals v. (Actually, it assumes a sequence of such functions—one for each n.) There are two natural choices for the value of $majority(v_1, \ldots, v_{n-1})$:

1. The majority value among the v_i if it exists, otherwise the value RETREAT;

2. The median of the v_i, assuming that they come from an ordered set.

The following algorithm requires only the aforementioned property of *majority*.

Algorithm OM(0)
1. The commander sends his value to every lieutenant.

2. Each lieutenant uses the value he receives from the commander, or uses the value RETREAT if he receives no value.

Alg. OM(m), $m > 0$
1. The commander sends his value to every lieutenant.

2. For each i, let v_i be the value Lieutenant i receives from the commander, or else be RETREAT if he receives no value. Lieutenant i acts as the commander in Algorithm OM($m - 1$) to send the value v_i to each of the $n - 2$ other lieutenants.

3. For each i, and each $j \neq i$, let v_j be the value Lieutenant i received from Lieutenant j in step (2) (using Algorithm OM($m - 1$)), or else RETREAT if he received no such value. Lieutenant i uses the value $majority(v_l, \ldots, v_{n-1})$.

To understand how this algorithm works, we consider the case $m = 1, n = 4$. Figure 3 illustrates the messages received by Lieutenant 2 when the commander sends the value v and Lieutenant 3 is a traitor. In the first step of OM(1), the commander sends v to all three lieutenants. In the second step, Lieutenant 1 sends the value v to Lieutenant 2, using the trivial algorithm OM(0). Also in the second step, the traitorous Lieutenant 3 sends Lieutenant 2 some other value x. In step 3, Lieutenant 2 then has $v_1 = v_2 = v$ and $v_3 = x$, so he obtains the correct value $v = majority(v, v, x)$.

Next, we see what happens if the commander is a traitor. Figure 4 shows the values received by the lieutenants if a traitorous commander sends three arbitrary

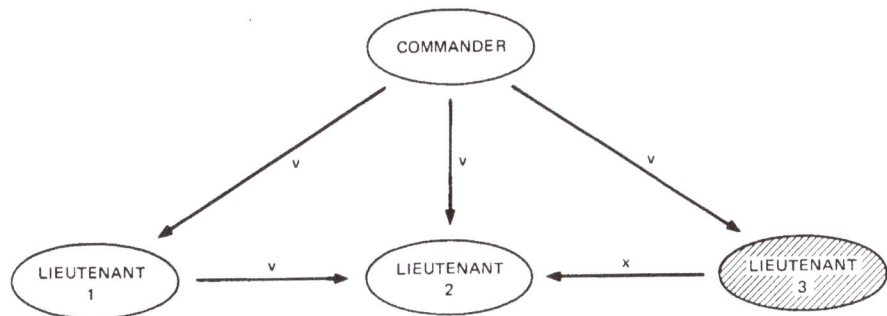

Figure 3 Algorithm OM(1); Lieutenant 3 a traitor.

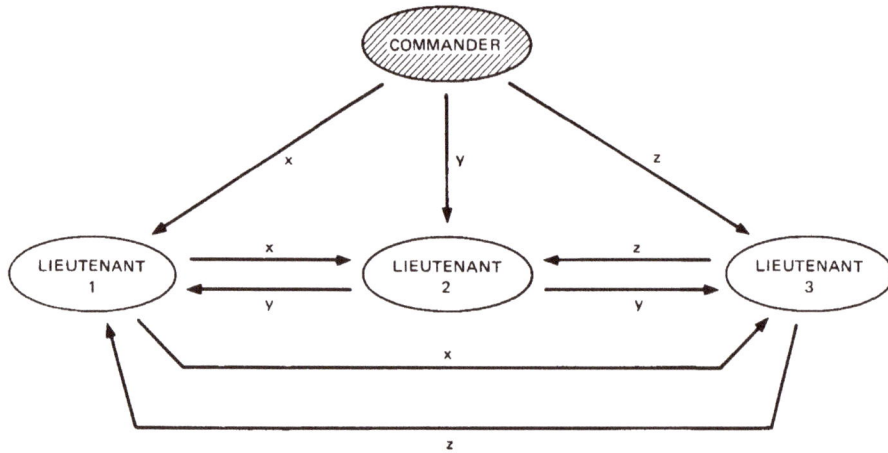

Algorithm OM(1); the commander a traitor.

values x, y, and z to the three lieutenants. Each lieutenant obtains $v_1 = x$, $v_2 = y$, and $v_3 = z$, so they all obtain the same value *majority*(x, y, z) in step (3), regardless of whether or not any of the three values x, y, and z are equal.

The recursive algorithm OM(m) invokes $n - 1$ separate executions of the algorithm OM($m - 1$), each of which invokes $n - 2$ executions of OM($m - 2$), etc. This means that, for $m > 1$, a lieutenant sends many separate messages to each other lieutenant. There must be some way to distinguish among these different messages. The reader can verify that all ambiguity is removed if each lieutenant i prefixes the number i to the value v_i that he sends in step (2). As the recursion "unfolds," the algorithm OM($m - k$) will be called $(n - 1) \cdots (n - k)$ times to send a value prefixed by a sequence of k lieutenants' numbers.

To prove the correctness of the algorithm OM(m) for arbitrary m, we first prove the following lemma.

Lemma 1   For any m and k, Algorithm OM(m) satisfies IC2 if there are more than $2k + m$ generals and at most k traitors.

Proof   The proof is by induction on m. IC2 only specifies what must happen if the commander is loyal. Using A1, it is easy to see that the trivial algorithm OM(0) works if the commander is loyal, so the lemma is true for $m = 0$. We now assume it is true for $m - 1$, $m > 0$, and prove it for m.

In step (1), the loyal commander sends a value v to all $n - 1$ lieutenants. In step (2), each loyal lieutenant applies OM($m - 1$) with $n - 1$ generals. Since by hypothesis $n > 2k + m$, we have $n - 1 > 2k + (m - 1)$, so we can apply the induction hypothesis to conclude that every loyal lieutenant gets $v_j = v$ for each loyal Lieutenant j. Since there are at most k traitors, and $n - 1 > 2k + (m - 1) \geq 2k$, a majority of the $n - 1$ lieutenants are loyal. Hence, each loyal lieutenant has $v_i = v$ for a majority of the $n - 1$ values i, so he obtains $majority(v_1, \ldots, v_{n-1}) = v$ in step (3), proving IC2. ∎

The following theorem asserts that Algorithm OM(m) solves the Byzantine Generals Problem.

Theorem 1 For any m, Algorithm OM(m) satisfies conditions IC1 and IC2 if there are more than $3m$ generals and at most m traitors.

Proof The proof is by induction on m. If there are no traitors, then it is easy to see that OM(0) satisfies IC1 and IC2. We therefore assume that the theorem is true for OM($m - 1$) and prove it for OM(m), $m > 0$.

We first consider the case in which the commander is loyal. By taking k equal to m in Lemma 1, we see that OM(m) satisfies IC2. IC1 follows from IC2 if the commander is loyal, so we need only verify IC1 in the case that the commander is a traitor.

There are at most m traitors, and the commander is one of them, so at most $m - 1$ of the lieutenants are traitors. Since there are more than $3m$ generals, there are more than $3m - 1$ lieutenants, and $3m - 1 > 3(m - 1)$. We may therefore apply the induction hypothesis to conclude that OM($m - 1$) satisfies conditions IC1 and IC2. Hence, for each j, any two loyal lieutenants get the same value for v_j in step (3). (This follows from IC2 if one of the two lieutenants is Lieutenant j, and from IC1 otherwise.) Hence, any two loyal lieutenants get the same vector of values $v_1, \ldots, v_{n-1}$, and therefore obtain the same value $majority(v_1, \ldots, v_{n-1})$ in step (3), proving IC1. ∎

4 A Solution with Signed Messages

As we saw from the scenario of Figures 1 and 2, it is the traitors' ability to lie that makes the Byzantine Generals Problem so difficult. The problem becomes easier to solve if we can restrict that ability. One way to do this is to allow the generals to send unforgeable signed messages. More precisely, we add to A1–A3 the following assumption:

A4 (a) A loyal general's signature cannot be forged, and any alteration of the contents of his signed messages can be detected.

(b) Anyone can verify the authenticity of a general's signature.

Note that we make no assumptions about a traitorous general's signature. In particular, we allow his signature to be forged by another traitor, thereby permitting collusion among the traitors.

Now that we have introduced signed messages, our previous argument that four generals are required to cope with one traitor no longer holds. In fact, a three-general solution does exist. We now give an algorithm that copes with m traitors for any number of generals. (The problem is vacuous if there are fewer than $m + 2$ generals.)

In our algorithm, the commander sends a signed order to each of his lieutenants. Each lieutenant then adds his signature to that order and sends it to the other lieutenants, who add their signatures and send it to others, and so on. This means that a lieutenant must effectively receive one signed message, make several copies of it, and sign and send those copies. It does not matter how these copies are obtained; a single message might be photocopied, or else each message might consist of a stack of identical messages which are signed and distributed as required.

Our algorithm assumes a function choice which is applied to a set of orders to obtain a single one. The only requirements we make for this function are

1. If the set V consists of the single element v, then $choice(V) = v$.

2. $choice(\emptyset) = \text{RETREAT}$, where $\emptyset$ is the empty set.

Note that one possible definition is to let $choice(V)$ be the median element of V—assuming that there is an ordering of the elements.

In the following algorithm, we let $x : i$ denote the value x signed by General i. Thus, $v : j : i$ denotes the value v signed by j, and then that value $v : j$ signed by i. We let General 0 be the commander. In this algorithm, each lieutenant i maintains a set V_i, containing the set of properly signed orders he has received so far. (If the commander is loyal, then this set should never contain more than a single element.) Do not confuse V_i, the set of orders he has received, with the set of messages that he has received. There may be many different messages with the same order.

Algorithm SM(m)   Initially $V_i = \emptyset$.

1. The commander signs and sends his value to every lieutenant.

2. For each i:

    (A) If Lieutenant i receives a message of the form $v : 0$ from the commander and he has not yet received any order, then
        (i) he lets V_i equal $\{v\}$;
        (ii) he sends the message $v : 0 : i$ to every other lieutenant.

(B) If Lieutenant i receives a message of the form $v : 0 : j_i : \cdots : j_k$ and v is not in the set V_i, then
   (i) he adds v to V_i;
   (ii) if $k < m$, then he sends the message $v : 0 : j_i : \cdots : j_k : i$ to every lieutenant other than $j_1, \ldots, j_k$.

3. For each i: When Lieutenant i will receive no more messages, he obeys the order $choice(V_i)$.

Note that in step (2), Lieutenant i ignores any message containing an order v that is already in the set V_i.

We have not specified how a lieutenant determines in step (3) that he will receive no more messages. By induction on k, one easily shows that for each sequence of lieutenants $j_1, \ldots, j_k$ with $k \leq m$, a lieutenant can receive at most one message of the form $v : 0 : j_1 : \cdots : j_k$ in step (2). If we require that Lieutenant j_k either send such a message or else send a message reporting that he will not send such a message, then it is easy to decide when all messages have been received. (By assumption A3, a lieutenant can determine if a traitorous lieutenant j_k sends neither of those two messages.) Alternatively, time-out can be used to determine when no more messages will arrive. The use of time-out is discussed in Section 6.

Note that in step (2), Lieutenant i ignores any messages that do not have the proper form of a value followed by a string of signatures. If packets of identical messages are used to avoid having to copy messages, this means that he throws away any packet that does not consist of a sufficient number of identical, properly signed messages. (There should be $(n - k - 2)(n - k - 3) \cdots (n - m - 2)$ copies of the message if it has been signed by k lieutenants.)

Figure 5 illustrates Algorithm SM(1) for the case of three generals when the commander is a traitor. The commander sends an "attack" order to one lieutenant and a "retreat" order to the other. Both lieutenants receive the two orders in step (2), so after step (2) $V_1 = V_2 = \{$"attack", "retreat"$\}$, and they both obey the order $choice(\{$"attack", "retreat"$\})$. Observe that here, unlike the situation in Figure 2, the lieutenants know the commander is a traitor because his signature appears on two different orders, and A4 states that only he could have generated those signatures.

In Algorithm SM(m), a lieutenant signs his name to acknowledge his receipt of an order. If he is the mth lieutenant to add his signature to the order, then that signature is not relayed to anyone else by its recipient, so it is superfluous. (More precisely, assumption A2 makes it unnecessary.) In particular, the lieutenants need not sign their messages in SM(1).

We now prove the correctness of our algorithm.

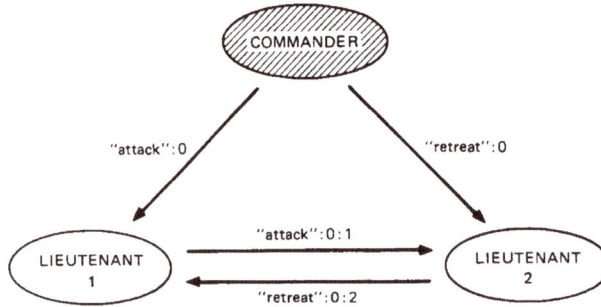

Figure 5   Algorithm SM(1); the commander a traitor.

Theorem 2   For any m, Algorithm SM(m) solves the Byzantine Generals Problem if there are at most m traitors.

Proof   We first prove IC2. If the commander is loyal, then he sends his signed order $v : 0$ to every lieutenant in step (1). Every loyal lieutenant will therefore receive the order v in step (2)(A). Moreover, since no traitorous lieutenant can forge any other message of the form $v' : 0$, a loyal lieutenant can receive no additional order in step (2)(B). Hence, for each loyal Lieutenant i, the set V_i obtained in step (2) consists of the single order v, which he will obey in step (3) by property 1 of the *choice* function. This proves IC2.

Since IC1 follows from IC2 if the commander is loyal, to prove IC1 we need only consider the case in which the commander is a traitor. Two loyal lieutenants i and j obey the same order in step (3) if the sets of orders V_i and V_j that they receive in step (2) are the same. Therefore, to prove IC1 it suffices to prove that, if i puts an order v into V_i in step (2), then j must put the same order v into V_j in step (2). To do this, we must show that j receives a properly signed message containing that order. If i receives the order v in step (2)(A), then he sends it to j in step (2)(A)(ii); so j receives it (by A1). If i adds the order to V_i in step (2)(B), then he must receive a first message of the form $v : 0 : j_1 : \cdots : j_k$. If j is one of the j_r, then by A4 he must already have received the order v. If not, we consider two cases:

1. $k < m$. In this case, i sends the message $v : 0 : j_1 : \cdots : j_k : i$ to j; so j must receive the order v.

2. $k = m$. Since the commander is a traitor, at most $m - 1$ of the lieutenants are traitors. Hence, at least one of the lieutenants $j_1, \ldots, j_m$ is loyal. This loyal lieutenant must have sent j the value v when he first received it, so j must therefore receive that value.

This completes the proof.   ■

5   Missing Communication Paths

Thus far, we have assumed that a general can send messages directly to every other general. We now remove this assumption. Instead, we suppose that physical barriers place some restrictions on who can send messages to whom. We consider the generals to form the nodes of a simple,[2] finite undirected graph G, where an arc between two nodes indicates that those two generals can send messages directly to one another. We now extend Algorithms OM(m) and SM(m), which assumed G to be completely connected, to more general graphs.

To extend our oral message algorithm OM(m), we need the following definition, where two generals are said to be *neighbors* if they are joined by an arc.

Definition 1   (a) A set of nodes $\{i_i, \ldots, i_p\}$ is said to be a *regular set of neighbors* of a node i if

       (i)   each i_j is a neighbor of i, and

       (ii)   for any general k different from i, there exist paths $\gamma_{j,k}$ from i_j to k not passing through i such that any two different paths $\gamma_{j,k}$ have no node in common other than k.

   (b) The graph G is said to be *p-regular* if every node has a regular set of neighbors consisting of p distinct nodes.

Figure 6 shows an example of a simple 3-regular graph. Figure 7 shows an example of a graph that is not 3-regular because the central node has no regular set of neighbors containing three nodes.

We extend OM(m) to an algorithm that solves the Byzantine Generals Problem in the presence of m traitors if the graph G of generals is $3m$-regular. (Note that a $3m$-regular graph must contain at least $3m + 1$ nodes.) For all *positive* integers m and p, we define the algorithm OM(m, p) as follows when the graph G of generals

---

2. A simple graph is one in which there is at most one arc joining any two nodes, and every arc connects two distinct nodes.

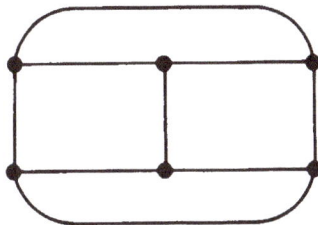

Figure 6   A 3-regular graph.

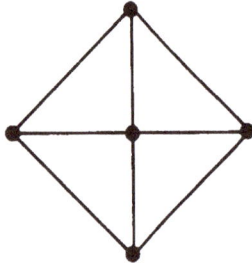

Figure 7   A graph that is not 3-regular.

is p-regular. (OM(m, p) is not defined if G is not p-regular.) The definition uses induction on m.

Alg. OM(m, p)   0. Choose a regular set N of neighbors of the commander consisting of p lieutenants.

1. The commander sends his value to every lieutenant in N.

2. For each i in N, let v_i be the value Lieutenant i receives from the commander, or else RETREAT if he receives no value. Lieutenant i sends v_i to every other lieutenant k as follows:

    (A) If $m = 1$, then by sending the value along the path $\gamma_{i,k}$ whose existence is guaranteed by part (a)(ii) of Definition 1.

    (B) If $m > 1$, then by acting as the commander in the algorithm OM($m - 1$, $p - 1$), with the graph of generals obtained by removing the original commander from G.

3. For each k, and each i in N with $i \neq k$, let v_i be the value Lieutenant k received from Lieutenant i in step (2), or RETREAT if he received no value. Lieutenant k uses the value $majority(v_{i_1}, \ldots, V_{i_p})$, where $N = \{i_1, \ldots, i_p\}$.

Note that removing a single node from a p-regular graph leaves a ($p - 1$)-regular graph. Hence, one can apply the algorithm OM($m - 1$, $p - 1$) in step (2)(B).

We now prove that OM(m, $3m$) solves the Byzantine Generals Problem if there are at most m traitors. The proof is similar to the proof for the algorithm OM(m) and will just be sketched. It begins with the following extension of Lemma 1.

Lemma 2   For any $m > 0$ and any $p \geq 2k + m$, Algorithm OM(m, p) satisfies IC2 if there are at most k traitors.

Proof   For $m = 1$, observe that a lieutenant obtains the value $majority(v_1, \ldots, v_p)$, where each v_i is a value sent to him by the commander along a path disjoint from the path used to send the other values to him. Since there are at most k traitors and $p \geq 2k + 1$, more than half of those paths are composed entirely of loyal lieutenants. Hence, if the commander is loyal, then a majority of the values v_i will equal the value he sent, which implies that IC2 is satisfied.

Now assume the lemma for $m - 1$, $m > 1$. If the commander is loyal, then each of the p lieutenants in N gets the correct value. Since $p > 2k$, a majority of them are loyal, and by the induction hypothesis each of them sends the correct value to every loyal lieutenant. Hence, each loyal lieutenant gets a majority of correct values, thereby obtaining the correct value in step (3).   ∎

The correctness of Algorithm OM$(m, 3m)$ is an immediate consequence of the following result.

Theorem 3   For any $m > 0$ and any $p \geq 3m$, Algorithm OM(m, p) solves the Byzantine Generals Problem if there are at most m traitors.

Proof   By Lemma 2, letting $k = m$, we see that OM(m, p) satisfies IC2. If the commander is loyal, then IC1 follows from IC2, so we need only prove IC1 under the assumption that the commander is a traitor. To do this, we prove that every loyal lieutenant gets the same set of values v_i in step (3). If $m = 1$, then this follows because all the lieutenants, including those in N, are loyal and the paths $\gamma_{i,k}$ do not pass through the commander. For $m > 1$, a simple induction argument can be applied, since $p \geq 3m$ implies that $p - 1 \geq 3(m - 1)$.   ∎

Our extension of Algorithm OM(m) requires that the graph G be $3m$-regular, which is a rather strong connectivity hypothesis.[3] In fact, if there are only $3m + 1$ generals (the minimum number required), then $3m$-regularity means complete connectivity, and Algorithm OM$(m, 3m)$ reduces to Algorithm OM(m). In contrast, Algorithm SM(m) is easily extended to allow the weakest possible connectivity hypothesis. Let us first consider how much connectivity is needed for the Byzantine Generals Problem to be solvable. IC2 requires that a loyal lieutenant obey a loyal commander. This is clearly impossible if the commander cannot communicate with the lieutenant. In particular, if every message from the commander to the lieutenant must be relayed by traitors, then there is no way to guarantee that the lieutenant gets the commander's order. Similarly, IC1 cannot be guaranteed if there

---

3. A recent algorithm of Dolev [2] requires less connectivity.

are two lieutenants who can only communicate with one another via traitorous intermediaries.

The weakest connectivity hypothesis for which the Byzantine Generals Problem is solvable is that the subgraph formed by the loyal generals be connected. We show that under this hypothesis, the algorithm SM($n - 2$) is a solution, where n is the number of generals—regardless of the number of traitors. Of course, we must modify the algorithm so that generals only send messages to where they can be sent. More precisely, in step (1), the commander sends his signed order only to his neighboring lieutenants; and in step (2)(B), Lieutenant i only sends the message to every *neighboring* lieutenant not among the j_r.

We prove the following more general result, where the diameter of a graph is the smallest number d such that any two nodes are connected by a path containing at most d arcs.

Theorem 4   For any m and d, if there are at most m traitors and the subgraph of loyal generals has diameter d, then Algorithm SM($m + d - 1$) (with the above modification) solves the Byzantine Generals Problem.

Proof   The proof is quite similar to that of Theorem 2 and is just sketched here. To prove IC2, observe that by hypothesis there is a path from the loyal commander to a lieutenant i going through $d - 1$ or fewer loyal lieutenants. Those lieutenants will correctly relay the order until it reaches i. As before, assumption A4 prevents a traitor from forging a different order.

To prove IC1, we assume the commander is a traitor and must show that any order received by a loyal lieutenant i is also received by a loyal lieutenant j. Suppose i receives an order $v : 0 : j_1 : \cdots : j_k$ not signed by j. If $k < m$, then i will send it to every neighbor who has not already received that order, and it will be relayed to j within $d - 1$ more steps. If $k \geq m$, then one of the first m signers must be loyal and must have sent it to all of his neighbors, whereupon it will be relayed by loyal generals and will reach j within $d - 1$ steps.   ■

Corollary   If the graph of loyal generals is connected, then SM($n - 2$) (as modified above) solves the Byzantine Generals Problem for n generals.

Proof   Let d be the diameter of the graph of loyal generals. Since the diameter of a connected graph is less than the number of nodes, there must be more than d loyal generals and fewer than $n - d$ traitors. The result follows from the theorem by letting $m = n - d - 1$.   ■

Theorem 4 assumes that the subgraph of loyal generals is connected. Its proof is easily extended to show that even if this is not the case, if there are at most m traitors, then the algorithm SM$(m + d - 1)$ has the following two properties:

1. Any two loyal generals connected by a path of length at most d passing through only loyal generals will obey the same order.

2. If the commander is loyal, then any loyal lieutenant connected to him by a path of length at most $m + d$ passing only through loyal generals will obey his order.

6 Reliable Systems

Other than using intrinsically reliable circuit components, the only way we know to implement a reliable computer system is to use several different "processors" to compute the same result, and then to perform a majority vote on their outputs to obtain a single value. (The voting may be performed within the system, or externally by the users of the output.) This is true whether one is implementing a reliable computer using redundant circuitry to protect against the failure of individual chips, or a ballistic missile defense system using redundant computing sites to protect against the destruction of individual sites by a nuclear attack. The only difference is in the size of the replicated "processor".

The use of majority voting to achieve reliability is based upon the assumption that all the nonfaulty processors will produce the same output. This is true so long as they all use the same input. However, any single input datum comes from a single physical component—for example, from some other circuit in the reliable computer, or from some radar site in the missile defense system—and a malfunctioning component can give different values to different processors. Moreover, different processors can get different values even from a nonfaulty input unit if they read the value while it is changing. For example, if two processors read a clock while it is advancing, then one may get the old time and the other the new time. This can only be prevented by synchronizing the reads with the advancing of the clock.

In order for majority voting to yield a reliable system, the following two conditions should be satisfied:

1. All nonfaulty processors must use the same input value (so they produce the same output).

2. If the input unit is nonfaulty, then all nonfaulty processes use the value it provides as input (so they produce the correct output).

These are just our interactive consistency conditions IC1 and IC2, where the "commander" is the unit generating the input, the "lieutenants" are the processors, and "loyal" means nonfaulty.

It is tempting to try to circumvent the problem with a "hardware" solution. For example, one might try to insure that all processors obtain the same input value by having them all read it from the same wire. However, a faulty input unit could send a marginal signal along the wire—a signal that can be interpreted by some processors as a 0 and by others as a 1. There is no way to guarantee that different processors will get the same value from a possibly faulty input device except by having the processors communicate among themselves to solve the Byzantine Generals Problem.

Of course, a faulty input device may provide meaningless input values. All that a Byzantine Generals solution can do is guarantee that all processors use the same input value. If the input is an important one, then there should be several separate input devices providing redundant values. For example, there should be redundant radars as well as redundant processing sites in a missile defense system. However, redundant inputs cannot achieve reliability; it is still necessary to insure that the nonfaulty processors use the redundant data to produce the same output.

In case the input device is nonfaulty but gives different values because it is read while its value is changing, we still want the nonfaulty processors to obtain a reasonable input value. It can be shown that, if the functions *majority* and *choice* are taken to be the median functions, then our algorithms have the property that the value obtained by the nonfaulty processors lies within the range of values provided by the input unit. Thus, the nonfaulty processors will obtain a reasonable value so long as the input unit produces a reasonable range of values.

We have given several solutions, but they have been stated in terms of Byzantine generals rather than in terms of computing systems. We now examine how these solutions can be applied to reliable computing systems. Of course, there is no problem implementing a "general's" algorithm with a processor. The problems lie in implementing a message passing system that meets assumptions A1–A3 (assumptions A1–A4 for Algorithm SM(m)). We now consider these assumptions in order.

A1. Assumption A1 states that every message sent by a nonfaulty processor is delivered correctly. In real systems, communication lines can fail. For the oral message algorithms OM(m) and OM(m, p), the failure of the communication line joining two processors is indistinguishable from the failure of one of the processors. Hence, we can only guarantee that these algorithms will work in the presence of up to m failures, be they processor or communication line failures. (Of course, the failure of several communication lines attached to the same processor is equivalent to a single processor failure.) If we assume that a failed communication line cannot result in the forgery of a signed message—an assumption which we will see below is quite reasonable, then our signed message algorithm SM(m) is insensitive to communication line failure. More precisely, Theorem 4 remains valid even with communication line failure. A failed communication line has the same effect as simply removing the communication line—it lowers the connectivity of the processor graph.

A2. Assumption A2 states that a processor can determine the originator of any message that it received. What is actually necessary is that a faulty processor not be able to impersonate a nonfaulty one. In practice, this means that interprocess communication be over fixed lines rather than through some message switching network. (If a switching network is used, then faulty network nodes must be considered, and the Byzantine Generals Problem appears again.) Note that assumption A2 is not needed if A4 is assumed and all messages are signed, since impersonation of another processor would imply forging its messages.

A3. Assumption A3 requires that the absence of a message can be detected. The absence of a message can only be detected by its failure to arrive within some fixed length of time—in other words, by the use of some time-out convention. The use of time-out to satisfy A3 requires two assumptions:

1. There is a fixed maximum time needed for the generation and transmission of a message.

2. The sender and receiver have clocks that are synchronized to within some fixed maximum error.

The need for the first assumption is fairly obvious, since the receiver must know how long he needs to wait for the message to arrive. (The generation time is how long it takes the processor to send the message after receiving all the input necessary to generate it.) The need for the second assumption is less obvious. However, it can be shown that either this assumption or an equivalent one is necessary to solve the Byzantine Generals Problem. More precisely, suppose that we allow algorithms in which the generals take action only in the following circumstances:

1. At some fixed initial time (the same for all generals).

2. Upon the receipt of a message.

3. When a randomly chosen length of time has elapsed. (I.e., a general can set a timer to a random value and act when the timer goes off.)

(This yields the most general class of algorithms we can envision which does not allow the construction of synchronized clocks.) It can be shown that no such algorithm can solve the Byzantine Generals Problem if messages can be transmitted arbitrarily quickly, even if there is an upper bound on message transmission delay. Moreover, no solution is possible even if we restrict the traitors so that the only incorrect behavior they are permitted is the failure to send a message. The proof of this result is beyond the scope of this paper. Note that placing a lower as well as an upper bound on transmission delay ahows processors to implement clocks by sending messages back and forth.

The above two assumptions make it easy to detect unsent messages. Let μ be the maximum message generation and transmission delay, and assume the nonfaulty processors have clocks that differ from one another by at most τ at any time. Then any message that a nonfaulty process should begin to generate by time T on its clock will arrive at its destination by time $T + \mu + \tau$ on the receiver's clock. Hence, if the receiver has not received the message by that time, then it may assume that it was not sent. (If it arrives later, then the sender must be faulty, so the correctness of our algorithms does not depend upon the message being sent.) By fixing the time at which the input processor sends its value, one can calculate until what time on its own clock a processor must wait for each message. For example, in Algorithm SM(m) a processor must wait until time $T_0 + k(\mu + \tau)$ for any message having k signatures, where T_0 is the time (on his clock) at which the commander starts executing the algorithm.

No two clocks run at precisely the same rate, so no matter how accurately the processors' clocks are synchronized initially, they will eventually drift arbitrarily far apart unless they are periodically resynchronlzed. We therefore have the problem of keeping the processors' clocks all synchronized to within some fixed amount, even if some of the processors are faulty. This is as difficult a problem as the Byzantine Generals Problem itself. Solutions to the clock synchronization problem exist which are closely related to our Byzantine Generals solutions. They will be described in a future paper.

A4. Assumption A4 requires that processors be able to sign their messages in such a way that a nonfaulty processor's signature cannot be forged. A signature is a piece of redundant information $S_i(M)$ generated by process i from a data item M. A message signed by i consists of a pair $(M, S_i(M))$. To meet parts (a) and (b) of A4, the function S_i must have the following two properties:

(a) If processor i is nonfaulty, then no faulty processor can generate $S_i(M)$.

(b) Given M and X, any process can determine if X equals $S_i(M)$.

Property (a) can never be guaranteed, since $S_i(M)$ is just a data item, and a faulty processor could generate any data item. However, we can make the probability of its violation as small as we wish, thereby making the system as reliable as we wish. How this is done depends upon the type of faults we expect to encounter. There are two cases of interest:

1. *Random Malfunction.* By making S_i a suitably "randomizing" function, we can make the probability that a random malfunction in a processor generates a correct signature essentially equal to the probability of its doing so through a random choice procedure—that is, the reciprocal of the number of possible signatures. The following is one method for doing this. Assume that messages are encoded as positive integers less than P, where P is a power of two. Let $S_i(M)$ equal $M * K_i \bmod P$, where K_i is a randomly chosen odd number less than P. Letting K_i^{-1} be the unique number less than P such that $K_i * K_i^{-1} \equiv 1 \bmod P$, a process can check that $X = S_i(M)$ by testing that $M \equiv X * K_i^{-1} \bmod P$. If another processor does not have K_i in its memory, then the probability of its generating the correct signature $M * K_i$ for a single (nonzero) message M should be $1/P$: its probability of doing so by random choice. (Note that if the processor could obtain K_i by some simple procedure, then there might be a larger probability of a faulty processor j forging i's signature by substituting K_i for K_j when trying to compute $S_j(M)$.)

2. *Malicious Intelligence.* If the faulty processor is being guided by a malicious intelligence—for example, if it is a perfectly good processor being operated by a human who is trying to disrupt the system—then the construction of the signature function S_i becomes a cryptography problem. We refer the reader to [1] and [4] for a discussion of how this problem can be solved.

Note that it is easy to generate the signature $S_i(M)$ if the process has already seen that signature. Hence, it is important that the same message never have to be signed twice. This means that, when using SM(m) repeatedly to distribute a sequence of values, sequence numbers should be appended to the values to guarantee uniqueness.

7 Conclusion

We have presented several solutions to the Byzantine Generals Problem, under various hypotheses, and shown how they can be used in implementing reliable computer systems. These solutions are expensive in both the amount of time and the number of messages required. Algorithms OM(m) and SM(m) both require message paths of length up to $m + 1$. In other words, each lieutenant may have to wait for messages that originated at the commander and were then relayed via m other lieutenants. Fischer and Lynch have shown that this must be true for any solution that can cope with m traitors, so our solutions are optimal in that respect. Our algorithms for a graph that is not completely connected require message paths of length up to $m + d$, where d is the diameter of the subgraph of loyal generals. We suspect that this is also optimal.

Algorithms OM(m) and SM(m) involve sending up to $(n - 1)(n - 2) \cdots (n - m - 1)$ messages. The number of separate messages required can certainly be reduced by combining messages. It may also be possible to reduce the amount of information transferred, but this has not been studied in detail. However, we expect that a large number of messages will still be required.

Achieving reliability in the face of arbitrary malfunctioning is a difficult problem, and its solution seems to be inherently expensive. The only way to reduce the cost is to make assumptions about the type of failure that may occur. For example, it is often assumed that a computer may fail to respond but will never respond incorrectly. However, when extremely high reliability is required, such assumptions cannot be made, and the full expense of a Byzantine Generals solution is required.

References

[1] DIFFIE, W., AND HELLMAN, M.E. New directions in cryptography. *IEEE Trans. Inf. Theory IT-22* (Nov. 1976), 644–654.

[2] DOLEV, D. The Byzantine generals strike again. *J. Algorithms 3,* 1 (Jan. 1982).

[3] PEASE, M., SHOSTAK, R., AND LAMPORT, L. Reaching agreement in the presence of faults. *J. ACM 27,* 2 (Apr. 1980), 228–234.

[4] RIVEST, R.L., SHAMIR, A., AND ADLEMAN, L. A method for obtaining digital signatures and public-key cryptosystems. *Commun.. ACM 21,* 2 (Feb. 1978), 120–126.

Received April 1980; revised November 1981; accepted November 1981

The Mutual Exclusion Problem: Part I—A Theory of Interprocess Communication

Leslie Lamport (Digital Equipment Corporation)

Abstract

A novel formal theory of concurrent systems that does not assume any atomic operations is introduced. The execution of a concurrent program is modeled as an abstract set of operation executions with two temporal ordering relations: "precedence" and "can causally affect". A primitive interprocess communication mechanism is then defined. In Part II, the mutual exclusion is expressed precisely in terms of this model, and solutions using the communication mechanism are given.

Categories and Subject Descriptors: B.3.m [**Memory Structures**]: Miscellaneous; B.4.m [**Input/Output and Data Communications**]: Miscellaneous; D.4.1 [**Operating Systems**]: Process Management—*concurrency; mutual exclusion*; F.3.m [**Logics and Meanings of Programs**]: Miscellaneous

Most of this work was performed while the author was at SRI International, where it was supported in part by the National Science Foundation under grant number MCS 78-16783.

Author's address: Digital Equipment Corporation, Systems Research Center, 130 Lytton Avenue, Palo Alto, CA 94301.

Paper originally published in *Journal of the Association for Computing Machinery,* 33(2), April 1986, pp. 313–326.

General Terms: Theory

Additional Key Words and Phrases: Nonatomic operations, readers/writers, shared variables

1 Introduction

The mutual exclusion problem was first described and solved by Dijkstra in [3]. In this problem, there is a collection of asynchronous processes, each alternately executing a critical and a noncritical section, that must be synchronized so that no two processes ever execute their critical sections concurrently. Mutual exclusion lies at the heart of most concurrent process synchronization and, apart from its practical motivation, the mutual exclusion problem is of great theoretical significance.

The concept of mutual exclusion is deeply ingrained in the way computer scientists think about concurrency. Almost all formal models of concurrent processing are based upon an underlying assumption of mutually exclusive atomic operations, and almost all interprocess communication mechanisms that have been proposed require some underlying mutual exclusion in their implementation. Hence, these models and mechanisms are not satisfactory for a fundamental study of the mutual exclusion problem. We have therefore been forced to develop a new formalism for talking about concurrent systems, and a new way of viewing interprocess communication. Part I is entirely devoted to this formalism, which we believe provides a basis for discussing other fundamental problems in concurrent processing as well; the mutual exclusion problem itself is discussed in Part II [9].

The formal model we have developed is radically different from commonly used ones, and will appear strange to computer scientists accustomed to thinking in terms of atomic operations. (It is a slight extension to the one we introduced in [6].) When diverging from the beaten path in this way, one is in great danger of becoming lost in a morass of irrelevance. To guard against this, we have continually used physical reality as our guidepost. (Perhaps this is why hardware designers seem to understand our ideas more easily than computer scientists.) We therefore give a very careful physical justification for all the definitions and axioms in our formalism. Although this is quite unusual in theoretical computer science, we feel that it is necessary in explaining and justifying our departure from the traditional approach.

2 The Model

We begin by describing a formal model in which to state the problem and the solution. Except for the one introduced by us in [6], all formal models of concurrent processes that we know of are based upon the concept of an indivisible atomic operation. The concurrent execution of any two atomic operations is assumed to have the same effect as executing them in some order. However, if two operations can affect one another—e.g., if they perform interprocess communication—then implementing them to be atomic is equivalent to making the two operations mutually exclusive. Hence, assuming atomic operations is tantamount to assuming a lower-level solution to the mutual exclusion problem. Any algorithm based upon atomic operations cannot be considered a fundamental solution to the mutual exclusion problem. We therefore need a formalism that is not based upon atomic operations. The one we use is a slight extension to the formalism of [6].

2.1 Physical Considerations

For our results to be meaningful, our formalism must accurately reflect the physical reality of concurrent processes. We therefore feel that it is important to justify the formalism on physical grounds. We do this in terms of the geometry of space-time, which lies at the foundation of all modern physics. We begin with a brief exposition of this geometry. A more thorough exposition can be found in [15] and [16], but for the more sophisticated reader we recommend the original works [4,11].

The reader may find the introduction of special relativity a bit far-fetched, since one is rarely, if ever, concerned with systems of processes moving at relativistic velocities relative to one another. However, the relativistic view of time is relevant whenever signal propagation time is not negligibly small compared to the execution time of individual operations, and this is certainly the case in most multiprocess systems.

Because it is difficult to draw pictures of four-dimensional space-time, we will discuss a three-dimensional space-time for a two-dimensional spatial universe. Everything generalizes easily to four-dimensional space-time.[1] We picture space-time as a three-dimensional Cartesian space whose points are called *events*, where the point (x, y, t) is the event occurring at time t at the point with spatial coordinates (x, y). Dimensional units are chosen so the speed of light equals 1.

The *world line* of a point object is the locus of all events (x, y, t) such that the object is at location (x, y) at time t. Since photons travel in a straight line with speed 1, the world line of a photon is a straight line inclined at 45° to the x-y plane. The forward light cone emanating from an event e is the surface formed by all possible world lines of photons created at that event. This is illustrated in

---

1. While it is even easier to draw pictures of a two-dimensional space-time with a single space dimension, a one-dimensional space has some special properties (such as the ability to send a light beam in only two directions) that can make such pictures misleading.

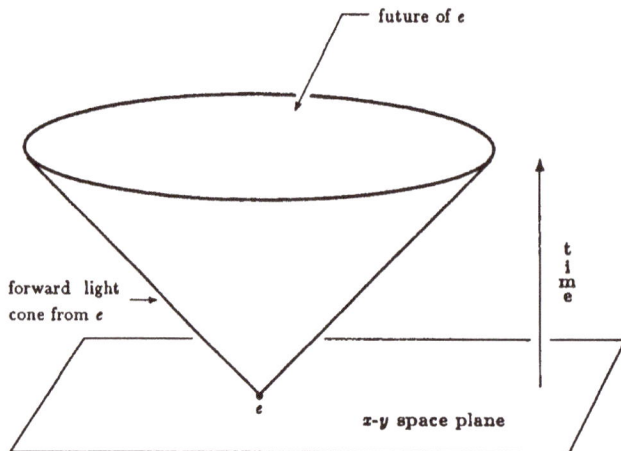

Figure 1   Space-time.

Figure 1. The *future* of event e consists of all events other than e itself that lie on or inside the future light cone emanating from e. It is a fundamental principle of special relativity that an event e can only influence the events in its future.

We say that an event e *precedes* an event f, written $e \longrightarrow f$, if f lies in the future of e. It is easy to see that $\longrightarrow$ is an irreflexive partial ordering—i.e., that (i) $e \nrightarrow e$ and (ii) $e \longrightarrow f \longrightarrow g$ implies $e \longrightarrow g$. Two events are said to be *concurrent* if neither precedes the other. Since objects cannot travel faster than light, two different events lying on the world-line of an object cannot be concurrent.

We can think of the vertical line through the origin as the world line of some standard clock, where the event $(0, 0, t)$ on this world line represents the clock "striking" time t. A horizontal plane, consisting of all events having the same t-coordinate, represents the universe at time t—as viewed by us. However, another observer may have a different view of which events occur at time t. We define a *space-like* plane to be a plane making an angle of less than $45°$ with the x-y plane. For an inertial observer, the set of events occurring at time t forms a space-like plane through $(0, 0, t)$. (An inertial observer is one traveling in a straight line at constant speed.) For different values of t, these planes are parallel (for the same observer). Any space-like plane represents a set of events that some inertial observer regards as all occurring at the same time. Such a plane defines an obvious partitioning of space-time into three sets: the future, the past, and the present (the plane itself).

It follows from these observations that an event e precedes an event f if and only if every inertial observer regards e as happening before f, and events e and f

are concurrent if and only if there is some observer who views them as happening at the same time.

2.2 System Executions

According to classical physics, the universe consists of a continuum of space-time events, each having no spatial or temporal extent. In computer science, one imposes a discrete structure upon this continuous universe, considering a system to consist of distinct *operation executions* such as reading a flip-flop or sending a message.[2] An infinite (usually bounded) set of space-time events is considered to be a single operation execution. For example, the operation execution of reading a flip-flop consists of events spatially located at the flip-flop and perhaps at some of the wires connected to it.

The boundary between the events of one operation execution and of other operation executions in the same processor is rather arbitrary; events occurring along the wire leading from the flip-flop can be included as part of the reading of the flip-flop or as part of a subsequent operation execution that uses the value that was read. The fine details of where the boundary is drawn do not matter; extending the region of space-time comprising the operation execution by a nanosecond here or a micron there makes no difference. However, the choice of which events belong to which operation executions can influence the properties we ascribe to the operations; the formalism used to describe a system can depend upon whether the events in the propagation of a value along a wire belong to the send or to the receive operation.

An execution of a system therefore consists of a set of operation executions, where each operation execution consists of a nonempty set of space-time events. We define the relations $\longrightarrow$ and $\dashrightarrow$ on the set of operation executions as follows:

$$A \longrightarrow B \overset{\text{def}}{=} \forall a \in A : \forall b \in B : a \longrightarrow b,$$

$$A \dashrightarrow B \overset{\text{def}}{=} \exists a \in A : \exists b \in B : a \longrightarrow b \quad \text{or} \quad a = b.$$

Thus, $A \longrightarrow B$ means that every event of A precedes every event of B, and $A \dashrightarrow B$ means that some event of A either precedes or is the same as some event of B. (If a read of a flip-flop occurs while the flip-flop is also being set, some space-time events located at the flip-flop may belong to both operation executions.)

---

2. Since the term "operation" often denotes a type of action that can be performed repeatedly, as in "the operation of addition", we write "operation execution" to emphasize that we are referring to a single instance of such an action.

Remembering the meaning of the precedence relation for events, we read $A \longrightarrow B$ as "A precedes B", and $A \dashrightarrow B$ as "A can causally affect B". However, we think of "can causally affect" as a purely temporal relation, independent of what the operations are doing. Thus, $A \dashrightarrow B$ can hold even if A and B are *read* operations that cannot actually influence one another. We say that A and B are *concurrent* if $A \not\longrightarrow B$ and $B \not\longrightarrow A$. In other words, two operation executions are concurrent unless one precedes the other.

The following properties of the relations $\longrightarrow$ and $\dashrightarrow$ on operation executions follow directly from the fact that the relation $\longrightarrow$ on events is an irreflexive partial ordering:

A1. The relation $\longrightarrow$ is an irreflexive partial ordering.

A2. If $A \longrightarrow B$, then $A \dashrightarrow B$ and $B \not\dashrightarrow A$.

A3. If $A \longrightarrow B \dashrightarrow C$ or $A \dashrightarrow B \longrightarrow C$, then $A \dashrightarrow C$.

A4. If $A \longrightarrow B \dashrightarrow C \longrightarrow D$, then $A \longrightarrow D$.

There are two kinds of operation executions—terminating ones, whose events all occur before some time (they are in the past of some space-like surface), and nonterminating ones that go on forever (their events do not lie in the past of any space-like surface). We make the following assumptions about these two classes of operation executions.

A5. For any terminating A, the set of B such that $A \not\longrightarrow B$ is finite.

A6. For any nonterminating A:

    (a) The set of B such that $B \longrightarrow A$ is finite.

    (b) For all B: $A \not\longrightarrow B$.

Properties A5 and A6 can be derived from the following assumptions.

- At any time, there are only a finite number of operation executions that have begun by that time—i.e., for any space-like surface, there are only a finite number of operation executions containing events in the past of that surface.

- There are only a finite number of operation executions concurrent with any terminating operation execution.

The second assumption means that the speed with which the system is "spreading out" in space is bounded by some value less than the speed of light.

We have described operation executions in terms of events in order to justify A1–A6. In computer science, one ignores the space-time events that comprise operation executions. A programmer does not care that machine instructions are composed of more primitive events. In our formalism, operation executions are considered primitives elements, and A1–A6 are taken as axioms. We define a *system execution* to consist of a set of operation executions, partitioned into terminating and non-terminating ones, together with relations $\longrightarrow$ and $\dashrightarrow$ that satisfy Axioms A1–A6.

2.3 Higher-Level Views

A system can be viewed at many different levels; the programmer may consider the execution of a *load accumulator from memory* instruction to be a single operation, while the hardware designer considers it to be a sequence of lower-level register-transfer operations. The fundamental task in computing is to implement higher-level operations with lower-level ones. A hardware designer implements machine-language operations with register-transfer operations; a compiler writer implements Pascal operations with machine-language operations; and an applications programmer implements funds-transferring operations with Pascal operations. One assumes that the lower-level, primitive operations are given and uses them to construct the higher-level ones.

A higher-level operation execution consists of a set of lower-level ones. If we view operation executions as sets of space-time events, a higher-level operation execution is the union of the events of the (lower-level) operation executions it is composed of. It is nonterminating if and only if it consists of a finite number of nonterminating operation executions. It is not hard to show that the relations $\longrightarrow$ and $\dashrightarrow$ between higher-level operation executions can be computed from those relations between the lower-level operation executions as follows:

$$
\begin{aligned}
R \longrightarrow S &= \forall A \in R : \forall B \in S : A \longrightarrow B, \\
R \dashrightarrow S &= \exists A \in R : \exists B \in S : A \dashrightarrow B \quad \text{or} \quad A = B.
\end{aligned}
\tag{2.1}
$$

Since events do not appear in our formalism, we cannot proceed in this way. Instead, we take (2.1) to be the definition of the relations $\longrightarrow$ and $\dashrightarrow$ between any two sets of operation executions. By identifying an operation execution A with the set $\{A\}$, this definition also applies when R or S is a single operation execution rather than a set of them. A set of operation executions is defined to be *terminating* if and only if it consists of a finite number of terminating operation executions.

Given a system execution, a higher-level view of that execution consists of a partitioning of its operation executions into sets, which represent higher-level operation executions. The machine-language view of a system is obtained by partitioning the register-transfer operations into executions of machine-language instructions. This need not be a true partition; a single register-transfer operation could be part of the execution of two separate machine-language instructions. We therefore define a *higher-level view* of a system execution to be a collection $\mathcal{H}$ of nonempty sets of operation executions such that each operation execution belongs to a finite number, greater than zero, of sets in $\mathcal{H}$. The elements of $\mathcal{H}$ (which are sets of operation executions) are called the operation executions of the higher-level view, or simply the *higher-level operation executions*.

Given a higher-level view of a system execution, we have defined the relations $\longrightarrow$ and $\dashrightarrow$ (by (2.1)) and the concept of termination on its high-level operation executions. Using these definitions and Axioms A1–A6 for the (lower-level) operation executions, it is easy to show that A1–A6 hold for the higher-level operation executions. Hence, the higher-level view of a system execution is itself a system execution.

In any study of computer systems, there is a lowest-level view that is of interest. The operation executions in that view will be called *elementary* operation executions. A set of elementary operation executions will be called an operation execution. (It is an operation execution in some higher-level view.)

3 Interprocess Communication

To achieve mutual exclusion, processes must be able to communicate with one another. We must therefore assume some interprocess communication mechanism. However, almost every communication primitive that has been proposed implicitly assumes mutual exclusion. For example, the first mutual exclusion algorithms assumed a central memory that can be accessed by all the processes, in which any two operations to a single memory cell occur in some definite order. In other words, they assumed mutually exclusive access to a memory cell. We will define an interprocess communication mechanism that does not assume any lower-level mutual exclusion. In order to explain our choice of a mechanism, we begin by examining the nature of interprocess communication.

The simplest form of interprocess communication is for a process i to send one bit of information to a process j. This can be done in two ways: by sending a message or by setting a bit. For example, if the physical communication medium is a wire, then "sending a message" might mean sending a pulse and "setting a bit" might mean setting a level. However, a message is a transient phenomenon, and j must be waiting for i's message in order to be sure of receiving it. We now show that with only this kind of transient communication, the mutual exclusion problem does not admit a solution in which the following two conditions hold:

- A process need communicate only when trying to enter or leave its critical section, not in its critical or noncritical sections.

- A process may remain forever in its noncritical section.

These conditions rule out algorithms in which processes take turns entering, or declining to enter, their critical section; such algorithms are really solutions to the producer/consumer problem [1].

Assume that a process i wants to enter its critical section first, while another process j is in its noncritical section. Since j could remain in its noncritical section forever, i must be able to enter its critical section without communicating with j. Assume that this has happened and i is in its critical section when j decides it wants to enter its critical section. Since i is not required to communicate while in its critical section, j cannot find out if i is in its critical section until i leaves the critical section. However, j cannot wait for a communication because i might be in, and remain forever in, its noncritical section. Hence, no solution is possible.

This conclusion is based upon the assumption that communication by transient messages can only be achieved if the receiving process is waiting for the message. This assumption may seem paradoxical since distributed systems often provide a message-passing facility with which a process can receive messages while engaged in other activity. A closer examination of such systems reveals that the receiving process actually consists of two concurrently executing subprocesses: a main subprocess that performs the process's major activity, and a communication subprocess that receives messages and stores them in a buffer to be read by the main subprocess, where one or more bits in the buffer may signal the main subprocess that it should interrupt its activity to process a message. The activity of the communication subprocess can be regarded as part of the sending operation, which effects the communication by setting bits in the buffer that can be read by the receiving process. Thus, this kind of message passing really involves the setting of bits at the remote site by the sender.

Hence, we assume that a process i communicates one bit of information to a process j by setting a communication bit that j can read. A bit that can be set but not reset can be used only once. Since there is no bound on the number of times a process may need to communicate, interprocess synchronization is impossible with a finite number of such "once only" communication bits. Therefore, we require that it be possible to reset the bit. This gives us three possibilities:

1. Only the reader can reset the communication bit.

2. Only the writer can reset the communication bit.

3. Both can reset the communication bit.

In case 1, with a finite number of bits, a process i can send only a bounded amount of information to another process j before j resets the bits. However, in the mutual exclusion problem, a process may spend arbitrarily long in its noncritical section, so process i can enter its critical section arbitrarily many times while process j is in its noncritical section. An argument similar to the one demonstrating that transient communication cannot be used shows that process i must communicate with process j every time it executes its critical section, so i may have to send an unbounded amount of information to j while j is in its noncritical section. Since a process need not communicate while in its noncritical section, the problem cannot be solved using the first kind of communication bit.[3]

Of the remaining two possibilities, we choose number 2 because it is more primitive than number 3. We are therefore led to the use of a communication bit that can be set to either of two values by one process and read by another—i.e., a boolean-valued communication variable with one writer and one reader. We let *true* and *false* denote the two values. We say that such a variable "belongs to" the process that can write it.

We now define the semantics of the operations of reading and writing a communication variable. A write operation execution for a communication variable has the form *write* $v := v'$, where v is the name of the variable, and v' denotes the value being written—either *true* or *false*. A read operation execution has the form *read* $v = v'$, where v' is the value obtained as the result of performing the read.

The first assumptions we make are:

C0. Reads and writes are terminating operation executions.

C1. A read of a communication variable obtains either the value *true* or the value *false*.

Physically, C1 means that no matter what state the variable is in when it is being read, the reader will interpret that state as one of the two possible values.

We require that all writes to a single communication variable be totally ordered by the $\longrightarrow$ relation. Since all of these writes are executed by the same process—the one that owns the variable—this is a reasonable requirement. We will see below that

---

3. However, it is possible to solve producer/consumer problems with it. In fact, an interrupt bit of an ordinary computer is precisely this kind of communication bit, and it is used to implement producer/consumer synchronization with its peripheral devices.

it is automatically enforced by the programming language in which the algorithms are described. This requirement allows us to introduce the following notation.

Definition 1 For any variable v we let $V^{[1]}$, $V^{[2]}$, ... denote the write operation executions to v, where

$$V^{[1]} \longrightarrow V^{[2]} \longrightarrow \cdots.$$

We let $v^{[i]}$ denote the value written by the operation execution $V^{[i]}$.

Thus $V^{[i]}$ is a *write* $v := v^{[i]}$ operation execution. We assume that the variable can be initialized to either possible value. (The initial value of a variable can be specified as part of the process's program.)

If a read is not concurrent with any write, then we expect it to obtain the value written by the most recent write—or the initial value if it precedes all writes. However, it turns out that we need a somewhat stronger requirement. To justify it, we return to our space-time view of operations. The value of a variable must be stored in some collection of objects. Communication is effected by the reads and writes acting on these objects—i.e., by each read and write operation execution containing events that lie on the world lines of these objects. A read or write operation may also contain "internal" events not on the world line of any of these shared objects. For example, if the variable is implemented by a flip-flop accessed by the reader and writer over separate wires, the flip-flop itself is the shared object and the events occurring on the wires are internal events. The internal events of a write do not directly affect a read. However, for a write to precede ($\longrightarrow$) a read, all events of the write, including internal events, must precede all events of the read.

For two operation executions A and B on the same variable, we say that A "effectively precedes" B if every event in A that lies on the world line of one of the shared objects precedes any events in B that lie on the same object's world line. For a read to obtain the value written by $V^{[k]}$, it suffices that (i) $V^{[k]}$ effectively precedes the read, and (ii) the read effectively precedes $V^{[k+1]}$. "Effectively precedes" is weaker than "precedes", since it does not specify any ordering on internal events, so this condition is stronger than requiring that the read obtain the correct value if it is not concurrent with any write.

This definition of "effectively precedes" involves events, which are not part of our formalism, so we cannot define this exact concept. However, observe that if events a and b lie on the same world line, then either $a \longrightarrow b$ or $b \longrightarrow a$. Hence, if A and B both have events occurring on the same world line, then $A \dashrightarrow B$ and/or $B \dashrightarrow A$. If $B \not\dashrightarrow A$, then no event in B precedes any event in A. Hence, $A \dashrightarrow B$ and

$B \not\dashrightarrow A$ imply that A effectively precedes B. We therefore are led to the following definition:

Definition 1   We say that two operation executions A and B are *effectively nonconcurrent* if either $A \dashrightarrow B$ or $B \dashrightarrow A$, but not both.

If two operation executions are effectively nonconcurrent according to this definition, then one "effectively precedes" the other according to the above definition in terms of events. We therefore expect a read that is effectively nonconcurrent with every write to obtain the correct value. This leads us to the following requirement.

> C2. A read R of v that is effectively nonconcurrent with every $V^{[i]}$ obtains the value $v^{[k]}$, where k is the largest number such that $V^{[k]} \dashrightarrow R$, or it obtains the initial value if there is no such k.

It follows from A2 and A5 that the set of k such that $V^{[k]} \dashrightarrow R$ is finite, so C2 specifies the value obtained by a read that is effectively nonconcurrent with every write. The only assumption we make about a read that is "effectively concurrent" with some write is that it obtain either the value *true* or the value *false* (by C1).

In the above space-time discussion of reading and writing, it is clear that for communication to take place, every pair of reads and writes must have events on the world line of the same object. The following requirement is therefore quite reasonable (although it may not be obvious why we need it).

> C3. If R is a read of the communication variable v, then for every write $V^{[i]}$ of v: $R \dashrightarrow V^{[i]}$ or $V^{[i]} \dashrightarrow R$ (or both).

It has been argued that the kind of communication variable we are assuming is equivalent to one in which reads and writes are atomic actions that cannot be concurrent. The reasoning used is as follows.

> If the value of the variable is not changed by a write, then there is no reason to do the write. We may therefore assume that a process executes a write only if it will change the value. By C1, a read that is concurrent with such a write must obtain either the old or the new value, since those are the only possible values. If the read obtains the old value, then we may consider it to have preceded the write, and if it obtains the new value then we may consider the write to have preceded it.[4]

---

4. In fact, we made this unfortunate claim in our original correctness proof for the bakery algorithm [5]. Happily, it was only the proof and not the algorithm that turned out to be incorrect.

This reasoning is fallacious under our assumptions because if two successive reads are concurrent with the same write, then the first read can obtain the new value and the second the old value. This is impossible if reads and writes are nonconcurrent atomic actions.

Several people have devised mutual exclusion algorithms using communication variables similar to ours, except with the stronger assumption that writing and reading are atomic operations [13,14]. We believe that these algorithms do not work with the more primitive type of communication variable that we are assuming.[5] Other than the ones mentioned here, we know of no published mutual exclusion algorithms that are correct using these communication variables.

4 Processes

An algorithm implements higher-level operations such as *request service* in terms of lower-level ones like reading and writing a one-bit variable. A synchronization problem is posed as a set of conditions on the higher-level system execution— for example, that each *request service* operation execution is followed by a *grant service* operation execution. A solution consists of a specification of a lower-level system execution together with a higher-level view—for example, an algorithm for generating reads and writes together with a specification of which sets of these lower-level operation executions correspond to *request service* and *grant service* executions. The system execution defined by this higher-level view must satisfy the problem conditions.

We now consider how the lower-level system execution is specified. We assume that the set of all elementary operation executions is partitioned into N sets called *processes*. A process is described by an ordinary program, each operation execution of the process being generated by the execution of some statement in its program. For example, suppose the program for a process contains the following program statement:

```
begin
    x := 1;
    z := y + z
end
```

5. We have found counterexamples to the simpler algorithms, and have no reason to expect the more complicated ones to work better.

Executing this statement might generate the following four elementary operation executions, with the indicated $\longrightarrow$ relations.

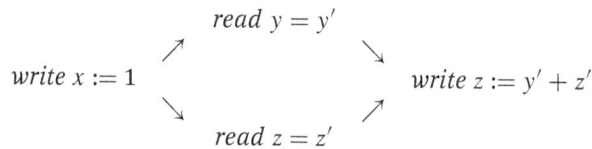

$$
\begin{array}{ccc}
 & read\ y = y' & \\
 & \nearrow \qquad \searrow & \\
write\ x := 1 & & write\ z := y' + z' \\
 & \searrow \qquad \nearrow & \\
 & read\ z = z' &
\end{array}
$$

Although we think of the program as generating the operation executions, formally the set of operation executions is given and the processes' programs provide a set of conditions on it. For example, if this statement were the only place where y is read, then it would provide the following formal condition:

For every *read* $y = y'$ operation execution, there must exist three operation executions *write* $x := 1$, *read* $z = z'$, and *write* $z := y' + z'$ such that the above $\longrightarrow$ relations hold.

Each process will be described by a program written in an Algol-like language with two kinds of program variables:

- *Private variables* read and written by that process only.
- *Communication variables* used for interprocess communication.

We can define a formal semantics for the programming language as follows. The elementary operation executions of a process are of the form *write* $v := v'$ or *read* $v = v'$, where v is a variable and v' is an element in the range of values of that variable. The variable v must be one that the process can write or read, respectively. For the critical section problem, there are also elementary operation executions of the form *critical section execution* and *noncritical section execution*.

We assume that C0–C3 hold for reads and writes of communication variables. We also assume that C0 and C2 hold for private variables. We will not need C1 or C3 because a read of a private variable will never be concurrent with a write of that variable. In fact, a read will not be concurrent with any write performed by the same process.

We now indicate how a process's program can be formally translated into a set of conditions on possible system executions. Syntactically, a program is composed of a hierarchy of program statements—more complicated statements being built up from simpler ones.[6] In any system execution, to each program statement cor-

---

6. If function calls are permitted, then we have to include expression evaluations as well as statement executions in this hierarchy.

responds a (not necessarily elementary) operation execution—intuitively, it is the set of elementary operation executions performed when executing that statement. The execution of the entire program, which is a single statement, is a single operation execution consisting of all the process's elementary operation executions. The semantics of each type of statement in the language is defined by a collection of axioms on the (set of elementary operation executions in the) execution of a statement of that type. For assignment statements, we have the following axiom:

An execution of the statement

$$v := F(v_1, \ldots, v_m)$$

consists of the elementary operation executions *read* $v_1 = v_1'$, ..., *read* $v_m = v_m'$, and *write* $v := F(v_1', \ldots, v_m')$, where each read precedes ($\longrightarrow$) the write.

This axiom, together with conditions C0–C3 for communication variables and C0 and C2 for private variables, defines the semantics of the simple assignment statement.

The following axioms define the semantics of the concatenation construction $S; T$. (Recall that a statement execution, being a set of elementary operation executions, is defined to terminate if and only if it consists of a finite number of terminating operation executions.)

An execution of $S; T$ is one of the following:

- A nonterminating execution of S.

- An operation execution of the form $A \cup B$, where
    - A is a terminating execution of S.
    - B is an execution of T.
    - $A \longrightarrow B$.

In this way, one can give a complete formal semantics for our programming language. However, we will not bother to do so, and will reason somewhat informally about system executions. We merely note the following properties:

- A write is not concurrent with any other operation generated by the same process. (However, it may be concurrent with operations generated by other processes.)

- Any elementary operation execution is concurrent with only a bounded number of elementary operation executions in the same process.

5 Multiple-Reader Variables

Thus far, we have assumed that communication variables can be read by only a single process. Using such variables, it is easy to construct a communication variable satisfying C0–C3 that can be read by several processes, though only written by one process. To implement a communication variable v that can be written by process i and read by processes $1, \ldots, N$, we use an array $v[1], \ldots, v[N]$ of variables, where $v[j]$ can be written by i and read by j. (All the $v[j]$ are communication variables except for $v[i]$, which is a private variable of process i.) Any statement $v := \ldots$ in process i's program is implemented as an operation of assigning the value of the right-hand expression to each element of the array, and any occurrence of the variable v in an expression within the program of process j is interpreted as an occurrence of $v[j]$. The fact that this construction works is implied by the following result, whose proof is left to the reader.

Theorem 1   For each $j \neq i$, let $v[j]$ be a communication variable that is written by process i and read by process j. Assume that for all j, j' and all k:

1. The initial values of $v[j]$ and $v[j']$ are equal;

2. $v[j]^{[k]} = v[j']^{[k]}$;

3. $V[j]^{[k]} \longrightarrow V[j']^{[k+1]}$.

Let the initial value of v be defined to equal the initial value of the $v[j]$, let $V^{[k]}$ be defined to be $\{V[1]^{[k]}, \ldots, V[N]^{[k]}\}$, and define a read of v by a process $j \neq i$ to be a read of $v[j]$. Then C0–C3 are satisfied by the variable v (where $\longrightarrow$ and $\dashrightarrow$ are defined for the set of operation executions $V^{[k]}$ by (2.1)).

Formally, we are defining a higher-level view whose operation executions are the same as those of the original system execution except that the reads and writes of the $v[j]$ are partitioned into reads and writes of v. This theorem shows that the resulting higher-level system execution satisfies C0–C3. We take the reads and writes of v to be elementary operation executions, ignoring the lower-level operation executions that comprise them.

We will therefore assume that a communication variable can be written by its owner and read by any process. However, we must remember that the "cost" of implementing such a communication variable may depend upon the number of processes that actually read it. If the physical communication mechanism involves wires that join two processors, then the number of wires needed to implement a communication variable equals the number of readers of that variable, so a variable read by r processes may be almost r times as expensive as one read by a single process. However, it is quite reasonable to suppose that the variable could be implemented with a single wire to which each reader is connected. In this case, the cost of an r-reader variable may not be much greater than the cost of a single-reader variable.

6 Discussion of the Assumptions

In this section, we have made some tacit assumptions that may have passed unnoticed. The most obvious of these is the assumption that each process knows in advance who it might communicate with. This assumption seems to us to be reasonable for an underlying physical model in which processors (the physical hardware that executes processes) are connected in pairs by direct physical connections—e.g., wires or optical fibers. In such a model, it is natural to assume that a processor knows the existence of every physical connection. Indeed, it is only for such a model that a communication variable owned by a single process is reasonable. Thus, our work is not applicable to systems of anonymous processors connected along a common wire, as in an Ethernet [10].

Our first two assumptions, C0 and C1, appear quite innocent. However, the fact that reading and writing are not synchronized means that the reader can become suspended for arbitrarily long in a meta-stable state if it happens to read at exactly the wrong time. This is the "arbiter problem" discussed in [2] and [12]. As explained in [2], one can construct a device in which the reader has probability zero of remaining in such a meta-stable state forever. Hence, our assumptions can be satisfied if we interpret truth to mean "true with probability one".

There is an additional subtle assumption hidden in the combination of C2 with the ordering of operation executions within a process that we have been assuming. Suppose $v := true; \ldots$ is part of the program for process i. We are assuming that the *write* $v := true$ generated by an execution of the first statement precedes any operation execution A generated by the subsequent execution of the next statement. Now suppose that this is the last *write* v generated by process i, and that there is a *read* v execution by another process that is preceded by A. By A1, the *read* v is preceded by the *write* $v := true$, and since this is the last *write* v operation execution, C2 implies that the *read* v must obtain the value *true*.

Let us consider what this implies for an implementation. To guarantee that the *read* v obtains the value *true*, after executing the *write* $v := true$ the writer must be sure that v has settled into a stable state before beginning the next operation. For example, if the value of v is represented by the voltage level on the wire joining two processors, then the writer cannot proceed until the new voltage has propagated to the end of the wire. If a bound cannot be placed upon the propagation time, then such a simple representation cannot be used. Instead, the value must be stored in a flip-flop local to the writer, and the reader must interrogate its value by sending a signal along the wire and waiting for a response. Since the flip-flop is located at the writing process, and is set only by that process, it is reasonable to assume a bound upon its settling time. The wire, with its unknown delay, becomes part of the reading process. Thus, although satisfying our assumption in a distributed process poses difficulties, they do not seem to be insurmountable. In any case, we know of no way to achieve interprocess synchronization without such an assumption.

7 Conclusion

In Section 2, we developed a formalism for reasoning about concurrent systems that does not assume the existence of atomic operations. This formalism has been further developed in [7], which addresses the question of what it means for a lower-level system to implement a higher-level one.

Section 3 considered the nature of interprocess communication, and argued that the simplest, most primitive form of communication that can be used to solve the mutual exclusion problem consists of a very weak form of shared register that can be written and read concurrently. Interprocess communication is considered in more detail in [8], where the form of shared register we have defined is called a *safe* register. Algorithms for constructing stronger registers from safe ones are given in [8].

Acknowledgments

Many of these ideas have been maturing for quite a few years before appearing on paper for the first time here. They have been influenced by a number of people during that time, most notably Carel Scholten, Edsger Dijkstra, Chuck Seitz, Robert Keller, and Irene Greif.

References

[1] BRINCH HANSEN, P. Concurrent programming concepts. *Comput. Surv. 5* (1973) 223–245, 1973.

[2] CHANEY, T. J. and MOLNAR, C. E. Anomalous behavior of synchronizer and arbiter circuits. *IEEE Trans. Comput. C-22* (Apr. 1973), 421–422.

[3] DIJKSTRA, E. W. Solution of a problem in concurrent programming control. *Commun. ACM 8*, 9 (Sept. 1965), 569.

[4] EINSTEIN, A. Zur electrodynamik bewegter korper. *Ann. Physik*, 17 (1905). Translated as: On the electrodynamics of moving bodies. In *The Principle of Relativity*, Dover, New York, pp. 35–65.

[5] LAMPORT, L. A new solution of Dijkstra's concurrent programming problem. *Commun. ACM 17*, 8 (Aug. 1974), 453–455.

[6] LAMPORT, L. A new approach to proving the correctness of multiprocess programs. *Prog. Lang. Syst. 1*, 1 (July 1979), 84–97.

[7] LAMPORT, L. On interprocess communication—Part I: Basic formalism. *Dist. Comput.* (to appear).

[8] LAMPORT, L. On interprocess communication—Part II: Algorithms. *Dist. Comput.* (to appear).

[9] LAMPORT, L. The mutual exclusion problem: Part II—Statement and solutions. *J. ACM 33*, 2 (Apr. 1986), 327–348.

[10] METCALFE, R. and BOGGS, D. R. Ethernet: distributed packet switching for local computer networks. *Commun. ACM 19*, 7 (July 1976), 395–404.

[11] MINKOWSKI, H. Space and Time. In *The Principle of Relativity*. Dover, New York, pp. 73–91.

[12] PALAIS, R. and LAMPORT, L. On the glitch phenomenon. Tech. Rep. CA-7611-0811, Massachusetts Computer Associates, Wakefield, Mass., Nov. 1976.

[13] PETERSON, G. and FISCHER, M. J. Economical solutions for the critical section problem in a distributed system. In *Proceedings of the 9th ACM Symposium on Theory of Computing* (Boulder, Colo., May 2–4). ACM, New York, 1977, pp. 91–97.

[14] RIVEST, R. L. and PRATT, V. R. The mutual exclusion problem for unreliable processes: Preliminary report. In *Proceedings of the IEEE Symposium on Foundations of Computer Science*. IEEE, New York, 1976, pp. 1–80.

[15] SCHWARTZ, J. T. *Relativity in Illustrations*. New York University Press, New York, 1962.

[16] TAYLOR, E. F. and WHEELER, J. A.. *Space-Time Physics*. W. H. Freeman, San Francisco, 1966.

The Mutual Exclusion Problem: Part II—Statement and Solutions

Leslie Lamport (Digital Equipment Corporation, Palo Alto, California)

Abstract

The theory developed in Part I is used to state the mutual exclusion problem and several additional fairness and failure-tolerance requirements. Four "distributed" N-process solutions are given, ranging from a solution requiring only one communication bit per process that permits individual starvation, to one requiring about $N!$ communication bits per process that satisfies every reasonable fairness and failure-tolerance requirement that we can conceive of.

Categories and Subject Descriptors: D.4.1 [**Operating Systems**]: Process Management—*concurrency; multiprocessing/multiprogramming; mutual exclusion; synchronization*; D.4.5 [**Operating Systems**]: Reliability—*fault-tolerance*

General Terms: Algorithms, Reliability, Theory

Additional Key Words and Phrases: Critical section, shared variables

Most of this work was performed while the author was at SRI International, where it was supported in part by the National Science Foundation under grant number MCS-78-16783.

Author's address: Digital Equipment Corporation, Systems Research Center, 130 Lytton Avenue, Palo Alto, CA 94301.

Paper originally published in *Journal of the Association for Computing Machinery,* 33(2), April 1986, pp. 327–348.

1 Introduction

This is the second part of a two-part paper on the mutual exclusion problem. In Part I [15], we described a formal model of concurrent systems and used it to define a primitive interprocess communication mechanism (communication variables) that assumes no underlying mutual exclusion. In this part, we consider the mutual exclusion problem itself.

The mutual exclusion problem was first described and solved by Dijkstra in [2]. In this problem, there is a collection of asynchronous processes, each alternately executing a critical and a noncritical section, that must be synchronized so that no two processes ever execute their critical sections concurrently. Dijkstra's original solution was followed by a succession of others, starting with [6].

These solutions were motivated by practical concerns—namely, the need to synchronize multiprocess systems using the primitive operations provided by the hardware. More recent computers usually provide sophisticated synchronization primitives that make it easy to achieve mutual exclusion, so these solutions are of less practical interest today. However, mutual exclusion lies at the heart of most concurrent process synchronization, and the mutual exclusion problem is still of great theoretical significance. This paper carefully examines the problem and presents new solutions of theoretical interest. Although some of them may be of practical value as well—especially in distributed systems—we do not concern ourselves here with practicality.

All of the early solutions assumed a central memory, accessible by all processes, which was typical of the hardware in use at the time. Implementing such a central memory requires some mechanism for guaranteeing mutually exclusive access to the individual memory cells by the different processes. Hence, these solutions assume a lower-level "hardware" solution to the very problem they are solving. From a theoretical standpoint, they are thus quite unsatisfactory as solutions to the mutual exclusion problem. The first solution that did not assume any underlying mutual exclusion was given in [7]. However, it required an unbounded amount of storage, so it too was not theoretically satisfying. The only other published solution we are aware of that does not assume mutually exclusive access to a shared resource is by Peterson [17].

Here, in Part II, we present four solutions that do not assume any underlying mutual exclusion, using the concurrently accessible registers defined in Part I [15]. They are increasingly stronger, in that they satisfy stronger conditions, and more expensive, in that they require more storage. The precise formulation of the mutual exclusion problem and of the various fairness and failure-tolerance assumptions, is based upon the formalism of Part I.

2 The Problem

We now formally state the mutual exclusion problem, including a number of different requirements that one might place upon a solution. We exclude from consideration only the following types of requirements:

—efficiency requirements involving space and time complexity;

—probabilistic requirements, stating that the algorithm need only work with probability one (solutions with this kind of requirement have recently been studied by Rabin [19]);

—generalizations of the mutual exclusion problem, such as allowing more than one process in the critical section at once under certain conditions [4, 8], or giving the processes different priorities [8].

Except for these exclusions and one other omission (*r*-bounded waiting) mentioned below, we have included every requirement we could think of that one might reasonably want to place upon a solution.

2.1 Basic Requirements

We assume that each process's program contains a noncritical section statement and a critical section statement, which are executed alternately. These statements generate the following sequence of elementary operation executions in process i:

$$NCS_i^{[1]} \longrightarrow CS_i^{[1]} \longrightarrow NCS_i^{[2]} \longrightarrow CS_i^{[2]} \longrightarrow \cdots$$

where $NCS_i^{[k]}$ denotes the kth execution of process i's noncritical section, $CS_i^{[k]}$ denotes the kth execution of its critical section, and $\longrightarrow$ is the precedence relation introduced in Part I. Taking $NCS_i^{[k]}$ and $CS_i^{[k]}$ to be elementary operation executions simply means that we do not assume any knowledge of their internal structure, and does not imply that they are of short duration.

We assume that the $CS_i^{[k]}$ are terminating operation executions, which means that process i never "halts" in its critical section. However, $NCS_i^{[k]}$ may be nonterminating for some k, meaning that process i may halt in its noncritical section.

The most basic requirement for a solution is that it satisfy the following:

Mutual Exclusion Property.   For any pair of distinct processes i and j, no pair of operation executions $CS_i^{[k]}$ and $CS_j^{[k']}$ are concurrent.

In order to implement mutual exclusion, we must add some synchronization operations to each process's program. We make the following requirement on these additional operations.

No other operation execution of a process can be concurrent with that process's critical or noncritical section operation executions.

This requirement was implicit in Dijkstra's original statement of the problem, but has apparently never been stated explicitly before.

The above requirement implies that each process's program may be written as follows:

> *initial declaration*;
> **repeat forever**
>   *noncritical section*;
>   *trying*;
>   *critical section*;
>   *exit*;
> **end repeat**

The *trying* statement is what generates all the operation executions between a noncritical section execution and the subsequent critical section execution, and the *exit* statement generates all the operation executions between a critical section execution and the subsequent noncritical section execution. The *initial declaration* describes the initial values of the variables. A solution consists of a specification of the *initial declaration*, *trying* and *exit* statements.

A process i therefore generates the following sequence of operation executions:

$$NCS_i^{[1]} \longrightarrow trying_i^{[1]} \longrightarrow CS_i^{[1]} \longrightarrow exit_i^{[1]} \longrightarrow NCS_i^{[2]} \longrightarrow \cdots$$

where $trying_i^{[1]}$ denotes the operation execution generated by the first execution of the *trying* statement, etc.

The second basic property that we require of a solution is that there be no deadlock. Deadlock occurs when one or more processes are "trying to enter" their critical sections, but no process ever does. To say that a process tries forever to enter its critical section means that it is performing a nonterminating execution of its *trying* statement. Since every critical section execution terminates, the absence of deadlock should mean that if some process's *trying* statement doesn't terminate, then other processes must be continually executing their critical sections. However, there is also the possibility that a deadlock occurs because all the processes are stuck in their *exit* statements. The possibility of a nonterminating *exit* execution complicates the statement of the properties and is of no interest here, since the *exit* statements in all our algorithms consist of a fixed number of terminating operations. We will therefore simply require of an algorithm that every *exit* execution terminates.

The absence of deadlock can now be expressed formally as follows:

> *Deadlock Freedom Property.*   If there exists a nonterminating *trying* operation execution, then there exist an infinite number of critical section operation executions.

These two properties, mutual exclusion and deadlock freedom, were the requirements for a mutual exclusion solution originally stated by Dijkstra in [2]. (Of course, he allowed mutually exclusive access to a shared variable in the solution.) They are the minimal requirements one might place on a solution.

2.2 Fairness Requirements

Deadlock freedom means that the entire system of processes can always continue to make progress. However, it does not preclude the possibility that some individual process may wait forever in its *trying* statement. The requirement that this cannot happen is expressed by:

> *Lockout Freedom Property.*   Every *trying* operation execution must terminate.

This requirement was first stated and satisfied by Knuth in [6].

Lockout freedom means that any process i trying to enter its critical section will eventually do so, but it does not guarantee when. In particular, it allows other processes to execute their critical sections arbitrarily many times before process i executes its critical section. We can strengthen the lockout freedom property by placing some kind of fairness condition on the order in which trying processes are allowed to execute their critical sections.

The strongest imaginable fairness condition is that if process i starts to execute its *trying* statement before process j does, then i must execute its critical section before j does. Such a condition is not expressible in our formalism because "starting to execute" is an instantaneous event, and such events are not part of the formalism. However, even if we were to allow atomic operations—including atomic reads and writes of communication variables—so our operations were actually instantaneous events, one can show that this condition cannot be satisfied by any algorithm. The reason is that with a single operation, a process can either tell the other processes that it is in its *trying* statement (by performing a write) or else check if other processes are in their *trying* statements (by performing a read), but not both. Hence, if two processes enter their *trying* statements at very nearly the same time, then there will be no way for them to decide which one entered first. This result can be proved formally, but we will not bother to do so.

The strongest fairness condition that can be satisfied is the following *first-come-first-served* (FCFS) condition. We assume that the *trying* statement consists of two substatements—a *doorway* whose execution requires only a bounded number of elementary operation executions (and hence always terminates), followed by a *waiting* statement. We can require that, if process i finishes executing its *doorway* statement before process j begins executing its *doorway* statement, then i must execute its critical section before j does. Letting $doorway_i^{[k]}$ and $waiting_i^{[k]}$ denote the kth execution of the *doorway* and *waiting* statements by process i, this condition can be expressed formally as follows:

First-Come, First-Served Property.   For any pair of processes i and j and any execution $CS_j^{[m]}$: if $doorway_i^{[k]} \longrightarrow doorway_j^{[m]}$, then $CS_i^{[k]} \longrightarrow CS_j^{[m]}$.

(The conclusion means that $CS_i^{[k]}$ is actually executed.)

The FCFS property states that processes will not execute their critical sections "out of turn". However, it does not imply that any process ever actually executes its critical section. In particular, FCFS does not imply deadlock freedom. However, FCFS and deadlock freedom imply lockout freedom, as we now show.

Theorem 1   FCFS and deadlock freedom imply lockout freedom.

Proof   Suppose $trying_i^{[k]}$ is nonterminating. Since there are a finite number of processes, the deadlock freedom property implies that some process j performs an infinite number of $CS_j^{[m]}$ executions, and therefore an infinite number of $doorway_j^{[m]}$ executions. It then follows from Axiom A5 of Part I that $doorway_i^{[k]} \longrightarrow doorway_j^{[m]}$ for some m. The FCFS property then implies the required contradiction.   ◾

The requirement that executing the doorway take only a bounded number of elementary operation executions means that a process does not have to wait inside its *doorway* statement. Formally, the requirement is that there be some *a priori* bound—the same bound for any possible execution of the algorithm—on the number of elementary operation executions in each $doorway_i^{[k]}$. Had we only assumed that the *doorway* executions always terminate, then any lockout-free solution is always FCFS, where the *doorway* is defined to be essentially the entire *trying* statement. This requirement seems to capture the intuitive meaning of "first-come, first-served". A weaker notion of FCFS was introduced in [18], where it was only required that a process in its *doorway* should not have to wait for a process in its critical or noncritical section. However, we find that definition rather arbitrary.

Michael Fischer has also observed that a FCFS algorithm should not force a process to wait in its *exit* statement. Once a process has finished executing its critical section, it may execute a very short noncritical section and immediately enter its *trying* statement. In this case, the *exit* statement is effectively part of the next execution of the *doorway*, so it should involve no waiting. Hence, any $exit_i^{[k]}$ execution should consist of only a bounded number of elementary operation executions for a FCFS solution. As we mentioned above, this is true of all the solutions described here.

An additional fairness property intermediate between lockout freedom and FCFS, called *r-bounded waiting*, has also been proposed [20]. It states that after process i has executed its *doorway*, any other process can enter its critical section at most r times before i does. Its formal statement is the same as the above statement of the FCFS property, except with $CS_j^{[m]}$ replaced by $CS_j^{[m+r]}$.

2.3 Premature Termination

Thus far, all our properties have been constraints upon what the processes may do. We now state some properties that give processes the freedom to behave in certain ways not explicitly indicated by their programs. We have already required one such property by allowing nonterminating executions of the noncritical section— i.e., we give the process the freedom to halt in its noncritical section. It is this requirement that distinguishes the mutual exclusion problem from a large class of synchronization problems known as "producer/consumer" problems [1]. For example, it prohibits solutions in which processes must take turns entering their critical section.

We now consider two kinds of behavior in which a process can return to its non-critical section from any arbitrary point in its program. In the first, a process stops the execution of its algorithm by setting its communication variables to certain default values and halting. Formally, this means that anywhere in its algorithm, a process may execute the following operation:

> **begin**
>   set all communication variables to their default values;
>   halt
> **end**

For convenience, we consider the final halting operation execution to be a non-terminating noncritical section execution. The default values are specified as part of the algorithm. For all our algorithms, the default value of every communication variable is the same as its initial value.

This type of behavior has been called "failure" in previous papers on the mutual exclusion problem. However, we reserve the term "failure" for a more insidious kind of behavior, and call the above behavior *shutdown*. If the algorithm satisfies a property under this type of behavior, then it is said to be *shutdown safe* for that property.

Shutdown could represent the physical situation of "unplugging" a processor. Whenever a processor discovers that another processor is unplugged, it does not try to actually read that processor's variables, but instead uses their default values. We require that the processor never be "plugged back in" after it has been unplugged. We show below that this is really equivalent to requiring that the processor remain unplugged for a sufficiently long time.

The second kind of behavior is one in which a process deliberately *aborts* the execution of its algorithm. Abortion is the same as shutdown except for three things:

—The process returns to its noncritical section instead of halting.

—Some of its communication variables are left unchanged. (Which ones are specified as part of the algorithm.)

—A communication variable is not set to its default value if it already has that value.[1]

Formally, an abortion is an operation execution consisting of a collection of writes that set certain of the process's communication variables to their default values, followed by ($\longrightarrow$) a noncritical section execution. (The noncritical section execution may then be followed by a *trying* statement execution—or by another abortion.) For our algorithms, the value of a communication variable is set by an abortion if there is an explicitly declared initial value for the variable, otherwise it is left unchanged by the abortion. If an algorithm satisfies a property with this type of behavior, then it is said to be *abortion safe* for that property.

2.4 Failure

Shutdown and abortion describe fairly reasonable kinds of behavior. We now consider unreasonable kinds of behavior, such as might occur in the event of process failure. There are two kinds of faulty behavior that a failed process could exhibit.

---

1. Remember that setting a variable to its old value is not a "no-op", since a read that is concurrent with that operation may get the wrong value. If communication variables were set every time the process aborted, repeated abortions would be indistinguishable from the "malfunctioning" behavior considered below.

—*unannounced death*, in which it halts undetectably;

—*malfunctioning*, in which it keeps setting its state, including the values of its communication variables, to arbitrary values.

An algorithm that can handle the first type of faulty behavior must use real-time clocks, otherwise there is no way to distinguish between a process that has died and one that is simply pausing for a long time between execution steps. An example of an algorithm (not a solution to our mutual exclusion problem) that works in the presence of such faulty behavior can be found in [10]. Consideration of this kind of behavior is beyond the scope of this paper.

A malfunctioning process obviously cannot be prevented from executing its critical section while another process's critical section execution is in progress. However, we may still want to guarantee mutual exclusion among the nonfaulty processes. We therefore assume that a malfunctioning process does not execute its critical section. (A malfunctioning process that executes its *critical section* code is simply defined not to be executing its critical section.)

A malfunctioning process can also disrupt things by preventing nonfaulty processes from entering their critical sections. This is unavoidable, since a process that malfunctions after entering its critical section could leave its communication variables in a state indicating that it is still in the critical section. What we can hope to guarantee is that if the process stops malfunctioning, then the algorithm will resume its normal operation. This leaves two types of behavior to be considered, which differ in how a process stops malfunctioning.

The first type of failure allows a failed process to execute the following sequence of actions.

—It malfunctions for a while, arbitrarily changing the values of its communication variables.

—It then aborts—setting all its communication variables to some default values.

—It then resumes normal behavior, never again malfunctioning.

This behavior represents a situation in which a process fails, its failure is eventually detected and it is shut down, and the process is repaired and restored to service. The assumption that it never again malfunctions is discussed below.

Formally, this means that each process may perform at most one operation execution composed of the following sequence of executions (ordered by the $\longrightarrow$ relation):

—a *malfunction* execution, consisting of a finite collection of writes to its communication variables.

—a collection of writes that sets each communication variable to its default value.

—a noncritical section execution.

The above operation execution will be called a *failure*. If a property of a solution remains satisfied under this kind of behavior, then the solution is said to be *fail-safe* for that property. Note that we do not assume failure to be detectable; one process cannot tell that another has failed (unless it can infer from the values of the other process's variables that a failure must have occurred).

The second type of failure we consider is one in which a process malfunctions, but eventually stops malfunctioning and resumes forever its normal behavior, starting in any arbitrary state. This behavior represents a transient fault.

If such a failure occurs, we cannot expect the system immediately to resume its normal operation. For example, the malfunctioning process might resume its normal operation just at the point where it is about to enter its critical section—while another process is executing its critical section. The most we can require is that after the process stops malfunctioning, the system *eventually* resumes its correct operation.

Since we are interested in the eventual operation, we need only consider what happens after every process has stopped malfunctioning. The state of the system at that time can be duplicated by starting all processes at arbitrary points in their program, with their variables having arbitrary values. In other words, we need only consider the behavior obtained by having each process do the following:

—execute a *malfunction* operation;

—then begin normal execution at any point in its program.

This kind of behavior will be called a *transient malfunction*. Any operation execution that is not part of the malfunction execution will be called a *normal* operation execution.

Unfortunately, deadlock freedom and lockout freedom cannot be achieved under this kind of transient malfunction behavior without a further assumption. To see why, suppose a malfunctioning process sets its communication variables to the values they should have while executing its critical section, and then begins normal execution with a nonterminating noncritical section execution. The process will always appear to the rest of the system as if it is executing its critical section, so no other process can ever execute its critical section.

To handle this kind of behavior, we must assume that a process executing its noncritical section will eventually set its communication variables to their default values. Therefore, we assume that instead of being elementary, the noncritical section executions are generated by the following program:

while ?
    do *abort* ;
        noncritical operation **od**

where the "?" denotes some unknown condition, which could cause the **while** to be executed forever, and every execution of the *noncritical operation* terminates. Recall that an *abort* execution sets certain communication variables to their default values if they are not already set to those values.

We now consider what it means for a property to hold "eventually". Intuitively, by "eventually" we mean "after some bounded period of time" following all the malfunctions. However, we have not introduced any concept of physical time. The only unit of time implicit in our formalism is the time needed to perform an operation execution. Therefore, we must define "after some bounded period of time" to mean "after some bounded number of operation executions". The definition we need is the following.

Definition 1   A *system step* is an operation execution consisting of one normal elementary operation execution from every process. An operation execution A is said to occur *after t system steps* if there exist system steps $S_1, \ldots, S_t$ such that $S_1 \longrightarrow \cdots \longrightarrow S_t \longrightarrow A$.

It is interesting to note that we could introduce a notion of time by defining the "time" at which an operation occurs to be the maximum t such that the operation occurs after t system steps (or 0 if there is no such t). Axioms A5 and A6 of Part I imply that this maximum always exists. Axiom A5 and the assumption that there are no nonterminating elementary operation executions imply that "time" increases without bound—i.e., there are operations occurring at arbitrarily large "times". Since we only need the concept of eventuality, we will not consider this way of defining "time".

We can now define what it means for a property to hold "eventually". Deadlock freedom and lockout freedom state that something eventually happens—for example, deadlock freedom states that so long as some process is executing its *trying* operation, then some process eventually executes its critical section. Since "eventually X eventually happens" is equivalent to "X eventually happens", requiring that these two properties eventually hold is the same as simply requiring that they hold.

We say that the mutual exclusion and FCFS properties eventually hold if they can be violated only for a bounded "length of time". Thus, the mutual exclusion property eventually holds if there is some t such that any two critical section executions $CS_i^{[k]}$ and $CS_j^{[m]}$ that both occur after t system steps are not concurrent. Similarly, the FCFS property holds eventually if it holds whenever both the *doorway* executions occur after t system steps. The value of t must be independent of the particular execution of the algorithm, but it may depend upon the number N of processes.

If a property eventually holds under the above type of transient malfunction behavior, then we say that the algorithm is *self-stabilizing* for that property. The concept of self-stabilization is due to Dijkstra [3].

Remarks on "Forever". In our definition of failure, we could not allow a malfunctioning process to fail again after it had resumed its normal behavior, since repeated malfunctioning and recovery can be indistinguishable from continuous malfunctioning. However, if an algorithm satisfies any of our properties under the assumption that a process may malfunction only once, then it will also satisfy the property under repeated malfunctioning and recovery—so long as the process waits long enough before malfunctioning again.

The reason for this is that all our properties require that something either be true at all times (mutual exclusion, FCFS) or that something happen in the future (deadlock freedom, lockout freedom). If something remains true during a malfunction, then it will also remain true under repeated malfunctioning. If something must happen eventually, then because there is no "crystal ball" operation that can tell if a process will abort in the future,[2] another malfunction can occur after the required action has taken place. Therefore, an algorithm that is fail-safe for such a property must also satisfy the property under repeated failure, if a failed process waits long enough before executing its *trying* statement again. Similar remarks apply to shutdown and transient malfunction.

3 The Solutions

We now present four solutions to the mutual exclusion problem. Each one is stronger than the preceding one in the sense that it satisfies more properties, and is more expensive in that it requires more communication variables.

---

2. Such operations lead to logical contradictions—for example, if one process executes "set x true if process i will abort", and process i executes "abort if x is never set true".

3.1 The Mutual Exclusion Protocol

We first describe the fundamental method for achieving mutual exclusion upon which all the solutions are based. Each process has a communication variable that acts as a synchronizing "flag". Mutual exclusion is guaranteed by the following protocol: in order to enter its critical section, a process must first set its flag true and then find every other process's flag to be false. The following result shows that this protocol does indeed ensure mutual exclusion, where v and w are communication variables, as defined in Part I, that represent the flags of two processes, and A and B represent executions of those processes' critical sections.

Theorem 2   Let v and w be communication variables, and suppose that for some operation executions A and B and some k and m:

—$V^{[k]} \longrightarrow read\ w = false \longrightarrow A$.

—$W^{[m]} \longrightarrow read\ v = false \longrightarrow B$.

—$v^{[k]} = w^{[m]} = true$.

—If $V^{[k+1]}$ exists then $A \longrightarrow V^{[k+1]}$.

—If $W^{[m+1]}$ exists then $B \longrightarrow W^{[m+1]}$.

Then A and B are not concurrent.

We first prove the following result, which will be used in the proof of the theorem. Its statement and proof use the formalism developed in Part I.

Lemma 1   Let v be a communication variable and R a $read\ v = false$ operation such that:

1. $v^{[k]} = true$

2. $V^{[k]} \dashrightarrow R$

3. $R \not\dashrightarrow V^{[k]}$

Then $V^{[k+1]}$ must exist and $V^{[k+1]} \dashrightarrow R$.

Proof   Intuitively, the assumptions mean that $V^{[k]}$ "effectively precedes" R, so R cannot see any value written by a write that precedes $V^{[k]}$. Since R does not obtain the value written by $V^{[k]}$, it must be causally affected by a later write operation $V^{[k+1]}$. We now formalize this reasoning.

By A3 and the assumption that the writes of v are totally ordered, hypothesis 2 implies that $V^{[i]} \dashrightarrow R$ for all $i \leq k$. If $R \dashrightarrow V^{[i]}$ for some $i < k$, then A3 would imply $R \dashrightarrow V^{[k]}$, contrary to hypothesis 3. Hence, we conclude that R is effectively nonconcurrent with $V^{[i]}$ for all $i \leq k$. If $V^{[k]}$ were the last write to v, hypothesis 2 and C2 would imply that R has to obtain the value $true$, contrary to hypothesis 1. Therefore, the operation $V^{[k+1]}$ must exist.

We now prove by contradiction that $V^{[k+1]} \dashrightarrow R$. Suppose to the contrary that $V^{[k+1]} \not\dashrightarrow R$. C3 then implies that $R \dashrightarrow V^{[k+1]}$, which by A3 implies $R \dashrightarrow V^{[i]}$ for all $i \geq k + 1$. A3 and the assumption that $V^{[k+1]} \not\dashrightarrow R$, implies that $V^{[i]} \not\dashrightarrow R$ for all $i \geq k + 1$. Since we have already concluded that $V^{[i]} \dashrightarrow R$ for all $i \leq k$, C2 implies that R must obtain the value *true*, which contradicts hypothesis 1. This completes the proof that $V^{[k+1]} \dashrightarrow R$. ∎

Proof of Theorem   By C3, we have the following two possibilities:

1. *read w = false* $\dashrightarrow W^{[m]}$.

2. $W^{[m]} \dashrightarrow$ *read w = false*.

(These are not disjoint possibilities.) We consider case (1) first. Combining (1) with the first two hypotheses of the theorem, we have

$$ V^{[k]} \longrightarrow read\ w = false \dashrightarrow W^{[m]} \longrightarrow read\ v = false $$

By A4, this implies $V^{[k]} \longrightarrow read\ v = false$. A2 and the lemma then imply that $V^{[k+1]}$ exists and $V^{[k+1]} \dashrightarrow read\ v = false$. Combining this with the fourth and second hypotheses gives

$$ A \longrightarrow V^{[k+1]} \dashrightarrow read\ v = false \longrightarrow B $$

By A4, this implies $A \longrightarrow B$, completing the proof in case (1).

We now consider case (2). Having already proved the theorem in case (1), we can make the additional assumption that case (1) does not hold, so *read w = false* $\not\dashrightarrow W^{[m]}$. We can then apply the lemma (substituting w for v and m for k) to conclude that $W^{[m+1]}$ exists and $W^{[m+1]} \dashrightarrow read\ w = false$. Combining this with the first and last hypotheses gives

$$ B \longrightarrow W^{[m+1]} \dashrightarrow read\ w = false \longrightarrow A $$

A4 now implies $B \longrightarrow A$, proving the theorem for this case. ∎

We have written the proof of this theorem in full detail to show how A1–A4 and C0–C3 are used. In the remaining proofs, we will be more terse, leaving many of the details to the reader.

3.2   The One-Bit Solution

We now use the above protocol to obtain a mutual exclusion solution that requires only the single (one-bit) communication variable x_i for each process i. Obviously, no solution can work with fewer communication variables. This solution was also

private variable: j **with range** $1 \ldots N$;
communication variable: x_i **initially** *false*;
repeat forever
    noncritical section;
l: $x_i := true$;
    for $j := 1$ **until** $i - 1$
        do if x_j **then** $x_i := false$;
                    while x_j **do od**;
                    goto l
            fi
        od;
    for $j := i + 1$ **until** N
        do while x_j **do od od**;
    critical section;
    $x_i := false$
end repeat

Figure 1   The one-bit algorithm: Process i.

discovered independently by Burns [1a]. The algorithm for process i is shown in Figure 1, and its correctness properties are given by the following result.

Theorem 3   The One-Bit Algorithm satisfies the mutual exclusion and deadlock freedom properties, and is shutdown safe and fail-safe for these properties.

Proof   To prove the mutual exclusion property, we observe that the above protocol is followed by the processes. More precisely, the mutual exclusion property is proved using Theorem 2, substituting x_i for v, x_j for w, $CS_i^{[k]}$ for A and $CS_j^{[k']}$ for B. This protocol is followed even under shutdown and failure behavior, so the algorithm is shutdown safe and fail-safe for mutual exclusion. To prove deadlock freedom, we first prove the following lemma.   ■

Lemma 2   Any execution of the second **for** loop must terminate, even under shutdown and failure behavior.

Proof   The proof is by contradiction. Let i be any process that executes a nonterminating second **for** loop. Then before entering the loop, i performs a finite number of *write* x_i executions, with the final one setting x_i true. We now prove by contradiction that every other process can also execute only a finite number of writes to its communication variable. Let k be the lowest-numbered process that performs an infinite number of *write* x_k executions. Process k executes statement l infinitely many times. Since every lower-numbered process j executes only a finite number of writes to x_j, A5, A2 and C2 imply that all but a finite number of reads of x_j by k must obtain its final value. For k to execute statement l infinitely many times (and not get trapped during an execution of the first **for** loop's **while** statement), this final value must be *false* for every $j < k$. This implies that k can execute its first **for** loop only finitely many times before it enters its second **for** loop. But since the final value of x_i is *true*, this means that $k < i$, and that k can execute its second **for** loop only finitely many times before being trapped forever in the "**while** x_i" statement in its second **for** loop. This contradicts the assumption that k performs an infinite number of *write* x_k executions.

We have thus proved that if the execution of the second **for** loop of any process is nonterminating, then every process can execute only a finite number of writes to its communication variable. The final value of a process's communication variable can be *true* only if the process executes its second **for** loop forever. Letting i be the highest-numbered process executing a nonterminating second **for** loop, so the final value of x_j is *false* for every $j > i$, we easily see that i must eventually exit this **for** loop, providing the required contradiction. Hence, every execution of the second **for** loop must eventually terminate. ▪

Proof of Theorem (continued). We now complete the proof of the theorem by showing that the One-Bit Algorithm is deadlock free. Assume that some process performs a nonterminating *trying* execution. Let i be the lowest numbered process that does not execute a nonterminating noncritical section. (There is at least one such process—the one performing the nonterminating *trying* execution.) Each lower numbered process j performs a nonterminating noncritical section execution after setting its communication variable false. (This is true for shutdown and failure behavior too.) It follows from A5, A2, and C2 that if i performs an infinite number of reads of the variable x_j, then all but a finite number of them must return the value *false*. This implies that every execution of the first **for** loop of process i must terminate. But, by the above lemma, every execution of its second **for** loop must also terminate. Since we have assumed that every execution of its noncritical section terminates, this implies that process i performs an infinite number of critical section executions, completing the proof of the theorem. ▪

The One-Bit Algorithm as written in Figure 1 is not self-stabilizing for mutual exclusion or deadlock freedom. It is easy to see that it is not self-stabilizing for deadlock freedom, since we could start all the processes in the **while** statement of the first **for** loop with their communication variables all true. It is not self-stabilizing for mutual exclusion because a process could be started in its second **for** loop with its communication variable false, remain there arbitrarily long, waiting as higher numbered processes repeatedly execute their critical sections, and then execute its critical section while another process is also executing its critical section.

The One-Bit Algorithm is made self-stabilizing for both mutual exclusion and deadlock freedom by modifying each of the **while** loops so they read the value of x_i and correct its value if necessary. In other words, we place

> **if** x_i **then** $x_i := false$

in the body of the first **for** loop's **while** statement, and likewise for the second **for** loop (except setting x_i true there). We now prove that this modification makes the One-Bit Algorithm self-stabilizing for mutual exclusion and deadlock freedom.

Theorem 4 With the above modification, the One-Bit Algorithm is self-stabilizing for mutual exclusion and deadlock freedom.

Proof It is easy to check that the proof of the deadlock freedom property in Theorem .3 is valid under the behavior assumed for self-stabilization, so the algorithm is self-stabilizing for deadlock freedom. To prove that it is self-stabilizing for mutual exclusion, we have to show that the mutual exclusion protocol is followed after a bounded number of system steps. It is easy to verify that this is true so long as every process that is in its second **for** loop (or past the point where it has decided to enter its second **for** loop) exits from that loop within a bounded number of system steps.[3] We prove this by "backwards induction" on the process number.

To start the induction, we observe that since its second **for** loop is empty, process N must exit that **for** loop within some bounded number $t(N)$ of system steps. To complete the induction step, we assume that if $j > i$, then process j must exit its second **for** loop within $t(j)$ system steps of when it entered, and we prove that if process i is in its second **for** loop (after the *malfunction*), then it must eventually exit. We define the following sets:

S_1: The set of processes waiting in their second **for** loop for a process numbered less than or equal to i.

S_2: The set of processes waiting in their first **for** loop for a process in S_1.

S_3: The set of processes in their *trying* statement.

---

3. In this proof, we talk about where a process is in its program immediately before and after a system step. This makes sense because a system step contains an elementary operation from every process.

If process i is in its second **for** loop, then within a bounded number of steps it either leaves that loop or else sets x_i true. In the latter case, no process that then enters its *trying* section can leave it before process i does. Each higher-numbered process that is in its second **for** loop must leave it in a bounded number of system steps, whereupon any other process that is in its second **for** loop past the test of x_i must exit that loop within a bounded number of system steps. It follows that within a bounded number of steps, if process i is still in its second **for** loop, then the system execution reaches a point at which each of the three sets S_m cannot get smaller until i sets x_i false. It is then easy to see that once this has happened, within a bounded number of steps, one of the following must occur:

—Process i exits its second **for** loop.

—Another process joins the set S_3.

—A process in S_3 joins S_1 or S_2.

Since there are only N processes, there is a bound on how many times the second two can occur. Therefore, the first possibility must occur within a bounded number of system steps, completing the proof that process i must exit its second **for** loop within a bounded number of system steps. This in turn completes the proof of the theorem. ◼

3.3 A Digression

Suppose N processes are arranged in a circle, with process 1 followed by process 2 followed by ... followed by process N, which is followed by process 1. Each process communicates only with its two neighbors using an array v of boolean variables, each $v(i)$ being owned by process i and read by the following process. We want the processes to continue forever taking turns performing some action—first process 1, then process 2, and so on. Each process must be able to tell whether it is its turn by reading just its own variable $v(i)$ and that of the preceding process, and must pass the turn on to the next process by complementing the value of $v(i)$ (which is the only change it can make).

The basic idea is to let it be process i's turn if the circle of variables $v(1), \ldots, v(N)$ changes value at i—that is, if $v(i) = \neg v(i-1)$. This doesn't quite work because a ring of values cannot change at only one point. However, we let process 1 be exceptional, letting it be 1's turn when $v(1) = v(N)$. The reader should convince himself that this works if all the $v(i)$ are initially equal.

It is obvious how this algorithm, which works for the cycle of all N processes arranged in order, is generalized to handle an arbitrary cycle of processes with one process singled out as the "first". To describe the general algorithm more formally, we need to introduce some notation. Recall that a *cycle* is an object of the form $\langle i_1, \ldots, i_m \rangle$, where the i_j are distinct integers between 1 and N. The i_j are called the *elements* of the cycle. Two cycles are the same if they are identical except for a cyclic permutation of their elements—e.g., $\langle 1, 3, 5, 7 \rangle$ and $\langle 5, 7, 1, 3 \rangle$ are two representations of the same cycle, which is not the same cycle as $\langle 1, 5, 3, 7 \rangle$. We define the *first element* of a cycle to be its smallest element i_j.

By a *Boolean function on a cycle* we mean a Boolean function on its set of elements. The following functions are used in the remaining algorithms. Note that $CG(v, \gamma, i)$ is the Boolean function that has the value *true* if and only if it is process i's turn to go next in the general algorithm applied to the cycle γ of processes.

Definition 2 Let v be a Boolean function on the cycle $\gamma = \langle i_1, \ldots, i_m \rangle$, and let i_1 be the first element of γ. For each element i_j of the cycle we define:

$$CGV(v, \gamma, i_j) \stackrel{\text{def}}{=} \neg v(i_{j-1}) \qquad \text{if} \quad j > 1;$$
$$v(i_m) \qquad \text{if} \quad j = 1.$$
$$CG(v, \gamma, i_j) \stackrel{\text{def}}{=} v(i_j) \equiv CGV(v, \gamma, i_j)$$

If $CG(v, \gamma, i_j)$ is true, then we say that v *changes value at* i_j.

The turn-taking algorithm, in which process i takes its turn when $CG(v, \gamma, i)$ equals *true*, works right when it is started with all the $v(i)$ having the same value. If it is started with arbitrary initial values for the $v(i)$, then several processes may be able to go at the same time. However, deadlock is impossible; it is always at least one process's turn. This is expressed formally by the following result, whose proof is simple and is left to the reader.

Lemma 3 Every Boolean function on a cycle changes value at some element—that is, for any Boolean function v on a cycle γ, there is some element i of γ such that $CG(v, \gamma, i)$ = *true*.

We shall also need the following definitions. A cycle $\langle i_1, \ldots, i_m \rangle$ is said to be *ordered* if, after a cyclic permutation of the i_j, $i_1 < \ldots < i_m$. For example, $\langle 5, 7, 2, 3 \rangle$ is an ordered cycle while $\langle 2, 5, 3, 7 \rangle$ is not. Any nonempty set of integers in the range 1 to N defines a unique ordered cycle. If S is such a set, then we let ORD S denote this ordered cycle.

3.4   The Three-Bit Algorithm

The One-Bit algorithm has the property that the lowest-numbered process that is trying to enter its critical section must eventually enter it—unless a still lower-numbered process enters the trying region before it can do so. However, a higher-numbered process can be locked out forever by lower-numbered processes repeatedly entering their critical sections. The basic idea of the Three-Bit Algorithm is for the processes' numbers to change in such a way that a waiting process must eventually become the lowest-numbered process.

Of course, we don't actually change a process's number. Rather, we modify the algorithm so that instead of process i's two **for** loops running from 1 up to (but excluding) i and $i + 1$ to N, they run cyclically from f up to but excluding i and from $i \oplus 1$ up to but excluding f, where f is a function of the communication variables, and $\oplus$ denotes addition modulo N. As processes pass through their critical sections, they change the value of their communication variables in such a way as to make sure that f eventually equals the number of every waiting process.

The first problem that we face in doing this is that if we simply replaced the **for** loops as indicated above, a process could be waiting inside its first **for** loop without ever discovering that f should have been changed. Therefore, we modify the algorithm so that when it finds x_j true, instead of waiting for it to become false, process i recomputes f and restarts its cycle of examining all the processes' communication variables.

We add two new communication variables to each process i. The variable y_i is set true by process i immediately upon entering its trying section, and is not set false until after process i has left its critical section and set x_i false. The variable z_i is complemented when process i leaves its critical section.

Finally, it is necessary to guarantee that while process i is in its trying region, a "lower-numbered" process that enters after i cannot enter its critical section before i does. This is accomplished by having the "lower-numbered" process wait for y_i to become false instead of x_i. This will still insure mutual exclusion, since x_i is false whenever y_i is.

Putting these changes all together, we get the algorithm of Figure 2. The "**for** $j := \ldots$ **cyclically to** $\ldots$" denotes an iteration starting with j equal to the lower bound, and incrementing j by 1 modulo N up to but excluding the upper bound. We let $*:=*$ denote an assignment operation that performs a write only if it will change the value of the variable—i.e., the right-hand side is evaluated, compared with the current value of the variable on the left-hand side, and an assignment performed only if they are unequal. The $*:=*$ operation is introduced because we have assumed nothing about the value obtained by a read that is concurrent with a write, even if the write does not change the value. For example, executing $v := true$

private variables: j, f **with range** $1 \ldots N$,
$\qquad\qquad$ γ **with range** cycles on $1 \ldots N$;
communication variables: x_i, y_i **initially** *false*, z_i;
repeat forever
$\quad$ noncritical section;
$\quad$ $y_i := true$;
$l1$: $x_i := true$;
$l2$: $\gamma := \mathrm{ORD}\{i : y_i = true\}$
$\quad$ $f := \text{minimum } \{j \in \gamma : CG(z, \gamma, j) = true\}$;
$\quad$ **for** $j := f$ **cyclically to** i
$\quad\quad$ **do if** y_j **then** $x_i *{:=}* false$;
$\quad\quad\quad\quad\quad\quad$ **goto** $l2$
$\quad\quad\quad$ **fi**
$\quad\quad$ **od**;
$\quad$ **if** $\neg x_i$ **then goto** $l1$ **fi**;
$\quad$ **for** $j := i \oplus 1$ **cyclically to** f
$\quad\quad$ **do if** x_j then **goto** $l2$ **fi od**;
$\quad$ *critical section*;
$\quad$ $z_i := \neg z_i$;
$\quad$ $x_i := false$;
$\quad$ $y_i := false$
end repeat

Figure 2 The three-bit algorithm: Process i

when v has the value *true* can cause a concurrent read of v to obtain the value *false*. However, executing $v *{:=}* true$ has absolutely no effect if v has the value *true*.

We let z denote the function that assigns the value z_j to j—so evaluating it at j requires a read of the variable z_j. Thus, $CG(z, \langle 1, 3, 5 \rangle, 3) = true$ if and only if $z_1 \neq z_3$. Note that i is always an element of the cycle γ computed by process i, so the cycle is nonempty and the argument of the minimum function is a nonempty set (by Lemma 3).

We now prove that this algorithm satisfies the desired properties. In this and subsequent proofs, we will reason informally about processes looping and things happening eventually. The reader can refer to the proof of Theorem 3 to see how these arguments can be made more formal.

Theorem 5 The Three-Bit Algorithm satisfies the mutual exclusion, deadlock freedom and lockout freedom properties, and is shutdown safe and fail-safe for them.

Proof To verify the mutual exclusion property, we need only check that the basic mutual exclusion protocol is observed. This is not immediately obvious, since process i tests either x_j or y_j before entering its critical section, depending upon the value of f. However, a little thought will show that processes i and j do indeed follow the protocol before entering their critical sections, process i reading either x_j or y_j, and process j reading either x_i or y_i. This is true for the behavior allowed under shutdown and failure safety, so the algorithm is shutdown safe and fail-safe for mutual exclusion.

To prove deadlock freedom, assume for the sake of contradiction that some process executes a nonterminating *trying* statement, and that no process performs an infinite number of critical section executions. Then eventually there must be some set of processes looping forever in their *trying* statements, and all other processes forever executing their noncritical sections with their x and y variables false. Moreover, all the "trying" processes will eventually obtain the same value for f. Ordering the process numbers cyclically starting with f, let i be the lowest-numbered trying process. It is easy to see that all trying processes other than i will eventually set their x variables false, and i will eventually enter its critical section, providing the necessary contradiction.

We now show that the algorithm is lockout free. There must be a time at which one of the following three conditions is true for every process:

—It will execute its critical section infinitely many times.

—It is and will remain forever in its *trying* statement.

—It is and will remain forever in its noncritical section.

Suppose that this time has been reached, and let $\beta = \langle j_1, \ldots, j_p \rangle$ be the ordered cycle formed from the set of processes for which one of the first two conditions holds. Note that we are not assuming j_1 to be the first element (smallest j_i) of β. We prove by contradiction that no process can remain forever in its trying section.

Suppose j_1 remains forever in its trying section. If j_2 were to execute its critical section infinitely many times, then it would eventually enter its *trying* section with z_{j_2} equal to $\neg CGV(z, \beta, j_2)$. When process j_2 then executes its statement $l2$, the cycle γ it computes will include the element j_1, and it will compute $CG(z, \gamma, j_2)$ to equal *false*. It is easy to see that the value of f that j_2 then computes will cause j_1 to lie in the index range of its first **for** loop, so it must wait forever for process j_1 to set y_{j_1} false.

We therefore see that if j_1 remains forever in its trying section, then j_2 must also remain forever in its trying section. Since this is true for any element j_1 in the cycle β (we did not assume j_1 to be the first element), a simple induction argument shows that if any process remains forever in its trying section, then all the processes $j_1, \ldots, j_p$ must remain forever in their trying sections. But this means that the system is deadlocked, which we have shown to be impossible, giving the required contradiction.

The above argument remains valid under shutdown and failure behavior, so the algorithm is shutdown safe and fail-safe for lockout freedom.   ∎

As with the One-Bit Algorithm, we must modify the Three-Bit Algorithm in order to make it self-stabilizing. It is necessary to make sure that process i does not wait in its *trying* section with y_i false. We therefore need to add the statement $y_i *{:=}*$ *true* somewhere between the label $l2$ and the beginning of the **for** statement. It is not necessary to correct the value of x_i because that happens automatically, and the initial value of z_i does not matter. We then have the following result.

Theorem 6   The Three-Bit Algorithm, with the above modification, is self-stabilizing for the mutual exclusion, deadlock freedom and lockout freedom properties.

Proof   Within a bounded number of system steps, each process will either have passed through point $l2$ of its program twice, or entered its noncritical section and reset its x and y variables. (Remember that for self-stabilization, we must assume that these variables are reset in the noncritical section if they have the value *true*.) After that has happened, the system will be in a state it could have reached starting at the beginning from a normal initial state.   ∎

3.5 FCFS Solutions

We now describe two FCFS solutions. Both of them combine a mutual exclusion algorithm ME that is deadlock free but not FCFS with an algorithm FC that does not provide a mutual exclusion but does guarantee FCFS entry to its "critical section". The mutual exclusion algorithm is embedded within the FCFS algorithm as follows.

```
repeat forever
    noncritical section;
    FC trying;
    FC critical section: begin
                            ME trying;
                            ME critical section;
                            ME exit
                         end;
    FC exit
end repeat
```

communication variables:
  y_i **initially** *false*,
  array z_i **indexed by** $\{1 \ldots N\} - \{i\}$;
private variables:
  array *after* **indexed by** $\{1 \ldots N\} - \{i\}$ **of boolean**,
  j **with range** $1 \ldots N$;
repeat forever
  noncritical section;
  doorway: **for all** $j \neq i$
              do $z_i[j] *:=* \neg CGV(z_{ij}, \text{ORD}\{i, j\}, i)$ **od**;
          for all $j \neq i$
              do *after*$[j] := y_j$ **od**;
          $y_i := true$;
  waiting: **for all** $j \neq i$
              do while *after*$[j]$
                do if $CG(z_{ij}, \text{ORD}\{i, j\}, i) \vee \neg y_j$
                        then *after*$[j] := false$ **fi od**
              od;
  critical section;
  $y_i := false$
end repeat

Figure 3   The N-Bit FCFS algorithm: Process i.

It is obvious that the entire algorithm satisfies the FCFS and mutual exclusion properties, where its doorway is the FC algorithm's doorway. Moreover, if both FC and ME are deadlock free, then the entire algorithm is also deadlock free. This is also true under shutdown and failure. Hence, if FC is shutdown safe (or fail-safe) for FCFS and deadlock freedom, and ME is shutdown safe (fail-safe) for mutual exclusion and deadlock freedom, then the entire algorithm is shutdown safe (fail-safe) for FCFS, mutual exclusion and deadlock freedom.

We can let ME be the One-Bit Algorithm, so we need only look for algorithms that are FCFS and deadlock free. The first one is the N-Bit Algorithm of Figure 3, which is a modification of an algorithm due to Katseff[5]. It uses N communication variables for each process. However, each of the $N - 1$ variables $z_i[j]$ of process i is read only by process j. Hence, the complete mutual exclusion algorithm using it and the One-Bit Algorithm requires the same number of single-reader variables as the Three-Bit Algorithm. The "**for all** j" statement executes its body once for each of the indicated values of j, with the separate executions done in any order (or interleaved). The function z_{ij} on the cycle ORD $\{i, j\}$ is defined by:

$$z_{ij}(i) \stackrel{\text{def}}{=} z_i[j],$$

$$z_{ij}(j) \stackrel{\text{def}}{=} z_j[i].$$

We now prove the following properties of this algorithm.

Lemma 4   The N-Bit Algorithm satisfies the FCFS and Deadlock Freedom properties, and is shutdown safe, abortion safe and fail-safe for them.

Proof   Informally, the FCFS property is satisfied because if process i finishes its doorway before process j enters its doorway, but i has not yet exited, then j must see y_i true and wait for i to reset y_i or change $z_i[j]$. This argument is formalized as follows.

Assume that $doorway_i^{[k]} \longrightarrow doorway_j^{[m]}$. Let $Y_i^{[k']}$ denote the write operation of y_i performed during $doorway_i^{[k]}$, let $Z_i[j]^{[k'']}$ be the last write of $z_i[j]$ performed before $Y_i^{[k']}$.

We suppose that $CS_j^{[m]}$ exists, but that $CS_i^{[k]} \nrightarrow CS_j^{[m]}$, and derive a contradiction. Let R be any read of y_i performed by process j during $trying_j^{[m]}$. Since $doorway_i^{[k]} \longrightarrow doorway_j^{[m]}$, we have $Y_i^{[k']} \longrightarrow R$. Since $CS_i^{[k]} \nrightarrow CS_j^{[m]}$, A4 implies that $Y_i^{[k'+1]} \nrightarrow R$. It then follows from C2 that the read R must obtain the value $y_i^{[k']}$, which equals *true*. A similar argument shows that every read of $z_i[j]$ during $trying_j^{[m]}$ obtains the value $z_i[j]^{[k'']}$. It is then easy to see that process j sets *after*$[i]$ true in its doorway and can never set it false because it always reads the same value of $z_i[j]$ in its *waiting* statement as it did in its *doorway*. Hence, j can never exit from its waiting section, which is the required contradiction.

We next prove deadlock freedom. The only way deadlock could occur is for there to be a cycle $\langle i_1, \ldots, i_m \rangle$ of processes, each one waiting for the preceding one—i.e., with each process $i_{j\oplus1}$ having *after*$[i_j]$ true. We assume that this is the case and obtain a contradiction. Let Ry_j denote the read of $y_{i_{j\ominus1}}$ and let Wy_j denote the write of y_{i_j} by process i_j in the last execution of its doorway. Since $Ry_j \longrightarrow Wy_j$ and the relation $\longrightarrow$ is acyclic, by A2 and A4 there must be some j such that $Wy_j \nrightarrow Ry_{j\oplus1}$. By C3, this implies that $Ry_{j\oplus1} \dashrightarrow Wy_j$.

Let Wy' be the write of y_{i_j} that immediately precedes Wy_j, and thus sets its value false. If Wy' did not exist (because Wy_j was the first write of y_{i_j}) or $Ry_{j\oplus1} \nrightarrow Wy'$, it would follow from C2 and C3 that $Ry_{j\oplus1}$ obtains the value *false*. But this is impossible because process $i_{j\oplus1}$ has set *after*$[i_j]$ true. Hence, there is such a Wy' and $Ry_{j\oplus1} \dashrightarrow Wy'$.

Using this result and A4, it is easy to check that the last write of $z_{i_{j\oplus 1}}[i_j]$ (during the last execution of the doorway of process $i_{j\oplus 1}$) must have preceded the reading of it by process i_j during the last execution of its doorway. It follows from this that in the deadlock state, $CG(z_{i_{j\oplus 1}}[i_j], \text{ORD}\{i_j, i_{j\oplus 1}\}, i_{j\oplus 1})$ must be true, contradicting the assumption that $i_{j\oplus 1}$ is waiting forever with $after[i_j]$ true. This completes the proof of deadlock freedom.

We leave it to the reader to verify that the above proofs remain valid under shutdown, abortion and failure behavior. The only nontrivial part of the proof is showing that the algorithm is abortion safe for deadlock freedom. This property follows from the observation that if no process enters its critical section, then eventually all the values of $z_i[j]$ will stabilize and no more writes to those variables will occur—even if there are infinitely many abortions.   ◾

Using this lemma and the preceding remarks about embedding a mutual exclusion algorithm inside a FCFS algorithm, we can prove the following result.

Theorem 7   Embedding the One-Bit Algorithm inside the N-Bit Algorithm yields an algorithm that satisfies the mutual exclusion, FCFS, deadlock freedom and lockout freedom properties, and is shutdown safe, abortion safe and fail-safe for these properties.

Proof   As we remarked above, the proof of the mutual exclusion, FCFS and deadlock freedom properties is trivial. Lockout freedom follows from these by Theorem 1. The fact that it is shutdown safe and fail-safe for these properties follows from the fact that the One-Bit and N-Bit algorithms are. The only thing left to show is that the entire algorithm is abortion safe for these properties even though the One-Bit algorithm is not. The FCFS property for the outer N-Bit algorithm implies that once a process has aborted, it cannot enter the One-Bit algorithm's *trying* statement until all the processes that were waiting there have either exited from the critical section or aborted. Hence, so far as the inner One-Bit algorithm is concerned, abortion is the same as shutdown until there are no more waiting processes. The shutdown safety of the One-Bit Algorithm therefore implies the abortion safety for the entire algorithm.   ◾

The above algorithm satisfies all of our conditions except for self-stabilization. It is not self-stabilizing for deadlock freedom because it is possible to start the algorithm in a state with a cycle of processes each waiting for the next. (The fact that this cannot happen in normal operation is due to the precise order in which variables are read and written.) In our final algorithm, we modify the N-Bit Algorithm to eliminate this possibility.

In the N-Bit Algorithm, process i waits for process j so long as the function z_{ij} on the cycle ORD $\{i, j\}$ does not change value at i. Since a function must change value at some element of a cycle, this prevents i and j from waiting for each other. However, it does not prevent a cycle of waiting processes containing more than two elements. We therefore introduce a function z_γ for every cycle γ, and we require that i wait for j only if for every cycle γ in which j precedes i: z_γ does not change value at i. It is easy to see that for any state, there can be no cycle γ in which each process waits for the preceding one, since z_γ must change value at some element of γ.

This leads us to the $N!$-Bit Algorithm of Figure 4. We use the notation that $CYC(i)$ denotes the set of all cycles containing i and at least one other element, and $CYC(j, i)$ denotes the set of all those cycles in which j precedes i. We let z_γ denote the function on the cycle γ that assigns the value $z_i[\gamma]$ to the element i.

Using the $N!$-Bit FCFS Algorithm, we can construct the "ultimate" algorithm that satisfies every property we have ever wanted from a mutual exclusion solution, as stated by the following theorem. Unfortunately, as the reader has no doubt noticed, this solution requires approximately $N!$ communication variables for each process, making it of little practical interest except for very small values of N.

Theorem 8 Embedding the One-Bit Algorithm inside the $N!$-Bit Algorithm yields an algorithm that satisfies the mutual exclusion, FCFS, deadlock freedom and lockout freedom properties, and is shutdown safe, abortion safe, fail-safe and self-stabilizing for these properties.

Proof The proof of all but the self-stabilizing condition is the same as for the previous solution using the N-Bit Algorithm. It is easy to see that since the One-Bit Algorithm is self-stabilizing for mutual exclusion and deadlock freedom, to prove self-stabilization for the entire algorithm it suffices to prove that the $N!$-Bit Algorithm is self-stabilizing for deadlock freedom. The proof of that is easily done using the above argument that there cannot be a cycle of processes each waiting endlessly for the preceding one. ∎

4 Conclusion

Using the formalism of Part I, we stated the mutual exclusion problem, as well as several additional properties we might want a solution to satisfy. We then gave four algorithms, ranging from the inexpensive One-Bit Algorithm that satisfies only the most basic requirements to the ridiculously costly $N!$-Bit Algorithm that satisfies every property we have ever wanted of a solution.

communication variables:
    y_i **initially** *false*,
    array z_i, **indexed by** $CYC(i)$;
private variables:
    j **with range** $1 \dots N$;
    γ **with range** $CYC(i)$,
    array *after* **indexed by** $1 \dots N$ **of booleans**;
repeat forever
    noncritical section;
    doorway: **for all** $\gamma \in CYC(i)$ **do**
                $z_i[\gamma] *{:=}* \neg CGV(z_\gamma, \gamma, j)$ **od**;
        for all $j \neq i$
            do *after*$[j] := y_j$ **od**;
    waiting: **for all** $j \neq i$
               do while *after*$[j]$
                  do *after*$[j] := y_j$;
                      for all $\gamma \in CYC(j, i)$
                        do if $\neg CG(z_\gamma, \gamma, i)$
                                then *after*$[j] := false$ **fi od**
                od
              od;
    critical section;
    $y_i := false$
end repeat

Figure 4 The $N!$-Bit FCFS Algorithm: Process i.

Our proofs have been done in the style of standard "journal mathematics", using informal reasoning that in principle can be reduced to very formal logic, but in practice never is. Our experience in years of devising synchronization algorithms has been that this style of proof is quite unreliable. We have on several occasions "proved" the correctness of synchronization algorithms only to discover later that they were incorrect. (Everyone working in this field seems to have the same experience.) This is especially true of algorithms using our nonatomic communication primitives.

This experience led us to develop a reliable method for proving properties of concurrent programs [9, 11, 16]. Instead of reasoning about a program's behavior, one reasons in terms of its state. When the first version of the present paper was written, it was not possible to apply this method to these mutual exclusion algorithms for the following reasons:

—The proof method required that the program be described in terms of atomic operations; we did not know how to reason about the nonatomic reads and writes used by the algorithms.

—Most of the correctness properties to be proved, as well as the properties assumed of the communication variables, were stated in terms of the program's behavior; we did not know how to apply our state-based reasoning to such behavioral properties.

Recent progress in reasoning about nonatomic operations [12] and in temporal logic specifications [13, 14] should make it possible to recast our definitions and proofs in this formalism. However, doing so would be a major undertaking, completely beyond the scope of this paper. We are therefore forced to leave these proofs in their current form as traditional, informal proofs. The behavioral reasoning used in our correctness proofs, and in most other published correctness proofs of concurrent algorithms, is inherently unreliable; we advise the reader to be skeptical of such proofs.

Acknowledgments.   Many of these ideas have been maturing for quite a few years before appearing on paper for the first time here. They have been influenced by a number of people during that time, most notably Carel Scholten, Edsger Dijkstra, Chuck Seitz, Robert Keller, Irene Greif, and Michael Fischer. The impetus finally to write down the results came from discussions with Michael Rabin in 1980 that led to the discovery of the Three-Bit Algorithm.

References

[1] BRINCH HANSEN, P. Concurrent programming concepts. *ACM Comput. Surv. 5* (1973), 223–245.

[1a] BURNS, J. Mutual exclusion with linear waiting using binary shared variables. *ACM SIGACT News* (Summer 1978), 42–47.

[2] DIJKSTRA, E. W. Solution of a problem in concurrent programming control. *Commun. ACM 8*, 9 (Sept. 1965), 569.

[3] DIJKSTRA, E. W. Self-stabilizing systems in spite of distributed control. *Commun. ACM 17*, 11 (Nov. 1974), 643–644.

[4] FISCHER, M. J., LYNCH, N., BURNS, J. E., AND BORODIN, A. Resource allocation with immunity to limited process failure. In *Proceedings of the 20th IEEE Symposium on the Foundations of Computer Science* (Oct.). IEEE, New York, 1979, pp. 234–254.

[5] KATSEFF, H. P. A new solution to the critical section problem. In *Conference Record of the 10th Annual ACM Symposium on the Theory of Computing* (San Diego, Calif., May 1–3). ACM, New York, 1978, pp. 86-88.

[6] KNUTH, D. E. Additional commments on a problem in concurrent program control. *Commun. ACM 9*, 5 (May 1966), 321–322.

[7] LAMPORT, L. A new solution of Dijkstra's concurrent programming problem. *Commun. ACM 17*, 8 (Aug. 1974), 453–455.

[8] LAMPORT, L. The synchronization of independent processes. *Acta Inf. 7*, 1 (1976), 15–34.

[9] LAMPORT, L. Proving the correctness of multiprocess programs. *IEEE Trans. Softw. Eng. SE-3*, 2 (Mar. 1977), 125–143.

[10] LAMPORT, L. The implementation of reliable distributed multiprocess systems. *Comput. Netw. 2* (1978), 95–114.

[11] LAMPORT, L. The 'Hoare logic' of concurrent programs. *Acta Inf. 14*, 1 (1980), 21–37.

[12] LAMPORT, L. Reasoning about nonatomic operations. In *Proceedings of the Tenth Annual ACM SIGACT-SIGPLAN Symposium on Principles of Programming Languages* (Austin, Tex., Jan. 24–26). ACM, New York, 1983, pp. 28–37.

[13] LAMPORT, L. Specifying concurrent program modules. *ACM Trans. Program. Lang. Syst. 5*, 2 (Apr. 1983), 190–222.

[14] LAMPORT, L. What good is temporal logic? In *Information Processing 83: Proceedings of the IFIP 9th World Congress* (Paris, Sept. 19–23). R. E. A. Mason, Ed. North Holland, Amsterdam, 1983.

[15] LAMPORT, L. The mutual exclusion problem: Part I—A theory of interprocess communication. *J. ACM 33*, 2 (Apr. 1986), 313–326.

[16] OWICKI, S. and LAMPORT, L. Proving liveness properties of concurrent programs. *ACM Trans. Program. Lang. Syst. 4*, 3 (July 1982), 455–495.

[17] PETERSON, G. L. A new solution to Lamport's concurrent programming problem. *ACM Trans. Program. Lang. Syst. 5*, 1 (Jan. 1983), 56–65.

[18] PETERSON, G. AND FISCHER, M. Economical solutions for the critical section problem in a distributed system. In *Proceedings of the 9th Annual ACM Symposium on the Theory Computing* (Boulder, Colo., May 2–4). ACM New York, 1977, pp. 91–97.

[19] RABIN, M. The choice coordination problem. *Acta Inf. 17* (1982), 121–134.

[20] RIVEST, R. L. AND PRATT, V. R. The mutual exclusion problem for unreliable processes: Preliminary report. *Proceedings of the IEEE Symposium on the Foundation of Computer Science*. IEEE, New York, 1976, pp. 1–8.

RECEIVED DECEMBER 1980; REVISED SEPTEMBER 1985; ACCEPTED SEPTEMBER 1985

The Part-Time Parliament

Leslie Lamport (Digital Equipment Corporation)

Recent archaeological discoveries on the island of Paxos reveal that the parliament functioned despite the peripatetic propensity of its part-time legislators. The legislators maintained consistent copies of the parliamentary record, despite their frequent forays from the chamber and the forgetfulness of their messengers. The Paxon parliament's protocol provides a new way of implementing the state machine approach to the design of distributed systems.

Categories and Subject Descriptors: C.2.4 [**Computer-Communications Networks**]: Distributed Systems—*Network operating systems*; D.4.5 [**Operating Systems**]: Reliability—*Fault-tolerance*; J.1 [**Computer Applications**]: Administrative Data Processing—*Government*

General Terms: Design, Reliability

Additional Key Words and Phrases: State machines, three-phase commit, voting

Author's address: Systems Research, Digital Equipment Corporation, 130 Lytton Avenue, Palo Alto, CA 94301.

Paper originally published in *ACM Transactions on Computer Systems,* 16(2), May 1998, pp. 133–169.

1   The Problem

1.1   The Island of Paxos

Early in this millennium, the Aegean island of Paxos was a thriving mercantile center.[1] Wealth led to political sophistication, and the Paxons replaced their ancient theocracy with a parliamentary form of government. But trade came before civic duty, and no one in Paxos was willing to devote his life to Parliament. The Paxon Parliament had to function even though legislators continually wandered in and out of the parliamentary Chamber.

The problem of governing with a part-time parliament bears a remarkable correspondence to the problem faced by today's fault-tolerant distributed systems, where legislators correspond to processes and leaving the Chamber corresponds to failing. The Paxons' solution may therefore be of some interest to computer scientists. I present here a short history of the Paxos Parliament's protocol, followed by an even shorter discussion of its relevance for distributed systems.

Paxon civilization was destroyed by a foreign invasion, and archeologists have just recently begun to unearth its history. Our knowledge of the Paxon Parliament is therefore fragmentary. Although the basic protocols are known, we are ignorant of many details. Where such details are of interest, I will take the liberty of speculating on what the Paxons might have done.

1.2   Requirements

Parliament's primary task was to determine the law of the land, which was defined by the sequence of decrees it passed. A modern parliament will employ a secretary to record its actions, but no one in Paxos was willing to remain in the Chamber throughout the session to act as secretary. Instead, each Paxon legislator maintained a *ledger* in which he recorded the numbered sequence of decrees that were passed. For example, legislator $\Lambda\breve{\iota}\nu\chi\partial$'s ledger had the entry

> 155: *The olive tax is 3 drachmas per ton*

if she believed that the 155th decree passed by Parliament set the tax on olives to 3 drachmas per ton. Ledgers were written with indelible ink, and their entries could not be changed.

---

1. It should not be confused with the Ionian island of Paxoi, whose name is sometimes corrupted to *Paxos*.

Sidebar 1

This submission was recently discovered behind a filing cabinet in the *TOCS* editorial office. Despite its age, the editor-in-chief felt that it was worth publishing. Because the author is currently doing field work in the Greek isles and cannot be reached, I was asked to prepare it for publication.

The author appears to be an archeologist with only a passing interest in computer science. This is unfortunate; even though the obscure ancient Paxon civilization he describes is of little interest to most computer scientists, its legislative system is an excellent model for how to implement a distributed computer system in an asynchronous environment. Indeed, some of the refinements the Paxons made to their protocol appear to be unknown in the systems literature.

The author does give a brief discussion of the Paxon Parliament's relevance to distributed computing in Section 4. Computer scientists will probably want to read that section first. Even before that, they might want to read the explanation of the algorithm for computer scientists by Lampson [1996]. The algorithm is also described more formally by De Prisco et al. [1997]. I have added further comments on the relation between the ancient protocols and more recent work at the end of Section 4.

Keith Marzullo
University of California, San Diego

The first requirement of the parliamentary protocol was the *consistency of ledgers*, meaning that no two ledgers could contain contradictory information. If legislator $\Phi\iota\sigma\partial\epsilon\rho$ had the entry

132: *Lamps must use only olive oil*

in his ledger, then no other legislator's ledger could have a different entry for decree 132. However, another legislator might have no entry in his ledger for decree 132 if he hadn't yet learned that the decree had been passed.

Consistency of ledgers was not sufficient, since it could be trivially fulfilled by leaving all ledgers blank. Some requirement was needed to guarantee that decrees were eventually passed and recorded in ledgers. In modern parliaments, the passing of decrees is hindered by disagreement among legislators. This was not the case in Paxos, where an atmosphere of mutual trust prevailed. Paxon legislators were willing to pass any decree that was proposed. However, their peripatetic propensity posed a problem. Consistency would be lost if one group of legislators passed the decree

37: *Painting on temple walls is forbidden*

and then left for a banquet, whereupon a different group of legislators entered the Chamber and, knowing nothing about what had just happened, passed the conflicting decree

> 37: *Freedom of artistic expression is guaranteed*

Progress could not be guaranteed unless enough legislators stayed in the Chamber for a long enough time. Because Paxon legislators were unwilling to curtail their outside activities, it was impossible to ensure that any decree would ever be passed. However, legislators were willing to guarantee that, while in the Chamber, they and their aides would act promptly on all parliamentary matters. This guarantee allowed the Paxons to devise a parliamentary protocol satisfying the following *progress condition*.

> If a majority of the legislators[2] were in the Chamber, and no one entered or left the Chamber for a sufficiently long period of time, then any decree proposed by a legislator in the Chamber would be passed, and every decree that had been passed would appear in the ledger of every legislator in the Chamber.

1.3 Assumptions

The requirements of the parliamentary protocol could be achieved only by providing the legislators with the necessary resources. Each legislator received a sturdy ledger in which to record the decrees, a pen, and a supply of indelible ink. Legislators might forget what they had been doing if they left the Chamber,[3] so they would write notes in the back of the ledgers to remind themselves of important parliamentary tasks. An entry in the list of decrees was never changed, but notes could be crossed out. Achieving the progress condition required that legislators be able to measure the passage of time, so they were given simple hourglass timers.

Legislators carried their ledgers at all times, and could always read the list of decrees and any note that had not been crossed out. The ledgers were made of the finest parchment and were used for only the most important notes. A legislator would write other notes on a slip of paper, which he might (or might not) lose if he left the Chamber.

---

2. In translating the progress condition, I have rendered the Paxon word $\mu\alpha\delta\zeta\partial\omega\rho\iota\tau\tilde{\iota}\sigma\epsilon\tau$ as *majority of the legislators*. Alternative translations of this word have been proposed and are discussed in Section 2.2.

3. In one tragic incident, legislator $T\omega\nu\epsilon\gamma$ developed irreversible amnesia after being hit on the head by a falling statue just outside the Chamber.

The acoustics of the Chamber were poor, making oratory impossible. Legislators could communicate only by messenger, and were provided with funds to hire as many messengers as they needed. A messenger could be counted on not to garble messages, but he might forget that he had already delivered a message, and deliver it again. Like the legislators they served, messengers devoted only part of their time to parliamentary duties. A messenger might leave the Chamber to conduct some business—perhaps taking a six-month voyage—before delivering a message. He might even leave forever, in which case the message would never be delivered.

Although legislators and messengers could enter and leave at any time, when inside the Chamber they devoted themselves to the business of Parliament. While they remained in the Chamber, messengers delivered messages in a timely fashion, and legislators reacted promptly to any messages they received.

The official records of Paxos claim that legislators and messengers were scrupulously honest and strictly obeyed parliamentary protocol. Most scholars discount this as propaganda, intended to portray Paxos as morally superior to its eastern neighbors. Dishonesty, although rare, undoubtedly did occur. However, because it was never mentioned in official documents, we have little knowledge of how Parliament coped with dishonest legislators or messengers. What evidence has been uncovered is discussed in Section 3.3.5.

2 The Single-Decree Synod

The Paxon Parliament evolved from an earlier ceremonial Synod of priests that was convened every 19 years to choose a single, symbolic decree. For centuries, the Synod had chosen the decree by a conventional procedure that required all priests to be present. But as commerce flourished, priests began wandering in and out of the Chamber while the Synod was in progress. Finally, the old protocol failed, and a Synod ended with no decree chosen. To prevent a repetition of this theological disaster, Paxon religious leaders asked mathematicians to formulate a protocol for choosing the Synod's decree. The protocol's requirements and assumptions were essentially the same as those of the later Parliament except that instead of containing a sequence of decrees, a ledger would have at most one decree. The resulting Synod protocol is described here; the parliamentary protocol is described in Section 3.

Mathematicians derived the Synod protocol in a series of steps. First, they proved results showing that a protocol satisfying certain constraints would guarantee consistency and allow progress. A *preliminary protocol* was then derived directly from these constraints. A restricted version of the preliminary protocol provided the *basic protocol* that guaranteed consistency, but not progress. The complete Synod protocol, satisfying the consistency and progress requirements, was obtained by restricting the basic protocol.[4]

The mathematical results are described in Section 2.1, and the protocols are described informally in Sections 2.2–2.4. A more formal description and correctness proof of the basic protocol appears in the appendix.

2.1   Mathematical Results

The Synod's decree was chosen through a series of numbered *ballots*, where a ballot was a referendum on a single decree. In each ballot, a priest had the choice only of voting for the decree or not voting.[5] Associated with a ballot was a set of priests called a *quorum*. A ballot succeeded if and only if every priest in the quorum voted for the decree. Formally, a ballot B consisted of the following four components. (Unless otherwise qualified, *set* is taken to mean *finite set*.[6])

B_{dec} A decree (the one being voted on).

B_{pot} A nonempty set of priests (the ballot's quorum).

B_{vot} A set of priests (the ones who cast votes for the decree).[7]

B_{bal} A ballot number.

A ballot B was said to be *successful* iff (if and only if) $B_{qrm} \subseteq B_{vot}$, so a successful ballot was one in which every quorum member voted.

Ballot numbers were chosen from an unbounded ordered set of numbers. If $B'_{bal} > B_{bal}$, then ballot B' was said to be *later* than ballot B. However, this indicated

---

4. The complete history of the Synod protocol's discovery is not known. Like modern computer scientists, Paxon mathematicians would describe elegant, logical derivations that bore no resemblance to how the algorithms were actually derived. However, it is known that the mathematical results (Theorems 1 and 2 of Section 2.1) really did precede the protocol. They were discovered when mathematicians, in response to the request for a protocol, were attempting to prove that a satisfactory protocol was impossible.

5. Like some modern nations, Paxos had not fully grasped the nature of Athenian democracy.

6. Although Paxon mathematicians were remarkably advanced for their time, they obviously had no knowledge of set theory. I have taken the liberty of translating the Paxons' more primitive notation into the language of modern set theory.

7. Only priests in the quorum actually voted, but Paxon mathematicians found it easier to convince people that the protocol was correct if, in their proof, they allowed any priest to vote in any ballot.

nothing about the order in which ballots were conducted; a later ballot could actually have taken place before an earlier one.

Paxon mathematicians defined three conditions on a set $\mathcal{B}$ of ballots, and then showed that consistency was guaranteed and progress was possible if the set of ballots that had taken place satisfied those conditions. The first two conditions were simple; they can be stated informally as follows.

$B1(\mathcal{B})$ Each ballot in $\mathcal{B}$ has a unique ballot number.

$B2(\mathcal{B})$ The quorums of any two ballots in $\mathcal{B}$ have at least one priest in common.

The third condition was more complicated. One Paxon manuscript contained the following, rather confusing, statement of it.

$B3(\mathcal{B})$ For every ballot B in $\mathcal{B}$, if any priest in B's quorum voted in an earlier ballot in $\mathcal{B}$, then the decree of B equals the decree of the latest of those earlier ballots.

Interpretation of this cryptic text was aided by the manuscript pictured in Figure 1, which illustrates condition $B3(\mathcal{B})$ with a set $\mathcal{B}$ of five ballots for a Synod consisting of the five priests A, B, Γ, Δ, and E. This set $\mathcal{B}$ contains five ballots, where for each ballot the set of voters is the subset of the priests in the quorum whose names are enclosed in boxes. For example, ballot number 14 has decree α, a quorum containing three priests, and a set of two voters. Condition $B3(\mathcal{B})$ has the form

#	decree	quorum and	voters

2	α	A B Γ [Δ]
5	β	A B [Γ] E
14	α	[B] Δ [E]
27	β	[A] [Γ] [Δ]
29	β	[B] Γ Δ

Figure 1   Paxon manuscript showing a set $\mathcal{B}$, consisting of five ballots, that satisfies conditions $B1(\mathcal{B})$–$B3(\mathcal{B})$. (Explanatory column headings have been added.)

"for every B in $\mathcal{B}:\ldots:$", where "$\ldots$" is a condition on ballot B. The conditions for the five ballots B of Figure ı are as follows.

2. Ballot number 2 is the earliest ballot, so the condition on that ballot is trivially true.

5. None of ballot 5's four quorum members voted in an earlier ballot, so the condition on ballot 5 is also trivially true.

14. The only member of ballot 14's quorum to vote in an earlier ballot is Δ, who voted in ballot number 2, so the condition requires that ballot 14's decree must equal ballot 2's decree.

27. (This is a successful ballot.) The members of ballot 27's quorum are A, Γ, and Δ. Priest A did not vote in an earlier ballot, the only earlier ballot Γ voted in was ballot 5, and the only earlier ballot Δ voted in was ballot 2. The latest of these two earlier ballots is ballot 5, so the condition requires that ballot 27's decree must equal ballot 5's decree.

29. The members of ballot 29's quorum are B, Γ, and Δ. The only earlier ballot that B voted in was number 14, priest Γ voted in ballots 5 and 27, and Δ voted in ballots 2 and 27. The latest of these four earlier ballots is number 27, so the condition requires that ballot 29's decree must equal ballot 27's decree.

To state $B1(\mathcal{B})$–$B3(\mathcal{B})$ formally requires some more notation. A *vote* v was defined to be a quantity consisting of three components: a priest v_{pst}, a ballot number v_{bal}, and a decree v_{dec}. It represents a vote cast by priest v_{pst} for decree v_{dec} in ballot number v_{bal}. The Paxons also defined *null* votes to be votes v with $v_{bal} = -\infty$ and $v_{dec} = \text{BLANK}$, where $-\infty < b < \infty$ for any ballot number b, and BLANK is not a decree. For any priest p, they defined $null_p$ to be the unique null vote v with $v_{pst} = p$.

Paxon mathematicians defined a total ordering on the set of all votes, but part of the manuscript containing the definition has been lost. The remaining fragment indicates that, for any votes v and v', if $v_{bal} < v'_{bal}$ then $v < v'$. It is not known how the relative order of v and v' was defined if $v_{bal} = v'_{bal}$.

For any set $\mathcal{B}$ of ballots, the set $Votes(\mathcal{B})$ of votes in $\mathcal{B}$ was defined to consist of all votes v such that $v_{pst} \in B_{vot}$, v_{bal}, and $v_{dec} = B_{dec}$ for some $B \in \mathcal{B}$. If p is a priest and b is either a ballot number or $\pm\infty$, then $MaxVote(b, p, \mathcal{B})$ was defined to be the largest vote v in $Votes(\mathcal{B})$ cast by p with $v_{bal} < b$, or to be $null_p$ if there was no such vote. Since $null_p$ is smaller than any real vote cast by p, this means that $MaxVote(b, p, \mathcal{B})$ is the largest vote in the set

$$\{v \in Votes(\mathcal{B}) : (v_{pst} = p) \land (v_{bal} < b)\} \cup \{null_p\}.$$

For any nonempty set Q of priests, $MaxVote(b, Q, \mathcal{B})$ was defined to equal the maximum of all votes $MaxVote(b, p, \mathcal{B})$ with p in Q.

Conditions $B1(\mathcal{B})$–$B3(\mathcal{B})$ are stated formally as follows.[8]

$$B1(\mathcal{B}) \triangleq \forall B, B' \in \mathcal{B} : (B \neq B') \Rightarrow (B_{bal} \neq B'_{bal})$$

$$B2(\mathcal{B}) \triangleq \forall B, B' \in \mathcal{B} : B_{qrm} \cap B'_{qrm} \neq \emptyset$$

$$B3(\mathcal{B}) \triangleq \forall B \in \mathcal{B} : (MaxVote(B_{bal}, B_{qrm}, \mathcal{B}_{bal}) \neq -\infty) \Rightarrow$$
$$B_{dec} = MaxVote(B_{bal}, B_{qrm}, \mathcal{B}_{dec})$$

Although the definition of $MaxVote$ depends upon the ordering of votes, $B1(\mathcal{B})$ implies that $MaxVote(b, Q, \mathcal{B})_{dec}$ is independent of how votes with equal ballot numbers were ordered.

To show that these conditions imply consistency, the Paxons first showed that $B1(\mathcal{B})$–$B3(\mathcal{B})$ imply that, if a ballot B in $\mathcal{B}$ is successful, then any later ballot in $\mathcal{B}$ is for the same decree as B.

Lemma   If $B1(\mathcal{B})$, $B2(\mathcal{B})$, and $B3(\mathcal{B})$ hold, then

$$((B_{qrm} \subseteq B_{vot}) \wedge (B'_{bal} > B_{bal})) \Rightarrow (B'_{dec} = B_{dec})$$

for any B, B' in $\mathcal{B}$.

Proof of Lemma   For any ballot B in $\mathcal{B}$, let $\Psi(B, \mathcal{B})$ be the set of ballots in $\mathcal{B}$ later than B for a decree different from B's:

$$\Psi(B, \beta) \triangleq \{B' \in \mathcal{B} : (B'_{bal} > B_{bal}) \wedge (B'_{dec} \neq B_{dec})\}$$

To prove the lemma, it suffices to show that if $B_{qrm} \subseteq B_{vot}$ then $\Psi(B, \mathcal{B})$ is empty. The Paxons gave a proof by contradiction. They assumed the existence of a B with $B_{qrm} \subseteq B_{vot}$ and $\Psi(B, \mathcal{B}) \neq \emptyset$, and obtained a contradiction as follows.[9]

1. Choose $C \in \Psi(B, \mathcal{B})$ such that $C_{bal} = \min\{B'_{bal} : B' \in \Psi(B, \mathcal{B})\}$.
   PROOF: C exists because $\Psi(B, \mathcal{B})$ is nonempty and finite.

2. $C_{bal} > B_{bal}$
   PROOF: By (1) and the definition of $\Psi(B, \mathcal{B})$.

3. $B_{vot} \cap C_{qrm} \neq \emptyset$
   PROOF: By $B2(\mathcal{B})$ and the hypothesis that $B_{qrm} \subseteq B_{vot}$.

---

8. I use the Paxon mathematical symbol $\triangleq$, which meant *equals by definition*.

9. Paxon mathematicians always provided careful, structured proofs of important theorems. They were not as sophisticated as modern mathematicians, who can omit many details and write paragraph-style proofs without ever making a mistake.

4. $MaxVote(C_{bal}, C_{qrm}, \mathcal{B})_{bal} \geq B_{bal}$
   PROOF: By (2), (3), and the definition of $MaxVote(C_{bal}, C_{qrm}, \mathcal{B})$.

5. $MaxVote(C_{bal}, C_{qrm}, \mathcal{B}) \in Votes(\mathcal{B})$
   PROOF: By (4) (which implies that $MaxVote(C_{bal}, C_{qrm}, \mathcal{B})$ is not a null vote) and the definition of $MaxVote(C_{bal}, C_{qrm}, \mathcal{B})$.

6. $MaxVote(C_{bal}, C_{qrm}, \mathcal{B})_{dec} = C_{dec}$
   PROOF: By (5) and $B3(\mathcal{B})$.

7. $MaxVote(C_{bal}, C_{qrm}, \mathcal{B})_{dec} \neq B_{dec}$
   PROOF: By (6), (1), and the definition of $\Psi(B, \mathcal{B})$.

8. $MaxVote(C_{bal}, C_{qrm}, \mathcal{B})_{bal} > B_{bal}$
   PROOF: By (4), since (7) and $B1(\mathcal{B})$ imply that $MaxVote(C_{bal}, C_{qrm}, \mathcal{B})_{bal} \neq B_{bal}$.

9. $MaxVote(C_{bal}, C_{qrm}, \mathcal{B}) \in Votes(\Psi(B, \mathcal{B}))$
   PROOF: By (7), (8), and the definition of $\Psi(B, \mathcal{B})$.

10. (10) $MaxVote(C_{bal}, C_{qrm}, \mathcal{B})_{bal} < C_{bal}$
    PROOF: By definition of $MaxVote(C_{bal}, C_{qrm}, \mathcal{B})$.

11. Contradiction
    PROOF: By (9), (10), and (1).   ∎

With this lemma, it was easy to show that, if $B1$–$B3$ hold, then any two successful ballots are for the same decree.

Theorem 1   If $B1(\mathcal{B})$, $B2(\mathcal{B})$, and $B3(\mathcal{B})$ hold, then

$$((B_{qrm} \subseteq B_{vot}) \wedge (B'_{qrm} \subseteq B'_{vot})) \;\Rightarrow\; (B'_{dec} = B_{dec})$$

for any B, B' in $\mathcal{B}$.

Proof of Theorem   If $B'_{bal} = B_{bal}$, then $B1(\mathcal{B})$ implies $B' = B$. If $B'_{bal} \neq B_{bal}$, then the theorem follows immediately from the lemma.   ∎

The Paxons then proved a theorem asserting that if there are enough priests in the Chamber, then it is possible to conduct a successful ballot while preserving $B1$–$B3$. Although this does not guarantee progress, it at least shows that a balloting protocol based on $B1$–$B3$ will not deadlock.

Theorem 2   Let b be a ballot number, and let Q be a set of priests such that $b > B_{bal}$ and $Q \cap B_{qrm} \neq \emptyset$ for all $B \in \mathcal{B}$. If $B1(\mathcal{B})$, $B2(\mathcal{B})$, and $B3(\mathcal{B})$ hold, then there is a ballot

B' with $B'_{bal} = b$ and $B'_{qrm} = B'_{vot} = Q$ such that $B1(\mathcal{B} \cup \{B'\})$, $B2(\mathcal{B} \cup \{B'\})$, and $B3(\mathcal{B} \cup \{B'\})$ hold.

Proof of Theorem   Condition $B1(\mathcal{B} \cup \{B'\})$ follows from $B1(\mathcal{B})$, the choice of B'_{bal}, and the assumption about b. Condition $B2(\mathcal{B} \cup \{B'\})$ follows from $B2(\mathcal{B})$, the choice of B'_{qrm}, and the assumption about Q. If $MaxVote(b, Q, B)_{bal} = -\infty$ then let B'_{dec} be any decree. Else let it equal $MaxVote(b, Q, B)_{dec}$. Condition $B3(\mathcal{B} \cup \{B'\})$ then follows from $B3(\mathcal{B})$.

∎

2.2   The Preliminary Protocol

The Paxons derived the *preliminary protocol* from the requirement that conditions $B1(\mathcal{B})$–$B3(\mathcal{B})$ remain true, where $\mathcal{B}$ was the set of all ballots that had been or were being conducted. The definition of the protocol specified how the set $\mathcal{B}$ changed, but the set was never explicitly calculated. The Paxons referred to $\mathcal{B}$ as a quantity observed only by the gods, since it might never be known to any mortal.

Each ballot was initiated by a priest, who chose its number, decree, and quorum. Each priest in the quorum then decided whether or not to vote in the ballot. The rules determining how the initiator chose a ballot's number, decree, and quorum, and how a priest decided whether or not to vote in a ballot were derived directly from the need to maintain $B1(\mathcal{B})$–$B3(\mathcal{B})$.

To maintain $B1$, each ballot had to receive a unique number. By remembering (with notes in his ledger) what ballots he had previously initiated, a priest could easily avoid initiating two different ballots with the same number. To keep different priests from initiating ballots with the same number, the set of possible ballot numbers was partitioned among the priests. While it is not known how this was done, an obvious method would have been to let a ballot number be a pair consisting of an integer and a priest, using a lexicographical ordering, where

$$(13, \; \Gamma\rho\alpha\breve{\iota}) < (13, \; \Lambda\iota\nu\sigma\epsilon\acute{\iota}) < (15, \; \Gamma\rho\alpha\breve{\iota})$$

since Γ came before Λ in the Paxon alphabet. In any case, it is known that every priest had an unbounded set of ballot numbers reserved for his use.

To maintain $B2$, a ballot's quorum was chosen to contain a $\mu\alpha\delta\zeta\partial\omega\rho\iota\tau\breve{\iota}\sigma\epsilon\tau$ of priests. Initially, $\mu\alpha\delta\zeta\partial\omega\rho\iota\tau\breve{\iota}\sigma\epsilon\tau$ just meant a simple majority. Later, it was observed that fat priests were less mobile and spent more time in the Chamber than thin ones, so a $\mu\alpha\delta\zeta\partial\omega\rho\iota\tau\breve{\iota}\sigma\epsilon\tau$ was taken to mean any set of priests whose total weight was more than half the total weight of all priests, rather than a simple majority of the priests. When a group of thin priests complained that this was unfair, actual weights were replaced with symbolic weights based on a priest's attendance record. The primary requirement for a $\mu\alpha\delta\zeta\partial\omega\rho\iota\tau\breve\iota\sigma\epsilon\tau$ was that any two sets containing a $\mu\alpha\delta\zeta\partial\omega\rho\iota\tau\breve\iota\sigma\epsilon\tau$ of priests had at least one priest in common. To maintain $B2$, the priest initiating a ballot B chose B_{qrm} to be a majority set.

Condition $B3$ requires that if $MaxVote(b, Q, B)_{dec}$ is not equal to BLANK, then a ballot with number b and quorum Q must have decree $MaxVote(b, Q, B)_{dec}$. If $MaxVote(b, Q, B)_{dec}$ equals BLANK, then the ballot can have any decree. To maintain $B3(B)$, before initiating a new ballot with ballot number b and quorum Q, a priest p had to find $MaxVote(b, Q, B)_{dec}$. To do this, p had to find $MaxVote(b, Q, B)$ for each priest q in Q.

Recall that $MaxVote(b, Q, B)$ is the vote with the largest ballot number less than b among all the votes cast by q, or $null_q$ if q did not vote in any ballot numbered less than b. Priest p obtains $MaxVote(b, q, B)$ from q by an exchange of messages. Therefore, the first two steps in the protocol for conducting a single ballot initiated by p are:[10]

1. Priest p chooses a new ballot number b and sends a $NextBallot(b)$ message to some set of priests.

2. A priest q responds to the receipt of a $NextBallot(b)$ message by sending a $LastVote(b, v)$ message to p, where v is the vote with the largest ballot number less than b that q has cast, or his null vote $null_q$ if q did not vote in any ballot numbered less than b.

Priest q must use notes in the back of his ledger to remember what votes he had previously cast.

When q sends the $LastVote(b, v)$ message, v equals $MaxVote(b, q, B)$. But the set B of ballots changes as new ballots are initiated and votes are cast. Since priest p is going to use v as the value of $MaxVote(b, q, B)$ when choosing a decree, to keep $B3(B)$ true it is necessary that $MaxVote(b, q, B)$ not change after q has sent the $LastVote(b, v)$ message. To keep $MaxVote(b, q, B)$ from changing, q must cast no new votes with ballot numbers between v_{bal} and b. By sending the $LastVote(b, v)$ message, q is promising not to cast any such vote. (To keep this promise, q must record the necessary information in his ledger.)

The next two steps in the balloting protocol (begun in step (1) by priest p) are:

---

10. Priests p and q could be the same. For simplicity, the protocol is described with p sending messages to himself in this case. In reality, a priest could talk to himself without the use of messengers.

3. After receiving a *LastVote*(*b*, *v*) message from every priest in some majority set *Q*, priest *p* initiates a new ballot with number *b*, quorum *Q*, and decree *d*, where *d* is chosen to satisfy *B3*. He then records the ballot in the back of his ledger and sends a *BeginBallot*(*b*, *d*) message to every priest in *Q*.

4. Upon receipt of the *BeginBallot*(*b*, *d*) message, priest *q* decides whether or not to cast his vote in ballot number *b*. (He may not cast the vote if doing so would violate a promise implied by a *LastVote*(*b'*, *v'*) message he has sent for some other ballot.) If *q* decides to vote for ballot number *b*, then he sends a *Voted*(*b*, *q*) message to *p* and records the vote in the back of his ledger.

The execution of step (3) is considered to add a ballot *B* to $\mathcal{B}$, where $B_{bal} = b$, $B_{qrm} = Q$, $B_{vot} = \emptyset$ (no one has yet voted in this ballot), and $B_{dec} = d$. In step (4), if priest *q* decides to vote in the ballot, then executing that step is considered to change the set $\mathcal{B}$ of ballots by adding *q* to the set B_{vot} of voters in the ballot $B \in \mathcal{B}$.

A priest has the option not to vote in step (4), even if casting a vote would not violate any previous promise. In fact, all the steps in this protocol are optional. For example, a priest *q* can ignore a *NextBallot*(*b*) message instead of executing step (2). Failure to take an action can prevent progress, but it cannot cause any inconsistency because it cannot make $B1(\mathcal{B})$–$B3(\mathcal{B})$ false. Since the only effect not receiving a message can have is to prevent an action from happening, message loss also cannot cause inconsistency. Thus, the protocol guarantees consistency even if priests leave the chamber or messages are lost.

Receiving multiple copies of a message can cause an action to be repeated. Except in step (3), performing the action a second time has no effect. For example, sending several *Voted*(*b*, *q*) messages in step (4) has the same effect as sending just one. The repetition of step (3) is prevented by using the entry made in the back of the ledger when it is executed. Thus, the consistency condition is maintained even if a messenger delivers the same message several times.

Steps (1)–(4) describe the complete protocol for initiating a ballot and voting on it. All that remains is to determine the results of the balloting and announce when a decree has been selected. Recall that a ballot is successful iff every priest in the quorum has voted. The decree of a successful ballot is the one chosen by the Synod. The rest of the protocol is:

5. If *p* has received a *Voted*(*b*, *q*) message from every priest *q* in *Q* (the quorum for ballot number *b*), then he writes *d* (the decree of that ballot) in his ledger and sends a *Success*(*d*) message to every priest.

6. Upon receiving a *Success*(*d*) message, a priest enters decree *d* in his ledger.

Steps (1)–(6) describe how an individual ballot is conducted. The preliminary protocol allows any priest to initiate a new ballot at any time. Each step maintains $B1(\mathcal{B})$–$B3(\mathcal{B})$, so the entire protocol also maintains these conditions. Since a priest enters a decree in his ledger only if it is the decree of a successful ballot, Theorem 1 implies that the priests' ledgers are consistent. The protocol does not address the question of progress.

In step (3), if the decree d is determined by condition $B3$, then it is possible that this decree is already written in the ledger of some priest. That priest need not be in the quorum Q; he could have left the Chamber. Thus, consistency would not be guaranteed if step (3) allowed any greater freedom in choosing d.

2.3 The Basic Protocol

In the preliminary protocol, a priest must record (1) the number of every ballot he has initiated, (2) every vote he has cast, and (3) every *LastVote* message he has sent. Keeping track of all this information would have been difficult for the busy priests. The Paxons therefore restricted the preliminary protocol to obtain the more practical *basic protocol* in which each priest p had to maintain only the following information in the back of his ledger:

lastTried[p] The number of the last ballot that p tried to initiate, or $-\infty$ if there was none.

prevVote[p] The vote cast by p in the highest-numbered ballot in which he voted, or $-\infty$ if he never voted.

nextBal[p] The largest value of b for which p has sent a *LastVote*(b, v) message, or $-\infty$ if he has never sent such a message.

Steps (1)–(6) of the preliminary protocol describe how a single ballot is conducted by its initiator, priest p. The preliminary protocol allows p to conduct any number of ballots concurrently. In the basic protocol, he conducts only one ballot at a time—ballot number *lastTried[p]*. After p initiates this ballot, he ignores messages that pertain to any other ballot that he had previously initiated. Priest p keeps all information about the progress of ballot number *lastTried[p]* on a slip of paper. If he loses that slip of paper, then he stops conducting the ballot.

In the preliminary protocol, each *LastVote*(b, v) message sent by a priest q represents a promise not to vote in any ballot numbered between v_{bal} and b. In the basic protocol, it represents the stronger promise not to cast a new vote in any ballot numbered less than b. This stronger promise might prevent him from casting a vote in step 4 of the basic protocol that he would have been allowed to cast in the preliminary protocol. However, since the preliminary protocol always gives

q the option of not casting his vote, the basic protocol does not require him to do anything not allowed by the preliminary protocol.

Steps (1)–(6) of the preliminary protocol become the following six steps for conducting a ballot in the basic protocol. (All information used by p to conduct the ballot, other than $lastTried[p]$, $prevVote[p]$, and $nextBal[p]$, is kept on a slip of paper.)

1. Priest p chooses a new ballot number b greater than $lastTried[p]$, sets $lastTried[p]$ to b, and sends a $NextBallot(b)$ message to some set of priests.

2. Upon receipt of a $NextBallot(b)$ message from p with $b > nextBal[q]$, priest q sets $nextBal[q]$ to b and sends a $LastVote(b, v)$ message to p, where v equals $prevVote[q]$. (A $NextBallot(b)$ message is ignored if $b \leq nextBal[q]$.)

3. After receiving a $LastVote(b, v)$ message from every priest in some majority set Q, where $b = lastTried[p]$, priest p initiates a new ballot with number b, quorum Q, and decree d, where d is chosen to satisfy $B3$. He then sends a $BeginBallot(b, d)$ message to every priest in Q.

4. Upon receipt of a $BeginBallot(b, d)$ message with $b = nextBal[q]$, priest q casts his vote in ballot number b, sets $prevVote[q]$ to this vote, and sends a $Voted(b, q)$ message to p. (A $BeginBallot(b, d)$ message is ignored if $b \neq nextBal[q]$.)

5. If p has received a $Voted(b, q)$ message from every priest q in Q (the quorum for ballot number b), where $b = lastTried[p]$, then he writes d (the decree of that ballot) in his ledger and sends a $Success(d)$ message to every priest.

6. Upon receiving a $Success(d)$ message, a priest enters decree d in his ledger.

The basic protocol is a restricted version of the preliminary protocol, meaning that every action allowed by the basic protocol is also allowed by the preliminary protocol. Since the preliminary protocol satisfies the consistency condition, the basic protocol also satisfies that condition. Like the preliminary protocol, the basic protocol does not require that any action ever be taken, so it does not address the question of progress.

The derivation of the basic protocol from $B1$–$B3$ made it obvious that the consistency condition was satisfied. However, some similarly "obvious" ancient wisdom had turned out to be false, and skeptical citizens demanded a more rigorous proof. Their Paxon mathematicians' proof that the protocol satisfies the consistency condition is reproduced in the appendix.

2.4   **The Complete Synod Protocol**

The basic protocol maintains consistency, but it cannot ensure any progress because it states only what a priest may do; it does not require him to do anything. The complete protocol consists of the same six steps for conducting a ballot as the basic protocol. To help achieve progress, it includes the obvious additional requirement that priests perform steps (2)–(6) of the protocol as soon as possible. However, to meet the progress condition, it is necessary that some priest be required to perform step (1), which initiates a ballot. The key to the complete protocol lay in determining when a priest should initiate a ballot.

Never initiating a ballot will certainly prevent progress. However, initiating too may ballots can also prevent progress. If b is larger than any other ballot number, then the receipt of a *NextBallot(b)* message by priest q in step (2) may elicit a promise that prevents him from voting in step 4 for any previously initiated ballot. Thus, the initiation of a new ballot can prevent any previously initiated ballot from succeeding. If new ballots are continually initiated with increasing ballot numbers before the previous ballots have a chance to succeed, then no progress might be made.

Achieving the progress condition requires that new ballots be initiated until one succeeds, but that they not be initiated too frequently. To develop the complete protocol, the Paxons first had to know how long it took messengers to deliver messages and priests to respond. They determined that a messenger who did not leave the Chamber would always deliver a message within 4 minutes, and a priest who remained in the Chamber would always perform an action within 7 minutes of the event that caused the action.[11] Thus, if p and q were in the Chamber when some event caused p to send a message to q, and q responded with a reply to p, then p would receive that reply within 22 minutes if neither messenger left the Chamber. (Priest p would send the message within 7 minutes of the event, q would receive the message within 4 more minutes, he would respond within 7 minutes, and the reply would reach p within 4 more minutes.)

Suppose that only a single priest p was initiating ballots, and that he did so by sending a message to every priest in step (1) of the protocol. If p initiated a ballot when a majority set of priests was in the chamber, then he could expect to execute step (3) within 22 minutes of initiating the ballot, and to execute step (5) within

---

11. I am assuming a value of 30 seconds for the $\delta\zeta\partial\iota\phi\tilde{\iota}$, the Paxon unit of time. This value is within the range determined from studies of hourglass shards. The reaction time of priests was so long because they had to respond to every message within 7 minutes (14 $\delta\zeta\partial\iota\phi\tilde{\iota}$), even if a number of messages arrived simultaneously.

another 22 minutes. If he was unable to execute the steps by those times, then either some priest or messenger left the Chamber after p initiated the ballot, or a larger-numbered ballot had previously been initiated by another priest (before p became the only priest to initiate ballots). To handle the latter possibility, p had to learn about any ballot numbers greater than $lastTried[p]$ used by other priests. This could be done by extending the protocol to require that if a priest q received a $NextBallot(b)$ or a $BeginBallot(b, d)$ message from p with $b < nextBal[q]$, then he would send p a message containing $nextBal[q]$. Priest p would then initiate a new ballot with a larger ballot number.

Still assuming that p was the only priest initiating ballots, suppose that he were required to initiate a new ballot iff (1) he had not executed step (3) or step (5) within the previous 22 minutes, or (2) he learned that another priest had initiated a higher-numbered ballot. If the Chamber doors were locked with p and a majority set of priests inside, then a decree would be passed and recorded in the ledgers of all priests in the Chamber within 99 minutes. (It could take 22 minutes for p to start the next ballot, 22 more minutes to learn that another priest had initiated a larger-numbered ballot, then 55 minutes to complete steps (1)–(6) for a successful ballot.) Thus, the progress condition would be met if only a single priest, who did not leave the chamber, were initiating ballots.

The complete protocol therefore included a procedure for choosing a single priest, called the *president*, to initiate ballots. In most forms of government, choosing a president can be a difficult problem. However, the difficultly arises only because most governments require that there be exactly one president at any time. In the United States, for example, chaos would result after the 1988 election if some people thought Bush had been elected president while others thought that Dukakis had, since one of them might decide to sign a bill into law while the other decided to veto it. However, in the Paxon Synod, having multiple presidents could only impede progress; it could not cause inconsistency. For the complete protocol to satisfy the progress condition, the method for choosing the president needed only to satisfy the following *presidential selection requirement*:

> If no one entered or left the Chamber, then after T minutes exactly one priest in the Chamber would consider himself to be the president.

If the presidential selection requirement were met, then the complete protocol would have the property that if a majority set of priests were in the chamber and no one entered or left the Chamber for $T + 99$ minutes, then at the end of that period every priest in the Chamber would have a decree written in his ledger.

The Paxons chose as president the priest whose name was last in alphabetical order among the names of all priests in the Chamber, though we don't know exactly how this was done. The presidential selection requirement would have been satisfied if a priest in the Chamber sent a message containing his name to every other priest at least once every $T - 11$ minutes, and a priest considered himself to be president iff he received no message from a "higher-named" priest for T minutes.

The complete Synod protocol was obtained from the basic protocol by requiring priests to perform steps (2)–(6) promptly, adding a method for choosing a president who initiated ballots, and requiring the president to initiate ballots at the appropriate times. Many details of the protocol are not known. I have described simple methods for selecting a president and for deciding when the president should initiate a new ballot, but they are undoubtedly not the ones used in Paxos. The rules I have given require the president to keep initiating ballots even after a decree has been chosen, thereby ensuring that priests who have just entered the Chamber learn about the chosen decree. There were obviously better ways to make sure priests learned about the decree after it had been chosen. Also, in the course of selecting a president, each priest probably sent his value of *lastTried*[p] to the other priests, allowing the president to choose a large enough ballot number on his first try.

The Paxons realized that any protocol to achieve the progress condition must involve measuring the passage of time.[12] The protocols given above for selecting a president and initiating ballots are easily formulated as precise algorithms that set timers and perform actions when time-outs occur—assuming perfectly accurate timers. A closer analysis reveals that such protocols can be made to work with timers having a known bound on their accuracy. The skilled glass blowers of Paxos had no difficulty constructing suitable hourglass timers.

Given the sophistication of Paxon mathematicians, it is widely believed that they must have found an optimal algorithm to satisfy the presidential selection requirement. We can only hope that this algorithm will be discovered in future excavations on Paxos.

3 The Multidecree Parliament

When Parliament was established, a protocol to satisfy its consistency and progress requirements was derived from the Synod protocol. The derivation and properties

---

12. However, many centuries were to pass before a rigorous proof of this result was given [Fischer et al. 1985].

of the original parliamentary protocol are described in Sections 3.1 and 3.2. Section 3.3 discusses the further evolution of the protocol.

3.1 The Protocol

Instead of passing just one decree, the Paxon Parliament had to pass a series of numbered decrees. As in the Synod protocol, a president was elected. Anyone who wanted a decree passed would inform the president, who would assign a number to the decree and attempt to pass it. Logically, the parliamentary protocol used a separate instance of the complete Synod protocol for each decree number. However, a single president was selected for all these instances, and he performed the first two steps of the protocol just once.

The key to deriving the parliamentary protocol is the observation that, in the Synod protocol, the president does not choose the decree or the quorum until step 3. A newly elected president p can send to some set of legislators a single message that serves as the *NextBallot(b)* message for all instances of the Synod protocol. (There are an infinite number of instances—one for each decree number.) A legislator q can reply with a single message that serves as the *LastVote* messages for step (2) of all instances of the Synod protocol. This message contains only a finite amount of information, since q can have voted in only a finite number of instances.

When the new president has received a reply from every member of a majority set, he is ready to perform step (3) for every instance of the Synod protocol. For some finite number of instances (decree numbers), the choice of decree in step (3) will be determined by $B3$. The president immediately performs step 3 for each of those instances to try passing these decrees. Then, whenever he receives a request to pass a decree, he chooses the lowest-numbered decree that he is still free to choose, and he performs step (3) for that decree number (instance of the Synod protocol) to try to pass the decree.

The following modifications to this simple protocol lead to the actual Paxon Parliament's protocol.

— There is no reason to go through the Synod protocol for a decree number whose outcome is already known. Therefore, if a newly elected president p has all decrees with numbers less than or equal to n written in his ledger, then he sends a *NextBallot(b, n)* message that serves as a *NextBallot(b)* message in all instances of the Synod protocol for decree numbers larger than n. In his response to this message, legislator q informs p of all decrees numbered greater than n that already appear in q's ledger (in addition to sending the usual *LastVote* information for decrees not in his ledger), and he asks *p* to send him any decrees numbered *n* or less that are not in his ledger.

— Suppose decrees 125 and 126 are introduced late Friday afternoon, decree 126 is passed and is written in one or two ledgers, but before anything else happens, the legislators all go home for the weekend. Suppose also that the following Monday, $\Delta\phi\omega\rho\kappa$ is elected the new president and learns about decree 126, but she has no knowledge of decree 125 because the previous president and all legislators who had voted for it are still out of the Chamber. She will hold a ballot that passes decree 126, which leaves a gap in the ledgers. Assigning number 125 to a new decree would cause it to appear earlier in the ledger than decree 126, which had been passed the previous week. Passing decrees out of order in this way might cause confusion—for example, if the citizen who proposed the new decree did so because he knew decree 126 had already passed. Instead, $\Delta\phi\omega\rho\kappa$ would attempt to pass

> 125: *The ides of February is national olive day*

a traditional decree that made absolutely no difference to anyone in Paxos. In general, a new president would fill any gaps in his ledger by passing the "olive-day" decree.

The consistency and progress properties of the parliamentary protocol follow immediately from the corresponding properties of the Synod protocol from which it was derived. To our knowledge, the Paxons never bothered writing a precise description of the parliamentary protocol because it was so easily derived from the Synod protocol.

3.2 Properties of the Protocol

3.2.1 The Ordering of Decrees

Balloting could take place concurrently for many different decree numbers, with ballots initiated by different legislators—each thinking he was president when he initiated the ballot. We cannot say precisely in what order decrees would be passed, especially without knowing how a president was selected. However, there is one important property about the ordering of decrees that can be deduced.

A decree was said to to be *proposed* when it was chosen by the president in step (3) of the corresponding instance of the Synod protocol. The decree was said to be *passed* when it was written for the first time in a ledger. Before a president could propose any new decrees, he had to learn from all the members of a majority set what decrees they had voted for. Any decree that had already been passed must have been voted for by at least one legislator in the majority set. Therefore, the president must have learned about all previously passed decrees before initiating any new decree. The president would not fill a gap in the ledgers with an important decree—that is, with any decree other than the "olive-day" decree. He would also not propose decrees out of order. Therefore, the protocol satisfied the following *decree-ordering property*.

> If decrees A and B are important and decree A was passed before decree B was proposed, then A has a lower decree number than B.

3.2.2 Behind Closed Doors

Although we don't know the details involved in choosing a new president, we do know exactly how Parliament functioned when the president had been chosen and no one was entering or leaving the Chamber. Upon receiving a request to pass a decree—either directly from a citizen or relayed from another legislator—the president assigned the decree a number and passed it with the following exchange of messages. (The numbers refer to the corresponding steps in the Synod protocol.)

3. The president sent a *BeginBallot* message to each legislator in a quorum.

4. Each legislator in the quorum sent a *Voted* message to the president.

5. The president sent a *Success* message to every legislator.

This is a total of three message delays and about $3N$ messages, assuming a parliament of N legislators and a quorum of about $N/2$. Moreover, if Parliament was busy, the president would combine the *BeginBallot* message for one decree with the *Success* message for a previous one, for a total of only $2N$ messages per decree.

3.3 Further Developments

Governing the island turned out to be a more complex task than the Paxons realized. A number of problems arose whose solutions required changes to the protocol. The most important of these changes are described below.

3.3.1 Picking a President

The president of parliament was originally chosen by the method that had been used in the Synod, which was based purely on the alphabetical ordering of names. Thus, when legislator $\Omega\kappa\iota$ returned from a six-month vacation, he was immediately made president—even though he had no idea what had happened in his absence. Parliamentary activity came to a halt while $\Omega\kappa\iota$, who was a slow writer, laboriously copied six months worth of decrees to bring his ledger up to date.

This incident led to a debate about the best way to choose a president. Some Paxons urged that once a legislator became president, he should remain president until he left the Chamber. An influential group of citizens wanted the richest legislator in the Chamber to be president, since he could afford to hire more scribes and other servants to help him with the presidential duties. They argued that once a rich legislator had brought his ledger up to date, there was no reason for him not to assume the presidency. Others, however, argued that the most upstanding citizen should be made president, regardless of wealth. Upstanding probably meant less likely to be dishonest, although no Paxon would publicly admit the possibility of official malfeasance. Unfortunately, the outcome of this debate is not known; no record exists of the presidential selection protocol that was ultimately used.

3.3.2 Long Ledgers

As the years progressed and Parliament passed more and more decrees, Paxons had to pore over an ever longer list of decrees to find the current olive tax or what color goat could be sold. A legislator who returned to the Chamber after an extended voyage had to do quite a bit of copying to bring his ledger up to date. Eventually, the legislators were forced to convert their ledgers from lists of decrees into law books that contained only the current state of the law and the number of the last decree whose passage was reflected in that state.

To learn the current olive tax, one looked in the law book under "taxes;" to learn what color goat could be sold, one looked under "mercantile law." If a legislator's ledger contained the law through decree 1298 and he learned that decree 1299 set the olive tax to 6 drachmas per ton, he just changed the entry for the olive-tax law and noted that his ledger was complete through decree 1299. If he then learned about decree 1302, he would write it down in the back of the ledger and wait until he learned about decrees 1300 and 1301 before incorporating decree 1302 into the law book.

To enable a legislator who had been gone for a short time to catch up without copying the entire law book, legislators kept a list of the past week's decrees in the back of the book. They could have kept this list on a slip of paper, but it was convenient for a legislator to enter decrees in the back of the ledger as they were passed and update the law book only two or three times a week.

3.3.3 Bureaucrats

As Paxos prospered, legislators became very busy. Parliament could no longer handle all details of government, so a bureaucracy was established. Instead of passing a decree to declare whether each lot of cheese was fit for sale, Parliament passed a decree appointing a cheese inspector to make those decisions.

It soon became evident that selecting bureaucrats was not as simple as it first seemed. Parliament passed a decree making $\Delta \breve{\iota} \kappa \sigma \tau \rho \alpha$ the first cheese inspector. After some months, merchants complained that $\Delta \breve{\iota} \kappa \sigma \tau \rho \alpha$ was too strict and was rejecting perfectly good cheese. Parliament then replaced him by passing the decree

> 1375: $\Gamma \omega \upsilon \delta \alpha$ *is the new cheese inspector*

But $\Delta \breve{\iota} \kappa \sigma \tau \rho \alpha$ did not pay close attention to what Parliament did, so he did not learn of this decree right away. There was a period of confusion in the cheese market when both $\Delta \breve{\iota} \kappa \sigma \tau \rho \alpha$ and $\Gamma \omega \upsilon \delta \alpha$ were inspecting cheese and making conflicting decisions.

To prevent such confusion, the Paxons had to guarantee that a position could be held by at most one bureaucrat at any time. To do this, a president included as part of each decree the time and date when it was proposed. A decree making $\Delta \breve{\iota} \kappa \sigma \tau \rho \alpha$ the cheese inspector might read

> 2716: 8:30 15 Jan 72—$\Delta \breve{\iota} \kappa \sigma \tau \rho \alpha$ *is cheese inspector for 3 months*

This declares his term to begin either at 8:30 on 15 January or when the previous inspector's term ended—whichever was later. His term would end at 8:30 on 15 March, unless he explicitly resigned by asking the president to pass a decree like

> 2834 9:15 3 Mar 72—$\Delta \breve{\iota} \kappa \sigma \tau \rho \alpha$ *resigns as cheese inspector*

A bureaucrat was appointed for a short term, so he could be replaced quickly—for example, if he left the island. Parliament would pass a decree to extend the bureaucrat's term if he was doing a satisfactory job.

A bureaucrat needed to tell time to determine if he currently held a post. Mechanical clocks were unknown on Paxos, but Paxons could tell time accurately to within 15 minutes by the position of the sun or the stars.[13] If $\Delta \breve{\iota} \kappa \sigma \tau \rho \alpha$'s term began at 8:30, he would not start inspecting cheese until his celestial observations indicated that it was 8:45.

It is easy to make this method of appointing bureaucrats work if higher-numbered decrees always have later proposal times. But what if Parliament passed the decrees

> 2854: 9:45 9 Apr 78—$\Phi \rho \alpha \upsilon \sigma \epsilon \zeta$ *is wine taster for 2 months*
> 2855: 9:20 9 Apr 78—$\Pi \upsilon \upsilon \epsilon \lambda \breve{\iota}$ *is wine taster for 1 month*

13. Cloudy days are rare in Paxos's balmy climate.

that were proposed between 9:30 and 9:35 by different legislators who both thought they were president? Such out-of-order proposal times are easily prevented because the parliamentary protocol satisfies the following property.

> If two decrees are passed by different presidents, then one of the presidents proposed his decree after learning that the other decree had been proposed.

To see that this property is satisfied, suppose that ballot number b was successful for decree D, ballot number b' was successful for decree D', and $b < b'$. Let q be a legislator who voted in both ballots. The balloting for D' began with a $NextBallot(b', n)$ message. If the sender of that message did not already know about D, then n is less than the decree number of D, and q's reply to the $NextBallot$ message must state that he voted for D.

3.3.4 Learning the Law

In addition to requesting the passage of decrees, ordinary citizens needed to inquire about the current law of the land. The Paxons at first thought that a citizen could simply examine the ledger of any legislator, but the following incident demonstrated that a more sophisticated approach was needed. For centuries, it had been legal to sell only white goats. A farmer named Δωλεφ got Parliament to pass the decree

> 77: *The sale of black goats is permitted*

Δωλεφ then instructed his goatherd to sell some black goats to a merchant named Σκεεν. As a law-abiding citizen, Σκεεν asked legislator Στωκμεῖρ if such a sale would be legal. But Στωκμεῖρ had been out of the Chamber and had no entry in his ledger past decree 76. He advised Σκεεν that the sale would be illegal under the current law, so Σκεεν refused to buy the goats.

This incident led to the formulation of the following *monotonicity condition* on inquiries about the law.

> If one inquiry precedes a second inquiry, then the second inquiry cannot reveal an earlier state of the law than the first.

If a citizen learns that a particular decree has been passed, then the process of acquiring that knowledge is considered to be an implicit inquiry to which this condition applies. As we will see, the interpretation of the monotonicity condition changed over the years.

Initially, the monotonicity condition was achieved by passing a decree for each inquiry. If $\Sigma\partial\nu\breve{\iota}\delta\epsilon\rho$ wanted to know the current tax on olives, he would get Parliament to pass a decree such as

      87: *Citizen $\Sigma\partial\nu\breve{\iota}\delta\epsilon\rho$ is reading the law*

He would then read any ledger complete at least through decree 86 to learn the olive tax as of that decree. If citizen $\Gamma\rho\epsilon\epsilon\varsigma$ then inquired about the olive tax, the decree for his inquiry was proposed after decree 87 was passed, so the decree-ordering property (Section 3.2.1) implies that it received a decree number greater than 87. Therefore, $\Gamma\rho\epsilon\epsilon\varsigma$ could not obtain an earlier value of the olive tax than $\Sigma\partial\nu\breve{\iota}\delta\epsilon\rho$. This method of reading the law satisfied the monotonicity condition when *precedes* was interpreted to mean that inquiry A precedes inquiry B iff A finished at an earlier time than B began.

Passing a decree for every inquiry soon proved too cumbersome. The Paxons realized that a simpler method was possible if they weakened the monotonicity condition by changing the interpretation of *precedes*. They decided that for one event to precede another, the first event not only had to happen at an earlier time, but it had to be able to causally affect the second event. The weaker monotonicity condition prevents the problem first encountered by farmer $\Delta\omega\lambda\epsilon\phi$ and merchant $\Sigma\kappa\epsilon\epsilon\nu$ because there is a causal chain of events between the end of the implicit inquiry by $\Delta\omega\lambda\epsilon\phi$ and the beginning of the inquiry by $\Sigma\kappa\epsilon\epsilon\nu$.

The weaker monotonicity condition was met by using decree numbers in all business transactions and inquiries. For example, farmer $\Delta\omega\lambda\epsilon\phi$, whose flock included many nonwhite goats, got Parliament to pass the decree

      277: *The sale of brown goats is permitted*

When selling his brown goats to $\Sigma\kappa\epsilon\epsilon\nu$, he informed the merchant that the sale was legal as of decree number 277. $\Sigma\kappa\epsilon\epsilon\nu$ then asked legislator $\Sigma\tau\omega\kappa\mu\epsilon\breve{\iota}\rho$ if the sale were legal under the law through at least decree 277. If $\Sigma\tau\omega\kappa\mu\epsilon\breve{\iota}\rho$'s ledger was not complete through decree 277, he would either wait until it was or else tell $\Sigma\kappa\epsilon\epsilon\nu$ to ask someone else. If $\Sigma\tau\omega\kappa\mu\epsilon\breve{\iota}\rho$'s ledger went through decree 298, then he would tell $\Sigma\kappa\epsilon\epsilon\nu$ that the sale was legal as of decree number 298. Merchant $\Sigma\kappa\epsilon\epsilon\nu$ would remember the number 298 for use in his next business transaction or inquiry about the law.

The Paxons had satisfied the monotonicity condition, but ordinary citizens disliked having to remember decree numbers. Again, the Paxons solved the problem by reinterpreting the monotonicity condition—this time, by changing the meaning of *state of the law*. They divided the law into separate areas, and a legislator was chosen as specialist for each area. The current state of each area of the law was determined by that specialist's ledger. For example, suppose decree 1517 changed the tariff law and decree 1518 changed the tax law. The tax law would change first if the tax-law specialist learned of both decrees before the tariff-law specialist learned of either, yielding a state of the law that could not be obtained by enacting the decrees in numerical order.

To avoid conflicting definitions of the current state, the Paxons required that there be at most one specialist at a time for any area. This requirement was satisfied by using the same method to choose specialists that was used to choose bureaucrats (see Section 3.3.3). If each inquiry involved only a single area of the law, monotonicity was then achieved by directing the inquiry to that area's specialist, who answered it from his ledger. Since learning that a law had passed constituted the result of an implicit inquiry, the Paxons required that a decree change at most one area of the law, and that notification of the decree's passage could come only from the area's specialist.

Inquiries involving multiple areas were not hard to handle. When merchant $\Lambda\iota\sigma\kappa\omega\phi$ asked if the tariff on an imported golden fleece was higher than the sales tax on one purchased locally, the tax-law and tariff-law specialists had to cooperate to provide an answer. For example, the tax specialist could answer $\Lambda\iota\sigma\kappa\omega\phi$ by first asking the tariff specialist for the tariff on golden fleeces, so long as he made no changes to his ledger before receiving a reply.

This method proved satisfactory until it became necessary to make a sweeping change to several areas of the law at one time. The Paxons then realized that the necessary requirement for maintaining monotonicity was not that a decree affect only a single area, but that every area it affects have the same specialist. Parliament could change several areas of the law with a single decree by first appointing a single legislator to be the specialist for all those areas. Moreover, the same area could have multiple specialists, so long as that area of the law was not allowed to change. Just before income taxes were due, Parliament would appoint several tax-law specialists to handle the seasonal flood of inquiries about the tax law.

3.3.5 Dishonest Legislators and Honest Mistakes

Despite official assertions to the contrary, there must have been a few dishonest legislators in the history of Paxos. When caught, they were probably exiled. By sending contradictory messages, a malicious legislator could cause different legislators' ledgers to be inconsistent. Inconsistency could also result from a lapse of memory by an honest legislator or messenger.

When inconsistencies were recognized, they could easily be corrected by passing decrees. For example, disagreement about the current olive tax could be eliminated by passing a new decree declaring the tax to have a certain value. The difficult problem lay in correcting inconsistent ledgers even if no one was aware of the inconsistency.

The existence of dishonesty or mistakes by legislators can be inferred from the redundant decrees that began appearing in ledgers several years after the founding of Parliament. For example, the decree

2605: *The olive tax is 9 drachmas per ton*

was passed even though decree 2155 had already set the olive tax to 9 drachmas per ton, and no intervening decree had changed it. Parliament apparently cycled through its laws every six months so that even if legislators' ledgers were initially inconsistent, all legislators would agree on the current law of the land within six months. It is believed that by the use of these redundant decrees, the Paxons made their Parliament self-stabilizing. (*Self-stabilizing* is a modern term due to Dijkstra [1974].)

It is not clear precisely what self-stabilization meant in a Parliament with legislators coming and going at will. The Paxons would not have been satisfied with a definition that required all legislators to be in the Chamber at one time before consistency could be guaranteed. However, achieving consistency required that if one legislator had an entry in his ledger for a certain decree number and another did not, then the second legislator would eventually fill in that entry.

Unfortunately, we don't know exactly what sort of self-stabilization property the Paxon Parliament possessed or how it was achieved. Paxon mathematicians undoubtedly addressed the problem, but their work has not yet been found. I hope that future archaeological expeditions to Paxos will give high priority to the search for manuscripts on self-stabilization.

3.3.6 Choosing New Legislators

At first, membership in Parliament was hereditary, passing from parent to child. When the elder statesman Παρνας retired, he gave his ledger to his son, who carried on without interruption. It made no difference to other legislators which Παρνας they communicated with.

As old families emigrated and new ones immigrated, this system had to change. The Paxons decided to add and remove members of Parliament by decree. This posed a circularity problem: membership in Parliament was determined by which decrees were passed, but passing a decree required knowing what constituted a majority set, which in turn depended upon who was a member of Parliament. The circularity was broken by letting the membership of Parliament used in passing decree n be specified by the law as of decree $n - 3$. A president could not try to pass decree 3255 until he knew all decrees through decree 3252. In practice, after passing the decree

> 3252: $\Sigma\tau\rho\omega\nu\gamma$ *is now a legislator*

the president would immediately pass the "olive-day" decree as decrees 3253 and 3254.

Changing the composition of Parliament in this way was dangerous and had to be done with care. The consistency and progress conditions would always hold. However, the progress condition guaranteed progress only if a majority set was in the Chamber; it did not guarantee that a majority set would ever be there. In fact, the mechanism for choosing legislators led to the downfall of the Parliamentary system in Paxos. Because of a scribe's error, a decree that was supposed to honor sailors who had drowned in a shipwreck instead declared them to be the only members of Parliament. Its passage prevented any new decrees from being passed—including the decrees proposed to correct the mistake. Government in Paxos came to a halt. A general named $\Lambda\alpha\mu\pi\sigma\omega\nu$ took advantage of the confusion to stage a coup, establishing a military dictatorship that ended centuries of progressive government. Paxos grew weak under a series of corrupt dictators, and was unable to repel an invasion from the east that led to the destruction of its civilization.

4 Relevance to Computer Science

4.1 The State Machine Approach

Although Paxos' Parliament was destroyed many centuries ago, its protocol is still useful. For example, consider a simple distributed database system that might be used as a name server. A state of the database consists of an assignment of values to names. Copies of the database are maintained by multiple servers. A client program can issue, to any server, a request to read or change the value assigned to a name. There are two kinds of read request: a *slow read*, which returns the value currently assigned to a name, and a *fast read*, which is faster but might not reflect a recent change to the database.

Table 1 shows the obvious correspondence between this database system and the Paxon Parliament: A client's request to change a value is performed by passing a decree. A *slow read* involves passing a decree, as described in Section 3.3.4. A

Table 1

Parliament		Distributed Database
legislator	↔	server
citizen	↔	client program
current law	↔	database state

command:	**read**(*name*, *client*)	**update**(*name*, *val*, *client*)
response:	(*client*, value of *name*)	(*client*, "ok")
new state:	Same as current state	Same as current state except value of *name* changed to *val*

Figure 2   State machine for simple database.

fast read is performed by reading the server's current version of the database. The Paxon Parliament protocol provides a distributed, fault-tolerant implementation of the database system,

This method of implementing a distributed database is an instance of the state machine approach, first proposed in Lamport [1978]. In this approach, one first defines a *state machine*, which consists of a set of states, a set of commands, a set of responses, and a function that assigns a response/state pair (a pair consisting of a response and a state) to each command/state pair. Intuitively, a state machine executes a command by producing a response and changing its state; the command and the machine's current state determine its response and its new state. For the distributed database, a state-machine state is just a database state. The state-machine commands and the function specifying the response and new state are described in Figure 2.

In the state machine approach, a system is implemented with a network of server processes. The servers transform client requests into state machine commands, execute the commands, and transform the state-machine responses into replies to clients. A general algorithm ensures that all servers obtain the same sequence of commands, thereby ensuring that they all produce the same sequence of responses and state changes—assuming they all start from the same initial state. In the database example, a client request to perform a *slow read* or to change a value is transformed into a state-machine **read** or **update** command. That command is executed, and the state-machine response is transformed into a reply to the client, which is sent to him by the server who received his request. Since all servers perform the same sequence of state-machine commands, they all maintain consistent versions of the database. However, at any time, some servers may have earlier versions than others because a state-machine command need not be executed at the same time by all servers. A server uses his current version of the state to reply to a *fast read* request, without executing a state-machine command.

The functionality of the system is expressed by the state machine, which is just a function from command/state pairs to response/state pairs. Problems of synchronization and fault-tolerance are handled by the general algorithm with which servers obtain the sequence of commands. When designing a new system, only the state machine is new. The servers obtain the state-machine commands by a standard distributed algorithm that has already been proved correct. Functions are much easier to design, and to get right, than distributed algorithms.

The first algorithm for implementing an arbitrary state machine appeared in Lamport [1978]. Later, algorithms were devised to tolerate up to any fixed number f of arbitrary failures [Lamport 1984]. These algorithms guarantee that, if fewer than f processes fail, then state machine commands are executed within a fixed length of time. The algorithms are thus suitable for applications requiring real-time response.[14] But if more than f failures occur, then different servers may have inconsistent copies of the state machine. Moreover, the inability of two servers to communicate with each other is equivalent to the failure of one of them. For a system to have a low probability of losing consistency, it must use an algorithm with a large value of f, which in turn implies a large cost in redundant hardware, communication bandwidth, and response time.

The Paxon Parliament's protocol provides another way to implement an arbitrary state machine. The legislators' law book corresponds to the machine state, and passing a decree corresponds to executing a state-machine command. The resulting algorithm is less robust and less expensive than the earlier algorithms. It does not tolerate arbitrary, malicious failures, nor does it guarantee bounded-time response. However, consistency is maintained despite the (benign) failure of any number of processes and communication paths. The Paxon algorithm is suitable for systems with modest reliability requirements that do not justify the expense of an extremely fault-tolerant, real-time implementation.

If the state machine is executed with an algorithm that guarantees bounded-time response, then time can be made part of the state, and machine actions can

---

14. These algorithms were derived from the military protocols of another Mediterranean state.

be triggered by the passage of time. For example, consider a system for granting ownership of resources. The state can include the time at which a client was granted a resource, and the state machine can automatically execute a command to revoke ownership if the client has held the resource too long.

With the Paxon algorithm, time cannot be made part of the state in such a natural way. If failures occur, it can take arbitrarily long to execute a command (pass a decree), and one command can be executed before (appear earlier in the sequence of decrees than) another command that was issued earlier. However, a state machine can still use real time the same way the Paxon Parliament did. For example, the method described in Section 3.3.3 for deciding who was the current cheese inspector can be used to decide who is the current owner of a resource.

4.2   Commit Protocols

The Paxon Synod protocol is similar to standard three-phase commit protocols [Bernstein 1987; Skeen 1982]. A Paxon ballot and a three-phase commit protocol both involve the exchange of five messages between a coordinator (the president) and the other quorum members (legislators). A commit protocol chooses one of two values—*commit* or *abort*—while the Synod protocol chooses an arbitrary decree. To convert a commit protocol to a Synod protocol, one sends the decree in the initial round of messages. A *commit* decision means that this decree was passed, and an *abort* decision means that the "olive-day" decree was passed.

The Synod protocol differs from a converted commit protocol because the decree is not sent until the second phase. This allows the corresponding parliamentary protocol to execute the first phase just once for all decrees, so the exchange of only three messages is needed to pass each individual decree.

The theorems on which the Synod protocol is based are similar to results obtained by Dwork, Lynch, and Stockmeyer [Dwork et al. 1988]. However, their algorithms execute ballots sequentially in separate rounds, and they seem to be unrelated to the Synod protocol.

Appendix: Proof of Consistency of the Synodic Protocol

A.1   The Basic Protocol

The Synod's basic protocol, described informally in Section 2.3, is stated here using modern algorithmic notation. We begin with the variables that a priest p must maintain. First come the variables that represent information kept in his

Sidebar 2

Much research has been done in the field since this article was written. The state-machine approach has been surveyed by Schneider [1990]. The recovery protocol by Keidar and Dolev [1996] and the totally-ordered broadcast algorithm of Fekete et al. [1997] are quite similar to the Paxon protocol described here. The author was also apparently unaware that the view management protocol by Oki and Liskov [1988] seems to be equivalent to the Paxon protocol.

Many of the refinements presented in this submission have also appeared in contemporary or subsequent articles. The method of delegation described in Section 3.3.3 is very similar to the leases mechanism of Gray and Cheriton [1989]. The technique of Section 3.3.4 in which the Paxons satisfy the monotonicity condition by using decree numbers is described by Ladin et al. [1992]. The technique of Section 3.3.6 for adding new legislators was also given by Schneider [1990].

K. M.

ledger. (For convenience, the vote $prevVote[p]$ used in Section 2.3 is replaced by its components $prevBal[p]$ and $prevDec[p]$.)

$outcome[p]$ The decree written in p's ledger, or BLANK if there is nothing written there yet.

$lastTried[p]$ The number of the last ballot that p tried to begin, or $-\infty$ if there was none.

$prevBal[p]$ The number of the last ballot in which p voted, or $-\infty$ if he never voted.

$prevDec[p]$ The decree for which p last voted, or BLANK if p never voted.

$nextBal[p]$ The number of the last ballot in which p agreed to participate, or $-\infty$ if he has never agreed to participate in a ballot.

Next come variables representing information that priest p could keep on a slip of paper:

$status[p]$ One of the following values:

  idle   Not conducting or trying to begin a ballot

  trying   Trying to begin ballot number $lastTried[p]$

  polling   Now conducting ballot number $lastTried[p]$

  If p has lost his slip of paper, then $status[p]$ is assumed to equal *idle* and the values of the following four variables are irrelevant.

prevVotes[*p*]	The set of votes received in *LastVote* messages for the current ballot (the one with ballot number *lastTried*[*p*]).
quorum[*p*]	If *status*[*p*] = *polling*, then the set of priests forming the quorum of the current ballot; otherwise, meaningless.
voters[*p*]	If *status*[*p*] = *polling*, then the set of quorum members from whom *p* has received *Voted* messages in the current ballot; otherwise, meaningless.
decree[*p*]	If *status*[*p*] = *polling*, then the decree of the current ballot; otherwise, meaningless.

There is also the history variable $\mathcal{B}$, which is the set of ballots that have been started and their progress—namely, which priests have cast votes. (A history variable is one used in the development and proof of an algorithm, but not actually implemented.)

Next come the actions that priest *p* may take. These actions are assumed to be atomic, meaning that once an action is begun, it must be completed before priest *p* begins any other action. An action is described by an enabling condition and a list of effects. The enabling condition describes when the action can be performed; actions that receive a message are enabled whenever a messenger has arrived with the appropriate message. The list of effects describes how the action changes the algorithm's variables and what message, if any, it sends. (Each individual action sends at most one message.)

Recall that ballot numbers were partitioned among the priests. For any ballot number *b*, the Paxons defined *owner*(*b*) to be the priest who was allowed to use that ballot number.

The actions in the basic protocol are allowed actions; the protocol does not require that a priest ever do anything. No attempt at efficiency has been made; the actions allow *p* to do silly things, such as sending another *BeginBallot* message to a priest from whom he has already received a *LastVote* message.

Try New Ballot
Always enabled.

- Set *lastTried*[*p*] to any ballot number *b*, greater than its previous value, such that *owner*[*b*] = *p*.
- Set *status*[*p*] to *trying*.
- Set *prevVotes*[*p*] to ∅.

Send *NextBallot* **Message**
Enabled whenever *status*[*p*] = *trying*.

- Send a *NextBallot*(*lastTried*[*p*]) message to any priest.

Receive *NextBallot(b) Message*

If $b \geq nextBal[p]$ then

- Set $nextBal[p]$ to b.

Send *LastVote* **Message**

Enabled whenever $nextBal[p] > prevBal[p]$.

- Send a *LastVote(nextBal[p], v)* message to priest $owner(nextBal[p])$, where $v_{pst} = p$, $v_{bal} = prevBal[p]$, and $v_{dec} = prevDec[p]$.

Receive *LastVote(b, v)* **Message**

If $b = lastTried[p]$ and $status[p] = trying$, then

- Set $prevVotes[p]$ to the union of its original value and $\{v\}$.

Start Polling Majority Set Q

Enabled when $status[p] = trying$ and $Q \subseteq \{v_{pst} : v \in prevVotes[p]\}$, where Q is a majority set.

- Set $status[p]$ to *polling*.
- Set $quorum[p]$ to Q.
- Set $voters[p]$ to $\emptyset$.
- Set $decree[p]$ to a decree d chosen as follows: Let v be the maximum element of $prevVotes[p]$. If $v_{bal} \neq -\infty$ then $d = v_{dec}$, else d can equal any decree.
- Set $\mathcal{B}$ to the union of its former value and $\{B\}$, where $B_{dec} = d$, $B_{qrm} = Q$, $B_{vot} = \emptyset$, and $B_{bal} = lastTried[p]$.

Send *BeginBallot* **Message**

Enabled when $status[p] = polling$.

- Send a *BeginBallot(lastTried[p], decree[p])* message to any priest in $quorum[p]$.

Receive *BeginBallot(b, d)* **Message**

If $b = nextBal[p] > prevBal[p]$ then

- Set $prevBal[p]$ to b.
- Set $prevDec[p]$ to d.
- If there is a ballot B in $\mathcal{B}$ with $B_{bal} = b$ [there will be], then choose any such B [there will be only one] and let the new value of $\mathcal{B}$ be obtained from its old value by setting B_{vot} equal to the union of its old value and $\{p\}$.

Send *Voted* **Message**

Enabled whenever $prevBal[p] \neq -\infty$.

- Send a $Voted(prevBal[p],\ p)$ message to $owner\,prevBal[p]$.

Receive *Voted*$(b,\ q)$ **Message**

$b = lastTried[p]$ and $status[p] = polling$, then

- Set $voters[p]$ to the union of its old value and $\{q\}$.

Succeed

Enabled whenever $status[p] = polling$, $participants[p] \subseteq voters[p]$, and $outcome[p] =$ BLANK.

- Set $outcome[p]$ to $decree[p]$.

Send *Success* **Message**

Enabled whenever $outcome[p] \neq$ BLANK.

- Send a $Success(outcome[p])$ message to any priest.

Receive *Success*(d) **Message**

If $outcome[p] =$ BLANL, then

- Set $outcome[p]$ to d.

This algorithm is an abstract description of the real protocol performed by Paxon priests. Do the algorithm's actions accurately model the actions of the real priests? There were three kinds of actions that a priest could perform "atomically": receiving a message, writing a note or ledger entry, and sending a message. Each of these is represented by a single action of the algorithm, except that **Receive** actions both receive a message and set a variable. We can pretend that the receipt of a message occurred when a priest acted upon the message; if he left the Chamber before acting upon it, then we can pretend that the message was never received. Since this pretense does not affect the consistency condition, we can infer the consistency of the basic Synod protocol from the consistency of the algorithm.

A.2   Proof of Consistency

To prove the consistency condition, it is necessary to show that whenever out-$come[p]$ and $outcome[q]$ are both different from BLANK, they are equal. A rigorous correctness proof requires a complete description of the algorithm. The description given above is almost complete. Missing is a variable $\mathcal{M}$ whose value is the multiset of all messages in transit.[15] Each **Send** action adds a message to this multiset and each **Receive** action removes one. Also needed are actions to represent the loss and duplication of messages, as well as a **Forget** action that represents a priest losing his slip of paper.

With these additions, we get an algorithm that defines a set of possible behaviors, in which each change of state corresponds to one of the allowed actions. The Paxons proved correctness by finding a predicate I such that

1. I is true initially.

2. I implies the desired correctness condition.

3. Each allowed action leaves I true.

The predicate I was written as a conjunction $I1 \wedge \ldots \wedge I7$, where $I1$–$I5$ were in turn the conjunction of predicates $I1(p)$–$I5(p)$ for all priests p. Although most variables are mentioned in several of the conjuncts, each variable except $status(p)$ is naturally associated with one conjunct, and each conjunct can be thought of as a constraint on its associated variables. The definitions of the individual conjuncts of I are given below, where a list of items marked by $\wedge$ symbols denotes the conjunction of those items. The variables associated with a conjunct are listed in bracketed comments.

The Paxons had to prove that I satisfies the three conditions given above. The first condition, that I holds initially, requires checking that each conjunct is true for the initial values of all the variables. While not stated explicitly, these initial values can be inferred from the variables' descriptions, and checking the first condition is straightforward. The second condition, that I implies consistency, follows from $I1$, the first conjunct of $I6$, and Theorem 1. The hard part was proving the third condition, the invariance of I, which meant proving that I is left true by every action. This condition is proved by showing that, for each conjunct of I, executing any action when I is true leaves that conjunct true. The proofs are sketched below.

Proof Sketch for $I1(p)$ $\mathcal{B}$ is changed only by adding a new ballot or adding a new priest to B_{vot} for some $B \in \mathcal{B}$, neither of which can falsify $I1(p)$. The value of $outcome[p]$ is changed only by the **Succeed** and **Receive** *Success* **Message** actions. The enabling condition and $I5(p)$ imply that $I1(p)$ is left true by the **Succeed** action. The enabling condition, $I1(p)$, and the last conjunct of $I7$ imply that $I1(p)$ is left true by the **Receive** *Success* **Message** action. ∎

---

15. A multiset is a set that may contain multiple copies of the same element.

$I1(p) \triangleq$ [Associated variable: $outcome[p]$]

$(outcome[p] \neq BLANK) \Rightarrow \exists B \in \mathcal{B}: (B_{qrm} \subseteq B_{vot}) \wedge (B_{dec} = outcome[p])$

$I2(p) \triangleq$ [Associated variable: $lastTried[p]$]

$\quad \wedge owner(lastTried[p]) = p$

$\quad \wedge \forall B \in \mathcal{B} : (owner(B_{bal}) = p) \Rightarrow$

$\qquad \wedge B_{bal} \leq lastTried[p]$

$\qquad \wedge (status[p] = trying) \Rightarrow (B_{bal} < lastTried[p])$

$I3(p) \triangleq$ [Associated variables: $prevBal[p], prevDec[p], nextBal[p]$]

$\quad \wedge prevBal[p] = MaxVote(\infty, p, \mathcal{B})_{bal}$

$\quad \wedge prevDec[p] = MaxVote(\infty, p, \mathcal{B})_{dec}$

$\quad \wedge nextBal[p] \geq prevBal[p]$

$I4(p) \triangleq$ [Associated variable: $prevVotes[p]$]

$(status[p] \neq idle) \Rightarrow$

$\forall v \in prevVotes[p] : \wedge v = MaxVote(lastTried[p], v_{pst}, \mathcal{B})$

$\qquad \wedge nextBal[v_{pst}] \geq lastTried[p]$

$I5(p) \triangleq$ [Associated variables: $quorum[p], voters[p], decree[p]$]

$(status[p] = polling) \Rightarrow$

$\quad \wedge quorum[p] \subseteq \{v_{pst} : v \in prevVotes[p]\}$

$\quad \wedge \exists B \in \mathcal{B} : \wedge quorum[p] = B_{qrm}$

$\qquad \wedge decree[p] = B_{dec}$

$\qquad \wedge voters[p] \subseteq B_{vot}$

$\qquad \wedge lastTried[p] = B_{bal}$

$I6 \triangleq$ [Associated variable: $\mathcal{B}$]

$\quad \wedge B1(\mathcal{B}) \wedge B2(\mathcal{B}) \wedge B3(\mathcal{B})$

$\quad \wedge \forall B \in \mathcal{B} : B_{qrm}$ is a majority set

$I7 \triangleq$ [Associated variable: $\mathcal{M}$]

$\quad \wedge \forall NextBallot(b) \in \mathcal{M} : (b \leq lastTried[owner(b)])$

$\quad \wedge \forall LastVote(b, v) \in \mathcal{M} : \wedge v = MaxVote(b, v_{pst}, \mathcal{B})$

$\qquad \wedge nextBal[v_{pst}] \geq b$

$\quad \wedge \forall BeginBallot(b, d) \in \mathcal{M} : \exists B \in \mathcal{B} : (B_{bal} = b) \wedge (B_{dec} = d)$

$\quad \wedge \forall Voted(b, p) \in \mathcal{M} : \exists B \in \mathcal{B} : (B_{bal} = b) \wedge (p \in B_{vot})$

$\quad \wedge \forall Success(d) \in \mathcal{M} : \exists p : outcome[p] = d \neq BLANK$

Figure 3   Individual conjuncts of predicate I.

Proof Sketch for $I2(p)$ This conjunct depends only on $lastTried[p]$, $status[p]$, and $\mathcal{B}$. Only the **Try New Ballot** action changes $lastTried[p]$, and only that action can set $status[p]$ to $trying$. Since the action increases $lastTried[p]$ to a value b with $owner(b) = p$, it leaves $I2(p)$ true. A completely new element is added to $\mathcal{B}$ only by a **Start Polling** action; the first conjunct of $I2(p)$ and the specification of the action imply that adding this new element does not falsify the second conjunct of $I2(p)$. The only other way $\mathcal{B}$ is changed is by adding a new priest to B_{vot} for some $B \in \mathcal{B}$, which does not affect $I2(p)$. ■

Proof Sketch for $I3(p)$ Since votes are never removed from $\mathcal{B}$, the only action that can change $MaxVote(\infty, p, \mathcal{B})$ is one that adds to $\mathcal{B}$ a vote cast by p. Only a **Receive** $BeginBallot$ **Message** action can do that, and only that action changes $prevBal[p]$ and $prevDec[p]$. The $BeginBallot$ conjunct of $I7$ implies that this action actually does add a vote to $\mathcal{B}$, and $B1(\mathcal{B})$ (the first conjunct of $I6$) implies that there is only one ballot to which the vote can be added. The enabling condition, the assumption that $I3(p)$ holds before executing the action, and the definition of $MaxVote$ then imply that the action leaves the first two conjuncts of $I3(p)$ true. The third conjunct is left true because $prevBal[p]$ is changed only by setting it to $nextBal[p]$, and $nextBal[p]$ is never decreased. ■

Proof Sketch for $I4(p)$ This conjunct depends only upon the values of $status[p]$, $prevVotes[p]$, $lastTried[p]$, $nextBal[q]$ for some priests q, and $\mathcal{B}$. The value of $status[p]$ is changed from $idle$ to not $idle$ only by a **Try New Ballot** action, which sets $prevVotes[p]$ to $\emptyset$, making $I4(p)$ vacuously true. The only other actions that change $prevVotes[p]$ are the **Forget** action, which leaves $I4(p)$ true because it sets $status[p]$ to $idle$, and the **Receive** $LastVote$ **Message** action. It follows from the enabling condition and the $LastVote$ conjunct of $I7$ that the **Receive** $LastVote$ **Message** action preserves $I4(p)$. The value of $lastTried[p]$ is changed only by the **Try New Ballot** action, which leaves $I4(p)$ true because it sets $status[p]$ to $trying$. The value of $nextBal[q]$ can only increase, which cannot make $I4(p)$ false. Finally, $MaxVote_{lastTried[p]} v_{pst} \mathcal{B}$ can be changed only if v_{pst} is added to B_{vot} for some $B \in \mathcal{B}$ with $B_{bal} < lastTried[p]$. But v_{pst} is added to B_{vot} (by a **Receive** $BeginBallot$ **Message** action) only if $nextBal v_{pst} = B_{bal}$, in which case $I4(p)$ implies that $B_{bal} \geq lastTried[p]$. ■

Proof Sketch for $I5(p)$ The value of $status[p]$ is set to $polling$ only by the **Start Polling** action. This action's enabling condition guarantees that the first conjunct becomes true, and it adds the ballot to $\mathcal{B}$ that makes the second conjunct true. No other action changes $quorum[p]$, $decree[p]$, or $lastTried[p]$ while leaving $status[p]$ equal to $polling$. The value of $prevVotes[p]$ cannot be changed while $status[p] = polling$, and $\mathcal{B}$ is changed only by adding new elements or by adding a new priest to B_{vot}. The only remaining possibility for falsifying $I5(p)$ is the addition of a new element to $voters[p]$ by the

Receive *Voted* **Message** action. The *Voted* conjunct of $I7$, $B1(\mathcal{B})$ (the first conjunct of $I6$), and the action's enabling condition imply that the element added to $voters[p]$ is in B_{vot}, where B is the ballot whose existence is asserted in $I5(p)$.   ■

Proof Sketch for *I6* Since B_{bal} and B_{qrm} are never changed for any $B \in \mathcal{B}$, the only way $B1(\mathcal{B})$, $B2(\mathcal{B})$, and the second conjunct of $I6$ can be falsified is by adding a new ballot to $\mathcal{B}$, which is done only by the **Start Polling Majority Set** Q action when $status[p]$ equals *trying*. It follows from the second conjunct of $I2(p)$ that this action leaves $B1(\mathcal{B})$ true; and the assertion, in the enabling condition, that Q is a majority set implies that the action leaves $B2(\mathcal{B})$ and the second conjunct of $I6$ true. There are two possible ways of falsifying $B3(\mathcal{B})$: changing $MaxVote(B_{bal}, B_{qrm}, \mathcal{B})$ by adding a new vote to $\mathcal{B}$, and adding a new ballot to $\mathcal{B}$. A new vote is added only by the **Receive** *BeginBallot* **Message** action, and $I3(p)$ implies that the action adds a vote later than any other vote cast by p in $\mathcal{B}$, so it cannot change $MaxVote(B_{bal}, B_{qrm}, \mathcal{B})$ for any B in $\mathcal{B}$. Conjunct $I4(p)$ implies that the new ballot added by the **Start Polling** action does not falsify $B3(\mathcal{B})$.   ■

Proof Sketch for *I7* $I7$ can be falsified either by adding a new message to $\mathcal{M}$ or by changing the value of another variable on which $I7$ depends. Since $lastTried[p]$ and $nextBal[p]$ are never decreased, changing them cannot make $I7$ false. Since $outcome[p]$ is never changed if its value is not BLANK, changing it cannot falsify $I7$. Since $\mathcal{B}$ is changed only by adding ballots and adding votes, the only change to it that can make $I7$ false is the addition of a vote by v_{pst} that makes the $LastVote(b, v)$ conjunct false by changing $MaxVote(b, v_{pst}, \mathcal{B})$. This can happen only if v_{pst} votes in a ballot B with $B_{bal} < b$. But v_{pst} can vote only in ballot number $nextBal[v_{pst}]$, and the assumption that this conjunct holds initially implies that $nextBal[v_{pst}] \geq b$. Therefore, we need check only that every message that is sent satisfies the condition in the appropriate conjunct of $I7$.

NextBallot: Follows from the definition of the **Send** *NextBallot* **Message** action and the first conjunct of $I2(p)$.

LastVote: The enabling condition of the **Send** *LastVote* **Message** action and $I3(p)$ imply that $MaxVote(nextBal[p], p, \mathcal{B}) = MaxVote(\infty, p, \mathcal{B})$, from which it follows that the *LastVote* message sent by the action satisfies the condition in $I7$.

BeginBallot: Follows from $I5(p)$ and the definition of the **Send** *BeginBallot* **Message** action.

Voted: Follows from $I3(p)$, the definition of *MaxVote*, and the definition of the **Send** *Voted* **Message** action.

Success: Follows from the definition of **Send** *Success* **Message**.   ■

Acknowledgments

Daniel Duchamp pointed out to me the need for a new state-machine implementation. Discussions with Martín Abadi, Andy Hisgen, Tim Mann, and Garret Swart led me to Paxos. $\Lambda\epsilon\omega\nu\acute{\iota}\delta\alpha\varsigma$ $\Gamma\kappa\acute{\iota}\mu\pi\alpha\varsigma$ provided invaluable assistance with the Paxon dialect.

References

Bernstein, P. A., Hadzilacos, V., and Goodman, N. 1987. *Concurrency Control and Recovery in Database Systems*. Addison-Wesley Longman Publ. Co., Inc., Reading, MA.

De Prisco, R., Lampson, B., and Lynch, N. 1997. Revisiting the Paxos algorithm. In *Proceedings of the 11th International Workshop on Distributed Algorithms*, M. Mavronicolas and P. Tsigas, Eds., Lecture Notes in Computer Science, vol. 1320. Springer-Verlag, Berlin, Germany, 111–125.

Dijkstra, E. W. 1974. Self-stabilizing systems in spite of distributed control. *Commun. ACM 17*, 11, 643–644.

Dwork, C., Lynch, N., and Stockmeyer, L. 1988. Consensus in the presence of partial synchrony. *J. ACM 35*, 2 (Apr.), 288–323.

Fekete, A., Lynch, N., and Shvartsman, A. 1997. Specifying and using a partitionable group communication service. In *Proceedings of the 16th Annual ACM Symposium on Principles of Distributed Computing*. ACM Press, New York, NY, 53–62.

Fischer, M. J., Lynch, N. A., and Paterson, M. S. 1985. Impossibility of distributed consensus with one faulty process. *J. ACM 32*, 1 (Jan.), 374–382.

Gray, C. and Cheriton, D. 1989. Leases: An efficient fault-tolerant mechanism for distributed file cache consistency. *SIGOPS Oper. Syst. Rev. 23*, 5 (Dec. 3-6), 202–210.

Keidar, I. and Dolev, D. 1996. Efficient message ordering in dynamic networks. In *Proceedings of the 15th Annual ACM Symposium on Principles of Distributed Computing*. ACM Press, New York, NY.

Ladin, R., Liskov, B., Shrira, L., and Ghemawat, S. 1992. Providing high availability using lazy replication. *ACM Trans. Comput. Syst. 10*, 4 (Nov.), 360–391.

Lamport, L. 1978. Time, clocks, and the ordering of events in a distributed system. *Commun. ACM 21*, 7, 558–565.

Lamport, L. 1984. Using time instead of timeout for fault-tolerant distributed systems. *ACM Trans. Program. Lang. Syst. 6*, 2 (Apr.), 254–280.

Lampson, B. W. 1996. How to build a highly available system using consensus. In *Distributed Algorithms*, O. Babaoglu and K. Marzullo, Eds. Springer Lecture Notes in Computer Science, vol. 1151. Springer-Verlag, Berlin, Germany, 1–17.

Oki, B. M. and Liskov, B. H. 1988. Viewstamped replication: A general primary copy. In *Proceedings of the 7th Annual ACM Symposium on Principles of Distributed Computing* (Toronto, Ontario, August 15–17, 1988). ACM Press, New York, NY, 8–17.

Schneider, F. B. 1990. Implementing fault-tolerant services using the state machine approach: A tutorial. *ACM Comput. Surv. 22*, 4 (Dec.), 299–319.

Skeen, M. D. 1982. Crash recovery in a distributed database system. Ph.D. thesis. University of California at Berkeley, Berkeley, CA.

References

M. Abadi and L. Lamport. 1991. The existence of refinement mappings. *Theor. Comput. Sci.*, 82(2):253–284. DOI: 10.1016/0304-3975(91)90224-P. 10, 113, 163

M. Abadi and L. Lamport. 1993. Composing specifications. *ACM Trans. Program. Lang. Syst.*, 15(1): 73–132. DOI: 10.1145/151646.151649. 114

M. Abadi and L. Lamport. 1994. Open systems in TLA. In J. H. Anderson, D. Peleg, and E. Borowsky (eds.), *Proceedings of the Thirteenth Annual ACM Symposium on Principles of Distributed Computing*, pp. 81–90. ACM. DOI: 10.1145/197917.197960. 114

M. Abadi and L. Lamport. 1995. Conjoining specifications. *ACM Trans. Program. Lang. Syst.*, 17(3): 507–534. DOI: 10.1145/203095.201069. 114

J.-R. Abrial. 1996. *The B-Book: Assigning Programs to Meanings*. Cambridge University Press. 115

J.-R. Abrial. 2010. *Modeling in Event-B*. Cambridge University Press. 115, 127

S. V. Adve and M. D. Hill. 1990. Weak ordering - A new definition. In *Proceedings of the 17th Annual International Symposium on Computer Architecture*. pp. 2–14, 1990. DOI: 10.1145/325096.325100. 46

Y. Afek, H. Attiya, D. Dolev, E. Gafni, M. Merritt, and N. Shavit. 1993. Atomic snapshots of shared memory. *J. ACM*, 40(4): 873–890. DOI: 10.1145/153724.153741. 64

M. Ahamad, G. Neiger, J. E. Burns, P. Kohli, and P. W. Hutto. 1995. Causal memory: Definitions, implementation, and programming. *Distributed Computing*, 9: 37–49. DOI: 10.1007/BF01784241. 53

B. Alpern and F. B. Schneider. 1985. Defining liveness. *Inf. Process. Lett.*, 21(4): 181–185. DOI: 10.1016/0020-0190(85)90056-0. 104

P. A. Alsberg and J. D. Day. 1976. A principle for resilient sharing of distributed resources. In *Proceedings of the 2nd International Conference on Software Engineering*, ICSE '76, pp. 562–570. IEEE Computer Society Press. 83, 85

American Mathematical Society. 2019a. AMS-LaTeX. http://www.ams.org/publications/authors/tex/amslatex; last retrieved 10 February 2019. 2, 145

American Mathematical Society. 2019b. AMS-TeX. http://www.ams.org/publications/authors/tex/amstex; last retrieved 10 February 2019. 145

K. R. Apt. 1981. Ten years of Hoare's logic: A survey—part 1. *ACM Trans. Prog. Lang. Syst.*, 3(4): 431–483, 1981. DOI: 10.1145/357146.357150. 109

P. C. Attie, N. Francez, and O. Grumberg. 1993. Fairness and hyperfairness in multi-party interactions. *Distributed Computing*, 6(4): 245–254, 1993. DOI: 10.1007/BF02242712. 104

H. Attiya, F. Ellen, and A. Morrison. 2015. Limitations of highly-available eventually-consistent data stores. In *Proceedings of the 2015 ACM Symposium on Principles of Distributed Computing, PODC '15*, pp. 385–394, New York. ACM. 53

H. Attiya and J. Welch. 1998. *Distributed Computing: Fundamentals, Simulations, and Advanced Topics*. McGraw-Hill International (UK), London, 1998. 37, 40

H. Attiya and J. Welch. 2004. *Distributed Computing: Fundamentals, Simulations, and Advanced Topics, Second Edition*. John Wiley & Sons, Hoboken, NJ, 2004. 37

H. Attiya and J. L. Welch. 1994. Sequential consistency versus linearizability. *ACM Trans. Comput. Syst.*, 12(2): 91–122. DOI: 10.1145/176575.176576. 46

N. Azmy, S. Merz, and C. Weidenbach. 2018. A machine-checked correctness proof for pastry. *Sci. Comput. Program.*, 158: 64–80. DOI: 10.1016/j.scico.2017.08.003. 127

R.-J. Back. 1981. On correct refinement of programs. *J. Comput. Syst. Sci.*, 23(1): 49–68, 1981. DOI: 10.1016/0022-0000(81)90005-2. 111

J. W. Backus, R. J. Beeber, S. Best, R. Goldberg, L. M. Haibt, H. L. Herrick, R. A. Nelson, D. Sayre, P. B. Sheridan, H. Stern. 1957 The Fortran automatic coding system. In *Papers presented at the February 26–28, 1957, Western Joint Computer Conference: Techniques for Reliability*, pp. 188–198. ACM. DOI: 10.1145/1455567.1455599. 133

C. Barrett and C. Tinelli. 2018. Satisfiability modulo theories. In E. M. Clarke, T. A. Henzinger, H. Veith, and R. Bloem (eds.), *Handbook of Model Checking*, pp. 305–343. Springer. 126

M. Ben-Or. 1983. Another advantage of free choice: Completely asynchronous agreement protocols (extended abstract). In *Proceedings of the Second Annual ACM Symposium on Principles of Distributed Computing, PODC '83*, pp. 27–30. ACM. DOI: 10.1145/800221.806707. 90

M. Ben-Or and R. El-Yaniv. 2003. Resilient-optimal interactive consistency in constant time. *Distributed Computing*, 16: 249–262. DOI: 10.1007/s00446-002-0083-3. 71

D. J. Bernstein, D. Hopwood, A. Hülsing, T. Lange, R. Niederhagen, L. Papachristodoulou, M. Schneider, P. Schwabe, and Z. Wilcox-O'Hearn. 2015. SPHINCS: Practical stateless hash-based signatures. In *Proceedings EUROCRYPT 2015*, pp. 368–397. DOI: 10.1007/978-3-662-46800-5_15. 81

I. Beschastnikh, P. Wang, Y. Brun, and M. D. Ernst. 2016. Debugging distributed systems. *Queue*, 14(2): 50. 53

K. Birman, A. Schiper, and P. Stephenson. August 1991. Lightweight causal and atomic group multicast. *ACM Trans. Comput. Syst.*, 9(3): 272–314. DOI: 10.1145/128738.128742. 53, 102

K. Birman. 1986. Isis: A system for fault-tolerant distributed computing. Technical report, Cornell University. 53

A. D. Birrell, A. Hisgen, C. Jerian, T. Mann, and G. Swart. September 1993. The Echo distributed file system. *Digital Systems Research Center Research Report 111*, 10. DOI: 10.1.1.43.1306. 148

R. L. Bocchino, Jr., V. S. Adve, S. V. Adve, and M. Snir. 2009. Parallel programming must be deterministic by default. In *Proceedings of the First USENIX Conference on Hot Topics in Parallelism*, HotPar'09, pp. 4–10, Berkeley, CA. USENIX Association. 86

W. J. Bolosky, J. R. Douceur, and J. Howell. 2007. The Farsite project: A retrospective. *Operating Systems Review*, 41(2): 17–26. DOI: 10.1145/1243418.1243422. 128

R. Bonichon, D. Delahaye, and D. Doligez. 2007. Zenon: An extensible automated theorem prover producing checkable proofs. In N. Dershowitz and A. Voronkov (eds.), *14th International Conference Logic for Programming, Artificial Intelligence, and Reasoning (LPAR)*, volume 4790 of *Lecture Notes in Computer Science*, pp. 151–165. Springer. DOI: 10.1007/978-3-540-75560-9_13. 126

F. V. Brasileiro, F. Greve, A. Mostéfaoui, and M. Raynal. 2001. Consensus in one communication step. In *Proceedings of the 6th International Conference on Parallel Computing Technologies*, PaCT '01, pp. 42–50. Springer-Verlag. DOI: 10.1007/3-540-44743-1_4.pdf. 93

E. A. Brewer. July 2000. Towards robust distributed systems (abstract). In *Proceedings of the Nineteenth Annual ACM Symposium on Principles of Distributed Computing*, p. 7. DOI: 10.1145/343477.343502. 50

J. A. Buchmann, E. Dahmen, and A. Hülsing. 2011. XMSS - A practical forward secure signature scheme based on minimal security assumptions. In *Proceedings Workshop on Post-Quantum Cryptography (PQC)*, volume 7071 of *Lecture Notes in Computer Science*, pp. 117–129. Springer. DOI: 10.1007/978-3-642-25405-5_8. 81

M. Burrows. January 2019. Personal communication. 150

M. Burrows. 2006. The Chubby lock service for loosely-coupled distributed systems. In *Proceedings of the 7th Symposium on Operating Systems Design and Implementation*, OSDI '06, pp. 335–350. USENIX Association. 9, 100

R. M. Burstall. 1974. Program proving as hand simulation with a little induction. In *Information Processing*, pp. 308–312. North-Holland Pub. Co. 105

V. Bush. 1945. As we may think. *The Atlantic Monthly*, 176(1): pp. 101–108. 131

C. Cachin, R. Guerraoui, and L. Rodrigues. 2011. *Introduction to Reliable and Secure Distributed Programming (Second Edition)*. Springer, 2011. 54, 69

C. Cachin, K. Kursawe, F. Petzold, and V. Shoup. August 2001. Secure and efficient asynchronous broadcast protocols. In *Advances in Cryptology - CRYPTO 2001, 21st Annual International Cryptology Conference*, pp. 524–541. 71

S. Chand, Y. A. Liu, and S. D. Stoller. 2016. Formal verification of multi-Paxos for distributed consensus. In J. S. Fitzgerald, C. L. Heitmeyer, S. Gnesi, and A. Philippou (eds.), *21st*

International Symposium Formal Methods (FM 2016), volume 9995 of *Lecture Notes in Computer Science*, pp. 119–136. DOI: 10.1007/978-3-319-48989-6_8. 127

T. D. Chandra, R. Griesemer, and J. Redstone. 2007. Paxos made live: An engineering perspective. In *Proceedings of the 26th ACM Symposium on Principles of Distributed Computing (PODC '07)*, pp. 398–407. ACM. DOI: 10.1145/1281100.1281103. 9, 99

T. D. Chandra and S. Toueg. 1996. Unreliable failure detectors for reliable distributed systems. *J. ACM*, 43(2): 225–267. DOI: 10.1145/226643.226647. 71

K. M. Chandy and L. Lamport. 1985. Distributed snapshots: Determining global states of distributed systems. *ACM Trans. Comput. Syst.*, 3(1): 63–75. DOI: 10.1145/214451 .214456. 7, 48, 59, 64, 143, 164

M. Chandy. July 2018. Personal communications (email), 16 and 30. 165

A. Condon and A. J. Hu. 2003. Automatable verification of sequential consistency. *Theory Comput. Syst.*, 36(5): 431–460. DOI: 10.1007/s00224-003-1082-x. 46

D. Cousineau, D. Doligez, L. Lamport, S. Merz, D. Ricketts, and H. Vanzetto. August 2012. TLA+ proofs. In D. Giannakopoulou and D. Méry (eds.), *FM 2012: Formal Methods - 18th International Symposium,* volume 7436 of *Lecture Notes in Computer Science*, pp. 147–154. Springer. 125

G. DeCandia, D. Hastorun, M. Jampani, G. Kakulapati, A. Lakshman, A. Pilchin, S. Sivasubramanian, P. Vosshall, and W. Vogels. 2007. Dynamo: Amazon's highly available key-value store. In *SOSP*. DOI: 10.1145/1323293.1294281. 53

D. Didona, R. Guerraoui, J. Wang, and W. Zwaenepoel. 2018. Causal consistency and latency optimality: Friend or foe? *PVLDB*, 11(11): 1618–1632. DOI: 10.14778/3236187 .3236210. 53

W. Diffie and M. E. Hellman. 1976. New directions in cryptography. *IEEE Transactions on Information Theory*, 22(6): 644–654. DOI: 10.1109/TIT.1976.1055638. 78, 140

E. W. Dijkstra. 1971. On the reliability of programs. https://www.cs.utexas.edu/users/EWD/ transcriptions/EWD03xx/EWD303.html. 159

E. W. Dijkstra. 1965. Solution of a problem in concurrent programming control. *CACM*, 8(9): 569. 4

E. W. Dijkstra. 1971. Hierarchical ordering of sequential processes. *Acta Inf.*, 1: 115–138. DOI: 10.1007/BF00289519. 30, 44

E. W. Dijkstra. 1976. *A Discipline of Programming*. Prentice Hall. 111

D. L. Dill, A. J. Drexler, A. J. Hu, and C. H. Yang. 1992. Protocol verification as a hardware design aid. In *IEEE International Conference Computer Design: VLSI in Computers and Processors*, pp. 522–525. IEEE Computer Society. 123

D. Dolev and N. Shavit. 1997. Bounded concurrent time-stamping. *SIAM J. Comput.*, 26(2): 418–455. DOI: 10.1137/S0097539790192647. 37, 40

D. Dolev and H. R. Strong. 1982 Polynomial algorithms for multiple processor agreement. In *Proceedings Symposium on Theory of Computing (STOC)*, pp. 401–407. DOI: 10.1145/ 800070.802215. 76

D. Dolev and H. R. Strong. 1983. Authenticated algorithms for Byzantine agreement. *SIAM J. Comput.* 12(4): 656–666. DOI: 10.1137/0212045. 76

D. Dolev and A. C. Yao. 1983. On the security of public key protocols. *IEEE Transactions on Information Theory*, 29(2): 198–207. DOI: 10.1109/TIT.1983.1056650. 78

D. Doligez, J. Kriener, L. Lamport, T. Libal, and S. Merz. 2014. Coalescing: Syntactic abstraction for reasoning in first-order modal logics. In C. Benzmüller and J. Otten (eds.), *Automated Reasoning in Quantified Non-Classical Logics,* volume 33 of *EPiC Series in Computing*, pp. 1–16. 126

J. Du, C. Iorgulescu, A. Roy, and W. Zwaenepoel. 2014. Gentlerain: Cheap and scalable causal consistency with physical clocks. In *Proceedings of the ACM Symposium on Cloud Computing*, SOCC '14, pp. 4: 1–4: 13. ACM. DOI: 10.1145/2670979.2670983. 53

C. Dwork, N. Lynch, and L. Stockmeyer. April 1988. Consensus in the presence of partial synchrony. *J. ACM*, 35(2): 288–323. DOI: 10.1145/42282.42283. 94

C. Dwork and O. Waarts. 1992. Simple and efficient bounded concurrent timestamping or bounded concurrent timestamp systems are comprehensible! In *Proceedings of the 24th Annual ACM Symposium on Theory of Computing*, pp. 655–666. DOI: 10.1145/129712.129776. 37, 40

C. A. Ellis. 1977. Consistency and correctness of duplicate database systems. In *Proceedings of the Sixth ACM Symposium on Operating Systems Principles*, SOSP '77, pp. 67–84. ACM. DOI: 10.1145/1067625.806548. 84

U. Engberg. 1996. *Reasoning in the Temporal Logic of Actions.* BRICS Dissertation Series. 151

U. Engberg, P. Grønning, and L. Lamport. 1992 Mechanical verification of concurrent systems with TLA. In G. von Bochmann and D. K. Probst (eds.), *Computer Aided Verification, Fourth International Workshop, CAV '92*, volume 663 of *Lecture Notes in Computer Science*, pp. 44–55. Springer. DOI: 10.1007/3-540-56496-9_5. 115

C. J. Fidge. 1988. Timestamps in message-passing systems that preserve the partial ordering. Dissertation, Australian National University. 53

M. J. Fischer, N. A. Lynch, and M. S. Paterson. April 1985. Impossibility of distributed consensus with one faulty process. *J. ACM*, 32(2): 374–382. DOI: 10.1145/3149.214121. 89, 148

M. Fitzi and J. A. Garay. 2003. Efficient player-optimal protocols for strong and differential consensus. In *Proceedings 22nd ACM Symposium on Principles of Distributed Computing (PODC)*, pp. 211–220. DOI: 10.1145/872035.872066. 70

R. W. Floyd. 1967. Assigning meanings to programs. In *Proceedings Symposium on Applied Mathematics*, volume 19, pp. 19–32. American Mathematical Society. 105

R. Friedman, A. Mostéfaoui, S. Rajsbaum, and M. Raynal. 2007. Asynchronous agreement and its relation with error-correcting codes. *IEEE Trans. Computers*, 56(7): 865–875. DOI: 10.1109/TC.2007.1043. 72

E. Gafni and L. Lamport. 2003. Disk Paxos. *Distributed Computing*, 16(1): 1–20. DOI: 10.1007/s00446-002-0070-8. 9, 100, 161

J. A. Garay and Y. Moses. 1998. Fully polynomial Byzantine agreement for $n > 3t$ processors in $t + 1$ rounds. 27(1): 247–290. DOI: 10.1137/S0097539794265232. 76

S. J. Garland and J. V. Guttag. 1988. LP: The Larch prover. In *International Conference on Automated Deduction*, pp. 748–749. Springer. DOI: 10.1007/BFb0012879. 151

S. Ghemawat, H. Gobioff, and S.-T. Leung. 2003. The Google file system. In *Proceedings of the Nineteenth ACM Symposium on Operating Systems Principles*, SOSP '03, pp. 29–43. ACM. DOI: 10.1145/1165389.945450. 101

P. B. Gibbons and E. Korach. 1997. Testing shared memories. *SIAM J. Comput.*, 26(4): 1208–1244. DOI: 10.1.1.107.3013. 46

P. B. Gibbons, M. Merritt, and K. Gharachorloo. 1991. Proving sequential consistency of high-performance shared memories (extended abstract). In *SPAA*, pp. 292–303. DOI: 10.1145/113379.113406. 46

S. Gilbert and N. Lynch. 2002. Brewer's conjecture and the feasibility of consistent, available, partition-tolerant web services. *SIGACT News*, 33(2): 51–59. DOI: 10.1145/564585.564601. 50

E. Gilkerson and L. Lamport. 2004. On hair color in France. *Annals of Improbable Research*, pp. 18–19. 165

P. Godefroid and P. Wolper. 1994. A partial approach to model checking. *Inf. Comput.*, 110(2): 305–326. DOI: 10.1006/inco.1994.1035. 127

C. Gray and D. Cheriton. 1989. Leases: An efficient fault-tolerant mechanism for distributed file cache consistency. In *Proceedings of the Twelfth ACM Symposium on Operating Systems Principles*, SOSP '89, pp. 202–210. ACM. DOI: 10.1145/74851.74870. 99

J. Gray and L. Lamport. 2006. Consensus on transaction commit. *ACM Trans. Database Syst.*, 31(1): 133–160, 2006. DOI: 10.1145/1132863.1132867. 162

D. Gries and F. B. Schneider. 1995. Avoiding the undefined by underspecification. In J. van Leeuwen, editor, *Computer Science Today*, volume 1000 of *Lecture Notes in Computer Science*, pp. 366–373. Springer. 116

Y. Gurevich. 1995. Evolving algebras 1993: Lipari guide. In E. Börger, editor, *Specification and validation methods*, pp. 9–36. Oxford University Press. 127

C. Hawblitzel, J. Howell, M. Kapritsos, J. R. Lorch, B. Parno, M. L. Roberts, S. T. V. Setty, and B. Zill. 2015. Ironfleet: Proving practical distributed systems correct. In E. L. Miller and S. Hand (eds.), *Proceedings 25th Symposium Operating Systems Principles, SOSP 2015*, pp. 1–17. ACM. DOI: 10.1145/2815400.2815428. 128

C. Hawblitzel, J. Howell, M. Kapritsos, J. R. Lorch, B. Parno, M. L. Roberts, S. T. V. Setty, and B. Zill. 2017. Ironfleet: Proving safety and liveness of practical distributed systems. *Commun. ACM*, 60(7): 83–92. DOI: 10.1145/3068608. 128

M. Herlihy. January 1991. Wait-free synchronization. *ACM Trans. Program. Lang. Syst.*, 13(1): 124–149. DOI: 10.1145/114005.102808. 4

M. Herlihy and J. M. Wing. July 1990. Linearizability: A correctness condition for concurrent objects. *ACM Trans. Prog. Lang. Syst.*, 12(3): 463–492. DOI: 10.1145/78969.78972. 5, 71

A. Hisgen, A. Birrell, T. Mann, M. Schroeder, and G. Swart. September 1989. Availability and consistency tradeoffs in the Echo distributed file system. In *Proceedings of the Second Workshop on Workstation Operating Systems*, pp. 49–54. IEEE Computer Society. DOI: 10.1109/WWOS.1989.109267. 96

G. J. Holzmann. 2003. *The SPIN Model Checker*. Addison-Wesley. 123

H. Howard, D. Malkhi, and A. Spiegelman. 2016. Flexible Paxos: Quorum intersection revisited. *arXiv preprint arXiv:1608.06696*. 162

P. Hunt, M. Konar, F. P. Junqueira, and B. Reed. 2010. Zookeeper: Wait-free coordination for internet-scale systems. In *USENIX ATC*. 9, 100

IBM. 1955. *IBM 705 EDPM Electronic Data Processing Machine*. Internation Business Machines Corp. 133

A. Israeli and M. Li. 1993. Bounded time-stamps. *Distributed Computing*, 6(4): 205–209. DOI: 10.1007/BF02242708. 37

A. Israeli and A. Shaham. 2005. Time and space optimal implementations of atomic multi-writer register. *Inf. Comput.*, 200(1): 62–106. 40

K. E. Iverson. 1962. A programming language. In *Proceedings of the Spring Joint Computer Conference*, pp. 345–351. ACM. 135

P. Jayanti. 2005. An optimal multi-writer snapshot algorithm. In *Proceedings of the Thirty-seventh Annual ACM Symposium on Theory of Computing*, pp. 723–732. ACM. DOI: 10.1145/1060590.1060697. 64

J. E. Johnson, D. E. Langworthy, L. Lamport, and F. H. Vogt. 2007. Formal specification of a web services protocol. *J. Log. Algebr. Program.*, 70(1): 34–52. DOI: 10.1016/j.jlap.2006.05.004. 128

P. R. Johnson and R. H. Thomas. 1975. The maintenance of duplicate databases. Network Working Group RFC 677. 6, 50, 53, 83, 137

R. Joshi, L. Lamport, J. Matthews, S. Tasiran, M. R. Tuttle, and Y. Yu. 2003. Checking cache-coherence protocols with TLA$^+$. *Formal Methods in System Design*, 22(2): 125–131. DOI: 10.1023/A:1022969405325. 123, 127

R. Koo and S. Toueg. 1987. Checkpointing and rollback-recovery for distributed systems. *IEEE Transactions on software Engineering*, (1): 23–31. DOI: 10.1109/TSE.1987.232562. 64

F. Kröger. 1977. LAR: A logic of algorithmic reasoning. *Acta Informatica*, 8: 243–266. DOI: 10.1007/BF00264469. 105

DEC WRL. October 2018. MultiTitan: Four architecture papers. http://www.hpl.hp.com/techreports/Compaq-DEC/WRL-87-8.pdf. 147

P. B. Ladkin, L. Lamport, B. Olivier, and D. Roegel. 1999. Lazy caching in TLA. *Distributed Computing*, 12(2–3): 151–174. DOI: 10.1007/s004460050063. 155

A. Lakshman and P. Malik. 2009. Cassandra: A decentralized structured storage system. In *SOSP Workshop on Large Scale Distributed Systems and Middleware (LADIS 2009)*. ACM. 100

L. Lamport. 1957 Braid theory. *Mathematics Bulletin of the Bronx High School of Science (1957)*, pp. 6,7,9. 132

L. Lamport. 1987. Distribution. Email message sent to a DEC SRC bulletin board at 12:23:29 PDT on 28 May 87. 163

L. Lamport. 2019. My writings. 3, 29, 67, 103, 132, 134, 135, 141, 142, 148, 150, 151, 158, 165

L. Lamport. 2018. Personal communication (recorded conversation). 144, 145

L. Lamport. 1970. Comment on Bell's quadratic quotient method for hash coded searching. *Commun. ACM*, 13(9): 573–574. DOI: 10.1145/362736.362765. 135

L. Lamport. 1973. The coordinate method for the parallel execution of DO loops. In *Proceedings 1973 Sagamore Comput. Conf*.

L. Lamport. 1974. A new solution of Dijkstra's concurrent programming problem. *Commun. ACM*, 17(8): 453–455. DOI: 10.1145/361082.361093. 3, 29, 30, 35, 136

L. Lamport. 1974. The parallel execution of DO loops. *Commun. ACM*, 17(2): 83–93. DOI: 10.1145/360827.360844. 135

L. Lamport. 1977. Concurrent reading and writing. *Commun. ACM*, 20(11): 806–811. DOI: 10.1145/359863.359878. 30, 36, 44

L. Lamport. 1977. Proving the correctness of multiprocess programs. *IEEE Trans. Software Eng.*, 3(2): 125–143. DOI: 10.1109/TSE.1977.229904. 30, 103, 104, 105, 106, 150

L. Lamport. 1978. The implementation of reliable distributed multiprocess systems. *Computer Networks*, 2: 95–114. DOI: 10.1016/0376-5075(78)90045-4. 84

L. Lamport. 1978. Time, clocks, and the ordering of events in a distributed system. *Commun. ACM*, 21(7): 558–565. DOI: 10.1145/359545.359563. 6, 48, 58, 103, 137, 163, 164

L. Lamport. 1979a. Constructing digital signatures from a one way function. *Technical Report CSL—98, Computer Science Laboratory, SRI International*. 68, 78

L. Lamport. 1979b. How to make a multiprocessor computer that correctly executes multiprocess programs. *IEEE Trans. Computers*, 28(9): 690–691. DOI: 10.1109/TC.1979.1675439. 5, 30, 44, 143, 150

L. Lamport. 1979c. A new approach to proving the correctness of multiprocess programs. *ACM Trans. Program. Lang. Syst.*, 1(1): 84–97. DOI: 10.1145/357062.357068. 103

L. Lamport. 1980. "Sometime" is sometimes "not never"—on the temporal logic of programs. In P. W. Abrahams, R. J. Lipton, and S. R. Bourne (eds.), *Conference Record of the Seventh Annual ACM Symposium on Principles of Programming Languages,* pp. 174–185. ACM Press. DOI: 10.1145/567446.567463. 106

L. Lamport. 1981. Password authentication with insecure communication. *Commun. ACM*, 24(11): 770–772. DOI: 10.1145/358790.358797. 68

L. Lamport. 1983. What good is temporal logic? In *IFIP Congress*, pp. 657–668. 111

L. Lamport. 1986a. The mutual exclusion problem: Part I: a theory of interprocess communication. *J. ACM*, 33(2): 313–326. DOI: 10.1145/5383.5384. 150

L. Lamport. 1986b. The mutual exclusion problem: Part II: statement and solutions. *J. ACM*, 33(2): 327–348. DOI: 10.1145/5383.5385. 150

L. Lamport. 1986c. On interprocess communication. Part I: basic formalism. *Distributed Computing*, 1(2): 77–85. DOI: 10.1007/BF01786227. 4, 29, 41, 42, 150

L. Lamport. 1986d. On interprocess communication. Part II: algorithms. *Distributed Computing*, 1(2): 86–101. DOI: 10.1007/BF01786228. 4, 29, 36, 37, 38, 39, 40, 42, 150

L. Lamport. 1987. A fast mutual exclusion algorithm. *ACM Trans. Comput. Syst.*, 5(1): 1–11. DOI: 10.1145/7351.7352. 147

L. Lamport. 1990. *win* and *sin*: Predicate transformers for concurrency. *ACM Trans. Program. Lang. Syst.*, 12(3): 396–428. DOI: 10.1145/78969.78970. 104

L. Lamport. 1991. The temporal logic of actions. *Research Report 79*, DEC Systems Research Center. 107

L. Lamport. 1992. Hybrid systems in TLA$^+$. In R. L. Grossman, A. Nerode, A. P. Ravn, and H. Rischel (eds.), *Hybrid Systems*, volume 736 of *Lecture Notes in Computer Science*, pp. 77–102. Springer. DOI: 10.1007/3-540-57318-6_25. 115

L. Lamport. June 1993. Verification and specification of concurrent programs. In J. W. de Bakker, W. P. de Roever, and G. Rozenberg (eds.), *A Decade of Concurrency, Reflections and Perspectives,* volume 803 of *Lecture Notes in Computer Science*, pp. 347–374. Springer. 151

L. Lamport. 1994. *L\#TEX—A Document Preparation System: User's Guide and Reference Manual, Second Edition*. Pearson/Prentice Hall. 11, 145

L. Lamport. 1994. The temporal logic of actions. *ACM Trans. Program. Lang. Syst.*, 16(3): 872–923. DOI: 10.1145/177492.177726. 107, 109, 151

L. Lamport. 1995. How to write a proof. *American Mathematical Monthly*, 102(7): 600–608. 125, 152, 154

L. Lamport. 1998. The part-time parliament. *ACM Trans. Comput. Syst.*, 16(2): 133–169. DOI: 10.1145/279227.279229. 9, 54, 96, 163

L. Lamport. 1999. Specifying concurrent systems with TLA$^+$. *Calculational System Design*. DOI: 10.1007%2F3-540-48153-2_6.pdf. 152, 156

L. Lamport. 2000. Fairness and hyperfairness. *Distributed Computing*, 13(4): 239–245. DOI: 10.1007/PL00008921. 104

L. Lamport. 2000. How (LA)TEX changed the face of mathematics. E-interview in DMV-Mitteilungen.

L. Lamport. 2001. Paxos made simple. *SIGACT News*, 32(4): 51–58. 98, 150

L. Lamport. 2002. *Specifying Systems: The TLA+ Language and Tools for Hardware and Software Engineers*. Addison-Wesley. 10, 115, 152, 156, 163

L. Lamport. 2002. A discussion with Leslie Lamport. *IEEE Distributed Systems Online* 3, 8.

L. Lamport. 2006c. Checking a multithreaded algorithm with $^+$CAL. In S. Dolev, editor, *Distributed Computing, 20th International Symposium,* volume 4167 of *Lecture Notes in Computer Science*, pp. 151–163. Springer. DOI: 10.1007/11864219_11. 159

L. Lamport. 2006b. Fast Paxos. *Distributed Computing*, 19(2): 79–103. DOI: 10.1007/s00446-006-0005-x. 161

L. Lamport. 2006. Measuring celebrity. *Annals of Improbable Research*, pp. 14–15. 165

L. Lamport. 2009. The PlusCal algorithm language. In M. Leucker and C. Morgan (eds.), *Theoretical Aspects of Computing*, volume 5684 of *Lecture Notes in Computer Science*, pp. 36–60. Springer. DOI: 10.1007/978-3-642-03466-4_2. 10, 120, 159

L. Lamport. 2011. Byzantizing Paxos by refinement. In D. Peleg, editor, *Distributed Computing - 25th International Symposium*, volume 6950 of *Lecture Notes in Computer Science*, pp. 211–224. Springer. 127, 162

L. Lamport. 2012. Buridan's principle. *Foundations of Physics*, 42(8): 1056–1066. DOI: 10.1007/s10701-012-9647-7. 142

L. Lamport. 2012. How to write a 21st century proof. *Journal of Fixed Point Theory and Applications*, March 6, 2012. DOI: 10.1007/s11784-012-0071-6. 163

L. Lamport. 2014. TLA^{+2}: A preliminary guide.

L. Lamport. 2015. The TLA^+ hyperbook. 115

L. Lamport. 2015a. Turing lecture: The computer science of concurrency: the early years. *Commun. ACM*, 58(6): 71–76. DOI: 10.1145/2771951.

L. Lamport. 2018. The TLA^+ video course. 115

L. Lamport. August 2018b. Personal communication (email). 131, 132

L. Lamport. 2018c. Personal communication (email), 9 October 2018. 152

L. Lamport. 2019. TLA+ tools. http://lamport.azurewebsites.net/tla/tools.html; last retrieved 11 February 2019. 160

L. Lamport and R. Levin. 2016. Lamport, Leslie. Oral history, part 1. https://www.computerhistory.org/collections/catalog/102717182. 2, 132, 133, 134, 135, 136, 137, 138, 139, 141, 142, 146, 148, 149, 159, 163

L. Lamport and R. Levin. 2016. Lamport, Leslie. Oral history, part 2. https://www.computerhistory.org/collections/catalog/102717246. 169

L. Lamport, D. Malkhi, and L. Zhou. 2009a. Vertical Paxos and primary-backup replication. In S. Tirthapura and L. Alvisi (eds.), *Proceedings of the 28th Annual ACM Symposium on Principles of Distributed Computing*, pp. 312–313. ACM. DOI: 10.1145/1582716.1582783. 9, 101, 162

L. Lamport, D. Malkhi, and L. Zhou. April 2009b. Stoppable Paxos. 162

L. Lamport, D. Malkhi, and L. Zhou. 2010. Reconfiguring a state machine. *SIGACT News*, 41(1): 63–73. DOI: 10.1145/1753171.1753191. 9, 102, 162

L. Lamport and M. Massa. 2004. Cheap Paxos. In *2004 International Conference on Dependable Systems and Networks*, pp. 307–314. IEEE Computer Society. 9, 101, 161

L. Lamport, J. Matthews, M. R. Tuttle, and Y. Yu. 2002. Specifying and verifying systems with TLA^+. In G. Muller and E. Jul (eds.), *Proceedings of the 10th ACM SIGOPS European Workshop*, pp. 45–48. ACM. 153, 154, 157

L. Lamport and P. M. Melliar-Smith. 1985. Synchronizing clocks in the presence of faults. *J. ACM*, 32(1): 52–78. DOI: 10.1145/2455.2457. 8, 76

L. Lamport and S. Merz. 2017. Auxiliary variables in TLA+. *CoRR*, abs/1703.05121. 113

L. Lamport and L. C. Paulson. 1999. Should your specification language be typed? *ACM Trans. Program. Lang. Syst.*, 21(3): 502–526. DOI: 10.1145/319301.319317. 116

L. Lamport, R. E. Shostak, and M. C. Pease. 1982. The Byzantine generals problem. *ACM Trans. Program. Lang. Syst.*, 4(3): 382–401. DOI: 10.1145/357172.357176. 7, 8, 67, 68, 69, 70, 72, 73, 75, 76, 105, 141, 163

L. Lamport. 1972. *The Analytic Cauchy Problem with Singular Data*. Ph.D. thesis, Brandeis University.

B. W. Lampson. 1996. How to build a highly available system using consensus. In *Workshop on Distributed Algorithms (WDAG)*, pp. 1–17. Springer. DOI: 10.1007/3-540-61769-8_1. 9

B. W. Lampson. 2018. Personal communication (email). 139, 140, 149, 150, 167

B. W. Lampson and H. E. Sturgis. 1979. Crash recovery in a distributed storage system. Unpublished manuscript. 162, 167

D. Langworthy. 2005. Personal communication (email). 158

The LaTeX Project. 2019. https://www.latex-project.org/; last retrieved 6 May 2019. 145

E. K. Lee and C. A. Thekkath. 1996. Petal: Distributed virtual disks. In *ACM SIGPLAN Notices*, volume 31, pp. 84–92. ACM. DOI: 10.1145/248209.237157. 100, 149

K. R. M. Leino. 2010. Dafny: An automatic program verifier for functional correctness. In E. M. Clarke and A. Voronkov (eds.), *16th International Conference Logic for Programming, Artificial Intelligence, and Reasoning*, volume 6355 of *Lecture Notes in Computer Science*, pp. 348–370. Springer. DOI: 10.1007/978-3-642-17511-4_20. 128

O. Lichtenstein and A. Pnueli. 1985. Checking that finite state concurrent programs satisfy their linear specification. In M. S. V. Deusen, Z. Galil, and B. K. Reid (eds.), *Proceedings Twelfth Ann. ACM Symposium Princ. Prog. Lang. (POPL 1985)*, pp. 97–107. ACM. DOI: 10.1145/318593.318622. 124

R. Lipton and J. Sandberg. 1988. PRAM: A scalable shared memory. Technical Report CS-TR-180-88, Computer Science Department, Princeton University. 46

B. Liskov and J. Cowling. 2012. Viewstamped replication revisited. 2012. 54

B. Liskov and R. Ladin. 1986. Highly available distributed services and fault-tolerant distributed garbage collection. In *Proceedings of the Fifth Annual ACM Symposium on Principles of Distributed Computing, PODC '86*, pp. 29–39. ACM. DOI: 10.1145/10590.10593. 53

W. Lloyd, M. J. Freedman, M. Kaminsky, and D. G. Andersen. 2011. Don't settle for eventual: Scalable causal consistency for wide-area storage with COPS. In *Proceedings of the Twenty-Third ACM Symposium on Operating Systems Principles*, SOSP '11, pp. 401–416, New York, NY. ACM. DOI: 10.1145/2043556.2043593. 53

W. Lloyd, M. J. Freedman, M. Kaminsky, and D. G. Andersen. 2013. Stronger semantics for low-latency geo-replicated storage. In *10th USENIX Symposium on Networked Systems Design and Implementation (NSDI 13)*, pp. 313–328. USENIX. 53

N. A. Lynch. 1996. *Distributed Algorithms*. Morgan Kaufmann, San Francisco. 76

D. Malkhi. 2018. Personal communication (recorded conversatino). 168

F. Mattern. 1989. Virtual time and global states of distributed systems. In M. Cosnard et al. (eds.), *Proceedings of the International Workshop on Parallel Algorithms*. Elsevier. 53, 64

K. McMillan. 1993. *Symbolic Model Checking*. Kluwer Academic Publishers. 123

R. C. Merkle. 1980. Protocols for public key cryptosystems. In *Proceedings IEEE Symposium on Security and Privacy*, pp. 122–134. DOI: 10.1109/SP.1980.10006. 80

S. Merz. 1999. A more complete TLA. In J. Wing, J. Woodcock, and J. Davies (eds.), *FM'99: World Congress on Formal Methods*, volume 1709 of *Lecture Notes in Computer Science*, pp. 1226–1244. Springer. DOI: 10.1007/3-540-48118-4_15. 110

S. Merz. 2008. The specification language TLA$^+$. In D. Bjørner and M. C. Henson (eds.), *Logics of Specification Languages*, Monographs in Theoretical Computer Science, pp. 401–451. Springer, Berlin-Heidelberg. DOI: 10.1007/978-3-540-74107-7_8. 115, 160

S. Merz. July 2018. Personal communication (email). 167

Microsoft Research. 2019. *TLA$^+$ Proof System*. https://tla.msr-inria.inria.fr/tlaps/content/Home.html; last retrieved 11 February 2019. 159

D. Milojicic. 2002. A discussion with Leslie Lamport. IEEE Distributed Systems Online 3, 8. https://www.microsoft.com/en-us/research/publication/discussion-leslie-lamport/; last retrieved 6 May 2019. 161

H. Minkowski. 2017. Translation:space and time—wikisource. [Online; accessed 15 March 2019]. 138

C. Morgan. 1990 *Programming from specifications*. Prentice Hall. 111

A. Mullery. December 1971. The distributed control of multiple copies of data. Technical Report RC 3642, IBM, Yorktown Heights, New York. 83

M. Naor and M. Yung. 1989. Universal one-way hash functions and their cryptographic applications. In *Proceedings Symposium on Theory of Computing (STOC)*, pp. 33–43. DOI: 10.1145/73007.73011. 80

National Institute of Standards and Technology. 2018. Post-quantum cryptography. Available at https://csrc.nist.gov/projects/post-quantum-cryptography/. 81

C. Newcombe. 2012. Post on TLA+ discussion group. https://groups.google.com/forum/#!searchin/tlaplus/professionalS20career/tlaplus/ZJCi-UF31fc/Mawvwi6U1CYJ 160

C. Newcombe, T. Rath, F. Zhang, B. Munteanu, M. Brooker, and M. Deardeuff. 2015. How Amazon web services uses formal methods. *CACM*, 58(4): 66–73. DOI: 10.1145/2699417. 128, 161

M. J. K. Nielsen. Titan system manual. http://www.hpl.hp.com/techreports/Compaq-DEC/WRL-86-1.pdf, last retrieved 15 October 2018. 147

B. M. Oki and B. H. Liskov. 1988. Viewstamped replication: A new primary copy method to support highly-available distributed systems. In *Proceedings of the Seventh Annual ACM Symposium on Principles of Distributed Computing*, pp. 8–17, ACM. DOI: 10.1145/62546.62549. 99, 149

D. Ongaro and J. Ousterhout. 2014. In search of an understandable consensus algorithm. In *Proceedings USENIX Annual Technical Conference ATC*. 54, 100

S. S. Owicki and D. Gries. 1976 Verifying properties of parallel programs: An axiomatic approach. *Commun. ACM*, 19(5): 279–285. DOI: 10.1145/360051.360224. 30, 44

S. S. Owicki and L. Lamport. Proving liveness properties of concurrent programs. *ACM Trans. Program. Lang. Syst.*, 4(3): 455–495, 1982. DOI: 10.1145/357172.357178. 106, 107, 108

D. S. Parker, G. J. Popek, G. Rudisin, A. Stoughton, B. J. Walker, E. Walton, J. M. Chow, D. Edwards, S. Kiser, and C. Kline. 1983. Detection of mutual inconsistency in distributed systems. *IEEE Transactions on Software Engineering*, (3): 240–247. DOI: 10.1109/TSE.1983.236733. 53

L. C. Paulson. 1994. *Isabelle: A Generic Theorem Prover*, volume 828 of Lecture Notes in Computer Science. Springer Verlag, Berlin, Heidelberg. See also the Isabelle home page at http://isabelle.in.tum.de/. 126

M. C. Pease, R. E. Shostak, and L. Lamport. 1980. Reaching agreement in the presence of faults. *J. ACM*, 27(2): 228–234. DOI: 10.1145/322186.322188. 7, 8, 67, 68, 75, 141, 163

A. Pnueli. 1977. The temporal logic of programs. In *Proceedings 18th Annual Symposium on the Foundations of Computer Science*, pp. 46–57. IEEE. DOI: 10.1109/SFCS.1977.32. 105

R. Prakash and M. Singhal. 1996. Low-cost checkpointing and failure recovery in mobile computing systems. *IEEE Transactions on Parallel and Distributed Systems*, 7(10):1035–1048. DOI: 10.1109/71.539735. 64

A. N. Prior. 1967. *Past, Present and Future*. Clarendon Press, Oxford, U.K. 105

Riak. Riak KV. http://basho.com/products/riak-kv. 53

R. L. Rivest, A. Shamir, and L. M. Adleman. 1978. A method for obtaining digital signatures and public-key cryptosystems. *Commun. ACM*, 21(2): 120–126. DOI: 10.1145/359340.359342. 80

T. R. Rodeheffer. 2018. Personal communication (recorded conversation and follow-up email), 9 October 2018 and 11 February 2019. 167

J. Rompel. 1990. One-way functions are necessary and sufficient for secure signatures. In *Proceedings Symposium on Theory of Computing (STOC)*, pp. 387–394. DOI: 10.1145/100216.100269. 80

J. H. Saltzer, D. P. Reed, and D. D. Clark. November 1984. End-to-end arguments in system design. *ACM Trans. Comput. Syst.*, 2(4): 277–288. DOI: 10.1145/357401.357402. 86

M. Satyanarayanan, J. J. Kistler, P. Kumar, M. E. Okasaki, E. H. Siegel, and D. C. Steere. 1990. Coda: A highly available file system for a distributed workstation environment. *IEEE Transactions on Computers*, 39(4): 447–459. DOI: 10.1109/12.54838. 53

F. B. Schmuck. 1988. The use of efficient broadcast protocols in asynchronous distributed systems. Ph.D. thesis, Cornell University. 53

F. Schneider. August 2018. Personal communication (email). 166

F. B. Schneider. 1982. Synchronization in distributed programs. *ACM Trans. Program. Lang. Syst.*, 4(2): 125–148. DOI: 10.1145/357162.357163. 139

F. B. Schneider. December 1990. Implementing fault-tolerant services using the state machine approach: A tutorial. *ACM Comput. Surv.*, 22(4): 299–319. DOI: 10.1145/98163.98167. 86, 139

R. L. Schwartz, P. M. Melliar-Smith, and F. H. Vogt. 1984. An interval-based temporal logic. In E. M. Clarke and D. Kozen (eds.), In *Proceedings Logics of Programs*, volume 164 of *Lecture Notes in Computer Science*, pp. 443–457. Springer. 106

R. Shostak. July 2018. Personal communication (email), 6–8. 140

A. K. Singh, J. H. Anderson, and M. G. Gouda. 1994. The elusive atomic register. *J. ACM*, 41(2): 311–339. 37

J. M. Spivey. 1992. *The Z Notation: A Reference Manual*. International Series in Computer Science. Prentice Hall, 2nd edition. 115

M. Suda and C. Weidenbach. 2012. A PLTL-prover based on labelled superposition with partial model guidance. In B. Gramlich, D. Miller, and U. Sattler (eds.), *6th International Joint Conference Automated Reasoning (IJCAR 2012)*, volume 7364 of *LNCS*, pp. 537–543. Springer. DOI: 10.1007/978-3-642-31365-3_42. 126

D. Terry, M. Theimer, K. Petersen, A. Demers, M. Spreitzer, and C. Hauser. 1995. Managing update conflicts in Bayou, a weakly connected replicated storage system. In *In Proceedings of the Fifteenth ACM Symposium on Operating Systems Principles*, pp. 172–183. DOI: 10.1145/224057.224070. 53

A. Valmari. June 1990. A stubborn attack on state explosion. In *2nd International Wsh. Computer Aided Verification*, volume 531 of *LNCS*, pp. 156–165, Rutgers. Springer. DOI: 10.1007/BF00709154. 127

R. van Renesse and F. B. Schneider. 2004. Chain replication for supporting high throughput and availability. In *Proceedings of the 6th Conference on Symposium on Operating Systems Design & Implementation*. USENIX Association. 84, 101

K. Vidyasankar. 1988. Converting Lamport's regular register to atomic register. *Inf. Process. Lett.*, 28(6): 287–290. DOI: 10.1016/0020-0190(88)90175-5. 39

P. M. B. Vitányi and B. Awerbuch. 1986. Atomic shared register access by asynchronous hardware (detailed abstract). In *27th Annual Symposium on Foundations of Computer Science*, pp. 233–243. 40

W. Vogels. 2009. Eventually consistent. *Commun. ACM*, 52(1): 40–44. DOI: 10.1145/1435417.1435432. 83

P. Voldemort. Voldemort. https://www.project-voldemort.com/voldemort. 53

S. A. Weil, S. A. Brandt, E. L. Miller, D. D. E. Long, and C. Maltzahn. 2006. Ceph: A scalable, high-performance distributed file system. pp. 307–320. 100

J. H. Wensley, L. Lamport, J. Goldberg, M. W. Green, K. N. Levitt, P. M. Melliar-Smith, R. E. Shostak, and C. B. Weinstock. 1978. Sift: Design and analysis of a fault-tolerant computer for aircraft control. *Proceedings of the IEEE*, 66(10): 1240–1255. DOI: 10.1109/PROC.1978.11114. 140, 164

J. H. Wensley, L. Lamport, J. Goldberg, M. W. Green, K. N. Levitt, P. M. Melliar-Smith, R. E. Shostak, and C. B. Weinstock. 1978. Synchronizing clocks in the presence of faults. *Proceedings of the IEEE*, 66(10): 1240–1255. 67

Wikipedia contributors. 2018a. Bravo (software)—Wikipedia, the free encyclopedia. https://en.wikipedia.org/w/index.php?title=Bravo_(software). [Online; accessed 25 February 2019]. 143

Wikipedia contributors. 2018b. Eckhard Pfeiffer—Wikipedia, the free encyclopedia. https://en.wikipedia.org/w/index.php?title=Eckhard_Pfeiffer, 2018. [Online; accessed 26 February 2019]. 155

Wikipedia contributors. 2018c. Scribe (markup language)—Wikipedia, the free encyclopedia. https://en.wikipedia.org/w/index.php?title=Scribe_(markup_language), 2018. [Online; accessed 25 February 2019]. 143

Wikipedia contributors. 2018d. UNIVAC—Wikipedia, the free encyclopedia. https://en.wikipedia.org/w/index.php?title=UNIVAC, 2018. [Online; accessed 24 February 2019]. 132

Wikipedia contributors. 2019a 1973 oil crisis—Wikipedia, the free encyclopedia. https://en.wikipedia.org/w/index.php?title=1973_oil_crisis. [Online; accessed 25 February 2019]. 140

Wikipedia contributors. 2019b. DEC Alpha—Wikipedia, the free encyclopedia. https://en.wikipedia.org/w/index.php?title=DEC_Alpha. [Online; accessed 25 February 2019]. 152

Wikipedia contributors. 2019c. Illiac—Wikipedia, the free encyclopedia. https://en.wikipedia.org/w/index.php?title=ILLIAC. [Online; accessed 25 February 2019]. 135

Wikipedia contributors. 2019d TeX—Wikipedia, the free encyclopedia. https://en.wikipedia.org/w/index.php?title=TeX. [Online; accessed 25 February 2019]. 144, 145

Y. Yu. August 2018. Personal communication (recorded conversation). 153, 166

M. Zawirski, N. Preguiça, S. Duarte, A. Bieniusa, V. Balegas, and M. Shapiro. 2015. Write fast, read in the past: Causal consistency for client-side applications. In *Proceedings of the 16th Annual Middleware Conference*, pp. 75–87. ACM. DOI: 10.1145/2814576.2814733. 53

L. Zhou. 2 August 2018. Personal communication (email). 165

G. Ziegler. January 2000. How (LA)TEX changed the face of mathematics: An e-interview with Leslie Lamport, the author of LATEX. Mitteilungen der Deutschen Mathematiker-Vereinigung, pp. 49–51. Personal communication (email), 2 August 2018. 145

Index

Footnotes are indicated by an 'n.'

Biographies

Dahlia Malkhi

Dahlia Malkhi received her Ph.D., an M.Sc. and a B.Sc. in computer science from the Hebrew University of Jerusalem. She is currently a lead researcher at Calibra. She is an ACM fellow (2011), serves on the Simons Institute Advisory Board, on the MIT Cryptocurrency Journal Advisory Board, and on the editorial boards of the Distributed Computing Journal. Her research career spans between industrial research and academia: 2014–2019, founding member and principal researcher at VMware Research; 2004–2014, principal researcher at Microsoft Research, Silicon Valley; 1999–2007, associate professor at the Hebrew University of Jerusalem; 1995–1999, senior researcher, AT&T Labs-Research, New Jersey. She has research interest in applied and foundational aspects of reliability and security in distributed systems.

Authors

Karolos Antoniadis is a Ph.D. candidate at EPFL under the supervision of Prof. Rachid Guerraoui. He holds an MSc in Computer Science from ETH Zurich.

Hagit Attiya received the B.Sc. degree in Mathematics and Computer Science from the Hebrew University of Jerusalem, in 1981, the M.Sc. and Ph.D. degrees in Computer Science from the Hebrew University of Jerusalem, in 1983 and 1987, respectively. She is a professor at the department of Computer Science at the Technion, Israel Institute of Technology, and holds the Harry W. Labov and Charlotte Ullman Labov Academic Chair. Before joining the Technion, she has been a post-doctoral research associate at the Laboratory for Computer Science at MIT. Her research interests are in distributed and concurrent computing. She is the editor-in-chief of Springer's journal Distributed Computing and a fellow of the ACM.

Christian Cachin is a professor of computer science at the University of Bern, where he leads the cryptology and data security research group since 2019. Before that he worked for IBM Research—Zurich during more than 20 years. With a background in cryptography, he is interested in all aspects of security in distributed systems, particularly in cryptographic protocols, consistency, consensus, blockchains, and cloud-computing security. He contributed to several IBM products, formulated security standards, and helped to create the Hyperledger Fabric blockchain platform.

Rachid Guerraoui received his Ph.D. from University of Orsay, and M.Sc from University of Sorbonne, both in Computer Science. He is currently professor in Computer Science at EPFL, Switzerland. His research interests are in the area of distributed computing.

Idit Keidar received her BSc (summa cum laude), MSc (summa cum laude), and Ph.D. from the Hebrew University of Jerusalem in 1992, 1994, and 1998, respectively. She was a Postdoctoral Fellow at MIT's Laboratory for Computer Science. She is currently a Professor at the Technion's Viterbi Faculty of Electrical Engineering, where she holds the Lord Leonard Wolfson Academic Chair. She serves as the Head of the Technion Rothschild Scholars Program for Excellence, and also heads the EE Faculty's EMET Excellence Program. Her research interests are in fault-tolerant distributed and concurrent algorithms and systems, theory and practice. Recently, she is mostly interested in distributed storage and concurrent data structures and transactions.

Roy Levin is a retired Distinguished Engineer, Managing Director, and founder of Microsoft Research Silicon Valley (2001–2014). Previously (1984–2001) he was a senior researcher and later Director of the Digital/Compaq Systems Research Center in Palo Alto, California. Before joining Digital, Levin was a researcher at Xerox's Palo Alto Research Center (1977–1984). His research focus was distributed computing systems. Levin holds a Ph.D. in Computer Science from Carnegie-Mellon University and a B.S. in Mathematics from Yale University. He is a Fellow of the Association for Computing Machinery (ACM) and a former chair of Special Interest Group on Operating Systems (SIGOPS).

Stephan Merz received his Ph.D. and habilitation in computer science from the University of Munich, Germany. He is currently a senior researcher and the head of science at Inria Nancy–Grand Est, France. His research interests are in formal verification of distributed algorithms and systems using model checking and theorem proving.

Robbert van Renesse received his Ph.D. in computer science, and an M.Sc. and a B.Sc. in mathematics from the Vrije Universiteit Amsterdam. He is currently a Research Professor at the Department of Computer Science at Cornell University and is Associate Editor of ACM Computing Surveys. He is an ACM fellow (since 2009). He was a researcher at AT&T Bell Labs in Murray Hill (1990) and served as Chair of ACM SIGOPS (2015–2019). His research interests include reliable distributed systems and operating systems.

Jennifer L. Welch received her S.M. and Ph.D. from the Massachusetts Institute of Technology and her B.A. from the University of Texas at Austin. She is currently holder of the Chevron II Professorship and Regents Professorship in the Department of Computer Science and Engineering at Texas A&M University, and is an ACM Distinguished Member. Her research interests are in the theory of distributed computing, algorithm analysis, distributed systems, mobile ad hoc networks, and distributed data structures.